Children in Migration and International Family Law

Stefan Arnold • Bettina Heiderhoff
Editors

Children in Migration and International Family Law

The Child's Best Interests Principle at the Interface of Migration Law and Family Law

Springer

Editors
Stefan Arnold
Institute of International Business Law, Chair for Private Law, Philosophy of Law, and Private International Law
University of Münster
Münster, Germany

Bettina Heiderhoff
Institute for German and International Family Law, Chair for Private International Law, International Civil Procedure Law and German Private Law
University of Münster
Münster, Germany

ISBN 978-3-031-71597-6 ISBN 978-3-031-71598-3 (eBook)
https://doi.org/10.1007/978-3-031-71598-3

This work was supported by European Commission (101090044 — FAMIMOVE 2.0 — JUST-2022-JCOO).

This Springer imprint is published by the registered company Springer Nature Switzerland AG
The registered company address is: Gewerbestrasse 11, 6330 Cham, Switzerland

If disposing of this product, please recycle the paper.

Acknowledgment

This open-access book has been co-funded by the European Commission as part of the FAMIMOVE project. Views and opinions expressed are however those of the authors only and do not necessarily reflect those of the European Union or the European Commission. Neither the European Union nor the granting authority can be held responsible for them.

First and foremost, we would like to extend our gratitude to all the authors who contributed to this book. We also thank all the FAMIMOVE project partners for their fruitful, friendly, and dedicated cooperation throughout the project's duration.

Our special thanks go to Kai Hüning, who coordinated and edited this volume with great care and patience.

Finally, we wish to thank the numerous stakeholders who enriched us with their contributions and knowledge at seminars, roundtables, and workshops. Without their input, neither this book nor the project itself would have been the same. Their reports have illustrated real people and their challenges to us, enabling us to focus our thoughts on reality. They have emphatically shown that much more needs to be done to serve the best interests of children and families at the intersection of migration law and family law.

Münster, 28.06.2024

Co-funded by
the European Union

Stefan Arnold
Bettina Heiderhoff

Contents

Contributors

Stefan Arnold Institute of International Business Law, Chair for Private Law, Philosophy of Law, and Private International Law, University of Münster, Münster, Germany

Leontine Bruijnen Institute for Private International Law, Ghent University, Ghent, Law and Development Research Group, University of Antwerp, Antwerp, Belgium

María Mayela Celis Aguilar Faculty of Law, Maastricht University, Maastricht, Netherlands

Iris Goldner Lang University of Zagreb – Faculty of Law, Zagreb, Croatia

María González Marimón Faculty of Law, Department of Private International Law, University of Valencia, Valencia, Spain

Bettina Heiderhoff Institute for German and International Family Law, Chair for Private International Law, International Civil Procedure Law and German Private Law, University of Münster, Münster, Germany

Kai Hüning Institute for German and International Family Law, University of Münster, Münster, Germany

Fabienne Jault-Seseke Faculty of Law and Political Science, Laboratory DANTE, University of Paris Saclay, Versailles Saint-Quentin-en-Yvelines, Paris, France

Ulf Maunsbach Faculty of Law, Lund University, Lund, Sweden

Martina Melcher Institute for Private Law, Foreign and International Private Law, University of Graz, Graz, Austria

Marta Pertegás Sender Chair for Private International Law and Transnational Law, Maastricht University, Maastricht, Netherlands

Giovanna Ricciardi International Social Service (ISS), Geneva, Switzerland

Orsolya Szeibert Department of Civil Law, Faculty of Law, Eötvös Loránd University, Budapest, Hungary

Alessia Voinich Faculty of Law, Milan Bicocca University, Milan, Italy

Jeannette Wöllenstein-Tripathi International Social Service (ISS), Geneva, Switzerland

Nadjma Yassari Swiss Institute of Comparative Law, Lausanne, Switzerland

Giovanni Zaccaroni Faculty of Law, Milan Bicocca University, Milan, Italy

Part I
Introduction

Children in Migration and International Family Law: An Introduction

Bettina Heiderhoff and Stefan Arnold

I. Aims of the Book and the FAMIMOVE Project

This book was written as part of the EU co-financed FAMIMOVE project. It is meant to shed light on the often overlooked legal difficulties at the interface between international family law and migration law. FAMIMOVE's central aim was to improve the situation of children and families migrating to the EU by reaching a better understanding and coordination between these policy areas. Marta Pertegás Sender describes the project in more detail in the following chapter (p. 23).

On the one hand, the legal situation can be improved simply by raising awareness for the interface issue in the first place — and by stakeholders in migration law and in international family law working together. Although both areas of law overlap so closely, the actors are almost always specialised in only one of the areas. As a result, migration authorities often act almost autonomously — without taking international family law into account and without co-operating with the relevant authorities. Similarly, family courts often decide cases with a migration law component without considering the possible migration law consequences of the decision.

On the other hand, there are also deficits in the legal structure. These can perhaps be remedied in part through changes in interpretation, but in part only through improved legislation. As far as interpretation is concerned, the Court of Justice of the European Union (CJEU) has already ruled several times on how to ensure the

B. Heiderhoff
Institute for German and International Family Law, Chair for Private International Law, International Civil Procedure Law and German Private Law, University of Münster, Münster, Germany
e-mail: bettina.heiderhoff@uni-muenster.de

S. Arnold (✉)
Institute of International Business Law, Chair for Private Law, Philosophy of Law, and Private International Law, University of Münster, Münster, Germany
e-mail: stefan.arnold@uni-muenster.de

S. Arnold, B. Heiderhoff (eds.), *Children in Migration and International Family Law*, https://doi.org/10.1007/978-3-031-71598-3_1

necessary protection for minors when applying European standards (see III. 3). However, the problem that an age assessment usually has to be repeated if the minor moves to another member state cannot be solved by interpretation. This is the case even if it was carried out in the previous country of residence with the help of an X-ray examination in accordance with the latest medical standards. Regulatory deficits are probably also the reason why even the Central Authorities currently have difficulties finding out whether a guardian has already been appointed for an unaccompanied minor in another member state.

The aim of this book is therefore to provide information on the applicable legal provisions and standards, but also to suggest improvements in interpretation and legislation. The focus will be on the principle of the best interests of the child and how this principle can be more effectively applied. It is striking that this principle, which applies in all areas of law — and all over the world — is often understood in very different ways by different stakeholders.

During the term of FAMIMOVE, a significant change in the legal situation has been determined by the EU. The New Pact on Asylum and Migration, with the core element of the Migration and Asylum Management Regulation[1] will make it much more difficult to protect the rights of unaccompanied minor refugees and families with children.[2] All contributions of this volume still refer to the old legal situation. Only in some cases could reference be made to the impending major changes due to the new legislation.

All internet sources cited are up to date as at 31 May 2024.

II. The Protection of the Best Interests of the Child: Deficits at the Interface of Migration Law and Family Law

1. Legal Complexity

When families migrate, the family relationships must be treated under private international law. This means that the authorities in the country of immigration cannot simply apply their own family law. Instead of applying domestic substantive law, such as the national rules on parentage or parental responsibility, it is necessary to apply the private international law first. The conflict of laws must be solved to find the law that is applicable to the particular legal issue. Private international law rules then often lead to foreign law having to be applied.

---

[1] Regulation (EU) 2024/1351 of the European Parliament and of the Council of 14 May 2024 on asylum and migration management, amending Regulations (EU) 2021/1147 and (EU) 2021/1060 and repealing Regulation (EU) No 604/2013 (Migration and Asylum Management Regulation).

[2] See for example B. Heiderhoff, A European Approach to Cross-Border Guardianship, in this volume, at p. 137.

In general terms, this application of foreign law — and in particular foreign family law — is indispensable to maintain respect for other legal systems and to avoid destroying family ties on whose stability the parties concerned rightly rely.

However, the application of foreign law is usually demanding in practice. It is a well-known problem that — in a first step — foreign law can be difficult to identify.[3] What is perhaps less known is that particularly concerning families, foreign law often contains legal institutions that are unknown in Europe and whose function is difficult to assess and therefore difficult to categorise legally. This is particularly true of kafāla and similar forms of care for a child by persons who are not the parents but who assume parental responsibility. Kafāla is an example of how this categorisation can vary widely across the EU. Therefore, it is a central object of investigation within the FAMIMOVE project and also in this book.

2. *Who Is a Child?*

Difficulties also arise when it comes to the question of who is a child. Almost worldwide, the age of 18 is now the legal age of majority. Even if this is still different in some countries of origin, this age limit is laid down in European legislation and also in the 1996 Child Protection Convention.[4]

Irrespective of this, there are still practical problems in determining the age of young refugees. It is often discussed, and unfortunately sometimes scandalised, that the age of young refugees cannot always be deduced from their identity documents and therefore has to be assessed by the competent authorities within the EU. In most cases, however, this age assessment is seen as a purely factual step, so that the recognition of an assessment made in one EU member state will usually have no effect in the other member states. What is more, it is often not even binding within the same member state. Kai Hüning addresses this issue in his contribution on age assessment (p. 75 of this book). He suggests adopting a truly European perspective: If we took Article 24 paras. 1 and 2 of the EU Charter[5] seriously, and followed the principle of mutual trust, we should assume that the age of a minor is no longer in doubt, once it has been established in one member state.

There is a reason why this proposal is mentioned here in the Introduction. It illustrates well how little mutual trust there is between member states in the area of migration law. And perhaps this lack of trust is somewhat justified. The methods used by member states to deal with minors, or presumed minors, vary widely. These

[3] With perspectives from many member states Esplugues Mota/Iglesias Buhigues/Palao Moreno (eds), Application of Foreign Law, 2011.

[4] Convention of 19 October 1996 on Jurisdiction, Applicable Law, Recognition, Enforcement and Co-operation in respect of Parental Responsibility and Measures for the Protection of Children (1996 Child Protection Convention).

[5] Charter of Fundamental Rights of the European Union (EU Charter).

differences do not always depend solely on the number of migrants, but also have political reasons. This becomes particularly evident in the case of guardianship for unaccompanied minor refugees and in the treatment of underage marriages (so-called "child-marriages"[6]). Those issues have, therefore, been chosen as topics for FAMIMOVE and this book.

III. The Child's Best Interests from Different Perspectives

1. Safeguarding in National Law, EU Law and International Conventions

Article 3 of the CRC[7] uses the term "best interests of the child". It states, that the best interests of the child shall be a *primary* consideration and, thereby, makes this the basic principle of all state action towards a child.

Just to make it explicitly clear once again, children here means all persons who have not yet reached the age of 18. If, contrary to this, only children under the age of 14 are taken into care and looked after in Hungary, while those over 14 only receive a Guardian *ad litem*, who takes over the legal representation when applying for asylum, this is not necessarily reassuring in light of the CRC. Children's rights are guaranteed in a very similar manner in the EU Charter. Article 24 para. 2 of the EU Charter states that in "all actions relating to children [. . .] the child's best interests must be a primary consideration." Based on this principle, the EU legislation regarding asylum law contains special provisions for the protection of children.

Particular attention is paid to minors in the Dublin III Regulation.[8] Article 6 of the Dublin III Regulation contains "Guarantees for minors" and the first paragraph repeats that "the best interests of the child shall be a primary consideration for Member States with respect to all procedures provided for in this Regulation". Individual aspects, such as the representation of minors, are addressed separately below. Unlike adults, minors are also largely free to choose the country in which they wish to submit their application in accordance with Article 8 of the Dublin III Regulation.

[6]See for the terminology used in this volume — "early marriage" — U. Maunsbach, Early marriages in Sweden. in this volume, 145 at pp. 145 f., S. Arnold, Early Marriage in Germany — Law and Politics of Cultural Demarcation, in this volume, 161, at p. 162 and M. Melcher, Early marriages in Austria — Private international law and ordre public assessment, in this volume, 183, at pp. 183 f.

[7]UN 1989 Convention of the Rights of the Child (CRC).

[8]Regulation (EU) No 604/2013 of the European Parliament and of the Council of 26 June 2013.

The directives also contain specific regulations concerning children and their protection. For instance, the Asylum Procedures Directive[9] regulates how children must be represented in the asylum procedure.

Iris Goldner Lang shows in her contribution, that the CJEU as well as the European Court of Human Rights (ECtHR) have already made many decisions that have secured and strengthened these rights. These include, in particular, the CJEU's decisions on the relevant age limits for family reunification and the judgement Camara by the ECtHR[10] on the need for legal representation of the child during the age assessment.

The European asylum regulations for dealing with families who migrate to Europe are therefore seemingly tight and orientated towards the best interests of the child and the protection of the family. However, it has already become clear that the reality in the EU does not always harmonise with these high standards of the law in the books.

2. Different Understandings by Different Actors: Different Views on the Best Interests of the Child in Family Law and Migration Law

In the context of FAMIMOVE, the handling of the best interests of the child principle can also be analysed from another exciting aspect. It can then be observed that the best interests of the child are also understood very differently within EU law — namely in international family law and asylum law. It is an astonishing discovery that even a fundamental concept as the best interests of the child can have such a different connotation in these two contexts.

In family law, the best interests of the child are understood as a completely individualised concept in most member states. In Germany, for example, the family courts always have to hear all children concerned by the proceedings. This is intended to give the judge a very individualised notion of what is the best solution for the specific child.

The participation of the child is not performed in exactly the same way in all member states — but it is common in family law to always think of the individual child.[11] Article 21 of the Brussels IIter Regulation[12] now contains provisions on the child's right to express their opinion. Although this does not mean that the court

---

[9]Directive 2013/32/EU of the European Parliament and of the Council of 26 June 2013 on common procedures for granting and withdrawing international protection.

[10]See for both I. Goldner Lang, The Principle of the Child's Best Interests in EU Law on Third-Country Nationals, in this volume, at p. 59.

[11]Schrama/Freemann/Taylor/Bruning (eds), International Handbook on Child Participation in Family Law, 2021.

[12]Council Regulation (EU) 2019/1111 of 25 June 2019 on jurisdiction, the recognition and enforcement of decisions in matrimonial matters and the matters of parental responsibility, and on international child abduction.

itself must hear the child, it makes clear that the child's individual views must be taken into account.[13] This means that the Brussels IIter Regulation now corresponds to Article 12 of the CRC, which stipulates that all children capable of forming their own views should have those views seriously considered in any decision that affects them. María González Marimón takes a closer look at the aspects of the best interests of the child in the Brussels IIter Regulation.

This individualised approach hardly exists in migration law. While it is true that a minor refugee is also heard in the asylum procedure, this hearing is restricted to the grounds for asylum. Being a minor can also take on significance in this context. However, in many other constellations in which children are affected, an individualised approach is dispensed with.

To illustrate the differences between the policy areas, it is worth taking a look at the decisions of the German Federal Constitutional Court (BVerfG). Since the best interests of the child are protected by constitutional law in Germany,[14] the way in which it is applied and the understanding of the term in detail have been refined by decisions of the BVerfG. The BVerfG has not only corrected family court judgements, but has also frequently corrected decisions by administrative courts concerning the protection of families and, in particular, the best interests of the child. In each case, it has explained how the best interests of the child are to be treated correctly. In this context, it can be said that the BVerfG acts as an "explainer" for both jurisdictions — but it explains the correct approach to the best interests of the child differently for administrative law and family law. On the one hand, for family law, it always requires that the individual circumstances must be clarified precisely — and the child must be heard anyway. For migration law, on the other hand, it has generalised statements. For example, in its established case law, it initially states unsuspiciously: "In the case of decisions on the right of residence that affect contact with a child, the child's point of view is decisive and it must be examined in each individual case whether there is actually a personal bond that the child depends on for its well-being."[15] That sounds easy to understand and would certainly be viewed similarly in family law. However, the subsequent procedure differs from family law. The BVerfG finds it perfectly normal for this assessment to be made in the abstract, without hearing the specific child. The administrative courts therefore have their own thoughts on what the child's perspective might be.[16]

Why these approaches are so different, cannot be explored in more detail here. As decisions in both family and migration law can involve the separation of a child from its parents, the differences do not seem completely comprehensible at first glance.

[13] T. Garber, In: Magnus/Mankowski (eds), ECPIL European Commentaries on Private International Law Commentary Volume IV Brussels IIter Regulation, 2023, Article 21 at paras. 12, 23.

[14] There is no provision guaranteeing the child's best interests explicitly. However, Article 2 paras. 1 and 2 and Article 6 para. 2 of the GG (German Basic Law) are the central rights from which the general protection of the child's best interests can be derived.

[15] Translation by the author, BVerfG 2 November 2023, 2 BvR 441/23, FamRZ 2024, 239 para. 23, ECLI:DE:BverfG:2023:rk20231102.2bvr044123.

[16] Applying the BVerfG's guidelines: VG Düsseldorf 17 March 2023, VG 27 L 990/22, NZFam 2023, 526, ECLI:DE:VGD:2023:0317.27L990.22.00.

However, it is advantageous for the understanding between the actors in the two areas of law to be at least aware of the divergent interpretation.

3. *Central Decisions of the CJEU*

a) Significance of the Case Law of the CJEU

As the CJEU has a monopoly on the interpretation of EU legal acts in accordance with Article 267 of the TFEU,[17] its decisions are of great importance for the application of EU asylum law. In international family law the number of European regulations and accordingly the influence of CJEU is equally high. In the context of migration, this primarily concerns the Brussels IIter Regulation, which regulates international jurisdiction and recognition in custody matters, but also greatly refines and shapes the 1980 Child Abduction Convention.[18] Overall, the influence of the CJEU is therefore very significant for the issues covered by FAMIMOVE.

b) Exemplary Decisions on the Best Interests of the Child in Migration Law

The CJEU is also strongly orientated towards the best interests of the child in its decision-making practice. Time and again, there have been important decisions that have raised the standard of the best interests of the child — at least in certain member states.

Germany and the Netherlands, for example, were directly involved in proceedings concerning the deadline for family reunification applications between minor children and their parents. The cases C-550/16,[19] C-273/20[20] and C-355/20 each concerned family reunification with a minor refugee who had entered the EU. The CJEU clearly stated that a person who was under the age of 18 at the time of entry and application for asylum and only reaches the age of majority during the asylum procedure is still to be regarded as a minor within the meaning of the definition in Article 2 lit. f of the Family Reunification Directive.[21]

Conversely, however, the CJEU has also specified the age limits in such a way that it is now clear that a child can still join a family member even if he or she has

[17] Treaty on the Functioning of the European Union (TFEU).

[18] Convention of 25 October 1980 on Civil Aspects of International Child Abduction (1980 Child Abduction Convention).

[19] CJEU 12 April 2018, case C-550/16, ECLI:EU:C:2018:248 (A. and S. versus the Netherlands).

[20] CJEU 1 August 2022, case C-273/20 and C-355/20, ECLI:EU:C:2022:617 (Bundesrepublik Deutschland).

[21] Council Directive 2003/86/EC of 22 September 2003 on the right to family reunification (Family Reunification Directive).

reached the age of majority during the lengthy reunification procedure. According to the ruling in case C-279/20,[22] the relevant point in time for determining whether a child is a minor in accordance with Article 4 para. 1 lit. c of the Family Reunification Directive is when the reunifying parent submitted their asylum application. In the same judgement, the CJEU also made statements on the existence of "living in a real family relationship" under Article 16 para. 1 lit. b of the Family Reunification Directive and clarified that mere kinship in the direct ascending line in the first degree is not sufficient, but that cohabitation is also not required. However, occasional visits can be sufficient proof.

Another important decision concerned Article 5 lit. a and lit. b of the Return Directive.[23] It prohibited the German legal practice of examining whether the best interests of the child are an obstacle to leaving Germany not when the return order is issued, but only shortly before the refugee is actually deported (§ 60a of the AufenthG (German Residence Act)). This practice is very stressful for refugees, as they receive a deportation order even though this is not really an option. The case in question concerned a deportation order for an infant whose father had a residence permit in Germany and whose mother was tolerated in Germany.

In its decision C-484/22 of 15 February 2023,[24] the CJEU ruled that the authorities must always fully consider the situation of the minor before issuing a return decision.

4. *Central Decisions of the ECtHR*

The ECtHR has jurisdiction only over violations of the Human Rights Convention.[25] When violations of the Human Rights Convention occur in the application of national or European migration law, the jurisdiction of the ECtHR overlaps with that of the CJEU. The ECtHR has consistently held that the right to private life enshrined in Article 8 of the Human Rights Convention includes the right to development and the right to establish relationships. Therefore, this fundamental right also significantly protects minors and families on the move.

The decision Darboe and Camara v. Italy shall be mentioned here as an important example.[26] In this judgement, the ECtHR explained the significance of the presumption of minority. Among other things, the ECtHR ruled that minor refugees must be

[22] CJEU 1 August 2022, case C-279/20, ECLI:EU:C:2022:618.

[23] Directive 2008/115/EC of the European Parliament and the Council of 16 December 2008 on common standards and procedures in Member States for returning illegally staying third-country nationals (Return Directive).

[24] CJEU 15 February 2023, case C-484/22, ECLI:EU:C:2023:122.

[25] European Convention on Human Rights.

[26] ECtHR 21 July 2022, 5797/17, ECLI:CE:ECHR:2022:0721JUD000579717 (Darboe und Camara versus Italy).

legally represented in the age assessment procedure. One of the minimum procedural guarantees is that the person concerned must still be granted a legal representative (for example a guardian *ad litem*) when filing an application against the determination of the age of majority by the authorities in charge.

5. Summary

To summarise, it can be seen that EU law has the best interests of the child in mind and also protects families. However, much of this is lost in the application by the authorities and courts of the member states. In some cases, this happens with reference to crisis situations. However, the high level of migration must not be used as an excuse. Instead, all efforts should be made to protect the best interests of the child in any case.

IV. On the Key Contents of the Contributions to This Book

The first part of this book (Part I) (*Marta Pertegás Sender*, An Introduction to FAMIMOVE, Its Accomplishments and Its Challenges) is dedicated to the FAMIMOVE-project and sets out the background, foundation and aims of FAMIMOVE.

The second part (Part II) explores general topics like the child's best interests principle in the context of EU family and migration law or age assessment.

The first chapter of the second part (*María González Marimón*, Child's best interests in international jurisdiction under the Brussels IIter Regulation) sheds light on the child's best interests in the area of international jurisdiction under the Brussels IIter Regulation. María González Marimón focuses on parental responsibility which is of paramount importance for the child's best interests in international settings and within migration contexts. She demonstrates how the Brussels IIter Regulation's jurisdiction model aims to reflect an accurate balance between abstract and concrete notions of the child's best interests. The article illustrates how this balance is achieved: The habitual residence of the child is generally the relevant factor for jurisdiction, but a range of exceptions to this general rule reflect experiences from practice and enables courts to achieve adequate solutions. María González Marimón also welcomes the jurisdiction regime as an enhancement of the child's best interests principle in its triple dimension as a substantive right, an inspiring principle, and as a procedural rule.

The next chapter (*Iris Goldner Lang*, The Principle of the Child's Best Interests in EU Law on Third-Country Nationals) demonstrates that the child's best interests principle is a paramount and intrinsic value of EU law, serving as an underlying rationale for EU legislation and judgments. Iris Goldner Lang examines how this fundamental principle impacts the rights of third-country nationals in the EU, with a focus on decisions related to family reunification as well as EU migration and asylum law. She develops a multidimensional understanding of the child's best interests principle, highlighting its threefold function as a substantive right, an interpretative tool, and a procedural rule. Based on this analysis, Iris Goldner Lang argues that the principle of the child's best interests will continue to gain importance in EU law on third-country nationals, due to its multidimensional nature and its role as a counterbalance to the ongoing trend of restricting the rights of migrants and asylum seekers across the EU.

The following chapter (*Kai Hüning*, Binding Effect of an Age Assessment) examines a difficult problem that is well-known in legal practice, namely the problem of age assessment in the perspective of the child's best interests principle. Kai Hüning illustrates the background of age assessment in the context of migration of minors and sheds light on the need for age assessment and its methods. The article's focus lies on the question of whether or not age assessment procedures carried out in one member state of the EU must be recognised by other member states. Kai Hüning invokes the Charter of Fundamental Rights of the European Union, the UN 1989 Convention on the Rights of the Child (CRC) and the Human Rights Convention for his approach to that problem: Kai Hüning argues for a binding effect in principle — an effect that must be incorporated by way of interpretation of the national provisions.

Guardianship is the topic of the book's third part (C). Two chapters explain the legal framework on guardianship for unaccompanied minor refugees from different national perspectives (Hungary and Germany). Here, family law is particularly closely connected with migration law. The chapters thus also analyse the respective migration law and focus on the the child's best interests principle in light of the respective national regulations and practice.

The first chapter (*Orsolya Szeibert*, Guardianship of children in the context of migration in Hungary) focuses on guardianship of unaccompanied minors in Hungary. Orsolya Szeibert gives an overview of the Hungarian asylum regime, its political background and complexity. She points out how the situation of children in Hungary was heavily affected by several legal acts in the mid-2010s that contained specific provisions for the "crisis situation caused by mass immigration". Orsolya Szeibert shows the (negative) effects of these provisions for minors and points out that the "crisis situation" has been continously prolonged since 2016 until today. She refers to criticisms of the Hungarian *status quo* in which unaccompanied minors between the age of 14 and 18 are effectively considered as adult asylum applicants.

The second chapter of the third part (*Bettina Heiderhoff*, Guardianship and other protective measures for minor refugees in Germany) emphasises the importance of protecting unaccompanied minor refugees and points out the connections of migration law, private international law and family law. Bettina Heiderhoff examines the central terms "minor" and "unaccompanied" in the perspective of German law, describes the procedures for the appointment of guardianship and other protective measures (in particular, the so-called provisional taking into care). She also analyses cases in which a minor refugee arrives in Germany after a guardian has been appointed in another member state. Bettina Heiderhoff shows that Germany combines several legal institutions to ensure the protection of unaccompanied minor refugees. Yet she also points to considerable problems, in particular a conflict of interest of the youth welfare office, the lack of special knowledge of the guardians as regards asylum law and certain difficulties as regards age assessment and responsibility.

Bettina Heiderhoff also concludes the third part with an outlook on the European perspective regarding guardianship (*Bettina Heiderhoff*, A European Approach to Cross-Border Guardianship). She emphasises that EU law only regulates specific aspects of migration law and private international law, while substantive family law remains under the jurisdiction of member states. Bettina Heiderhoff argues that the opportunities for EU law to directly influence guardianship practices are limited. Nonetheless, she points out potential refinements, particularly in the application of the Brussels IIter Regulation.

The book's fourth part (D) is dedicated to early marriage, a topic analysed from various national perspectives (Sweden, Germany, and Austria). The authors have chosen to use the neutral term "early marriage" to avoid the stereotypical images and ideas associated with the problematic term "child marriage." The visibility of early marriage in Europe has been increased by families on the move. This topic also illustrates how deeply intertwined law and politics can be.

The first chapter (*Ulf Maunsbach*, Early Marriages in Sweden) explains recent developments in Sweden, where early marriages validly concluded abroad are generally not recognised. Ulf Maunsbach shows that there is a very narrow exception to this non-recognition principle: recognition is possible only in exceptional cases when there are extraordinary reasons. He argues that the application of the non-recognition principle may vary across different institutional settings, such as asylum proceedings, family law, or inheritance proceedings. Ulf Maunsbach explains that for the purposes of registering status relationships in the Swedish population registration database, the exception to the non-recognition principle will rarely apply since the Tax Agency's examination relies solely on written documentation and does not include specific investigations into the circumstances surrounding the marriage. He also highlights a general lack of case law, which makes it even more difficult to evaluate the situation. Ulf Maunsbach argues for allowing individual exceptions to enable authorities and courts to make carefully considered decisions.

The second chapter of the fourth part (*Stefan Arnold*, Early Marriage in Germany — Law and Politics of Cultural Demarcation) examines the German law on early marriage with a focus on the recent statute effective from 1 July 2024. Stefan Arnold argues that the recent German law on early marriage is emblematic of symbolic politics and cultural demarcation, highlighting the detrimental power of symbolic lawmaking. He shows that the law's turbulent recent history has been written by an an unfortunate interplay between courts, politicians, and interest groups. He argues that before the recent legislative interventions, just and differentiated solutions were achieved by the courts through the application of the ordre public clause. Stefan Arnold shows that such solutions are no longer attainable, as German law now adheres to a strict policy of non-recognition of early marriages when a spouse was under the age of 16 at the time of marriage. He argues that the political debate and the law's resort to a symbolic outlawing of early marriages abroad have significantly worsened the position of those deserving protection, particularly the young women concerned and the children born from such marriage.

The third chapter of the fourth part (*Martina Melcher*, Early Marriages in Austria) explains the Austrian legal framework regarding early marriages. Martina Melcher shows that the issue of a valid marriage arises not only in family law matters, but most often in family reunification and asylum proceedings. This part reveals that, unlike in Germany, early marriage has not yet been the subject of intense political and academic debates in Austria. Martina Melcher points out that Austrian Law enables courts to carefully consider the individual circumstances of each case. She notes that there is no violation of the Austrian ordre public if both spouses are adults at the time of the assessment, want to uphold their marriage, and there was neither coercion nor lack of will at the time of the marriage's conclusion. She emphasises that explicit legislation may not be necessary and argues for a careful, individual, and conscious analysis of all relevant aspects of the situation. At the same time, Martina Melcher calls for legislative action regarding certain aspects, particularly the consequences of early marriages in cases where they are not recognised.

The fourth part concludes with a contribution on early marriage from a European perspective (*Stefan Arnold*, Early Marriage: A European Perspective). Stefan Arnold particularly compares Sweden's and Germany's strict non-recognition approach with Austria's flexible ordre public approach regarding early marriages validly concluded abroad. He argues that the Austrian approach is preferable, as it enables courts to achieve just solutions based on an individual case-by-case analysis. Based on the chapter's comparative evaluation, Stefan Arnold develops proposals for potential legislative measures with an emphasis on institutional solutions that promote justice and prioritise the needs of those worthy of protection.

The book's fifth part (E) is dedicated to kafāla. Five contributions explain kafāla and related institutes from different perspectives (Islamic law, France, the Netherlands, Belgium and International Social Services). The contributions also explain the respective migration case law and migration legal framework. The chapter is rounded up by a chapter on a European approach to kafāla.

The fifth part's first chapter (*Nadjma Yassari*, Beyond kafāla: How parentless children are placed in new homes) explores the various legal options available in Muslim jurisdictions for placing parentless children into new homes. She identifies four categories of these options: complete incorporation of a child into a new family, wide-ranging incorporation, structures for the temporary care of abandoned or orphaned children, and jurisdictions where caretaking occurs informally, with minimal state supervision or intervention. Nadjma Yassari reviews several Muslim jurisdictions and demonstrates how they have developed alternative caretaking arrangements for parentless children based on these categories. She discusses how these jurisdictions navigate the prohibition of tabannī (adoption) in Islamic law while still finding ways to provide children with stable homes. Nadjma Yassari highlights Tunisia as the only country to formally regulate and accept tabannī, allowing for complete incorporation of a child into a new family. She also notes the absence of a formalised legal framework for placing parentless children in new homes in some Muslim jurisdictions, such as Lebanon.

The second chapter in the fifth part (*Fabienne Jault-Seseke*, Kafāla in France) provides a French perspective on kafāla. Fabienne Jault-Seseke highlights the practical importance of kafāla in France: Many individuals of Moroccan or Algerian nationality living in France assume responsibility for a child born in their country of origin through kafāla. Fabienne Jault Seseke explains how such arrangements intend to compensate for the absence of parents or to offer the child better living conditions and education. Additionally, as the chapter shows, kafāla serves as an alternative to adoption, which is prohibited in Morocco and Algeria. Jault-Seseke argues that despite kafāla not constituting adoption, it should be regulated similarly to ensure the protection of fundamental rights for all parties involved. She emphasises that Article 33 of the 1996 Hague Convention on parental responsibility and protection of children provides the necessary framework for this regulation.

The fifth part's third chapter (*Mayela Celis Aguilar*, Kafāla in the Netherlands) explains the legal framework and case law on kafāla in the Netherlands where most cases originate from Morocco. Mayela Celis Aguilar points out a change of policy in 2013 following which kafāla is no longer treated as adoptions but, with some caution, similar to foster care measures. She expounds the Dutch legislation and Article 33 of the 1996 Hague Convention that are applied in the Netherlands. Mayela Celis Aguilar evaluates the Dutch policy with regard to the recognition of kafālas as generally coherent and in line with the applicable international instruments. Yet she also points to concerns about the use of kafāla to circumvent adoption and immigration policies and regulations.

The fourth chapter of the fifth part (*Leontine Bruijnen*, Kafāla in Belgium: private international law as an essential tool to establish migration law consequences?) discusses how a kafāla can be characterised and recognised in Belgium, whether or not it should be converted into an adoption or whether kafāla is equal to foster care. She points out that a kafāla should be characterised as a child protection measure according to the 1996 Child Protection Convention yet that the Convention did not solve all kafāla-related issues — particularly as regards migration law consequences. Leontine Bruijnen explains the relevant legal framework as well as the Belgian family and migration case law. She offers a solution based on the general recognition rules for kafālas falling outside the scope of the 1996 Child Protection Convention. Leontine Bruijnen further argues that the private international law framework should be taken into account to determine whether a makfūl (ward) can be considered an unaccompanied minor.

The fifth part's fifth chapter (*Giovanna Ricciardi/Jeannette Wöllenstein-Tripathi*, Principles to ensure a cross-border kafāla placement is in the best interests of the child) highlights the principles and recommended practices drawn from the International Social Services (ISS) Kafalah study 2020. These principles are aimed at guiding states in ensuring that cross-border kafāla placements prioritise the best interests of the child. The authors emphasise that protecting children's rights has always been central to the ISS mission. They caution that European debates on kafāla often reflect Western perspectives that equate kafāla with institutions like adoption, guardianship, or foster care. The authors underscore the importance of maintaining continuity in the child's situation across borders, ensuring legal security, and respecting the child's fundamental human rights.

The fifth part's sixth and final chapter (*Fabienne Jault-Seseke*, Recognition of kafāla in European member states — need for a uniform approach?) addresses whether and under what conditions a kafāla issued in an Islamic state may be recognised in European member states. Jault-Seseke highlights the diverse approaches taken by member states and the lack of a uniform EU legislative approach. She argues that any European solution must uphold the EU Charter, the CRC, and the 1996 Child Protection Convention, and respect the cultural context of the child. She concludes that kafāla should not not be equated with adoption and that the best interests of the child must be taken into account at both the pronouncement of kafāla and recognition stages.

The book's sixth part (F) is dedicated to two practically important topics at the intersection of family law, migration law and private international law.

The first chapter of the sixth part (*Alessia Voinich*, The Role of the Court of Justice in Shaping the Right to Maintain Family Unity for Beneficiaries of International Protection) examines how the CJEU addresses member states' flexibility in establishing more favorable national regimes. It explores the connection between the rights of family members and the asylum rights of their relatives who are beneficiaries of international protection, as well as situations where different member states bear responsibility for international protection and ensuring family unity. The chapter also assesses the impact of recent reforms within the Common European Asylum System (CEAS). Alessia Voinich underscores the high standards of protection for the right to family unity provided by EU secondary law and highlights the CJEU's efforts to prioritise the best interests of the child as a guiding principle. She argues that the CJEU's future decisions will be pivotal in achieving a balanced approach between uniformity and necessary flexibility in individual cases.

The second chapter of the sixth part (*Giovanni Zaccaroni*, Polygamous marriages and reunification of families on the move under EU law: an overview) is dedicated to polygamous marriages that are usually associated with countries outside the EU. Giovanni Zaccaroni shows how questions of the recognition of polygamous marriages and possible rights attached to the status of the spouses have led to intense discussions in the EU. He argues that the prohibition of family reunification under EU law represents an obstacle to free movement and family reunification of migrant families, and, potentially, also to the best interests of the child. But, as Giovanni Zaccaroni argues, at the same time it is rooted in the necessity to protect and promote equal treatment between men and women, enshrined in the EU Charter of Fundamental Rights as well as in the national constitutions. The contribution highlights the need to protect the rights of the weaker parts of the relationship and to avoid the creation of partners of first and second class, thus discriminating among persons in a similar situation and violating their fundamental rights.

V. Other Sources and Important Actors

1. Preliminary Remark

Given the complexity of the legal situation at the interface between migration law and family law, it is not surprising that the number of governmental bodies, NGOs and expert groups working in this field is large and diverse. The following overview is an attempt to identify at least some of the main actors and their roles or activities. It may also provide some guidance as to which organisations are appropriate contacts when legal issues relating to child refugees arise at the intersection of family law and migration law.

It should be pointed out that no claim can be made to the completeness of this list.

2. EPAPFR

First of all, EPAPFR (European Platform for Access to Personal and Family Rights) shall be mentioned. EPAPFR was a project that could almost be seen as a "predecessor project" to FAMIMOVE. It also concerned the interface between international family law and public administrative law in the EU. Just like FAMIMOVE, it was co-funded by the Justice Programme of the EU.

However, the focus of EPAPFR differed from that of FAMIMOVE in various respects. Above all, it was not just about refugees, but about families in the EU in general. Similar to FAMIMOVE, however, the aim was to improve "coordination and cooperation between public and private systems providing legal and social services in Member States". In this context, the visualisation of contact persons and responsible actors played an important role in EPAPFR. The result can be found on the EPAPFR website, where many important public and private actors can now be easily found.[27]

3. Important Actors and Their Specialisations

a) Central Authorities and EJN

aa) General Function

In all EU member states, many cross-border co-operation tasks are bundled together at the central authorities. These are national authorities set up by the member states, in particular, to take on tasks relating to communication and counselling in

[27] https://epapfr.com/en/useful-websites/.

cross-border legal relations. These Central Authorities are not only provided for in the Brussels IIter Regulation, but also in the 1996 Child Protection Convention in order to facilitate the implementation of cooperation between the member states and contracting states.

In the context of refugee minors, the Central Authority is particularly important when it comes to recognising protection measures already taken abroad.

This concerns guardianships, curatorships, adoptions and similar procedures in the home country or a third country — above all the kafāla, which is of particular interest in the context of FAMIMOVE.

To a certain extent, the Central Authority works in both directions. It can be used for communication with foreign authorities and courts if a child is to travel to another member state. The aim may be to ensure that protective measures can be taken immediately in the host country.

However, it can also be an important point of contact if a child has travelled to another country and the aim is to find out whether measures have already been taken to protect a child in another member state.

bb) Structure and Tasks Under the Brussels IIter Regulation and the 1996 Child Protection Convention

The Central Authorities must be designated by the participating member states under Article 76 of the Brussels IIter Regulation and by the contracting states under Article 29 of the 1996 Child Protection Convention. The Brussels IIter Regulation (Recital 72) explicitly recommends to entrust the same body for both legal acts. The Central Authorities are financed by the member states and the assistance provided by them is free of charge (see Article 83 para 1 of the Brussels IIter Regulation; Article 38 of the 1996 Child Protection Convention). They may impose reasonable charges only for additional services (such as psychological expert opinions or carrying out supervised contact).

Under the Brussels IIter Regulation, the Central Authorities support courts and competent authorities. However, in certain cases, in particular in abduction situations, they also provide direct assistance to the holders of parental responsibility. The task covers many important functions in cross-border procedures, such as, for example, promoting the amicable resolution of family disputes.

The tasks under the 1996 Child Protection Convention are set out in Articles 29 et seq. of the 1996 Child Protection Convention. Just like under the Brussels IIter Regulation, communication and cooperation between the contracting states and the acting courts and authorities are of central importance. Additionally, under Article 33 of the 1996 Child Protection Convention, any decision on the placement or taking into care of a child in another contracting state must be prepared and agreed by the Central Authorities.

cc) EJN (European Judicial Network)

The European Judicial Network, which was founded in 1998, is best known for its functions in the area of criminal law. However, it also has a strong branch in family law. Article 77 and Article 84 of the Brussels IIter Regulation provide for co-operation between judges and authorities through the European Judicial Network. So-called contact points are to be designated in all member states, from which foreign authorities can obtain expert advice. This includes, in particular, the liaison magistrates who, as judges, form a network in which direct communication can take place successfully.[28]

b) European Union Agency for Asylum (EUAA)

In contrast to the Central Authorities, the EUAA is an authority of the EU itself.[29]

The EUAA has the task of ensuring the harmonisation of asylum systems and the practical application of European asylum law in all EU member states. However, it has no actual authority to intervene but rather acts in an assisting capacity. Its activities are also entirely focused on supporting the member states and are not aimed at individuals.

In particular, the EAUU offers the EU member states practical and legal support in various formats. This includes a considerable amount of general information, such as analytical reports. However, the EAUU also organises expert networks and training services. Operational assistance is central here, in which the member states are supported — sometimes over several years — in further improving the capacities and expertise of their reception and asylum systems.

c) Council of Europe and European Court of Human Rights (ECtHR)

The Council of Europe is not a body of the EU, but has 46 member states, including the UK, Turkey and Azerbaijan. An important part of the Council of Europe is the European Court of Human Rights, which monitors compliance with the Human Rights Convention.

The Council of Europe also supports many projects aimed at improving human rights. The problem of unaccompanied minor refugees[30] is a constant concern in this context. In December 2022, the Council of Europe Committee of Ministers adopted a Recommendation on Age Assessment in the Context of Migration.[31] In particular,

[28] https://e-justice.europa.eu/431/EN/about_the_network.

[29] https://euaa.europa.eu/.

[30] https://www.coe.int/en/web/children/migration.

[31] https://rm.coe.int/0900001680ab501f.

it emphasises the assumption of minority and also warns against making medical examinations the norm.

There has also been an Action Plan on Protecting Refugee and Migrant Children in Europe, which ran from 2017 to 2019.[32] One of the issues was that children should not be held in places that were "ill-adapted to the presence of children".

Currently an Action Plan on Protecting Vulnerable Persons in the Context of Migration and Asylum in Europe (2020–2025) is running.[33] This deals in particular with the coordination between the various competent authorities.

d) Selected Independent Actors

aa) EU Agency for Fundamental Rights (FRA)

FRA calls itself "the independent centre of reference and excellence for promoting and protecting human rights in the EU".[34] It is funded by the EU and covers, among other things, the human rights situation of unaccompanied minor refugees. In particular, FRA has specialised in the collection and distribution of information. It has also set itself the task of strengthening co-operation between fundamental rights actors.

Overall, a lot of important information can be found on the FRA website. For example, one can find a complete list of the respective national authorities responsible for coordinating the protection of children's rights.[35]

Various studies should be emphasised here, which provide detailed information on the situation of unaccompanied minor refugees in the EU. This applies in particular to the publication "Guardianship systems for unaccompanied children in the the European Union: developments since 2014".[36] This report is an update of a former study. It shows that positive legislative changes have taken place in many member states. However, quite in accordance with FAMIMOVE's findings, it also shows that national guardianship systems continue to face challenges.

In January 2024, the FRA published a study on "Mapping Child Protection Systems in the EU".[37] This study, too, is an update of a former study. Quite similar to the issue of guardianship, most member states have amended their national

---

[32] https://www.coe.int/en/web/special-representative-secretary-general-migration-refugees/action-plan.

[33] https://edoc.coe.int/en/refugees/10241-council-of-europe-action-plan-on-protecting-vulnerable-persons-in-the-context-of-migration-and-asylum-in-europe-2021-2025.html.

[34] https://fra.europa.eu.

[35] https://fra.europa.eu/en/content/central-authority-national-coordinating-role.

[36] https://fra.europa.eu/en/publication/2022/guardianship-systems-children-update.

[37] https://fra.europa.eu/en/publication/2024/mapping-child-protection-systems-eu-update-2023?page=7.

legislation regarding children in the context of migration since 2014. It underlines that often child protection and migration legislation are not aligned.

Finally, it should be mentioned that FRA and EUAA have jointly published a series of information brochures aimed at helping guardians in the representation of unaccompanied minors.[38]

bb) ISS

The International Social Service (ISS) is a globally active umbrella organisation for social NGOs.[39] The overarching objective of the ISS is to ensure that respect for human rights is accorded to every individual, especially to children. The ISS is focusing on resolving international child protection cases. On the one hand, this involves a high standard of social protection for minors, but on the other hand the ISS also specialises in the legal aspects of international cases.

FAMIMOVE has worked closely with the ISS. This volume contains a contribution by Jeannette Woellenstein and Giovanna Ricciardi, which emerged from the ISS' Kafalah study.[40]

cc) Other Large Organisations and Networks

There are a large number of other international organisations that provide considerable support to refugee families and unaccompanied minors. An example is The Red Cross (TRC). The Red cross not only works in the field of emergency care and accommodation but is also particularly well known for its Tracing Service for refugees. It therefore plays an important role in the area of family reunification and subsequent immigration of relatives.

However, it should be noted that there are a large number of specialised networks working intensively on the situation of minor refugees in the EU, sometimes in particular with a legal focus.

This includes, for example the Separated Children in Europe Programme (SCEP).[41] SCEP is a European NGO-Network of 31 organisations from 28 European countries. It is specialised in supporting unaccompanied children. It aims to ensure through research, a shared policy and advocacy at national and regional levels that age assessment and guardianship are subject to appropriate standards and that durable solutions are found.

---

[38] https://fra.europa.eu/en/publication/2024/practical-tool-guardians-transnational-procedures-framework-international.

[39] https://iss-ssi.org/.

[40] https://www.iss-ssi.org/storage/2023/03/ISS_Kafalah_ENG.pdf.

[41] https://www.separated-children-europe-programme.org/.

The European Council on Refugees and Exiles (ECRE) is an alliance of 125 NGOs across 40 European countries.[42] ECRE is not only generally working in the field of flight and exile, but it has also effected several projects specifically related to minor refugees. These were, however, carried out some time ago.[43]

The organisation Missing Children Europe is more specialised and aims at protecting unaccompanied children from abuse and child trafficking.[44] It also focuses on children in migration.

Finally, the European Guardianship Network (EGN) aims to improve guardianship services for unaccompanied and separated children in the EU member states.[45]

[42] https://ecre.org/.

[43] https://ecre.org/our-work/the-rights-of-refugee-children/.

[44] https://missingchildreneurope.eu.

[45] https://www.egnetwork.eu/.

An Introduction to FAMIMOVE, Its Accomplishments and Its Challenges

Marta Pertegás Sender

FAMIMOVE is the acronym of a two-year project carried out by a consortium of seven universities on behalf of the European Commission from January 2023 to December 2024. FAMIMOVE stands for "Families on the Move: The Coordination between international family law and migration law". The project's objectives are twofold: depicting the intersections between these two areas of the law and seeking to contribute to a better coordination between them.

In this introductory chapter, I have been asked to contextualise FAMIMOVE as a project, looking at its origins, its implementation and its (intended) results.

1. Getting to FAMIMOVE

FAMIMOVE stems from a joint academic initiative of several experts working in different EU member states in the areas of international family law, international migration and human rights. What unites them is their intention of implementing the recommendations of earlier studies published in June 2017 by the European Parliament's Committee on Legal Affairs.[1] These studies recommended further work on specific actions for a better articulation of the EU private international law instruments in a migratory context. In response to this recommendation, a FAMIMOVE project proposal was submitted by a consortium of seven universities under the

[1] To be completed: two short-term studies commissioned by the JURI committee of the European Parliament on "Private International Law in a Context of Increasing International Mobility: Challenges and Potential" and "Children on the Move: A Private International Law Perspective" (https://www.europarl.europa.eu/thinktank).

M. Pertegás Sender (✉)
Maastricht University, Maastricht, Netherlands
e-mail: m.pertegassender@maastrichtuniversity.nl

S. Arnold, B. Heiderhoff (eds.), *Children in Migration and International Family Law*, https://doi.org/10.1007/978-3-031-71598-3_2

coordination of Maastricht University. Further to the European Commission's decision of funding this proposal under the JUST-2022-JCOO programme, FAMIMOVE started in January 2023 as a research-based action plan with interconnected work packages project for a duration of 24 months.

2. FAMIMOVE as a Project

The project relates to two distinct policy areas such as migration and international family protection. These two policy areas share an essential factor: they affect the lives of individuals whose personal and family status are uncertain when crossing borders. Despite their common feature, these areas operate separately and their underlying legal frameworks do not readily interact. Previous work had already made clear that the lack of concerted action may be detrimental to the concerned individuals. Against this framework, FAMIMOVE sets out some minimum objectives: a higher mutual awareness of the intersections between these policy areas, a better reciprocal understanding of their respective legal frameworks and more dialogue between stakeholders in the different areas. More specifically, the implementation of FAMIMOVE was designed to respond to the specific objectives as follows:

- mapping how relevant authorities responsible for migration issues apply the instruments of international family law;
- assessing the level of knowledge about relevant instruments from the international framework on child protection that authorities possess;
- planning and delivering interventions to relevant authorities that fill any knowledge gaps and make sure they are updated with new developments;
- ensuring collaboration and connection among migration caseworkers, international child protection authorities, and affiliated stakeholders; and
- connecting the fields of international family law and migration law through targeted activities involving practitioners from each field.

In response to these objectives, FAMIMOVE put in place a series of interconnected actions piloted by different partner universities and with combined participation of other project researchers and external experts. In five interconnected work packages, the project design focused on three types of activities.

First, the respective project partners contacted the relevant instances and individuals involved in the field of international family law and migration law. It became clear that not all stakeholders appreciated the (challenging) intersection between their respective legal fields. This confirmed the need for awareness-raising and mapping work carried out under the FAMIMOVE project. In particular, the project's work package two, under the coordination of Lund University (Sweden), included a series of awareness-raising seminars in each of the seven countries represented in FAMIMOVE (Belgium, France, Germany, Hungary, Italy, the Netherlands, and Sweden). In each country, the project team brought together representatives of institutions involved in handling cases with migrant children. These seminars confirmed the insufficient dialogue between instances in charge of different responsibility areas (e.g. the Immigration Services and the units responsible for international family cases). Furthermore, the participants reported that administrative authorities and other entities concerned with migrant children, such as youth welfare offices and migration authorities, often do not cooperate because the persons working in these areas do not know each other or each other's responsibilities.

While much more structural work is needed, the reports of the seven FAMIMOVE "awareness-raising seminars" make clear that these events indeed contributed to a better understanding of the respective challenges faced by the stakeholders. Furthermore, these events were instrumental for the collection of detailed insights from practice about the problems the key players are confronted with. As such, these events were a necessary stepping stone for the project's subsequent implementation. Above all, the active participation of the relevant stakeholders, their clear intentions to use these initial contacts in future case management and the stakeholders' commitment towards subsequent project activities confirm that the work carried out at the domestic level was beneficial.

Secondly, FAMIMOVE carried out transnational work around three previously identified questions: guardianship, child marriage[2] and the treatment of kafāla. Under the direction of Ghent University (Belgium), the project team collected comparative empirical data in previously identified key jurisdictions for each of these topics and conducted dedicated sessions to those questions. The meetings took place in Paris, Muenster and Milan, involved experts from three or more different jurisdictions, and resulted in very comprehensive reports. These reports provide a wealth of information about the difficulties that practitioners encounter in practice. At the same time, they clearly identify practices or ideas that could be rolled out more generally, as they are aligned with the overall objective of a consolidated action with due attention to both the migratory context and the international child protection context. For instance, regarding the appointment of guardianship, the experts signalled the ineffective doubling of procedures, with a possible risk of conflicting results and the imperative need for a local guardian. Much of this is actually possible under the relevant legal instruments on international judicial and administrative cooperation, including the Brussels IIter Regulation[3] and the 1996 Child Protection Convention.[4] For the portability of child protection arrangements such as kafāla, or

[2] See for the terminology used in this volume—"early marriage"—U. Maunsbach, Early marriages in Sweden. in this volume, 145, at pp. 145 f., S. Arnold, Early Marriage in Germany—Law and Politics of Cultural Demarcation, in this volume, 161, at p. 162 and M. Melcher, Early marriages in Austria—Private international law and ordre public assessment, in this volume, 183, at pp. 183 f.

[3] Council Regulation (EU) 2019/1111 of 25 June 2019 on jurisdiction, the recognition and enforcement of decisions in matrimonial matters and the matters of parental responsibility, and on international child abduction.

[4] Convention of 19 October 1996 on Jurisdiction, Applicable Law, Recognition, Enforcement and Co-operation in respect of Parental Responsibility and Measures for the Protection of Children (1996 Child Protection Convention).

the legal treatment of child marriage, the reports show remarkable differences in the EU jurisdictions under review. As such, the transnational roundtables underscore the need for case-specific and child-centred approaches to migrant children, rather than categorical rules banning any legal effect to such foreign marriages or other institutions, for instance in the context of a family reunification request. Furthermore, the discussions made clear that the individuals and families are "on the move", not only towards the EU, but also within the EU. The intra-EU mobility of these migrant individuals brings to the fore the relevance of the freedom of movement within the EU. When domestic authorities implement their policies based on their domestic legislation, they cannot lose sight of the EU legal framework. The transnational roundtables and the resulting reports provide much food for further action in the interface of migration law and private international law.

Thirdly, FAMIMOVE put in place a number of supporting actions to ensure the project's outreach. The project website (https://famimove.unimib.it/), run by the University of Milano-Bicocca (Italy), became the project's main information hub. Furthermore, the FAMIMOVE Newsletter ensures a rapid dissemination of the project's main findings and other relevant news among a growing legal community seeking to contribute to the project's objectives. In the final stages of the project, all partners, under the coordination of partner Milano-Bicocca, have convened a general conference in Brussels, in the hope that the European Commission as the main funding institution of FAMIMOVE can take stock of the work carried out under the project and the ensuing recommendations. In the same vein, the project partners will produce tailor-made policy briefs to ensure that the main project results are translated into specific recommendations for the relevant caseworkers and other authorities in a more targeted way. Last but not least, FAMIMOVE's academic learnings are compiled in this book as the project's main academic output under the direction of the University of Muenster.

3. Intended Results

At the time of writing, three quarters of the project's implementation time have lapsed so venturing some comments about what was done and what was (so far) achieved seems possible.

FAMIMOVE brought together a relatively large group of entities (7 universities each based in a different member state) and around 20 researchers (with diverse dedication to the project, from full-time to very part-time dedication to the project) worked on the project. It seems that the clearcut division of tasks, with the project management entrusted to the University of Maastricht as the project's coordinator and the substantive work distributed among all partners, yielded satisfactory results. Furthermore, a consultative body composed of international independent experts (FAMIMOVE's Advisory Body) provided external insights on the way to maximise the benefits for all stakeholders, and in particular for practitioners involved with migrant children. The role of the Advisory Body was key in supporting the consortium and ensuring a practical focus of actions and recommendations in line with the project's long-term objectives.

More importantly, some of the anticipated outcomes have materialised or they are expected to materialise upon the project's conclusion.

In particular, FAMIMOVE contributed to a better dissemination of the rules of the Brussels IIter Regulation, the 1996 Child Protection Convention and other international child protection instruments among lawyers, judges and authorities handling cases involving migrant children.

A short-term project like FAMIMOVE cannot achieve an ideal articulation between migration law and international child protection. However, it has achieved concrete improvements as the experts involved in joint activities have gained awareness about the intersections between the relevant legal areas and they have expressed their willingness to establish durable networks.

With regard to the specific case studies under scrutiny, FAMIMOVE has contributed to a better understanding of varying legal frameworks and practices. At the same time, the study makes clear the need for the recognition of guardianship or parental responsibility arrangements established in a non-EU member state and recognised in an EU member state. In the same vein, it recalls that the recognition of guardianship decisions rendered in one member state in other member states is possible under the applicable legal framework.

A more nuanced approach is advocated for married migrant children or for migrant children under a protection measure unknown to the domestic legal system (such as the kafāla from the perspective of EU member states). Several FAMIMOVE outputs underscore the importance of assessing the individual circumstances of the case to determine the best interests of the child. The general framework of control and regulation of migration should not stand in the way of the protection of the best interests of the individual child.

The following chapters in this book describe how these objectives were pursued and which concrete actions were deployed. They take us closer to a fully implemented FAMIMOVE project and, as such, to a better application of the relevant instruments of international child protection for all children crossing borders.

Part II
General Topics

The Child's Best Interests in International Jurisdiction Under the Brussels IIter Regulation

María González Marimón

I. Introduction

Within the European Union (EU), the mobility of family groups, sometimes consisting of members of different nationalities and origins, has led the EU legislator to consider the uniform regulation of certain family law aspects as necessary for the proper functioning of the internal market. Thus, the EU legislator has sought to provide families in the EU with uniform and coherent rules. These rules are supposed to give them a secure answer regarding, inter alia, the question of which courts they should go to in the event of a dispute arising in certain aspects and areas that affect them.

When it comes to the children involved in transnational situations,[1] the issue of parental responsibility is particularly relevant. The concept of "parental responsibility" is dynamic and covers, in its plurality, various situations with their own singularity, with the child in the centre. In this respect, the Brussels IIbis Regulation[2]

[1] For an overall vision of the EU children protection system see: R. Espinosa Calabuig/L. Carballo Piñeiro, Child Protection in European Family Law, In: Pfeiffer/Lobach/Rapp (eds), Facilitating Cross-Border Family Life — Towards a Common European Understanding: EUFams II and Beyond, 2021, at pp. 49–90; R. Espinosa Calabuig, Cross-border Family Issues in the EU: Multiplicity of Instruments, Inconsistencies and Problems of Coordination, In: Ruiz Abou-Nigm/ Noodt Taquela (eds), Diversity and Integration in Private International Law, 2019, at pp. 65 ff.

[2] Council Regulation (EC) No 2201/2003 of 27 November 2003 concerning jurisdiction and the recognition and enforcement of judgments in matrimonial matters and the matters of parental responsibility, repealing Regulation (EC) No 1347/2000.

M. González Marimón (✉)
Faculty of Law, Department of Private International Law, University of Valencia, Valencia, Spain
e-mail: maria.gonzalez-marimon@uv.es

S. Arnold, B. Heiderhoff (eds.), *Children in Migration and International Family Law*, https://doi.org/10.1007/978-3-031-71598-3_3

and its successor, the Brussels IIter Regulation,[3] have articulated a system of international jurisdiction in matters of parental responsibility that seeks to provide a predictable, flexible and appropriate response to this complex problem.[4] Therefore, the Brussels IIter Regulation jurisdiction rules are an essential tool to offer solutions to the different situations that migrant children may face regarding parental responsibility issues.[5]

In this context, the aim of this chapter is to present the jurisdiction model on parental responsibility matters of the Brussels IIter Regulation from the necessary children-based approach that should be paramount in any case involving children, including Private International Law rules.[6] This overview will reflect on how the jurisdiction rules seek to respond to the complexity of international movement of families through the articulation of the best interests of the child principle.

[3]Council Regulation (EU) 2019/1111 of 25 June 2019 on jurisdiction, the recognition and enforcement of decisions in matrimonial matters and the matters of parental responsibility, and on international child abduction (recast).

[4]For the definition of parental responsibility see Articles 1 and 2 para. 2 no. 7 of the Brussels IIter Regulation.

[5]Increasing attention is paid to the necessary link between Private International Law rules and Migration Law. On the topic see, among others, A. Fiorini, The Protection of the Best Interests of Migrant Children — Private International Law Perspectives, In: Biagioni/Ippolito (eds), Migrant Children in the XXI Century. Selected Issues of Public and Private International Law, 2016, at pp. 379–418; V. Van Den Eeckhout, Private International Law Questions that Arise in the Relation between Migration Law (in the Broad Sense of the Word) and Family Law: Subjection of PIL to Policies of Migration Law?, Background Paper, PILAGG-Presentation (20 January 2013).

[6]For the connection of human rights and Private International Law see J.J. Fawcett/M. Ní Shúilleabháin/S. Shah, Human Rights and Private International Law, 2016; R. Michaels/V. Ruiz Abou-Nigm/H. Van Loon, Introduction: The Private Side of Transforming our World — UN Sustainable Development Goals 2030 and the Role of Private International Law, In: Michaels/Ruiz Abou-Nigm/Van Loon (eds), The Private Side of Transforming our World: UN Sustainable Development Goals 2030 and the Role of Private International Law, 2021, at pp. 1–27; S. Vrells, Quelques réflexions sur l'influence des droits fondamentaux en droit international privé, Revue Internationale de Droit Comparé, n.° 1, 2017, at pp. 47–64; P. Franzina, The Place of Human Rights in Private International Law of the Union in Family Matters, In: Bergamini/Ragni (eds), Fundamental Rights and Best Interests of the Child in Transnational Families, 2019, at pp. 141–156; R. Espinosa Calabuig, Derecho Internacional privado europeo y protección de grupos vulnerables, Revista General de Derecho Europeo, n.° 54, 2021, at p. 2; R. Baratta, Derechos fundamentales y Derecho internacional privado de familia, Anuario español de Derecho Internacional privado, t. XVI, 2016, at pp. 103–126.

II. The Anchoring of the Brussels IIter Regulation Jurisdiction Rules in the Principle of the Best Interests of the Child

The rationale of any rule dealing with children is precisely to ensure that the principle of the best interests of the child is safeguarded to the maximum extent possible. The rules on international jurisdiction in matters of parental responsibility are no exception and therefore share this objective.[7]

This is precisely the case for the rules on international jurisdiction in matters of parental responsibility of the Brussels IIter Regulation,[8] which are based on respect for, and the safeguarding of, the principle of the best interests of the child.[9] Thus, the rules of jurisdiction are not only designed in accordance with this principle but must also be interpreted in the light of Article 3 para.1 of the CRC[10] and Article 24 para. 2 of the EU Charter.[11,12] In the area of international jurisdiction, this principle is embodied by the EU legislator in the criterion of proximity.[13]

In fact, references to the best interests of the child as a guide and limit to the functioning of the Brussels IIter Regulation can be found in its Recitals 19, 20, 23, 26, 27, 30, 39, 47, 48, 55, 57 and 84 as well as in various Articles of the Regulation (Articles 10, 12, 13, 15, 25, 27, 39, 56, 66 and 68 of the Brussels IIter

[7] A. Grammaticaki-Alexiou, Best Interests of the Child in Private International Law, Recueil Des Cours, Collected Courses, Tome 412, 2020; P. Hammje, L'intérêt de l'enfant face aux sources internationals du droit international privé, In: Jobard-Bachellier/Mayer et al (eds), Le droit international privé: esprit et méthodes. Mélanges en l'honneur de Paul Lagarde, 2005, 365, at pp. 371–373; A. Borrás Rodríguez, El «interés del menor» como factor de progreso y unificación del Derecho internacional privado (discurs d'ingrés), 1993, at p. 14; M. Herranz Ballesteros, El interés del menor en los Convenios de La Haya de Derecho Internacional Privado, 2004, at p. 118.

[8] The reinforcement of the principle of the best interests of the child has been, precisely, one of the main goals of the Brussels IIbis Recast. However, of course, this principle was already mentioned in the aforementioned instrument, in particular, see Recitals 12, 13 and 33; and Articles 13 and 15 of the Brussels IIbis Regulation.

[9] This has been stated on several occasions by the Court of Justice of the European Union (CJEU). See e.g. CJEU 1 October 2014, case C-436/13, ECLI:EU:C:2014:2246 (E.) para. 45: "It follows that jurisdiction in matters of parental responsibility must be determined, above all, in the best interests of the child".

[10] UN 1989 Convention on the Rights of the Child (CRC).

[11] EU Charter of Fundamental Rights (EU Charter).

[12] See Recital 19 of the Brussels IIter Regulation. Irrespective of the debate on the value of Recitals in EU instruments, this Recital reinforces the general obligation to apply and interpret EU law in accordance with the EU Charter, which derives from the post-Lisbon Treaty legal regime, L. Carpaneto, Impact of the Best Interests of the Child on the Brussels IIter Regulation, In: Bergamini/Ragni (eds), Fundamental Rights and Best Interests of the Child in Transnational Families, 2019, 265, at p. 275.

[13] As it is reminded by Recital 20 of the Brussels IIter Regulation, and previously, by Recital 12 of the Brussels IIbis Regulation.

Regulation). In all of them, the best interests of the child are considered to be the "paramount consideration"[14] for the functioning of the system.

Focusing on the international jurisdiction model on parental responsibility matters in the Brussels IIter Regulation, the best interests of the child are considered in a double sense. The system of the Brussels IIter Regulation is structured around the general rule of the habitual residence of the child, linked to the criterion of proximity. However, it is acknowledged that the practical reality is extremely rich. This is projected in the Brussels IIter Regulation through the articulation of exceptions to the general rule of habitual residence. In these exceptions, the concept of proximity is either relativised or simply ignored. The first group of precisions to the general rule refers to cases of a legal or illegal modification of the habitual residence of the child, while the second category of forums involves the design of exceptions, opting for criteria other than habitual residence, such as party autonomy. This logic reflects the interplay between the best interests of the child *in abstracto* and *in concreto*.[15]

The attempt to improve the consideration of the best interests of the child in the jurisdiction rules of the Brussels IIter Regulation is undoubtedly one important step forward introduced by this instrument.[16] Having said that, the truth is that the new Regulation does not introduce far-reaching changes in the jurisdiction rules model on parental responsibility issues.[17] On the contrary, the Brussels IIbis system and its flexibility is maintained, with of course some modifications with certain nuances and updates, and with constant references to the principle of the best interests of the child.

[14] Recital 84 of the Brussels IIter Regulation.

[15] In this sense also G. Biagioni, Jurisdiction in matters of parental responsibility between legal certainty and children's fundamental rights, European Papers, v. 4, n.° 1, 2019, 285, at p. 289; L. Carpaneto, La ricerca di una (nuova) sintesi tra interesse superior del minore «in astratto» e «in concreto» nella riforma del Regolamento bruxelles ii-bis, Rivista di diritto internazionale privato e processuale, n°. 4, 2018, 944, at p. 960.

[16] In fact, as opposed to Recital 12 of the Brussels IIbis Regulation, and the aforementioned new Recital 20 of the Brussels IIter Regulation, it reflects this balance in the jurisdiction rules in a much more precise way, thus responding to certain criticisms from the doctrine. I.e.: "The term "best interests of the child" is used in different senses, depriving it of sensible meaning. This magical term provides the basis of the jurisdiction rules, but at the same time also the basis for its exceptions. This confusion should be rectified by a rephrasing of the Recitals. It should be clear that the best interests of the child are paramount and that they do not necessarily coincide with the criterion of proximity", T. Kruger/L. Samyn, Brussels II bis: successes and suggested improvements, Journal of Private International Law, v. 12, n.° 1, 2016, 132, at p. 155.

[17] In this sense as well L. Carpaneto, In: Bergamini/Ragni (fn. 12), at p. 275.

III. The Triple Equation of the Best Interests of the Child, the Proximity and the Habitual Residence of the Child: The General Forum in Matters of Parental Responsibility

1. The Plural Role of the Habitual Residence of the Child in the Brussels IIter Regulation

The Brussels IIter Regulation — and its predecessor — following the trend of other international texts, such as the 1996 Child Protection Convention[18] assume in the design of their solutions, in general, the equation of habitual residence of the child, greater proximity and better safeguarding of the best interests of the child.[19]

In this context, the child's habitual residence fulfils a dual function. It acts as a criterion for the attribution of international jurisdiction in matters of parental responsibility,[20] and it also plays a central role when determining the wrongful nature of a child's removal or retention to another member state in cases of international jurisdiction.[21] Additionally, it should be borne in mind that the assessment of the habitual residence is also a key element for determining the relationship of the different sources of the parental responsibility legal framework, particularly in the case of the 1996 Child Protection Convention.[22]

Article 7 para. 1 of the Brussels IIter Regulation establishes the general rule of jurisdiction in matters of parental responsibility, equating the best interests of the child with the criterion of proximity for the majority of cases. Following this logic, in general, the jurisdiction system of the Brussels IIter Regulation attributes competence in matters of parental responsibility to the courts of the member state where the child is habitually resident at the time the court is seised.

This is because it is understood that these courts are the closest to the child's living situation and, therefore, the best placed to determine questions relating to

---

[18] Convention of 19 October 1996 on Jurisdiction, Applicable Law, Recognition, Enforcement and Co-operation in Respect of Parental Responsibility and Measures for the Protection of Children (1996 Child Protection Convention).

[19] A discussion about the evolution of the use of the criterion of the habitual residence of the child can be found in A. Bucher, L'enfant en droit international privé, 2003, at p. 1.

[20] C. Chalas, Précisions sur la résidence habituelle et la procédure de retour de l'enfant dans le règlement Bruxelles II bis, Revue Critique de Droit International privé, n.° 1, 2018, para. 7.

[21] See Article 2 para. 2 no. 11 and Chapter III of the Brussels IIter Regulation. The need to establish the habitual residence of the child as a pre-condition in any international child abduction case has also been outlined by the CJEU. See CJEU 8 June 2017, case C-111/17 PPU, ECLI:EU:C:2017:436 (O. L.), in particular paras. 38, 52 and 53.

[22] Generally speaking, the Brussels IIter Regulation will be applicable when the child is habitually resident in a member state. However, Article 97 of the Brussels IIter Regulation has clarified certain exceptional situations in which, despite the fact that the child is habitually resident in an EU member state, the 1996 Child Protection Convention shall be applied.

parental responsibility issues.[23] This choice of jurisdiction in favour of the habitual residence of the child corresponds to the principle of the best interests of the child in the abstract (*in abstracto*), i.e., what the legislator — in this case the EU legislator — considers to be in the best interests of the child in the ordinary case.[24] Consequently, by using the forum of the habitual residence of the child, the principle of the best interests of the child would already have been taken into account implicitly, and it will not be necessary, in general, to justify the reasons why it is being used.

In line with the legislative option adopted by the EU legislator in the Brussels IIbis Regulation, the Brussels IIter Regulation does not incorporate any definition of the child's habitual residence.[25] It is assumed that it is a factual notion which must, therefore, be determined on the basis of the circumstances of the individual case by the courts of the EU countries, as an inherent characteristic of the criterion of proximity.[26] This operation of concretion has resulted to be one of the most litigated issues in the practice of the Brussels IIbis Regulation and this will, predictably, continue to be the case in the new Regulation.

The maintenance of the child's habitual residence as a factual notion in the new Brussels IIter Regulation provides a flexible and adequate response to the circumstances of each individual child involved in a cross-border case. Having said that, the legislator could have also opted, perhaps, to introduce the interpretative criteria of the CJEU in the new text, or at least in a Recital.[27] In any case, a highly recommended option would be to incorporate them into a future good practices guide.

---

[23] If not the closest connection, at least, a close connection, P. Lagarde, Le principe de proximité dans le droit international privé contemporain, RCADI, t. 196, 1986, at pp. 25 ff.

[24] This idea has been stated by the CJEU on several occasions. See, for example, CJEU 15 February 2017, case C-499/15, ECLI:EU:C:2017:118 (W. and V.) para. 51, and the opinion of Advocate General Bot, 1 December 2016, case C-499/15, ECLI:EU:C:2016:920 para 50: "The grounds of jurisdiction in matters of parental responsibility which Regulation No 2201/2003 establishes are shaped in the light of the best interests of the child, in particular on the criterion of proximity. It is for that reason that, pursuant to Article 8 of that regulation, jurisdiction in such matters lies, in the first place, with the courts of the member state in which the child is habitually resident at the time the court is seised. Indeed, because of their geographical proximity, it is those courts that are generally the best placed to assess the measures to be taken in the interests of the child".

[25] Following, as well, the 1996 Child Protection Convention. When these Conventions were drafted, habitual residence was considered to be a de facto criterion, so that a legal definition had no practical value. Following A. Limante/I. Kunda, Jurisdiction in Parental Responsibility Matters (Articles 8, 9 and 13, 14), In: Honorati (ed), Jurisdiction in Matrimonial Matters, Parental Responsibility and International Abduction. A Handbook on the Application of Brussels IIa Regulation in National Courts, 2017, 61, at p. 64.

[26] On the topic see T. Kruger, Finding a Habitual Residence, In: Viarengo/Villata (eds), Planning the Future of Cross Border Families. A Path Through Coordination, 2020, at pp. 117–132.

[27] Nonetheless, legal operators already handle them properly in practice, as evidenced by Spanish case law. For an analysis of this case law see M. González Marimón, Menor y responsabilidad parental en la Unión Europea, 2021, at pp. 149–153.

2. *The Notion of the Habitual Residence of the Child in the CJEU Case Law*

In this task of determining the autonomous notion of the child's habitual residence, the broad case law of the CJEU has been of enormous relevance in setting up uniform interpretative criteria. It is a special and unique notion that finds an additional significance, precisely, because of children's conditions: children are subjects with their own rights and whose interests need to be safeguarded. Their vital, social and family factual circumstances differ from those of adults.

The CJEU has recalled several times that the habitual residence of the child is an EU law autonomous concept[28] as well as a factual notion.[29] Therefore, it is for the courts of the member states to establish the habitual residence of the child on the basis of all the circumstances specific to each individual case,[30] by carrying out an overall analysis of all the particular factual circumstances surrounding the child in each case.[31] Moreover, these circumstances ought to be, mainly, objective.[32]

The key element in the process of determining the child's habitual residence is his/her social and family integration in a member state: that is, where his or her centre of life is located.[33] Therefore, the mere physical presence of the child in a member state is not sufficient to establish the habitual residence of the child.[34] It has to come with a presence that is not temporary or intermittent and which shows "some degree of integration in a social and family environment".[35]

---

[28] See for example CJEU 22 November 2010, case C-497/10 PPU, ECLI:EU:C:2010:829 (Mercredi) paras. 45 and 46. This autonomous interpretation must be uniform for all the articles in the Brussels IIter Regulation (CJEU 9 October 2014, case C-376/14 PPU, ECLI:EU:C:2014:2268 (C.) para. 55; CJEU 8 June 2017, case C-111/17 PPU, ECLI:EU:C:2017:436 (O. L.) para. 41) but not necessarily to other EU Regulations (CJEU 2 October 2009, case C-523/07, ECLI:EU:C:2009:225 (A) para. 36). In consequence, there is not a common notion of habitual residence in the EU Regulations. See A. Limante/I. Kunda, In: Honorati (fn. 25), at p. 65.

[29] See for example CJEU 8 June 2017, case C-111/17 PPU, ECLI:EU:C:2017:436 (O. L.) para. 51.

[30] CJEU 2 October 2009, case C-523/07, ECLI:EU:C:2009:225 (A.) para. 37.

[31] According to Lenaerts, the CJEU, with this balancing of the circumstances of the specific case, is modulating the principle of legal certainty in such a way as to guarantee the requirements of the principle of the best interests of the child in conjunction with the criterion of proximity. The CJEU thereby avoids a fixed and watertight concept of the child's habitual residence, which would not necessarily guarantee the best interests of the child in every specific case. K. Lenaerts, The Best Interests of the Child Always Come First: the Brussels II *bis* Regulation and the European Court of Justice, Jurisprudencija/Jurisprudence, v. 20, n.° 4, 2013, at p. 1307.

[32] CJEU 28 June 2018, case C-512/17, ECLI:EU:C:2018:513 (H. R.) para. 64.

[33] CJEU 2 October 2009, case C-523/07, ECLI:EU:C:2009:225 (A.) para. 44.

[34] CJEU 2 October 2009, case C-523/07, ECLI:EU:C:2009:225 (A.) para. 33.

[35] CJEU 2 October 2009, case C-523/07, ECLI:EU:C:2009:225 (A.) para. 38. For this purpose some detailed factors are listed by the CJEU: "In particular, the duration, regularity, conditions and reasons for the stay on the territory of a member state and the family's move to that State, the child's nationality, the place and conditions of attendance at school, linguistic knowledge and the family

Departing from this general premise, it has also been accepted that, under certain circumstances, some factual elements allow the solution to be nuanced or modulated in the light of the circumstances of the particular case. Notably, this has been the case for the age of the child[36] or the subjective requirement of the will or intention of the parents.[37] It also applies to the mandatory physical presence of the child in an EU member state to establish his or her habitual residence there,[38] which has been the discussed issue of the latest pronouncements of the CJEU.[39]

and social relationships of the child in that State must be taken into consideration", CJEU 2 October 2009, case C-523/07, ECLI:EU:C:2009:225 (A.) para. 39.

[36]The age of the child directly influences the social and family integration of the child. For instance, the situation of a child in school age and the one of an infant are not the same. The environment of a young child is essentially a family environment (CJEU 22 November 2010, case C-497/10 PPU, ECLI:EU:C:2010:829 (Mercredi) paras. 53–55). Notwithstanding the fact that an infant's environment is largely determined by the parent with whom he/she resides on a daily basis, the other parent may also be an important factor to be considered, for instance if he/she lives in the same city and has a regular relationship with the child (CJEU 28 June 2018, case C-512/17, ECLI:EU:C:2018:513 (H. R.) para. 48). The relevance of the age of the child is also addressed in CJEU 8 June 2017, case C-111/17 PPU, ECLI:EU:C:2017:436 (O. L.).

[37]The CJEU has known different cases regarding the parents' intention. They concern both the existence of a willingness to move to a different country expressed in the past — before the habitual residence has been changed — as well as projected into the future — i.e. the future intention to change the habitual residence. In this regard, the CJEU establishes that in cases of young children, "the parents' intention to settle permanently with the child in another member state, manifested by certain tangible steps such as the purchase or lease of a residence in the host member state, may constitute an indicator of the transfer of the habitual residence" (CJEU 2 October 2009, case C-523/07, ECLI:EU:C:2009:225 (A.) para. 40). Despite the fact that the parent and the child are in the new place of residence for a short period of time, in this case, the lack of the objective criterion of "habituality" is compensated by the subjective criterion of the intention of the parent (CJEU 22 November 2010, case C-497/10 PPU, ECLI:EU:C:2010:829 (Mercredi) paras. 41–51). However, in other cases the CJEU has been reluctant to attribute too much weight to the intention of the parent, as this could be detrimental to legal certainty (following G. Biagioni (fn. 15), at p. 293). Therefore, the intention of the parents is an important factor to be considered, but it cannot be the only factor. It must be weighted together with all the circumstances of the case. Other external circumstances may have more relevance in a particular case, such as the presence of the child in the member state concerned since birth, his or her schooling, or the fact that he or she maintains a close relationship with the parent with whom he or she does not live (CJEU 28 June 2018, case C-512/17, ECLI:EU:C:2018:513 (H. R.)); or the provisional nature of a judgment (CJEU 9 October 2014, case C-376/14 PPU, ECLI:EU:C:2014:2268 (C.) para. 57).

[38]For instance, in CJEU 15 February 2017, case C-499/15, ECLI:EU:C:2017:118 (W. and V.), even if one of the nationalities of the child was that of a specific EU member state — in this case Lithuania — the child's habitual residence can never be established there, since he or she has never been physically present there.

[39]As this might have seen to clarify the CJEU's interpretation of the circumstance of the physical presence, two more cases were presented regarding this point. The peculiarity of both cases lies in the fact that the habitual residence of a young child who has resided in a single state since birth must be determined. Despite this indisputable geographical connection between the child and the territory of a specific state, on both occasions, the national courts have asked the CJEU to disregard this objective circumstance as a determining factor in establishing the habitual residence of the child, given the existence of other weighty factors that would cast doubt on the determining nature of such

This rigid requirement for the physical presence of the child in order to establish his or her habitual residence in an EU member state for the application of the general rule of the Brussels IIter Regulation, although reasonable for guaranteeing legal certainty,[40] may cause some frictions. For instance, it may have an important impact on international child abduction cases as it establishes a clear difference in treatment before and after the child is born.[41] In addition, it should be borne in mind that a divergence between the terminology of the EU Regulation and other legal sources, especially the 1996 Child Protection Convention or the 1980 Child Abduction Convention,[42] is always possible. For these instruments, the courts of other contracting parties might interpret that the physical presence is not a mandatory circumstance for the establishment of the habitual residence of the child.

To sum up, the CJEU requires the concurrence of two indispensable conditions — objective and subjective — in order to be able to affirm that a child has a habitual residence in a given member state: on the one hand, an objective criterion, the physical presence of the child in the territory together with the requirement of a certain degree of integration in the social and family environment, and on the other hand, a subjective criterion, a certain degree of (proven) intention to create a stable life in a given member state.[43] Therefore, this double condition should be met in order to apply the general rule of jurisdiction on matters of parental responsibility to a migrant child.

---

a link. In CJEU 8 June 2017, case C-111/17 PPU, ECLI:EU:C:2017:436 (O. L.), the other factor was the past intention of the parents to establish the habitual residence of the child where they lived — Italy — after the birth of the child — which was in Greece. More worryingly, in CJEU 17 October 2018, case C-393/18 PPU, ECLI:EU:C:2018:835 (U. D.), it is asked whether "circumstances such as those in the main proceedings, assuming that they are proven, that is to say, first, the fact that the father's coercion of the mother had the effect of her giving birth to their child in a third country where she has resided with that child ever since, and, secondly, the breach of the mother's or the child's rights, have any bearing in that regard" (para. 43). For the first time, the CJEU must assess whether an alleged infringement of fundamental rights, protected by the EU Charter, can constitute a factor capable of counterbalancing the priority given hitherto to the physical presence of the child in a place — as an exponent of the criteria of proximity and legal certainty. However, the CJEU concludes that these circumstances "do not have any bearing" for the determination of the habitual residence of the child for the application of Article 8 para. 1 of the Brussels IIbis Regulation (para. 70). Instead, it suggests the possible application of Article 14 of the Brussels IIbis Regulation, verifying the possibility of the jurisdiction of the national courts under their national laws (para. 66).

[40] G. Biagioni (fn. 15), at pp. 294–295; T. Kruger/L. Samyn, Journal of Private International Law, v. 12, n.° 1, 2016, 132, at p. 147.

[41] In practice, the paradox of a totally different response can occur in the case of a pregnant mother moving to any other state, and a parent moving after the child is born. Under the Regulation, the first case could not be qualified as a wrongful removal or retention, whereas the second case could.

[42] Convention of 25 October 1980 on the Civil Aspects of International Child Abduction (1980 Child Abduction Convention).

[43] A. Limante/I. Kunda, In: Honorati (fn. 25), at p. 68.

IV. The Exceptions to the Habitual Residence of the Child as the General Rule: In Search of the Best Interests of the Child *In Concreto*

The EU legislator designs a series of nuances to the general rule of the habitual residence of the child, seeking to achieve maximum flexibility and adaptability to the complex practical reality. Therefore, it allows other courts within the EU than the one of the habitual residence of the child to hear a particular case when it is clear from the circumstances that this is precisely in the child's best interests. That is to say that, together with the general forum, the EU legislator articulates a series of alternative or complementary forums in order to safeguard the principle of best interests *in concreto*; that is the best interests of a child in a given case, which does not necessarily have to correspond, in all cases and on all occasions, to what is considered best for him or her in general. As the exceptional circumstances that they are, it will be necessary to justify on each occasion that the application of these forums constitutes the option that best guarantees the best interests of the child in that particular case.[44]

This idea would explain why an express reference to the best interests of the child is added in most of the special grounds for jurisdiction, in one form or another. This is not even explicitly mentioned in the general rule although it is true that it is mentioned in the Recitals, but not in the provision relating to the general rule. Thus, when applying the special rules, the judge must take into account the circumstances surrounding the specific situation in order to ensure that the exercise of jurisdiction is the most appropriate option for guaranteeing the best interests of the child.

1. The Nuances to the Habitual Residence of the Child Jurisdiction Rule: Lawful vs. Unlawful Relocation

The first two exceptions provided by the Brussels IIter Regulation find their justification, precisely, on the change in the location of the child. The reply provided depends on the lawful or unlawful nature of the movement of the child to another member state.

[44] Also on the need to justify the application of the best interests *in concreto*, L. Carpaneto, Rivista di diritto internazionale privato e processuale, n°. 4, 2018, 944, at p. 960.

a) First Situation: The Lawful Change of the Habitual Residence of the Child

In a cross-border context, the mobility of families and children is a very common reality which can also alter the life of the child in different ways. Reality thus shows the presence of multiple situations in which a child changes its location. And therefore, that could also entail the modification of his or her habitual residence. This could lead, sometimes, to tense situations. Precisely, the so-called relocation disputes are a particularly problematic example: situations in which holders of parental responsibility of the child, and in particular the holders of the rights of custody,[45] do not agree on his/her place of residence.

In this context, while the EU legal framework provides a strong answer to cases of international child abduction, it hardly regulates the procedure for a parent to request a legal change of his or her child's habitual residence. Consequently, the EU law leaves this question to the domestic legislation of each member state.[46] Perhaps at this point, the EU legislator could have opted for a more proactive approach, since this problem has a direct impact on the mobility of families within the EU.

The rules of international jurisdiction in matters of parental responsibility confront this issue indirectly when they address the child's legal change of habitual residence. In this regard, certain exceptions to the general forum of the child's habitual residence are designed which seek to take into account and respond to different specific situations which may affect the child.

The treatment of the child's lawful relocation is designed around two forums which have not undergone major changes in the Brussels IIter Regulation: the general forum of the child's habitual residence[47] and the forum on continuing jurisdiction in relation to access rights[48] in the event of a legal change in the child's habitual residence.

Regarding the first one, in the recast of the Brussels IIbis Regulation the maintenance of *perpetuatio iurisdictionis* or *perpetuatio fori* principle was called into question.[49] According to this principle, and as a general rule, for procedures already

[45] This is understood, in terms of the Regulation, as the right to determine place of residence of the child. See Article 2 para. 2 no. 9 of the Brussels IIter Regulation.

[46] For instance, in Spain there has been different case law of the Supreme Court analysing the criteria for a legal change of the habitual residence of the child — both internal and international. On this topics see C. González Beilfuss, El traslado lícito de menores: las denominadas relocation disputes, Revista Española de Derecho Internacional, v. LXII, n.° 2, 2010, at pp. 51–75; M. Herranz Ballesteros, Traslado del domicilio del menor a otro país. Doctrina del Tribunal Supremo, In: Calvo Caravaca/Carrascosa González (eds), El Tribunal Supremo y el Derecho Internacional Privado. Volumen 2, Rapid Centro Color, 2019, at pp. 567–586.

[47] See Article 7 para. 1 of the Brussels IIter Regulation.

[48] See Article 8 of the Brussels IIter Regulation.

[49] In fact, the suppression of the *perpetuatio fori* principle was proposed. See European Commission, Proposal for a Council Regulation on jurisdiction, the recognition and enforcement of decisions in matrimonial matters and the matters of parental responsibility, and on international child abduction (recast), COM/2016/0411 final — 2016/0190 (CNS), at p. 39 and Recital 15. De

pending, the courts of the member state in which the proceedings have been initiated shall have jurisdiction until they have rendered a judgment that is final and no longer open to appeal, even if in the course of that procedure the child changes his or her habitual residence.[50] This solution differs from the general jurisdiction rule contained in Article 5 para. 2 of the 1996 Child Protection Convention,[51] where the courts of the new habitual residence of the child immediately have jurisdiction even if there are pending proceedings in the previous contracting state. However, the EU legislator has finally chosen to maintain on the 2019 instrument the regime existing in the Brussels IIbis Regulation, although nuancing the principle[52] as well as clarifying the diverse possible situations and their treatment.[53] Therefore, this represents one example of the different treatment for intra-EU mobility and mobility

---

Boer is highly critical of this system and believes that the EU legislator introduced the *perpetuatio fori* principle with intra-European movements in mind, not movements with third states. Above all, in this group of cases, the author believes that there may be negative consequences for the interests of the child and for the criterion of proximity. Fundamentally, the risk of parallel proceedings and the refusal to recognise and enforce the possible judgment of the EU member state. T. M. De Boer, What we should not expect from a recast of the Brussels IIbis Regulation, Nederlands Internationaal Privaatrecht, no. 1, 2015, 10, at pp. 15–18. Equally see H. Van Loon, The Brussels IIa Regulation: towards a review?, in European Parliament: Cross-border activities in the EU-Making life easier for citizens, Workshop for the JURI Committee, Directorate General for internal policies. Policy Department C: Citizens' Rights and Constitutional Affairs, 2015, 178, at p. 192; E. Rodríguez Pineau, La refundición del Reglamento Bruselas II bis: de nuevo sobre la función del Derecho Internacional privado europeo, Revista Española de Derecho Internacional, v. 69, no. 1, 2017, 139, at p. 156.

[50] CJEU 22 November 2010, case C-497/10 PPU, ECLI:EU:C:2010:829 (Mercredi), confirmed that the habitual residence of the child must be determined at the time when the case is brought before the court in question, in accordance with Article 8 of the Brussels IIbis Regulation.

[51] Article 5 para. 2 of the 1996 Child Protection Convention establishes that: "Subject to Article 7, in case of a change of the child's habitual residence to another contracting State, the authorities of the State of the new habitual residence have jurisdiction". In this sense A. Borrás Rodríguez, Article 9. Continuing jurisdiction of the child's former habitual residence, In: Magnus/Mankowski (eds), ECPIL European Commentaries on Private International Law Commentary Volume IV Brussels IIbis Regulation, 2017, at p. 117; N. Lowe/M. Nicholls, The 1996 Hague Convention on the Protection of Children, Family Law, at p. 38; H. Setright/D. Williams et al, International Issues in Family Law. The 1996 Hague Convention on the Protection of Children and the Brussels IIa, Family Law, at p. 33.

[52] In this sense C. Honorati, La proposta di revisione del regolamento bruxelles ll-bis: Piu' tutela per i minori e piu' efficacia nell'Esecuzione delle decisioni, Rivista di diritto internazionale privato e processuale, v. 52, no. 2, 2017, 247, at p. 251.

[53] See Article 7 para. 1 and Recital 21 of the Brussels IIter Regulation. The Recital suggests a differentiated solution depending on whether or not there is a pending case at the time of a change in the habitual residence of the child. In particular, it leaves the door open to a possible transfer of jurisdiction despite the existence of a pending case. However, unlike the Commission and Parliament proposals, it does not leave this power to the agreement of the parties, but to the court. Campuzano Díaz understands that a proper balance between legal certainty and flexibility has been achieved, B. Campuzano Díaz, El nuevo Reglamento (UE) 2019/1111: análisis de las mejoras en las relaciones con el Convenio de La Haya de 19 de octubre de 1996 sobre responsabilidad parental, Cuadernos de Derecho Transnacional, v. 12, no. 2, 97, at pp. 110–111.

towards a third country contracting state of the 1996 Child Protection Convention.[54]

b) Second Situation: The Protection of the General Forum in Cases of International Child Abduction

Secondly, in cases of international child abduction,[55] the jurisdiction rule set forth in Article 9 of the Brussels IIter Regulation in practically identical terms as in its predecessor is articulated on a general rule and certain exceptions. They seek to provide a flexible response by dividing the competences between the two EU member states potentially affected by such a situation.[56] In general, this forum enhances the general rule of the habitual residence of the child,[57] but conversely, in certain justified circumstances, it allows the transfer of the jurisdiction on the substance to the courts of the member state in which the child is wrongfully located.[58]

Therefore, the balance of the best interests of the child *in abstracto* and *in concreto* is reproduced and adapted to the inner logic of international child abduction cases, which face special problems both from a social and systemic point of view. In general, in the event of a wrongful removal or retention of a child to another state — in our case, within the EU — in breach of custody rights, it is understood that what

[54] Indeed, like its predecessor, once the habitual residence of the child has been acquired in a third state party to the 1996 Child Protection Convention, the latter instrument will apply, as specified in Article 97 para. 1 lit. a of the Brussels IIter Regulation. Therefore, with the new version of the Brussels IIter Regulation we continue to have this difference in treatment in the institutional and conventional regime when the child moves to a third state party to the 1996 Child Protection Convention once the proceedings have been initiated, as established in CJEU 14 July 2022, case C-572/21, ECLI:EU:C:2022:562 (CC) for the Brussels IIbis Regulation. In this sense too T. Garber, Article 7 General Jurisdiction, In: Magnus/Mankowski (eds), ECPIL European Commentaries on Private International Law Commentary Volume IV Brussels IIter Regulation, 2023, at pp. 141 and 143. For an in-depth analysis of this topic see M. González Marimón, La movilidad de niños y niñas más allá de las fronteras de la Unión (traslado lícito e ilícito de menores de un Estado miembro a un Estado tercero), Bitácora Millenium DIPr, 2023, no. 18, at pp. 10–21.

[55] See Article 2 para. 2 no. 11 of the Brussels IIter Regulation for the definition of wrongful retention or removal of a child.

[56] This forum might only come into action when the wrongful retention or removal is produced from one EU member state to another. CJEU 24 March 2021, case C-603/20 PPU, ECLI:EU:C:2021:231 (M. C. P.).

[57] Therefore, the court of a member state where the child is wrongfully present does not have jurisdiction to hear an application for custody of the child, in the absence of any indication that the other parent has consented to the removal of the child or has not lodged an application for the child's return. See CJEU 10 April 2018, case C-85/18 PPU, ECLI:EU:C:2018:220 (C. V.) para. 57.

[58] In other words, a wrongful removal or retention of a child will not affect the determination of jurisdiction except in certain very limited circumstances. C. Honorati/A. Limante, Jurisdiction in Child Abduction Proceedings (Article 10, 11), In: Honorati (ed), Jurisdiction in Matrimonial Matters, Parental Responsibility and International Abduction. A Handbook on the Application of Brussels IIa Regulation in National Courts, 2017, 93, at p. 105.

best corresponds to his or her best interests is, precisely, his or her immediate return to the place of previous habitual residence. However, although this premise remains true in most cases, the answer must be weighted in the light of the circumstances of the particular case, in which the interests of the child involved may not be identified with that immediate return. This is precisely the equilibrium established by the 1980 Child Abduction Convention, by which the EU Regulation is inspired.[59]

The legal response to international child abduction in the EU shows a landscape of a plurality of legal sources seeking to discourage this phenomenon. It is mainly a tripartite legal framework consisting of the interplay between the Brussels IIter Regulation and the 1980 Child Abduction Convention, which is supplemented by the timely interaction of the 1996 Child Protection Convention. The EU legislator opted for a peculiar regulation of international child abduction, consisting in the reference by the Brussels IIbis — now Brussels IIter — Regulation to the 1980 Child Abduction Convention, but with certain modifications. It goes without saying that to properly understand this rule of jurisdiction, it is also essential to study the legal framework of international child abduction, and in particular, the other provisions regarding international child abduction in the Brussels IIter Regulation, notably Chapter III.[60]

Nowadays, a necessary redefinition of the legal framework of international child abduction is suggested, seeking to adapt it to new realities and nuances. In this line, there is a need to face the profound social changes of recent decades, reflected in the consolidation of different family models, or in the already targeted greater children rights centred approach, over his or her parents' rights. That is why recent cases are showing that the immediate return of the child might not always be the best solution for the child involved.[61] Just as a paradigmatic example of the complexity of these cases, there is an increasing awareness of how to deal with cases where domestic or gender-based violence is alleged as a ground for denial of the return of the child.[62]

---

[59] Article 9 of the Brussels IIter Regulation is very similar to Article 7 of the 1996 Child Protection Convention, both of them are clearly inspired by the 1980 Child Abduction Convention system for the return of the child, and its general rules and exceptions (Articles 12, 13 and 20 of the 1980 Child Abduction Convention).

[60] For a general study of the international child abduction regime in the EU see M. González Marimón, La sustracción internacional de menores en el espacio jurídico europeo, 2022; for a specific work on the novelties introduced by the Brussels IIter Regulation see M. González Marimón, La regulación de la sustracción internacional de menores en el Reglamento Bruselas II ter y sus principales novedades: hacia una mejor protección del interés superior del menor, Cuadernos de Derecho Transnacional, 2022, v. 14, no. 1, at pp. 286–312.

[61] In this sense see M. Herranz Ballesteros, El retorno seguro del menor: ¿puente entre la excepción de grave riesgo y la obligación de devolución?, Bitácora Millenium DIPr: Derecho Internacional Privado, n°. 19, 2024; and I. Pretelli, Una reinterpretación del Convenio de La Haya sobre la sustracción de menores para proteger a los niños de la exposición al sexismo, la misoginia y la violencia contra las mujeres, Cuadernos de Derecho Transnacional, v. 14, n°. 2, 2022, pp. 1310–1337.

[62] K. Trimmings et al (eds), Domestic Violence and Parental Child Abduction, 2022. Directly related to the object of this book, particularly interesting is CJEU 2 August 2021, case C-262/21

2. *The Special Grounds of Jurisdiction in Matters of Parental Responsibility Proceedings*

As it has already been stated, the general forum of the habitual residence of the child is based on the premise that it is identified as the one that best guarantees the best interests of the child *in abstracto*. However, in certain circumstances, the best interests of the child *in concreto* may recommend that the courts of another member state have jurisdiction. On that basis, the Brussels IIter Regulation proceeds to make that rule more flexible by articulating a number of exceptions to it, two of which have presented a special relevance in practice.

Specifically, we are referring to the choice of court forum and the forum relating to transfer of proceedings to a court better placed to hear the case. Both of them share the fact that they are based on the principle of flexibility that is characteristic of questions of parental responsibility, seeking to provide a response adapted to the intrinsic complexity of this matter.

a) Choice of Court Forum: The Best Interests of the Child as a Limit to Party Autonomy in Matters of Parental Responsibility

Party autonomy in Private International Family Law is known to be a developing sector with an increasing — but unequal — role in the EU.[63] In line with this tendency, and specifically in relation to international jurisdiction, the EU legislator has improved and advanced its regulation in the Brussels IIbis Regulation recast process towards the Brussels IIter Regulation. Although the spirit of the previous legislation is maintained, certain relevant modifications have been introduced.

PPU, ECLI:EU:C:2021:640 (A.), connecting European Asylum Law, domestic violence and a removal of a child to another member state. See B. Heiderhoff, Geflüchtete und HKÜ, IPRax, Issue 6/2022, 1, at pp. 1–3; S. Corneloup, Demande de retour d'un enfant enlevé et principe de non-refoulement des réfugiés: lorsque la Convention de La Haye de 1980 rencontre la Convention de Genève de 1951, Revue Critique de Droit International Privé, no. 4, 2021, aT pp. 773–787; C. Ruiz Sutil, International Removals in Contexts of Violence between European Asylum Law and the Best Interests of the Child. The CJEU case a. V. B., of 2 august 2021, Yearbook of Private International Law, v. 23, 2021/2022, at pp. 349–363.

[63] González Beilfuss talks about an "emerging tendency", specially thanks to the EU Regulations in family law: C. González Beilfuss, Reflexiones en torno a la función de la autonomía de la voluntad conflictual en el Derecho internacional privado de familia, Revista Española de Derecho Internacional, v. 72, no. 1, 2020, 101, at pp. 101–102. There are plenty of academic works on the topic, for all see C. González Beilfuss, Party Autonomy in International Family Law, 2020; E. Jayme, Party autonomy in International Family and Succession Law: New tendencies, Yearbook of Private International Law, v. 11, 2009, at pp. 1–10; L. Walker, Party Autonomy, Inconsistency and the Specific Characteristics of Family Law in the EU, Journal of Private International Law, v. 14, no. 2, 2018, 225, at pp. 225–261; J. Gray, Party Autonomy in EU Private International Law, 2021.

As a first visual change, the reference to the "prorogation of jurisdiction" of Article 12 of the Brussels IIbis Regulation is abandoned in Article 10 of the Brussels IIter Regulation to speak directly of "choice of court". Additionally, and reflecting the CJEU transcendent case law in this area, one of the major innovations is the suppression of any reference to the prorogation of jurisdiction on matrimonial or substantially connected grounds.[64] Instead, the text generically refers to the choice of forum, so that proceedings in matters of parental responsibility acquire their own autonomy.[65]

This demonstrates the significant advance of party autonomy in international jurisdiction in matters of parental responsibility. That autonomy, however, is clearly limited, finding the child's best interests as an impassable limit. This conditionality translates into the presence of three cumulative requirements, which are remarkably similar to the wording of the former Article 12 of the Brussels IIbis Regulation: (1) the substantial connection of the child with the member state in question,[66] (2) the acceptance by all the parties of the choice of forum — freely and expressly,[67] (3) and finally, logically, that the exercise of the choice of forum is in the best interests of the child.[68]

The intense CJEU case law regarding the application of these requirements in the Brussels IIbis Regulation perfectly shows the difficulties in properly assessing the best interests of the child in each particular case. And more importantly, the judgments highlight the difficulties in establishing common guidelines that ensure

---

[64] Article 12 of Brussels IIbis Regulation contained different concrete situations where the prorogation of jurisdiction was allowed: prorogation of jurisdiction on cases of matrimonial matters linked to parental responsibility issues (Article 12 para. 1), prorogation of jurisdiction in cases of a substantial connection of the child with another member state (Article 12 para. 3) and prorogation in cases where the child has his or her habitual residence in the territory of a third state which is not a contracting party to the 1996 Child Protection Convention (Article 12 para. 4). However, although the first two situations no longer appear in the provision, they are still referred to in Recital 23 of the new Regulation. On the contrary, the reference of 12 para. 4 of the Brussels IIbis Regulation is supressed in the new regime.

[65] As established by CJEU 12 November 2014, case C-656/13, ECLI:EU:C:2014:2364 (L. versus M.) para. 45. In this sense C. Honorati, Rivista di diritto internazionale privato e processuale, v. 52, no. 2, 2017, 247, at p. 254; C. González Beilfuss, Party Autonomy in International Family Law, 2020, at p. 160.

[66] "In particular by virtue of the fact that: (i) at least one of the holders of parental responsibility is habitually resident in that Member State; (ii) that Member State is the former habitual residence of the child; or (iii) the child is a national of that Member State" (Article 10 para. 1 lit. a of the Brussels IIter Regulation).

[67] Article 10 para. 1 lit. b of the Brussels IIter Regulation. This requisite is the manifestation of the line of thought which revendicates the need to adapt party autonomy in family law to the logic and notions of family relations. For instance, family relations are not horizontal but rather interdependent, and they usually develop in a context of cooperation, altruism and solidarity. The theory of vulnerability is an example, situating the caring works at the centre, which have been traditionally influenced by gender roles. On this topic see C. González Beilfuss (fn. 65), at pp. 193–201; L. Walker (fn. 63), at pp. 244–245.

[68] Article 10 para. 1 lit. c of the Brussels IIter Regulation.

certain legal certainty in their application. As in other European instruments, the Brussels IIter Regulation has assumed the various pronouncements of the CJEU in interpreting the requirements for the activation of the forum.[69] It can certainly be stated that the Brussels IIter Regulation has improved the structure and procedure of the aforementioned forum, as well as the formulation of other points relating to the extent of the parties' consent, the moment of exercising it, or the formal requirements of the agreement.[70]

However, this new provision leaves some open questions. Particularly noteworthy is Article 10 para. 4 of the Brussels IIter Regulation, which provides that competence granted in accordance with one of the modalities of acceptance shall be exclusive.[71] Perhaps this is the most controversial uncertainty of the new forum, because it raises doubts about the scope, and even nature of that exclusive character.[72] Finally, a further unanswered aspect by the new regulation, which might have a direct impact on migrant families, is whether it is possible to apply the elective forum of Brussels IIter when the child has his/her habitual residence in a third country — non-party of the 1996 Child Protection Convention. This question is accentuated by the fact that Article 12 para. 4 of the Brussels IIbis Regulation, which specifically addressed this situation, has been suppressed.

---

[69] CJEU 1 October 2014, case C-436/13, ECLI:EU:C:2014:2246 (E.); CJEU 12 November 2014, case C-656/13, ECLI:EU:C:2014:2364 (L. versus M.); CJEU 21 October.2015, case C-215/15, ECLI:EU:C:2015:710 (Gogova); CJEU 19 April 2018, case C-565/16, ECLI:EU:C:2018:265 (Saponaro); CJEU 16 January 2018, case C-6044/17, ECLI:EU:C:2018:10 (P. M. versus A. H.); CJEU 3 October 2019, case C-759/18, ECLI:EU:C:2019:816 (O. F. versus P. G.).

[70] Focusing on the aforementioned conditions, the Article 12 of the Brussels IIbis Regulation clause "the jurisdiction of the courts has been accepted expressly or otherwise in an unequivocal manner" has been particularly problematic, as well as the concretion of the moment when such consent must be controlled by the chosen court. These points have now been clarified by the EU legislator, albeit incorporating a quite complex regulation. It distinguishes between two modalities of acceptance, depending on the moment when it takes place: before the procedure — including, therefore, choice of court agreements (Article 10 para. 1 lit. b i) of the Brussels IIter Regulation); or during the procedure, as a novelty to the previous regime (Article 10 para.1 lit. b ii) of the Brussels IIter Regulation). The formal requirements are established by Article 10 para. 2 of the Brussels IIter Regulation.

[71] Article 10 para. 4 and para. 1 lit. b ii) of the Brussels IIter Regulation.

[72] Regarding, in particular, the possibility to transfer the proceedings and in cases of lis pendens. See Articles 12 para. 5, 20 paras. 4 and 5, and Recital 38 of the Brussels IIter Regulation. It also might imply a different treatment of the previously mentioned two modalities of acceptance, and the possible effect on choice of court agreements. Therefore, it is still unclear whether exclusive prorogation is possible beyond the cases named in Article 10 para. 4 of the Brussels IIter Regulation. Legal doctrine has also identified this issue, see B. Heiderhoff: Das Sorgerechtsverfahren nach der EuEheVO 2019 — Beschwörungen, Kompromisse und Hoffnungen, IPRax, Issue 4/2023, 333, at p. 334; S. Corneloup/T. Kruger, Le Règlement 2019/1111, Bruxelles II: la protection des enfants gagne du ter(rain), Revue Critique de Droit International Privé, no. 2, 2020, 215, at pp. 229–230; B. Campuzano Díaz, Los acuerdos de elección de foro en materia de responsabilidad parental: un análisis del art. 10 del Reglamento (UE) 2019/1111, Revista Electrónica de Estudios Internacionales, n.° 40, 2020, at p. 31.

b) The Transfer of Proceedings to a Better Court to Hear the Case as a Paradigmatic Example of the Best Interests of the Child in Concreto: The Flexibilisation of the Response

The Brussels IIter Regulation system also foresees the transfer of jurisdiction, inspired by the figure of *forum non conveniens,* and directly based on the principle of flexibility. Therefore, this ground of jurisdiction represents the paradigmatic example of the balance between the best interests of the child *in abstracto* and *in concreto*. It also demonstrates the need to strike the great balance between legal certainty and the proper guarantee of the principles of the best interests of the child and of proximity. This delicate balance leads to allowing, in certain exceptional circumstances, or for practical reasons, that the transfer of jurisdiction constitutes the best response to the specific case.[73]

As a novelty, the new Regulation, in line with the 1996 Child Protection Convention, abandons the asymmetry of the previous text and articulates the transfer of jurisdiction in two provisions. One relates to the transfer of jurisdiction by the competent court as set out in Article 12 of the Brussels IIter Regulation. The other asks for such a transfer as stipulated in Article 13 of the aforementioned Regulation. Moreover, it improves its procedural functioning by clarifying some problematic issues which have been raised in practice, and resolved by the CJEU.[74]

As far as the transfer of jurisdiction is concerned, according to the CJEU's case law, it must be interpreted restrictively.[75] The strong presumption in favour of the court having jurisdiction is questioned just in the light of the circumstances of the particular case. In order to ensure such an exceptional application, Article 12 para. 1 of the Brussels IIter Regulation establishes three requisites: (1) the child's particular connection with the member state concerned,[76] (2) that the court is better placed

[73] E. Pataut, Article 15. Transfer to a court better placed to hear the case, In: Magnus/Mankowski (fn. 51), at p. 175; C. Honorati/A. Limante, Transfer of Proceedings (Article 15), In: Honorati (ed), Jurisdiction in Matrimonial Matters, Parental Responsibility and International Abduction. A Handbook on the Application of Brussels IIa Regulation in National Courts, 2017, 199, at pp. 202–203.

[74] On the interpretation of Article 15 of the Brussels IIbis Regulation see CJEU 27 October 2016, case C-428/15, ECLI:EU:C:2016:819 (D.); CJEU 4 October 2018, case C-478/17, ECLI:EU:C:2018:812 (I. Q.); CJEU 10 July 2019, case C-530/18, ECLI:EU:C:2019:583 (E. P.). And after the entry into force of Brussels IIter Regulation CJEU 27 April 2023, case C-372/22, ECLI:EU:C:2023:364 (C. M. versus D. N.); CJEU 13 July 2023, case C-87/22, ECLI:EU:C:2023:571 (T. T.).

[75] CJEU 27 October 2016, case C-428/15, ECLI:EU:C:2016:819 (D.), para. 29.

[76] Article 12 para. 4 of the Brussels IIter Regulation further establishes an exhaustive list of the concrete situations of particular connection and proximity between the child and the member state. However, the CJEU recalls that the existence of this proximity does not necessarily mean that the other two requisites are met in the particular case. CJEU 27 October 2016, case C-428/15, ECLI:EU:C:2016:819 (D.), paras. 52–55.

to hear the case,[77] (3) and finally, and again quite logically, that the transfer is found to be in the best interests of the child.[78]

In addition to these three conditions, the question of which court is qualified to activate the transfer could be added as a sort of prerequisite to them. On this point, and although the new regulatory text is not entirely coherent in some points, it may be concluded that any court having jurisdiction under the Regulation is entitled to activate the transfer and not just the court which has assumed jurisdiction on the basis of the child's habitual residence.[79]

Similarly, doubts have also been raised in the case law as to whether a court already having jurisdiction under the Regulation is entitled to receive the transfer of jurisdiction if it accomplishes the three mandatory conditions. Regarding this point, the CJEU's firm negative response has been reflected in the new Regulation in its Article 12.[80] Additionally, this restriction is now accompanied by a second one, since the transfer of jurisdiction may only be requested by the court of the habitual residence of the child, as established by Article 13 of the Brussels IIter Regulation.

Even if it is true that the EU legislator has merely incorporated the CJEU's interpretation on this point, perhaps it should be re-evaluated to what extent so many limitations could undermine the very purpose of the mechanism of transfer of jurisdiction: that is, to provide flexibility to the system of international jurisdiction schemed by the Regulation.

3. The Closing Forums in Matters of Parental Responsibility: The Protection of the Child Involved in Migratory Flows

The reality of international families, with their complexities and heterogeneities, can in practice lead to a situation in which neither the general forum of the child's habitual residence nor the various special forums on parental responsibility set out in the Regulation are applicable to the specific case. This could ultimately lead to a potential situation of lack of protection for the child involved. By way of example, the situation of many children may not allow to confirm that they have had a habitual residence in an EU member state, irrespective of any links their parents may have

[77] On this condition the CJEU has stated that "the court having jurisdiction must determine whether the transfer of the case to that other court is such as to provide genuine and specific added value...", CJEU 27 October 2016, case C-428/15, ECLI:EU:C:2016:819 (D.), para. 57.

[78] The CJEU has clarified that the assessment of the best interests of the child is a requirement in its own. That is to say, it should not be assessed together with the requirement of the court better placed to hear the case. CJEU 27 October 2016, case C-428/15, ECLI:EU:C:2016:819 (D.), paras. 58–59.

[79] In this regard see Article 12 para. 1 and Recital 26 of the Brussels IIter Regulation.

[80] See CJEU 4 October 2018, case C-478/17, ECLI:EU:C:2018:812 (I. Q.). This option has been said to go against the finality of this forum, see S. Álvarez González, De nuevo sobre la interpretación y alcance del artículo 15 del Reglamento Bruselas II bis (Una alternativa efímera a la STJ de 4 de octubre de 2018), LA LEY Unión Europea, no. 66, enero 2019, at p. 11.

with a member state of the EU. Migration of people from third countries also aggravates the problem of unaccompanied children arriving in the EU without a known habitual residence.[81]

In order to provide an adequate response to all types of situations, the Brussels IIter Regulation system closes with the design of residual forums in matters of parental responsibility that allow for the protection of children who are in a particularly vulnerable situation. These forums, in contrast to what has happened with other solutions included in the 2019 text, remain practically unchanged after the recasting process of the Brussels IIbis Regulation. These forums are, on the one hand, the forum based on the presence of the child and, on the other hand, the residual forum that refers to the national law of the member states.

a) Jurisdiction Based on the Presence of the Child: Protecting Migrant Children

Practice shows the potential existence of situations where it is very complex or not feasible at all to determine the habitual residence of the child. The migration crisis of recent years in the EU is an additional reason for this. The need to deal with these situations, avoiding the insecurity generated by the possible lack of regulatory response, is resolved through Article 11 of the Brussels IIter Regulation — a forum that accepts the mere presence of the child in a member state as a criterion of competence for this type of case.

This forum is subsidiary, so that it only comes into operation where it is neither possible to determine the habitual residence of the child in the case in question, nor is there a choice of court agreement in accordance with Article 10 of the Brussels IIter Regulation.[82]

Article 11 para. 2 of the Brussels IIter Regulation has been slightly modified by introducing the following terms: "The jurisdiction under paragraph 1 shall also apply to refugee children or children internationally displaced because of disturbances occurring in their Member State of habitual residence". Therefore, the previous term "their country" has been modified by "Member State of habitual residence".[83]

This modification introduced by the 2019 text has clarified the relationship of the EU Regulation with the 1996 Child Protection Convention in these situations, as the

[81] M. Requejo Isidro, La protección del menor no acompañado solicitante de asilo: entre Estado competente y Estado responsable, Cuadernos de Derecho Transnacional, v. 19, no. 2, 2017, 482, at pp. 482–505.

[82] Particular emphasis should be placed on the idea that the court should not be able to determine the habitual residence of the child on the basis of the available circumstances. Consequently, the mere presence of the child in a member state is not sufficient to trigger the forum in question, but the child must not be habitually resident in another state — member state or non-member state.

[83] While Article 13 para. 2 of Brussels IIbis Regulation established that: "Paragraph 1 shall also apply to refugee children or children internationally displaced because of disturbances occurring in their country".

conventional text has a very similar forum in Article 6.[84] Indeed, as Recital 25 of the Brussels IIter Regulation recalls, Article 11 of this legal text might only be applied when the child has his/her habitual residence in another EU member state. On the contrary, if the child has his/her habitual residence in a third country before the displacement — we ought to suppose therefore, both contracting and non-contracting parties of the 1996 Child Protection Convention — the 1996 Child Protection Convention is applicable.[85]

More worryingly, further doubts have been raised as to the personal scope of the application of the presence forum. And, in particular, it is unclear if the expression "refugee children and children internationally displaced because of disturbances" might leave outside some other categories of children in similar circumstances, and hence in need of protection. Notably, the question arises whether or not children seeking asylum, children whose asylum applications have been rejected, or simply those children who arrive in an EU member state from a third state for economic reasons may or may not be included in this ground of jurisdiction.

Regarding the protection of migrant children, the European Parliament proposed in the Recast procedure to include a new Recital with the aim to clarify that the Brussels IIter Regulation jurisdiction rules "(...) should also be applicable to all children who are present on Union territory and whose habitual residence cannot be established with certainty. The scope of such rules should extend in particular to cover refugee children and children who have been internationally displaced either for socioeconomic reasons or because of disturbances occurring in their country".[86]

However, this proposal has not been included in the final text, perhaps as a symbolic sign of the little importance that is given to migration in Private International Law rules. Even if it had been desirable to include an open formula that would clearly have embraced the inclusion of all migrant children, it is still possible to interpret the presence forum broadly. Precisely, if we are dealing with a residual forum whose aim is to fill in the gaps in the system of jurisdiction of the Brussels IIter Regulation and to offer protection to all children, it would be logical that, despite the limited wording of the provision, it was to be interpreted broadly. It can

---

[84] This amendment would be prompted by doubts as to which instrument applies — Regulation or Convention — when the child was habitually resident prior to the movement in a third state — not a party to the 1996 Child Protection Convention. J. Pirrung, Article 61, In: Magnus/Mankowski (fn. 51), at p. 467; A. L. Calvo Caravaca/J. Carrascosa González, Derecho Internacional Privado, Volumen II, Comares, Granada, 18ª ed., 2018, at pp. 431–432. Anyway, the problem had little practical impact, as both instruments contain the same solution, B. Campuzano Díaz, Cuadernos de Derecho Transnacional, v. 12, no. 2, 97, at p. 108.

[85] See Recital 25 of the Brussels IIter Regulation.

[86] European Parliament, European Parliament legislative resolution of 18 January 2018 on the proposal for a Council regulation on jurisdiction, the recognition and enforcement of decisions in matrimonial matters and matters of parental responsibility, and on international child abduction (recast) (COM(2016)0411 — C8-0322/2016 — 2016/0190(CNS)), Amendment 6.

hence be understood as including any child "on the move" in need of protection, irrespective of their specific situation.[87]

b) The Residual Forum in Matters of Parental Responsibility as a Solution for Separated Families in a Migratory Context

Closing the system of jurisdiction in matters of parental responsibility, Article 14 of the Brussels IIter Regulation allows jurisdiction to be determined, in each member state, by the laws of that member state. Like the previous forum, it has a residual character. Consequently, it will again only be activated when jurisdiction cannot be determined by virtue of the other grounds for jurisdiction contained in the Brussels IIter Regulation. Nor will this forum be applicable when the child is habitually resident in a third state party to the 1996 Child Protection Convention, since in that case, the latter legal instrument would apply.[88]

The use of this forum in practice is therefore infrequent, almost marginal, given its nature and the peculiarities of its design. Nevertheless, in practice there have been some cases in which the residual forum has been applied, those in which the child is habitually resident in a third state not party to the 1996 Child Protection Convention — and again if no other forum of the Brussels IIter Regulation was applicable.[89] Indeed, this has been the forum used in some cases where the habitual residence of the child in a member state could not be established because the child had not been physically present in an EU member state.[90] In addition, another example of the application of the residual forum concerns foreign parents residing in an EU member state who ask the courts of this member state to apply measures on parental responsibility for their children, who maintain their residence in the state of origin.[91]

---

[87] In this sense A. Limante/I. Kunda, In: Honorati (fn. 25), at p. 88.

[88] As Recital 29 of the Brussels IIter Regulation clarifies: "The term 'laws of that Member State' should include international instruments in force in that Member State".

[89] The application of the Brussels IIbis Regulation to children residing in third states is an issue that has raised doubts in the legal doctrine. J. Pirrung, Article 61, In: Magnus/Mankowski (fn. 51), at p. 467.

[90] See, for example, CJEU 17 October 2018, case C-393/18 PPU, ECLI:EU:C:2018:835 (U. D.) para. 66. In this case the CJEU held that the habitual residence of a child born in Pakistan cannot be fixed in the UK because it has never physically been in the former state, but affirmed that the application of the residual forum of Article 14 of the Brussels IIbis Regulation is possible.

[91] Thus, in Spain, this case has typically arisen in respect of persons originally from third states who work in Spain, but whose children reside in the country of origin in the care of a relative. In the Spanish system, if the Brussels IIter Regulation, the 1996 Child Protection Convention or any other international convention ratified by Spain are not applicable, Article 22 *quáter* d) — or even Article 22 *Octies* para. 3 — of the Ley Orgánica del Poder Judicial would then be applicable. I.e. SAP de León 18 July 2018, 232/2018, ECLI: ES:APLE:2018:841, this case concerns the divorce of two Pakistani nationals residing in Spain, whose daughter resides in Pakistan with her maternal grandparents. Equally see SAP de Barcelona 31 May 2018, 400/2018, ECLI:ES:APB:2018:5395, which applies the residual forum to an application for divorce by a Spanish national resident in

It, therefore, provides a solution to the reality of thousands of families subject to complex migratory processes, in which the family does not necessarily remain united.

V. Further Modifications to Reinforce Children's Rights in the Brussels IIter Regulation

The Brussels IIter Regulation designs a set of mechanisms of different nature in support of its practice. They have been affected by the new text of 2019, seeking to ensure the achievement of the objectives of the regulatory text, and specifically, the better and faster safeguarding of the rights of the child and his or her best interests. Three areas particularly show the EU legislator's aim to better protect children's rights in international cases.

1. Provisional, Including Protective, Measures in Urgent Cases as a Guarantee for the Best Interests of the Child

Provisional and interim measures provide an immediate response aimed at temporarily protecting the child while the procedure is pending. Moreover, they play an additional role in rebalancing two relevant approaches to the best interests of the child. On one side, as a rule of procedure, this principle translates into the need for speed and effectiveness of judicial proceedings. On the other side, from a substantial approach, it requires that all the circumstances surrounding the child's particular situation are carefully evaluated.[92]

The practical projection of the provisional and interim model in matters of parental responsibility in the Brussels IIbis Regulation has not escaped from certain

---

Spain against a Spanish national who is also resident in India, together with her three children. For an in-depth analysis of this matter see M. Herranz Ballesteros, Proyección de la competencia de las autoridades de los Estados miembros sobre menores residentes en terceros Estados: la experiencia española, Revista General de Derecho Europeo, no. 52, 2020, at p. 15; A. Del Ser López and Carrizo Aguado, D., Reglas de competencia judicial internacional en materia de responsabilidad parental: análisis del foro de la "residencia habitual del menor" y estudio de la "competencia residual", Revista Aranzadi Unión Europea, no. 10, 2019, at pp. 62 ff.

[92] In Sandrini's words: "the conflict between speed and thoroughness is heightened in matters of parental responsibility, and is balanced within domestic legal systems by procedural rules that provide for interim measures of protection". L. Sandrini, Provisional Measures and the Best Interests of the Child in the Field of Parental Responsibility, In: Bergamini/Ragni (eds), Fundamental Rights and Best Interests of the Child in Transnational Families, 2019, 287, at p. 288.

doubts and tension, as evidenced by the practice of the CJEU.[93] In particular, doubts have focused on the faculty of the non-competent courts on the substance of the matter, under the Regulation, to issue provisional and interim measures. In addition to this, the scope of such measures has been questioned, both in terms of their content and their subsequent effectiveness in other EU member states.

As far as the international jurisdiction system is concerned, the new regime improves its predecessor both in terms of its clarity and its technical precision, facilitating its future implementation, also, thanks to the interpretation of the CJEU regarding the requirements for implementing it. Thus, Article 15 of the Brussels IIter Regulation is systematically placed within the set of rules of international jurisdiction, thereby clarifying the doubts surrounding its nature in the previous regime.[94]

2. The Formal Improvement in the Brussels IIter Regulation of the Fundamental Right of Children to Express Their Views

Secondly, the right of the child to express his or her opinions in accordance with his or her age and maturity constitutes one of the greatest exponents of the new conception of children as right holders.[95] However, despite the importance of this right, recognised both at the international and national level, the practice of the Brussels IIbis Regulation has shown that its regulation has very important limitations which are now being addressed in the Brussels IIter text.[96]

---

[93] See Article 20 of the Brussels IIbis Regulation and the CJEU's interpretation of this Article in CJEU 2 October 2009, case C-523/07, ECLI:EU:C:2009:225 (A.); CJEU 23 December 2009, case C-403/09 PPU, ECLI:EU:C:2009:810 (Detiček); CJEU 15 July 2010, case C-256/09, ECLI:EU: C:2010:437 (Purrucker); CJEU 26 April 2012, case C-92/12 PPU, ECLI:EU:C:2012:255 (Health Service Executive). On this topic see A. Dutta/A. Schulz, First Cornerstones of the EU Rules on Cross-Border Child Cases: The Jurisprudence of the Court of Justice of the European Union on the Brussels IIa Regulation From C to Health Service Executive, Journal of Private International Law, v. 10, no. 1, 2014, 1, at pp. 14–15; M. Requejo Isidro, El artículo 20 Reglamento (CE) número 2201/2003 ante el TJCE, Diario La Ley, no. 7479, 2010, at pp. 1–15.

[94] Maintaining the EU requirements relating to the urgency and the provisional nature, the new Regulation restricts the subjective requirement to the person of the child, compared to the old reference to "persons", thereby correcting a dubious interpretation of the CJEU. For an in-depth analysis of the new regime of provisional measures see I. Pretelli, Provisional Measures in Family Law and the Brussels IIter Regulation, Yearbook of Private International Law, v. 20, 2018–2019, at pp. 113–148.

[95] See Article 12 of the CRC; Article 3 of the 1996 European Convention on the Exercise of Children's Rights of the Council of Europe; Article 24 of the EU Charter.

[96] The Commission's 2016 Proposal identifies the right of the child to be heard as one of the six main shortcomings in the practical functioning of the Brussels IIbis Regulation (European Commission, Proposal for a Council Regulation (fn. 49), at p. 5. On the topic see B. Ubertazzi, The hearing of the child in the Brussels IIa Regulation and its Recast Proposal, Journal of Private International Law, v. 13, no. 3, 2017, at pp. 568–601.

The Brussels IIbis Regulation did not generally proclaim, for all decisions on parental responsibility, the right of the child to express his or her views. This deficiency has now been adequately resolved in the Brussels IIter Regulation. This Regulation introduces a provision which emphasises the importance of giving children a real and effective possibility to be heard in accordance with the requirements of the CRC and the EU Charter.[97] Hereby, the new Brussels IIter Regulation improves the children's protection by stressing and recognising the importance of listening to children in all matters affecting them, including as well, cross-border parental responsibility and international child abduction procedures, although they are more complex than in internal proceedings.

It can be concluded that the right of the child to express his or her views is improved at the legislative and theoretical level, even though it is also true that such standards were previously already applicable in accordance with the CRC and the EU Charter. Nevertheless, it is considered that to achieve a proper functioning and protection of this right, the existence of some minimum common standards in both material and procedural rules for the hearing of the child will continue to be necessary: without such minimum standards, it is extremely difficult to create a real climate of trust between courts of the EU countries.[98]

That is why, in addition to strengthening the right of the child to be heard at the legislative level, it should be enhanced and promoted by the EU institutions through a whole range of complementary measures. Examples could be the training of judges and other legal professionals involved, the creation of common guides of best practices, and in general, the promulgation and development of child-friendly civil procedures.[99]

---

[97] Article 21, situated in Section 3 "Common Provisions" of Chapter II of the Brussels IIter Regulation. See also Recital 39 of this legal instrument.

[98] A further limitation identified in the Brussels IIbis Regulation in relation to the hearing of the child is the absence of a minimal EU harmonisation of both procedural and material rules on the matter (for a comparison of the different national procedural laws in this area see B. Ubertazzi, The Child's Right to Be Heard in the Brussels System, European Papers, v. 2, no. 1, 2017, at pp. 64 ff.). This has greatly affected the establishment of an adequate climate of trust between the judicial administrations of member states (this is concluded in European Commission, Study on the assessment of Regulation (EC) No 2201/2003 and the policy options for its amendment, Directorate-General for Justice and Consumers, 2015, at p. 47). Furthermore, it has shown to have a negative impact on the regime for the recognition and enforcement of foreign judgments, and even on the very consideration of the principle of the best interests of the child. See on this regard CJEU 22 December 2010, case C-491/10 PPU, ECLI:EU:C:2010:828 (Aguirre Zárraga).

[99] This generic reference to the right of the child to be heard might be useful to accelerate the necessary change of mentality still required in some member states regarding this right, as stated by C. Honorati, Rivista di diritto internazionale privato e processuale, v. 52, no. 2, 2017, 247; T. Kruger, Brussels IIa Recast moving forward, Nederlands internationaal privaatrecht, v. 35, no. 3, 2017, 462, at p. 466.

3. A Shy Commitment of Promoting Mediation as a Way to Solve Parental Responsibility Disputes

Finally, in the context of the growing global trend towards exploring alternative routes to state courts, also promoted by the EU,[100] the new Brussels IIter Regulation introduces a shy — but clear — commitment to its promotion in the context of conflict resolution in matters of parental responsibility, and more precisely, in international child abduction cases.[101] Leaving behind the almost absolute silence in the area of its predecessor,[102] the new Regulation represents a step forward in the regulation of this issue, introducing in Article 25 *intra judicial* mediation.[103] It, therefore, gives an active role to the courts in the search of an agreement between the parties, which is a clear sign of the change of philosophy.[104]

There remains, however, a basic problem regarding the circulation of these agreements within the EU — and that is also shared in the Brussels IIter Regulation — which is the nature of the agreement reached and the need for it to be enforceable. On this premise, which severely limits the steps taken by the Regulation in this area, the new model of recognition and enforcement of the Brussels IIter Regulation will benefit the circulation of mediation agreements, once they have been given the

[100] Vid. S. Barona/C. Esplugues, ADR Mechanisms and Their Incorporation into Global Justice in the Twenty-First Century: Some Concepts and Trends, In: Barona/Esplugues (eds), Global Perspectives on ADR, 2014, 1, at pp. 7–16.

[101] It should be borne in mind that the relevant Article is in Chapter III of the Regulation, dedicated specifically to International Child Abduction. However, Recital 43 of the Brussels IIter Regulation refers to both parental responsibility procedures and those relating to the international child abduction: "In all cases concerning children, and in particular in cases of international child abduction, courts should consider the possibility of achieving solutions through mediation and other appropriate means (. . .)".

[102] Only Article 55 lit. e of the Brussels IIbis Regulation mentioned cooperation of Central Authorities to "facilitate agreement between holders of parental responsibility through mediation or other means, and facilitate cross-border cooperation to this end". This article is reproduced in Article 79 of the Brussels IIter Regulation.

[103] Article 25 of the Brussels IIter Regulation: "As early as possible and at any stage of the proceedings, the court either directly or, where appropriate, with the assistance of the Central Authorities, shall invite the parties to consider whether they are willing to engage in mediation or other means of alternative dispute resolution, unless this is contrary to the best interests of the child, it is not appropriate in the particular case or would unduly delay the proceedings". For an in-depth analysis of this new provision see M. González Marimón, El fomento de la mediación en casos de sustracción internacional de menores en el Reglamento Bruselas II ter, In: Barona Vilar (ed), Meditaciones sobre mediación (Med+), 2022, at pp. 399–418; P. Diago Diago, Artículo 25 Formas alternativas de resolución de conflictos, In: Palao Moreno/González Marimón (eds), El nuevo marco europeo en materia matrimonial, responsabilidad parental y sustracción de menores Comentarios al Reglamento (UE) n° 2019/1111, 2022, at pp. 283 ff.

[104] See in this regard C. Esplugues Mota, El Reglamento Bruselas II ter y el recurso a los MASC inmateria de responsabilidad parental y sustracción internacional de menores, Cuadernos de Derecho Transnacional, v. 13, no. 2, 2021, 132, at p. 159.

necessary enforceability.[105] There is a second issue likely to arise in these cases: namely the fragmentation of international jurisdiction for the homologation of a mediation agreement when such an agreement is reached not only on the (non-) return of the child, but also on parental responsibility.[106]

VI. Final Remarks

Cross-border conflicts dealing with parental responsibility matters have a wide diversity which is projected in the Brussels IIter Regulation international jurisdiction model. In particular, the system is based on the principle of the best interests of the child, linked to the criterion of proximity. Following this logic, the Brussels IIter Regulation, inheriting the system from its predecessor, reflects a much more accurate balance between the two conceptions of the best interests of the child, *in abstracto* and *in concreto*. This is achieved thanks to the articulation of a general rule, based on the notion of habitual residence of the child, as an exponent of the criterion of proximity. This general rule must be seen together with a range of exceptions to this general forum, in which the aforementioned notion of the child's habitual residence is either relativised or simply ignored. This set of forums designed by the EU legislator takes into account the practice of the Brussels IIbis Regulation and seeks to address some of the problems and limitations identified in its practice.

One of the main challenges of the Brussels IIbis Regulation recast is considered to be the harmonisation of the integration objectives with a better protection of children's rights and their best interests. In this sense, the new Brussels IIter Regulation evolves towards the recognition of a greater centrality of the child and his or her rights in resolving cross-border cases in the EU. It thereby constitutes a clear manifestation of the growing influence of the principle of the best interests of the child in all areas and issues affecting them, also from the perspective of Private International Law as well as the tendency to accept a greater influence of human rights in this discipline.

Overall, the Brussels IIter Regulation reflects a better and greater enhancement not only of the principle of the best interests of the child *in abstracto* and *in concreto*, but also in its triple dimension as a substantive right, an inspiring principle, and as a procedural rule. Firstly, it is the child's subjective right to have his or her best

---

[105] In this regard, see Article 2 and Chapter IV of the Brussels IIter Regulation. In depth on the new regime of recognition and enforcement of judgments and authentic instruments in matters of parental responsibility see M. González Marimón, Menor y responsabilidad parental en la Unión Europea, at pp. 331 ff.

[106] In the new regime this problem may be resolved thanks to the choice of court forum, see Articles 9 and 10 of the Brussels IIter Regulation. C. González Beilfuss, La sustracción de menores en el nuevo Reglamento 2019/1111, In: Álvarez González/Arenas García et al (eds), Relaciones transfronterizas, globalización y Derecho. Homenaje al Prof. Dr. José Carlos Fernández Rozas, 2020, 383, at p. 389.

interests as a primary consideration in all cross-border matters of parental responsibility in the EU. Secondly, the concept of the child's best interests acts as an inspiring principle of the Regulation, both in the drafting of its PIL rules and in its subsequent application by the national courts and by the CJEU. Thirdly, the best interests can be regarded as a procedural rule, which in jurisdiction is identified with the existence of effective mechanisms, but also with flexible clauses. Within this approach, the fulfilment of the right of the child to be heard also in cross-border matters is particularly important.

That is why it can be concluded that the EU legislator advances towards a deeper level of cooperation in the context of the Private International Law harmonisation in family law. This will imply, undoubtedly, an improvement of transnational families' realities, including those of migrant children.

The Principle of the Child's Best Interests in EU Law on Third-Country Nationals

Iris Goldner Lang

I. Introduction

The principle of the child's best interests has been recognised as an intersecting and unifying legal principle in EU law that crosses the boundaries set by other legal provisions and connects member states' national, supranational (EU) and international law obligations.[1] The importance of this principle is attested by EU primary and secondary law and case law of the Court of Justice (CJEU). Articles 3 para. 3 and para. 5 TEU[2] list the protection of the rights of the child as one of the Union's aims.[3] The child's best interests have also been proclaimed in Article 24 para. 2 of the EU Charter[4] as "a primary consideration" in all actions relating to children, no matter whether taken by public or private authorities.[5] The CJEU often reads this article in conjunction with Article 7 of the EU Charter, which provides that "everyone has the right to respect for his or her private and family life, home and communications".

[1] I. Goldner Lang, The Child's Best Interests as a Gap Filler and Expander of EU Law in Internal Situations, In: Ziegler/Neuvonen/Moreno-Lax (eds), Research Handbook on General Principles of EU Law, 2022, at pp. 562–573.

[2] Treaty on the European Union (TEU).

[3] Article 3 para. 3 TEU states that the Union shall promote the "protection of the rights of the child".

[4] Charter of Fundamental Rights of the European Union (EU Charter).

[5] Article 24 para. 2 of the EU Charter provides that "in all actions relating to children, whether taken by public authorities or private institutions, the child's best interests must be a primary consideration". Article 24 para. 3 of the EU Charter further states that "every child shall have the right to maintain on a regular basis a personal relationship and direct contact with both his or her parents, unless that is contrary to his or her interests". Additionally, Article 7 protects the right to family life; Article 14 the right to education, Article 32 stipulates prohibition of child labour and protection of young people at work and Article 33 family and professional life.

I. Goldner Lang (✉)
Faculty of Law, University of Zagreb, Zagreb, Croatia
e-mail: iris.goldner@pravo.unizg.hr

S. Arnold, B. Heiderhoff (eds.), *Children in Migration and International Family Law*, https://doi.org/10.1007/978-3-031-71598-3_4

Additionally, the wording of Article 24 para. 2 of the EU Charter derives from a principle of international law.[6] It has been taken from the CRC,[7] the most important international instrument regulating the rights of the child and ratified by all EU member states, which provides in its Article 3 para. 1 that "the best interests of the child shall be a primary consideration".[8]

The Union's commitment to protect the best interests of the child is also applicable in the area of EU migration and asylum law, as confirmed in a number of EU documents, including the EU Strategy on the Rights of the Child, which states that "the principle of best interests of the child must be the primary consideration in all actions or decisions concerning children in migration".[9] Additionally, the child's best interests have been explicitly stated or indirectly relied upon in a number of EU secondary law instruments and policy documents, including a number of acts in the area of EU migration and asylum law.[10] As an example, the Reception Conditions Directive[11] refers to this principle in its recitals 9 and 22 and Article 2 lit. j, 11 para. 2, Article 23 paras. 1, 2 and 5, and Article 24 para. 1, 2 and 3. The Dublin III Regulation[12] mentions the child's best interests in recitals 13, 16, 24 and 35, and Article 2 lit. k, Article 6, Article 8 and Article 20 para. 3. Further, the Asylum

[6]On the discussion of external principles being sources of EU law, see A. Arnull, What is a General Principle of EU Law?, In: de la Feria/Vogenauer (eds), Prohibition of Abuse of Law. A New General Principle of EU Law, 2011, at p. 7.

[7]UN 1989 Convention on the Rights of the Child (CRC).

[8]In the explanations of the EU Charter, it is explicitly stated that Article 24 "is based on the New York Convention on the Rights of the Child signed on 20 November 1989 and ratified by all the Member States, particularly Articles 3, 9, 12 and 13 thereof". See Text of the explanations relating to the complete text of the EU Charter as set out in CHARTE 4487/00 CONVENT 50, In: CHARTE 4473/00, http://www.europarl.europa.eu/charter/pdf/04473_en.pdf.

[9]Communication from the Commission to the European Parliament, the Council, the European Economic and Social Committee and the Committee of the Regions: EU Strategy on the Rights of the Child, COM/2021/142 final, 9 March 2021, at p. 13; See also the Council Conclusions on the EU Strategy on the rights of the child, 10024/22, 9 June 2022 and the Communication from the Commission to the European Parliament and the Council on the protection of children in migration, 12 April 2017, COM(2017) 211 final.

[10]For the list of EU acquis and policy documents on the rights of the child, see Annex 2 to the EU Strategy on the Rights of the Child: EU Acquis and Policy Documents on the Rights of the Child, available at: https://commission.europa.eu/document/download/e32422b2-6ba3-4dbf-931b-d3204877f78a_en?filename=childrights_annex2_2021_4_digital.pdf. See also EASO Practical guide on the best interests of the child in asylum procedures, available at: https://euaa.europa.eu/sites/default/files/Practical_Guide_on_the_Best_Interests_of_the_Child_EN.pdf.

[11]Directive 2013/33/EU of the European Parliament and of the Council of 26 June 2013 laying down standards for the reception of applicants for international protection (recast) (Reception Conditions Directive).

[12]Regulation (EU) No. 604/2013 of the European Parliament and of the Council of 26 June 2013 establishing the criteria and mechanisms for determining the Member State responsible for examining an application for international protection lodged in one of the Member States by a third-country national or a stateless person (recast) (Dublin III Regulation).

Procedures Directive[13] invokes this principle in its recital 33, as well as in Article 2 lit. n and Article 25 para. 1 lit. a and para. 6. Finally, the Qualification Directive[14] refers to the child's best interests in its recitals 18, 19, 27 and 38, and Article 20 para. 5 and Article 31 paras. 4 and 5.

The principle of the child's best interests has also been relied on in recent years in a number of judgments of the CJEU and opinions of Advocates General.[15] Based on Article 51 para. 1 of the EU Charter, its provisions apply to member states' actions "when they are implementing Union law". In other words, the situation needs to fall within the scope of EU law for the application of the principle of the child's best interests, stipulated by Article 24 para. 2 of the EU Charter.[16] This is particularly important in the context of family reunification rights of EU citizens and third-country nationals, where the situation is linked to only one member state (internal situations), as will be discussed later in the text. However, in the area of migration and asylum law, it is not disputable that EU Charter rights, including the best interests of the child, apply in most cases, as this area has been extensively stipulated by EU law.[17] When applicable, EU Charter rights have the same legal value as the Treaties, as provided by Article 6 para. 1 TEU, thus carrying significant weight as part of EU primary law.

Additionally, Article 52 para. 3 of the EU Charter stipulates that the rights it contains have the same meaning and scope as those granted by the Human Rights Convention,[18] provided they correspond, but that this does not prevent EU law from providing more extensive protection. Accordingly, the CJEU has confirmed on several occasions that Article 7 of the EU Charter, which must be read in conjunction with Article 24 para. 2 thereof, has the same meaning and scope as the identically

[13] Directive 2013/32/EU of the European Parliament and of the council of 26 June 2013 on common procedures for granting and withdrawing international protection (Asylum Procedures Directive).

[14] Directive 2011/95/EU of the European Parliament and of the Council of 13 December 2011 on standards for the qualification of third-country nationals or stateless persons as beneficiaries of international protection, for a uniform status for refugees or for persons eligible for subsidiary protection, and for the content of the protection granted (recast) (Qualification Directive).

[15] See the discussion further in text.

[16] The Court's confirmation of this, see for example CJEU 13 September 2016, case C-165/14, ECLI:EU:C:2016:675 (Alfredo Rendón Marín v Administración del Estado), para. 81.

[17] Generally speaking, the Court interprets extensively the word "implement" contained in Article 51 para. 1 of the EU Charter to place a wider range of member states' activities within the field of application of the EU Charter (see, for example, CJEU 7 May 2013, case C-617/10, ECLI:EU:C:2013:280 [Åklagaren versus Hans Åkerberg Fransson]). For an example of non-application of EU Charter rights in the area of migration and asylum law, see CJEU 7 March 2017, case C-638/16 PPU, ECLI:EU:C:2017:173 (X and X versus État belge). For the discussion of "X and X", see I. Goldner Lang, Towards 'Judicial Passivism' in EU Migration and Asylum Law?, In: Ćapeta/Goldner Lang/Perišin (eds), The Changing European Union: A Critical View on the Role of Law and the Courts, 2022, at pp. 175–192.

[18] Convention for the Protection of Human Rights and Fundamental Freedoms (Human Rights Convention).

worded Article 8 of the Human Rights Convention.[19] On the other hand, the European Court of Human Rights (ECtHR) has, in its judgments, confirmed that "there is a broad consensus, including in international law, in support of the idea that in all decisions concerning children, their best interests are of paramount importance".[20] It further added that "a child shall not be separated from his or her parents against their will, except when competent authorities subject to judicial review determine [. . .] that such separation is necessary for the best interests of the child".[21] Due to the obligation contained in Article 52 para. 3 of the EU Charter, this reasoning needs to be the guiding principle in all the judgments of the CJEU, including the ones involving third-country nationals.

The aim of this chapter is to examine the functioning and impacts of the principle of the child's best interests on the rights of third-country nationals in the EU. This analysis will be done by exploring the use of the child's best interests in two groups of cases decided by the CJEU: the ones on family reunification of EU citizens and third-country nationals, relying on Article 20 of the TFEU[22] or the Citizenship Directive,[23] as their legal bases, and the ones on EU migration and asylum law, relying on EU secondary legislation in the area of migration and asylum. It will be shown that the principle of the child's best interests has a multidimensional function for third-country nationals in the EU, which corresponds to its threefold function, as defined by the UN Committee on the Rights of Children.[24] First, it is a substantive right to have the child's best interests taken as a primary consideration against other interests that might be at stake, and it is applicable whenever a situation is within the scope of EU law. Second, it is an interpretative tool, meaning that other provisions of EU law have to be interpreted in a manner that most effectively serves the child's best interests.[25] This function of the principle of the child's best interests has been used to expand the reach of EU law to situations which would otherwise be outside

---

[19] CJEU 26 March 2019, case C-129/18, ECLI:EU:C:2019:248 (SM versus Entry Clearance Officer, UK Visa Section), para. 65; CJEU 5 October 2010, case C-400/10 PPU, ECLI:EU:C:2010:582 (J. McB. versus L. E.), para. 53; CJEU 5 June 2018, case C-673/16, EU:C:2018:385 (Coman and Others versus Inspectoratul General pentru Imigrări and Ministerul Afacerilor Interne), para. 49.

[20] ECtHR 10 September 2019, no. 37283/13, ECLI:CE:ECHR:2019:0910JUD003728313 (Strand Lobben and Others versus Norway), para. 204.

[21] Ibid., para. 207.

[22] Treaty on the Functioning of the European Union (TFEU).

[23] Directive 2004/38/EC of the European Parliament and of the Council of 29 April 2004 on the right of citizens of the Union and their family members to move and reside freely within the territory of the Member States (Citizenship Directive).

[24] In its interpretation of Article 3 para. 1, entitled "The General comment on the right of the child to have his or her best interests taken as a primary consideration", the UN Committee on the Rights of Children states that the child's best interests are a threefold concept comprising a substantive right, *a fundamental, interpretative legal principle*, and a rule of procedure (para. 6 of the General Comment No. 14, 2013, on the right of the child to have his or her best interests taken as a primary consideration (Article 3 para. 1), adopted by the Committee on the Rights of the Children).

[25] To that effect, see para. 6 lit. b of the General Comment.

its scope, by enabling the protection of family reunification rights of EU citizens and third-country nationals in internal situations. Thirdly, the principle of the child's best interests serves as a rule of procedure in cases involving children, in which all procedural rules need to be assessed and aligned with the child' best interests. The fact that a number of EU instruments invoke the CRC in the context of the child's best interests, implies that they embrace not only the concept itself, but also its function and legal nature, as interpreted by the UN Committee.[26]

The structure of this chapter will follow the threefold function by dividing the discussion into three sections, proceeding this introduction. The second section will approach the principle of the child's best interests as a substantive right of third-country nationals in the EU and explore the case law of the CJEU from this perspective. The third section will concentrate on the child's best interests as a rule of procedure in cases involving third-country nationals, while the fourth section will focus on the interpretative function of this principle. The final section will summarise the main findings and offer some concluding remarks. It will be suggested that the three-dimensional character of the child's best interests contributes to its recognition as one of the core, intrinsic values of EU law and as an underlying rationale of EU legislation and judgments. It will also be concluded that the child's best interests serve as a gap-filler and expander of EU law and of individual rights, as well as a corrective mechanism that can rectify some of its anomalies. The concluding section will suggest that the principle of the child's best interests will continue to gain importance in EU law on third-country nationals. Two reasons for this development will be put forth, the first being its multidimensional and intersecting character which connects different areas of EU law. Second, it will be put forth that the growing importance of the child's best interests will be the result of its role to counterweigh the continuing trend of restricting migrants' and asylum seekers' rights in the EU.

II. The Child's Best Interests as a Substantive Right

The following discussion of the case law of the CJEU related to third-country nationals aims to show that the principle of the child's best interests constitutes a substantive right which precludes other interests that might be at stake and applies whenever a situation is within the scope of EU law. When having to balance the child's best interests with public policy and national/public security, the Court has given priority to the former. This approach was taken in "M.D.", a case dealing with the issue of lawfulness of entry and residence bans on grounds of national security

[26] For EU legal instruments that invoke the UN Convention on the Rights of the Child, in the context of the child's best interests, see, e.g., recital 18 of the Qualification Directive; recital 33 of the Asylum Procedures Directive; Article 28 of the Citizenship Directive; and recital 13 of the Dublin III Regulation.

against a third-country national who had been residing in Hungary as a family member of a minor EU citizen.[27] In its judgment, the Court stated that where there is a relationship of dependency between the third-country national and its EU citizen family member, "the Member State concerned may ban entry and stay in European Union territory of that national for reasons of public order or national security only after having taken into account all the relevant circumstances and, in particular, where appropriate, the best interests of the minor child, who is a Union citizen".[28] It continued that "Article 5 of [the Return Directive[29]] precludes the adoption of an entry ban decision [. . .] in respect of a third-country national without consideration being given, beforehand, to [. . .] the best interests of his or her minor child".[30] The judgment in "M.D." testifies that the child's best interests are tangible rights which prevail over other important state and public interests.

The Court followed a similar line of reasoning in its earlier judgments in "K.A. and Others", "Alfredo Rendón Marín" and "C.S.". The case "K.A. and Others" concerned seven third-country nationals who have been subject to orders to leave Belgium based on national legislation transposing the Return Directive, which establishes common standards and procedures for member states for returning illegally staying third-country nationals.[31] Having received orders to leave and entry bans, all seven third-country nationals applied for residence permits for the purpose of family reunification with Belgian nationals who had never exercised their free movement rights. In four cases, applications were made for family reunification between a third-country national parent and an EU citizen minor child. In two cases, the family reunification applications were made on the basis of a relationship between an adult third-country national, who was a child of an EU citizen parent. Finally, in one case the application was made for the purpose of family reunification between an adult third-country national and an adult EU citizen cohabitee. According to Belgian administrative practice, if third-country national was issued with a valid and final ban on entry of at least 3 years, the subsequent application for family reunification with an EU citizen would not be examined at all, and there would be no leeway to take into consideration the best interests of the child or the EU citizenship status of the family member.

As will be shown in section four of this chapter, the Grand Chamber judgment also testifies the interpretative function of the principle of the child's best interests. However, this section will exclusively deal with the part of the judgment affirming that the child's best interests are a substantive right. In this respect, the Court

---

[27] CJEU 27 April 2023, case C-528/21 ECLI:EU:C:2023:341 (M.D. versus Országos Idegenrendészeti Főigazgatóság Budapesti és Pest Megyei Regionális Igazgatósága).

[28] Ibid., para. 69.

[29] Directive 2008/115/EC of the European Parliament and of the Council of 16 December 2008 on common standards and procedures in Member States for returning illegally staying third-country nationals (Return Directive).

[30] CJEU 27 April 2023, case C-528/21 ECLI:EU:C:2023:341 (M.D. versus Országos Idegenrendészeti Főigazgatóság Budapesti és Pest Megyei Regionális Igazgatósága), para. 91.

[31] CJEU 8 May 2018, case C-82/16, ECLI:EU:C:2018:308 (K.A. and Others).

concluded that Article 5 of the Return Directive precludes the adoption of a return decision for a third-country national, who had previously been the subject of a return decision and an entry ban that remains in force, "without any account being taken of the details of his or her family life, and in particular the interests of a minor child of that third-country national".[32] In other words, the Court needs to do this assessment and substantiate its decision accordingly.

Similarly, in "Alfredo Rendón Marín" and "C.S.", the Court pointed to the need to balance the interests of public policy and security with the right to respect for private and family life and the child's best interests.[33] It ruled that Article 20 of the TFEU has to take into account the child's best interests, recognised in Article 24 para. 2 of the EU Charter, consequently precluding a member state from automatically refusing to grant a residence permit to a third-country national on the sole ground that he has a criminal record, where that refusal has the consequence of requiring the EU citizen child to leave the Union territory.[34] Consequently, the child's best interests need to take precedence over other legitimate public interest.

The only limit to the member states' obligation to protect the best interests of the child in the area of EU migration and asylum law has been set by the CJEU in "M.A. and Others", where the Court stated that the provision on the best interests of the child contained in the Dublin III Regulation does not require a member state which is not responsible under the Dublin criteria for examining an application for international protection to take into account the best interests of the child and to take over the responsibility for the examination.[35] On the other hand, in "L.G.", the Court confirmed that the discretionary clause contained in Article 17 para. 1 of the Dublin III Regulation does not preclude a member state to examine an asylum application, on the sole ground of the best interests of the child, even though the respective member state would otherwise not be responsible for the examination, based on the Dublin criteria.[36] Consequently, when given a margin of discretion, member states are entitled to provide an even stronger degree of protection of the child's best interests, if they so choose.

[32] Ibid., para. 107.

[33] CJEU 13 September 2016, C-165/14, ECLI:EU:C:2016:675 (Alfredo Rendón Marín v Administración del Estado); CJEU 13 September 2016, case C-304/14, ECLI:EU:C:2016:674 (Secretary of State for the Home Department versus CS), para. 81.

[34] Ibid., para. 88.

[35] CJEU 23 January 2019, case C-661/17, ECLI:EU:C:2019:53 (M.A. and Others), para. 72.

[36] CJEU 16 February 2023, case C-745/21, ECLI:EU:C:2023:113 (L.G. versus Staatssecretaris van Justitie en Veiligheid), para. 54.

III. The Child's Best Interests as a Rule of Procedure

The principle of the child's best interests is also a rule of procedure, meaning that all procedural rules need to be assessed and aligned with the child's best interests. This was confirmed in "K, L versus Netherlands", where the Court stated that "the best interests of the child must not only be taken into account in the substantive assessment of applications concerning children, but must also influence the decision-making process leading to that assessment".[37] The Court continued that, when deciding upon an asylum application submitted by a minor, the national authorities have to "concretely determine(d) the best interests of that minor in the context of an individual assessment".[38]

The procedural obligation to take into consideration the child's best interests was also confirmed in the context of issuing a return decision against an unaccompanied minor, where a member state "must, at all stages of the procedure, necessarily take into account the best interests of the child".[39]

The same procedural requirement to respect the child's best interests at all stages of the decision-making process related to third-country nationals, was followed in "X, Y, A, B versus Belgium", a recent case dealing with a Belgian rule which required, without exception, that an application for family reunification be submitted in person at a competent diplomatic post.[40] The case dealt with Ms X and her children, who submitted, via email and letter, an application for entry and residence for the purposes of family reunification with Mr Y, who was a refugee in Belgium. They claimed that it was not possible for them to travel to a competent Belgian diplomatic post and that an application submitted by email and letter should be accepted under EU law. The CJEU first stated that member states should show flexibility in order to enable individuals to submit applications for family reunification in good time.[41] Having said this, the Court concluded that "a national provision that requires, without exception, that the sponsor's family members appear in person in order to submit an application for family reunification, even where that is impossible or excessively difficult, infringes the right to respect for the family unit [. . .] in conjunction with [the best interests of the child]".[42]

---

[37] CJEU 11 June 2024, case C-646/21, ECLI:EU:C:2024:487 (K, L versus Staatssecretaris van Justitie en Veiligheid), para. 73.

[38] Ibid., para. 84.

[39] CJEU 14 January 2021, case C-441/19, ECLI:EU:C:2021:9 (TQ v Staatssecretaris van Justitie en Veiligheid), para. 44.

[40] CJEU 18 April 2023, case C-1/23 PPU, ECLI:EU:C:2023:296 (X, Y, A, B versus État belge), ECLI:EU:C:2023:296.

[41] Ibid., para. 51.

[42] Ibid., para. 56.

IV. The Child's Best Interests as an Interpretative Tool[43]

The principle of the child's best interests also has an important interpretative function, as it requires other provisions of EU law to be interpreted in a manner that most effectively serves the child's best interests. The interpretative function of the child's best interests has expanded the reach of both EU migration and asylum rules and of EU citizenship provisions, extending the protection granted to third-country nationals.

The judgment in "X versus Belgische Staat" exemplifies this interpretative function in the area of EU migration and asylum law.[44] The case concerned two actions of annulment, brought by a third-country national, against decisions by Belgian authorities refusing to grant her a visa for family reunification with her minor daughter (who was married at the age of 15 and recognised as a refugee in Belgium), and refusing to issue humanitarian visas for her two minor sons. In its preliminary reference, the national court asked the CJEU to interpret the term "unaccompanied minor", contained in the Family Reunification Directive.[45] In particular, it asked whether a minor refugee who resides in a member state, must be "unmarried" under national law in order to enjoy the right to family reunification with relatives in the direct ascending line. By stating that the provisions of the Family Reunification Directive need to be interpreted in the light of the right to family life, contained in Article 7 of the EU Charter, and the best interests of the child, contained in Article 24 para. 2 of the EU Charter, the Court concluded that an "unaccompanied refugee minor residing in a member state does not have to be unmarried in order to acquire the status of sponsor for the purposes of family reunification with his or her first-degree relatives in the direct ascending line".[46]

On the other hand, the interpretative function of the child's best interests has played an even more significant role in family reunification cases involving EU citizens and third-country nationals, which are based on Article 20 of the TFEU and/or the Citizenship Directive. The Grand Chamber judgment in "SM" illustrates the interpretative function of the child's best interests for the Citizenship Directive.[47] The case concerned a third-country national minor who was under a permanent legal guardianship of Union citizens under kafāla. The question put to the CJEU was whether such a child was encompassed by the term "direct descendant" under Article 2 para. 2 lit. c of the Citizenship Directive, meaning that it would be considered as a family member under EU law and granted the right to enter and reside in the EU. The

[43] This section is partly based on my previous publication: I. Goldner Lang, In: Ziegler/Neuvonen/Moreno-Lax (Fn. 1), at pp. 562–573.

[44] CJEU 17 November 2022, case C-230/21, ECLI:EU:C:2022:887 (X versus Belgische Staat).

[45] Directive 2003/86/EC of 22 September 2003 on the right to family reunification (Family Reunification Directive).

[46] Ibid., paras. 47 and 49.

[47] CJEU 26 March 2019, case C-129/18, ECLI:EU:C:2019:248 (SM versus Entry Clearance Officer, UK Visa Section).

Court first asserted that such a child could not be covered by the concept "direct descendant", because that placement did not create any parent-child relationship between them.[48] However, the Court then continued that "it is for the competent national authorities to facilitate the entry and residence of such a child as one of the other family members of a citizen of the Union pursuant to Article 3(2)(a) of [the Citizenship] directive, read in the light of Article 7 and Article 24(2) of the Charter, by carrying out a balanced and reasonable assessment [. . .] in particular, of the best interests of the child concerned".[49] Obviously, the CJEU found a way to accommodate the kafāla relationship within the sphere of family reunification provisions, by relying on the principle of the best interests of the child as an underlying objective and interpretative tool.

On the other hand, the proceeding paragraphs will show that the interpretative function of the child's best interests was even more imperative for the evolution of Article 20 of the TFEU in the context of its application to family reunification cases involving third-county national parents or stepparents of minor EU citizens who have never exercised their free movement rights and could, thus, be characterised as internal situations. Even though the CJEU in "Ruiz Zambrano" did not mention the child's best interests,[50] it relied on the criterion of the dependency of EU citizen children on their third-country national parent as the crucial factor for determining whether the refusal to grant a residence permit to a third-country national parent would deprive its EU citizen children of the right to reside in the EU.[51]

The first family reunification cases confined to internal situations, which mentioned the child's best interests, were joined cases "O, S & L" decided on 6 December 2012.[52] The cases concerned two third-country national women residing in Finland. Both women were first married to Finnish nationals with whom they had Finnish children, but then divorced and remarried third-country nationals with whom they had third-country national children. The third-country national husbands were refused the right to reside in Finland. Here, the main issue was whether EU citizenship provisions precluded a member state from refusing to grant a third-country national a residence permit on the basis of family reunification, where that third-country national wishes to reside with his third-country national wife and child, and where the wife resides lawfully in the host member state and is the mother of an EU citizen child from a previous marriage. The question put by the national court was whether the EU citizenship provision contained in Article 20 of the TFEU

---

[48] Ibid., para. 73.

[49] Ibid., para. 73.

[50] CJEU 8 March 2011, case C-34/09, ECLI:EU:C:2011:124 (Gerardo Ruiz Zambrano versus Office national de l'emploi [ONEm]).

[51] On the discussion of Ruiz Zambrano and the proceeding case-law on family reunification in internal situations, see I. Goldner Lang, The Reach of EU Citizenship Rights for 'Static' EU Citizens: Time to Move On?, In: Dourado (ed), Movement of Persons and Tax Mobility in the European Union: Changing Winds, 2014, at pp. 307–328.

[52] CJEU 6 December 2012, joined Cases C-356/11 and C-357/11, ECLI:EU:C:2012:776 (O, S & L).

precludes the third-country national — who lives together with his third-country national spouse and her EU citizen child, of whom he is not the biological father and does not have custody — from being refused a residence permit because of a lack of means of subsistence.

The Court first ascertained that the principle established in "Ruiz Zambrano" is not confined to situations in which there is a blood relationship between the third-country national for whom the right of residence is sought and the minor EU citizen from whom that right is derived.[53] However, relying on the criterion of dependency, the Court determined that there is no legal, financial or emotional dependency between the minor EU citizens and the third-country nationals for whom the right of residence was sought.[54] Consequently, the Court stated that Article 20 of the TFEU does not preclude member states from refusing to grant a residence permit to a third-country national who resides with his spouse, who is the mother of an EU citizen child from her previous marriage. This is provided that such a refusal does not entail, for the minor EU citizen concerned, the denial of the genuine enjoyment of the substance of its EU citizenship rights.[55]

Interestingly, when interpreting EU citizenship rights, the Court did not invoke the child's best interests, but seemed to imply that — since there is no dependency between the Finnish children and their third-country national stepfathers — there is no violation of the child's best interests, if the third-country national stepfathers are denied the right to reside in the EU. The concept of the child's best interests, therefore, seems to be entailed in the notion of dependency and applied once dependency has been established or presumed. On the other hand, the non-existence of dependency between EU citizen children and their third-country national stepfathers places the situation outside the scope of Article 20 of the TFEU, since there is no breach of the genuine enjoyment of the substance of the children's EU citizenship rights.

In contrast, in "O, S & L", the Court did rely on the child's best interests when addressing the applicability of the Family Reunification Directive, even though the national court did not refer a preliminary question on the interpretation of this Directive. The Court established the applicability of the Directive to the present case and followed the Opinion of Advocate General Bot by ascertaining that the Directive must be applied in the light of Articles 7 and 24 of the EU Charter.[56] The Court did not go as far as AG Bot, who quoted the ECtHR, when saying that "only exceptional circumstances may lead to a severing of the family ties and that everything must be done to preserve personal relations and family unity or to 'rebuild' the family".[57] It, nevertheless, concluded that the national court is obliged

[53] Ibid., para. 55.

[54] Ibid., para. 56.

[55] Ibid., para. 58.

[56] Opinion of AG Bot, joined cases C-356/11 and C-357/11, ECLI:EU:C:2012:595 (O, S & L) para. 80.

[57] Ibid., para. 73.

to "make a balanced and reasonable assessment of all the interests in play, taking particular account of the interests of the children concerned".[58] Obviously, the Court's choice to rely on the child's best interests in relation to the Family Reunification Directive and not in relation to Article 20 of the TFEU, suggests that the Court starts from the premise that the relationship of dependency of third-country national children on their third-country national fathers, who are refused the right of residence in Finland, is much stronger than the relationship of dependency between the same third-country nationals and their EU citizen stepchildren. It seems that, in this case, blood relationship does play a role after all.

On the other hand, "Alfredo Rendón Marín" and "C.S.", which were mentioned previously in Section II, display well the interpretative function of the child's best interests.[59] Here, the Court explicitly stated that the reading of Article 20 of the TFEU has to take into account the child's best interests, recognised in Article 24 para. 2 of the EU Charter.[60] In another judgment in this line of cases, "Chavez-Vilchez and Others", the Court reiterated the importance of interpreting Article 20 of the TFEU by taking into account the existence of a relationship of dependency between the EU citizen child and the third-country national parent, which entails the concept of the child's best interests.[61] The case concerned Ms. Chavez-Vilchez and seven other individuals who were all third-country national mothers of one or more Dutch children whose fathers were also Dutch. All the children lived mainly or exclusively with their mothers. Except for the child of Ms. Chavez-Vilchez, the other EU citizen children had never exercised their free movement rights, so the situations were "purely internal". The question posed by the national courts was whether the third-country national mothers could acquire the right of residence based on Article 20 of the TFEU, as that would enable, where appropriate, them to acquire social assistance or child benefits under Dutch law. The national court, in particular, wanted to know whether it mattered that the children were entirely legally, financially and/or emotionally dependent on the third-country national mothers and that it could not be excluded that the Dutch national fathers might, in fact, be able to care for the children.

In its judgment, the Court elaborated that the right of residence in the Union of an EU citizen child can be violated, even if the child is theoretically not forced to leave the EU, due to the fact that one parent is entitled to stay but the other is not. According to the Court, this can happen in a situation where the child would in practice be compelled to leave the EU, due to the child's legal, financial and/or emotional dependency on the third-country national parent. The Court thus states

[58] Ibid., para. 81.

[59] CJEU 13 September 2016, case C-165/14, ECLI:EU:C:2016:675 (Alfredo Rendón Marín v Administración del Estado); CJEU 13 September 2016, case C-304/14, ECLI:EU:C:2016:674 (Secretary of State for the Home Department versus CS).

[60] CJEU 13 September 2016, case C-165/14, ECLI:EU:C:2016:675 (Alfredo Rendón Marín v Administración del Estado), para. 81.

[61] CJEU 10 May 2017, case C-133/15, ECLI:EU:C:2017:354 (Chavez-Vilchez and Others).

that the fact that the EU citizen parent is "able and willing to assume sole responsibility for the primary day-to-day care of the child is a relevant factor, but it is not in itself a sufficient ground for a conclusion that there is not, between the third-country national parent and the child, such a relationship of dependency" that the child would be compelled to leave the EU, if the third-country national parent was refused the right of residence.[62] The Court further elaborated that "such an assessment must take into account, in the best interests of the child concerned, all the specific circumstances, including the age of the child, the child's physical and emotional development, the extent of his emotional ties both to the Union citizen parent and to the third-country national parent, and the risks which separation from the latter might entail for the child's equilibrium".[63]

In other words, if depriving the third-country national parent of the right of residence would be against the child's best interests, due to the child's dependency on the third-country national parent, the parent has a derived right of residence in the EU, based on Article 20 of the TFEU.

Finally, the Grand Chamber in "K.A. and Others", which was discussed previously, in Section II, holds incompatible with Article 20 of the TFEU a national practice of not examining an application for residence for the purpose of family reunification, solely on the ground that the third-country national family member is the subject of an entry ban, without examining the individual circumstances of the case and, in particular, the relationship of dependency between the EU citizen and the third-country national.[64] Additionally, the Court seized the opportunity and tried to consolidate its previous case law on family reunification of EU citizens and third-country nationals in internal situations, starting from "Ruiz Zambrano" onwards. The Court repeated its statement contained in "Chavez-Vilchez",[65] where it ascertained that the relationship of dependency "must be based on consideration, in the best interest of the child, of all the specific circumstances, including the age of the child, the child's physical and emotional development, the extent of his emotional ties to each of his parents, and the risks which separation from the third-country national parent might entail for that child's equilibrium".[66]

Obviously, these considerations cover not only "exceptional circumstances", where separation "is not possible" (as the test the Court applies to adult family members), but also where separation is possible, but not desirable, as it is contrary to the best interests of the child due to the child's dependency on the third-country national parent. Consequently, if keeping the family together is in the child's best interests, due to child's dependency on the third-country national family member, then it would be a valid reason for a derived right of residence of a third-country

[62] Ibid., para. 72.

[63] Ibid., para. 72.

[64] CJEU 8 May 2018, case C-82/16, ECLI:EU:C:2018:308 (K.A. and Others), para. 62.

[65] CJEU 10 May 2017, case C-133/15, ECLI:EU:C:2017:354 (Chavez-Vilchez and Others), para. 72.

[66] CJEU 8 May 2018, case C-82/16, ECLI:EU:C:2018:308 (K.A. and Others), paras. 72 and 76.

national family member based on Article 20 of the TFEU, interpreted in the light of Articles 7 and 24 para. 2 of the EU Charter.

V. Conclusion

The preceding discussion has displayed the concept of the child's best interests as a powerful substantive right, rule of procedure and interpretative tool in EU law involving third-country nationals. The three-dimensional character of the child's best interests contributes to its recognition as one of the core, intrinsic values of EU law and as an underlying rationale of EU legislation and judgments. It also enables the child's best interests to serve a triple function in EU law. First, they have an important gap-filling function, which has enabled EU law to expand to a new category of internal situations, which would have otherwise been left out of the scope of EU law, as illustrated by the "Ruiz Zambrano" line of cases, discussed in Section IV.

Second, and linked to the first point, the principle of the child's best interests serves as a corrective mechanism that can rectify some of the anomalies of EU law. It provides a standard of validity of EU secondary law and can, thus, be relied upon as a ground for judicial review. As a result, EU legislation that violates the child's best interests may be set aside, as attested in the Family Reunification Directive "European Parliament versus Council" case.[67] Finally, the child's best interests cannot restrict, but only expand individual rights. This was confirmed by the CJEU in "X", where the Court stated that the "best interests [of the child] could be relied on not in order to reject an application for a residence permit but, on the contrary, to preclude the adoption of a decision that compelled that child to leave the territory of the European Union".[68]

One can expect that the principle of the child's best interests will continue to gain importance in EU law on third-country nationals, for two reasons, the first being its multidimensional and intersecting character which connects different areas of EU law. Second, the growing importance of the child's best interests in EU law involving third-country nationals will be the result of its effect as a counterweight to the continuing trend of restricting migrants' and asylum seekers' rights across the EU.

[67] CJEU 27 June 2006, case C-540/03, ECLI:EU:C:2006:429 (European Parliament versus Council). This was an action for annulment of the Family Reunification Directive, where the Court of Justice decided to dismiss the action, because it considered that the Family Reunification Directive did not go against the child's best interests (see in particular paras. 58 and 59).

[68] CJEU 22 June 2023, case C-459/20, ECLI:EU:C:2023:499 (X v Staatssecretaris van Justitie en Veiligheid), para. 43.

Binding Effect of an Age Assessment

Kai Hüning

I. Introduction

The assessment of age is one of the most challenging aspects when unaccompanied refugees, who are potentially minors, arrive in their country of destination. A particular problem arises when authorities in different countries or different authorities within the same country have doubts about whether a refugee is a minor.

To illustrate this, imagine the following situation: A is a person from Sudan seeking protection. On arrival in Italy, he states that he is 17 years old. At first sight, it is not clear whether A is an adult or a minor. The Italian authorities go through the local age assessment procedure with him, including a medical examination, and conclude that A is between 17 and 19 years old. They therefore assume that he is a minor in accordance with Article 25 para. 5 subpara. 1 of the Asylum Procedures Directive.[1] An asylum application is submitted for A in Italy. Before the asylum procedure is completed, A hears that a friend of his is in Berlin and therefore travels on to Germany. Once in Berlin, A could apply for asylum again as a minor (due to Article 8 para. 4 of the Dublin III Regulation[2]) and would not have to return to Italy.[3]

[1] Directive 2013/32/EU of the European Parliament and of the Council of 26 June 2013 on common procedures for granting and withdrawing international protection (recast) (Asylum Procedures Directive).

[2] Regulation (EU) No 604/2013 of the European Parliament and of the Council of 26 June 2013 establishing the criteria and mechanisms for determining the Member State responsible for examining an application for international protection lodged in one of the Member States by a third-country national or a stateless person (recast) (Dublin III Regulation).

[3] CJEU 6 June 2013, case C-648/11, ECLI:EU:C:2013:93 (MA, BT, DA versus Secretary of State for the Home Department), NVwZ-RR 2013, 735 paras. 53 ff.

K. Hüning (✉)
Institute for German and International Family Law, University of Münster, Münster, Germany
e-mail: k_huen03@uni-muenster.de

S. Arnold, B. Heiderhoff (eds.), *Children in Migration and International Family Law*, https://doi.org/10.1007/978-3-031-71598-3_5

Like the Italian authorities, the German authorities doubt that A is a minor. The German authorities now wonder whether they can carry out another age assessment procedure. Or — after an administrative age assessment has already been carried out in the EU — can they only conclude that the age cannot be determined again because the age determined in another member state must be recognised or is binding?

The aim of this chapter is to examine this question. First, an overview of the need for age assessment and its methods will be given. Then the question will be addressed with the possibility of recognition through explicit provisions. Subsequently, legal policy considerations and the approach to interpreting national provisions will be presented. The EU Charter[4] will be used for this purpose in conjunction with the CRC[5] and the Human Rights Convention.[6]

II. Need for an Age Assessment

An age assessment is carried out if there is uncertainty as to whether the unaccompanied refugee is minor or adult. This is a question that can arise in any member state.

It is necessary to ascertain whether a person is minor or adult in order to apply the special (protection) regulations and privileges that apply to minors or refugee minors. Minority can take on significance at various points.

Firstly, the status of minority is relevant for possible protective measures taken by the state against a minor.[7] If a refugee who may be a minor arrives in Germany and is unaccompanied, the youth welfare office provisionally takes the minor into care. As part of the provisional taking into care, it is then clarified whether the person concerned is a minor, is still being distributed and will be taken into care permanently. The age is also relevant to whether the person concerned is placed in an initial reception facility specifically for minors or an initial reception facility for adults.

Then the question of whether the person is a minor can become important in family law. This applies in particular in the context of guardianship.[8]

Minority is also of significance in various areas of asylum and migration law. It is relevant for determining the responsibility of a state for an asylum application within the framework of the Dublin III Regulation. According to Article 8 para. 4 of the

[4]Charter of Fundamental Rights of the European Union (EU Charter).

[5]UN 1989 Convention on the Rights of the Child (CRC).

[6]Convention for the Protection of Human Rights and Fundamental Freedoms (Human Rights Convention).

[7]A. Schwedler, In: Rolfs/Jox/Wellenhofer (eds), beck-online.Großkommentar, ed. 2024, Section 42f of the SGB VIII (German Youth Welfare Act) para. 2: e.g. in Germany the taking into care of the person concerned.

[8]See Section 1773 of the BGB (German Civil Code).

Dublin III Regulation, a minor does not have to file an application in their country of first arrival, but can also file an application in their country of residence.[9]

Minority may also be relevant in the context of deportation. Article 10 of the Return Directive[10] contains special conditions for the return decision and removal. According to Article 10 para. 2 of the Return Directive, removal is only possible if it is ensured that the minor will be returned to a member of his or her family, a nominated guardian or adequate reception facilities.[11] Minority is also relevant for family reunification. Unaccompanied minors with refugee status can be reunited with their parents in accordance with Article 10 para. 3 lit. a of the Family Reunification Directive[12] without having to fulfil any special additional requirements.[13]

Finally, being a minor can also be relevant in various other areas, e.g. juvenile criminal law.

III. Legal Underpinning for Age Assessment

In principle, age assessment is a procedure that has barely been harmonised at European level, but is regulated by the member states.[14] This means that the various national legislations are of great importance in their respective countries.

Age assessment is only given limited coverage in European regulations. Only Article 25 para. 5 of the Asylum Procedures Directive outlines a few guarantees in the context of medical age assessments,[15] e.g. in cases of doubt, the person concerned must be assumed to be a minor. Article 25 para. 5 of the Asylum Procedures Directive does not specify any requirements for non-medical methods of age assessment.

---

[9] CJEU 6 June 2013, case C-648/11, ECLI:EU:C:2013:93 (MA, BT, DA versus Secretary of State for the Home Department), NVwZ-RR 2013, 735 paras. 53 ff.

[10] Directive 2008/115/EC of the European Parliament and of the Council of 16 December 2008 on common standards and procedures in Member States for returning illegally staying third-country nationals (Return Directive).

[11] More detailed information on the German implementation (Section 58 Ia of the AufenthG (German Residence Act)): BVerwG 13 June 2013, 10 C 13/12, NVwZ 2013, 1489, ECLI:DE: BVerwG:2013:130613U10C13.12.0.

[12] Council Directive 2003/86/EC of 22 September 2003 on the right to family reunification (Family Reunification Directive).

[13] CJEU 12 April 2018, case C-550/16, ECLI:EU:C:2018:248 (A. and S. versus the Netherlands): Clarifies that the relevant date for the age of majority is the date of entry into the country of asylum.

[14] In Germany, age assessment is regulated both in child and youth welfare law (Section 42f of the SGB VIII) and in residence law (Section 49 para. 3 of the AufenthG).

[15] L. Blahová/J. Kapounová/J. Šeba, Age Assessment: Rights of Children, methods, and challenges, In: Van Heddeghem (ed), EJTN Themis Annual Journal 2022, Volume 4 Issue 1, 76, at p. 78.

The EU Charter may also be relevant in the context of age assessments. In particular, Article 24 paras. 1 and 2 (The rights of the child), Article 3 para. 1 (Right to integrity of the person) and Article 7 para. 1 (Respect for private life) of the EU Charter may require consideration. In addition, Article 3 para. 1 and 2 (Guarantee of the best interests of the child), Article 22 para. 1 (Children as refugees) and Article 24 para. 1 (Protection of health) of the CRC and Article 3 (Prohibition of torture) and Article 8 para. 1 (Right to respect for private life) of the Human Rights Convention may also require consideration.

IV. Methods of Age Assessment

There are various methods available for determining age. These will now be briefly presented. However, the catalogue of suitable methods is limited. It is useful here to make an initial categorisation. The methods differ in terms of accuracy, reliability and degree of intrusiveness.[16]

1. (Official) Documents

Firstly, the authority or court can view (official ID) documents that contain the age of the person concerned, such as a passport or birth certificate. The advantage of this method is that it requires little time and effort, is not very invasive and promises a very accurate result. The biggest disadvantage of this logical option is that documents are often either not available at all or are not credible.[17] For example, the Afghan Tazkira is regularly categorised as a non-credible document in Germany.[18]

2. Physical Appearance and Minor-Sensitive Interview

Another method of age assessment is the (minor-sensitive) interview. As part of such an interview, an overall view of the person concerned is taken.[19] The person

[16] L. Blahová/J. Kapounová/J. Šeba, EJTN Themis Annual Journal 2022 (fn. 15), at p. 78.

[17] A. Schwedler, beck-online.Großkommentar (fn. 7), Section 42f of the SGB VIII para. 4; K. Tillmanns, In: Münchener Kommentar zum BGB, Volume 10, 9th ed. 2024, Section 42f of the SGB VIII para. 5.

[18] OVG Bremen 19 August 2016, 1 B 169/16, ECLI:DE:OVGHB:2016:0819.1B169.16.0A, para. 8; different for the e-Tazkira: VG München 7 September 2023, M 18 S7 23.3329, ECLI:DE:VGMUENC:2023:0907.M18S723.3329.00, para. 28.

[19] T. Trenczek, In: Münder/Meysen/Trenczek (eds), Frankfurter Kommentar SGB VIII, 9th ed. 2022, Section 42f of the SGB VIII para. 6.

concerned is looked at and asked about their life and their flight in order to reconstruct the course of their life.[20] The reconstruction of the biography is then used to estimate how old the person concerned is. The term "interview" can have a very broad understanding. Depending on the national interpretation, all forms of evidence may be considered, i.e. photos or documents such as school reports or similar, as well as information from contact persons.[21]

The advantage of this method is that it does not interfere with the physical integrity of the person concerned. However, this method also has two major disadvantages. Firstly, it is disadvantageous that personality and privacy rights are infringed, when discussing the life story. This is because they have to talk about various formative life experiences, in particular the reasons for fleeing and the often traumatising flight with experience of violence, lack of acceptance, fear, war, etc.[22] These topics are covered in such interviews, so that the interviews represent a high psychological burden for the person concerned. Having said that, this method is not very accurate in most cases — the refugees may have lost their sense of time due to the psychological stress of flight, and certain inconsistencies are to be expected in the statements. It is also a subjective assessment by the interviewer.[23]

In order to conduct this interview in a (minor-)sensitive and successful manner, language mediation is required first and foremost. Furthermore, consideration must be given to the traumatic experiences and vulnerable situation of the person concerned, so that ideally staff trained in dealing with minors should conduct the interview.[24] Finally, the four-eyes principle should be observed to ensure a minimum degree of objectivity.[25]

3. *Medical Assessment by a Doctor or Dentist*

In this method, the person concerned is medically examined by a doctor or dentist. The analysis of the development of the teeth (wisdom teeth) is particularly relevant here,[26] but the mere physical examination as well as genital examinations also fall

[20] L. Blahová/J. Kapounová/J. Šeba, EJTN Themis Annual Journal 2022 (fn. 15), at p. 86.

[21] L. Blahová/J. Kapounová/J. Šeba, EJTN Themis Annual Journal 2022 (fn. 15), at p. 85; K. Tillmanns, In: Münchener Kommentar zum BGB (fn. 17), Section 42f of the SGB VIII para. 4: In Germany, a very broad understanding is applied here and any evidence that the youth welfare office considers necessary is taken into account.

[22] Giving a general overview: L. Blahová/J. Kapounová/J. Šeba, EJTN Themis Annual Journal 2022 (fn. 15), at p. 86; M. Weinand, Das Verfahren zur Altersfeststellung bei unbegleiteten jungen Ausländern (§ 42f SGB VIII), 2022, at pp. 162 ff.

[23] L. Blahová/J. Kapounová/J. Šeba, EJTN Themis Annual Journal 2022 (fn. 15), at p. 86.

[24] L. Blahová/J. Kapounová/J. Šeba, EJTN Themis Annual Journal 2022 (fn. 15), at p. 86.

[25] Bundesarbeitsgemeinschaft der Landesjugendämter, Handlungsempfehlungen zum Umgang mit unbegleiteten Minderjährigen, 3. Fassung 2020, at p. 38.

[26] M. Weinand (fn. 22), at pp. 93 f.

into this category. Once again, the advantage of this method is that it does not interfere with physical integrity. However, the disadvantage of this method is again obvious: although a doctor or dentist will probably be able to estimate the age of the person concerned more accurately than a youth welfare officer through physical examination, the result is also rather inaccurate and prone to error. In particular, wisdom teeth can also break through at the age of 17.[27] Furthermore, there are also strong ethical and legal concerns about genital examinations.[28]

4. X-ray Diagnostics

This method involves an X-ray (radiography) examination of the affected person. The knee, wrist and hand bones, third molars (wisdom teeth), collar bone or hip are usually x-rayed and then compared with the existing empirical values for dental/ skeletal development.[29] Here, it must be considered that the empirical values may differ depending on ethnic origin.[30] During an X-ray examination, ionising radiation is used, which affects the body of the person concerned.[31] The disadvantage of this method is that it can cause damage to the health.[32] The informative value and accuracy of this method is also limited: it only works with high standard deviations and can therefore only indicate age ranges.[33] Its great advantage is that it is one of the most reliable methods within this standard deviation.[34]

---

[27] A. Schmeling/G. Geserick, Forensische Altersdiagnostik bei Lebenden, In: Madea (ed), Rechtsmedizin, 4th ed. 2024, 721, at p. 724.

[28] European Asylum Support Office (EASO), Practical Guide on age assessment 2nd ed. 2018, at p. 55; L. Blahová/J. Kapounová/J. Šeba, EJTN Themis Annual Journal 2022 (fn. 15), at pp. 87 f.; M. Weinand (fn. 19) sees no possibility of justifying genital examinations, at pp. 220 ff.

[29] L. Blahová/J. Kapounová/J. Šeba, EJTN Themis Annual Journal 2022 (fn. 15), at p. 86.

[30] L. Blahová/J. Kapounová/J. Šeba, EJTN Themis Annual Journal 2022 (fn. 15), at p. 82.

[31] L. Blahová/J. Kapounová/J. Šeba, EJTN Themis Annual Journal 2022 (fn. 15), at p. 88.

[32] Joint Research Centre, Medical Age Assessment of Juvenile Migrants (2018), at pp. 22 f.; M. Weinand (fn. 22), at pp. 172 ff.; Meier/Schmeling/Loose/Vieth, Altersdiagnostik und Strahlenexposition, Rechtsmedizin 2015, 30, at p. 33.

[33] A. Schwedler, beck-online.Großkommentar (fn. 7), Section 42f of the SGB VIII paras. 3, 12; L. Blahová/J. Kapounová/J. Šeba, EJTN Themis Annual Journal 2022 (fn. 15), at pp. 87 f.; K. Tillmanns, In: Münchener Kommentar zum BGB (fn. 17), Section 42f of the SGB VIII para. 6.

[34] M. Weinand (fn. 22), at pp. 111 f.

5. *Methods of the Future*

Magnetic resonance imaging (MRI) examinations, ultrasound examinations and DNA analyses can be considered as possible methods of the future.[35]

MRI scans have not yet been conclusively studied, but have great potential.[36] A major advantage of MRI examinations is that they do not involve radiation.[37] The method is, however, unsuitable for refugees with tattoos or metal parts in their body.[38] In addition, the psychological stress that an MRI examination can cause, especially for traumatised people, should not be ignored.[39] The studies to date also point to a not inconsiderable degree of inaccuracy.[40] For this reason, it is sometimes recommended to combine MRI examinations with other methods.[41]

Ultrasound examinations and DNA analyses also have the advantage that they do not require radiation, but have so far proven to be far too inaccurate.[42]

6. *Use of Methods in Europe*

There is no standardised procedure for determining age in the European Union.[43] Different methods are used in the member states to assess age. What many member states have in common is that, where possible, they first use identity documents and then conduct a (minor-sensitive) interview.[44] In some member states, however, a medical examination is also carried out immediately.[45] The Netherlands and Portugal were the only member states to state that they look at EURODAC and check the age of majority information there.[46]

---

[35] M. Weinand (fn. 22), at pp. 105 ff.

[36] M. Weinand (fn. 22), at pp. 108 f.

[37] European Asylum Support Office (fn. 28), at p. 52.

[38] European Asylum Support Office (fn. 28), at p. 53.

[39] M. Weinand (fn. 22), at p. 109.

[40] For more details see M. Weinand (fn. 22), at pp. 108 f.: As a result, although there is a high probability that the child has reached the age of majority when bone growth is complete, the possibility that the child is a minor cannot be ruled out.

[41] This is already done in Sweden, for example: European Asylum Support Office (fn. 28), at pp. 53 f.

[42] European Asylum Support Office (fn. 28), at p. 54; M. Weinand (fn. 22), at p. 110.

[43] European Economic and Social Committee Opinion SOC/634 of 18 September 2020, at 4.6.

[44] For example in Croatia, Estonia and Germany: EMN, AD HOC QUERY ON 2021.10 Unaccompanied minors — age assessment methods used by Member States (2021), initiated in 2021 by the EMN National Contact Point for the Czech Republic, available at https://ec.europa.eu/home-affairs/system/files/2021-05/202110_unaccompanied_minors_age_assessment_methods_used_by_member_states.pdf.

[45] For example in Bulgaria and Finland: EMN, AD HOC QUERY ON 2021.10 (fn. 44).

[46] EMN, AD HOC QUERY ON 2021.10 (fn. 44).

V. Is the Result of an Age Assessment Carried Out in the EU Binding?

1. Legal Regulation

Consideration needs to be given to how recognition might be normatively incorporated into an age assessment.

At EU and international law level, there is no provision that explicitly stipulates the recognition of such a determination by the authorities in the case of an age assessment. At first glance, this is also plausible, because age assessment throughout Europe is not usually carried out as a decision by a judge,[47] but is a mere factual finding (within an official procedure) and the recognition of such factual findings is unknown to the EU system.

However, a binding effect could also be stipulated at national level. With regard to the question of whether there is a binding effect on the result of an age determination by a national authority within Germany, the opinion is generally shared both in German case law and in German doctrine that there is no such binding effect.[48]

In German practice, however, there is sometimes an internal administrative instruction to adhere to the result of the (national) age assessment.[49] Nevertheless, there is a consensus in case law and literature that the absence of a formal obligation does not preclude the first national age assessment procedure from being taken into account.[50]

---

[47] See also: ECtHR 21 July 2022, 5797/17, ECLI:CE:ECHR:2022:0721JUD000579717 (Darboe and Camara versus Italy), para. 148: In this case in Italy, neither an authority nor a court decision was made, meaning that it was not possible to appeal against the age assessment in isolation; A. Schwedler, beck-online.Großkommentar (fn. 7), Section 42f of the SGB VIII para. 15: In the German national implementation in child and youth welfare law, the person concerned cannot act against the age assessment in isolation, but rather must challenge the decision of the entire procedure.

[48] OVG Saarlouis 23 November 2020, 2 D 268/20, ECLI:DE:OVGSL:2020:1123.2D268.20.00, BeckRS 2020, 32458 para. 11; OVG Koblenz 6 December 2018, 7 a 10777/18, ECLI:DE:OVGRLP:2018:1206.7A10777.18.00, BeckRS 2018, 40449 para. 25; OVG Bremen 2 March 2017, 1 B 331/16, ECLI:DE:OVGHB:2017:0302.1B331.16.0A, BeckRS 2017, 104,245 para. 11; KG Berlin 13 November 2019, 3 UF 107/19, ECLI:DE:KG:2019:1113.3UF107.19.00, FamRZ 2020, 842, 845; G. Kirchhoff, In: Schlegel/Voelzke (eds), jurisPK SGB VIII, 3rd ed. 2022, Section 42f of the SGB VIII para. 8; K. Neundorf, Die Altersbestimmung bei unbegleiteten Minderjährigen — rechtliche Grundlagen und Debattenüberblick, ZAR 2018, 238, 241; M. Erb-Klünemann/M. Kößler, Unbegleitete minderjährige Flüchtlinge — eine verstärkte familiengerichtliche Herausforderung, FamRB 2016, 160, 163.

[49] For example at the BAMF, but as a counter-example Brandenburg, Bundestags-Drucksache 18/5564 of 15 July 2015, at p. 73; G. Kirchhoff, In: Schlegel/Voelzke (fn. 48), Section 42f of the SGB VIII para. 8.

[50] OVG Bremen 2 March 2017, 1 B 331/16, ECLI:DE:OVGHB:2017:0302.1B331.16.0A, BeckRS 2017, 104,245 para. 11; G. Kirchhoff, In: Schlegel/Voelzke (fn. 48), Section 42f of the SGB VIII para. 8; Neundorf ZAR 2018, 238, at p. 241.

If a binding effect within Germany is already rejected by case law and the prevailing doctrine, it can be assumed that, a fortiori, no binding effect is assumed as a result of an age assessment carried out in another member state.

It should therefore first be noted that there is no legal regulation — either under European law or, at least in Germany, at national level — that expressly stipulates a binding effect. Applied to the introductory case, this would mean that the German authorities would be entitled to assess A's age again.

2. *Problems of Current Practice and the EU As an Area of Mutual Trust*

A general argument in favour of a binding effect is the protection of the potential minor. If there is a binding effect, the refugee does not have to undergo a second age assessment. It is easy to imagine that the age assessment procedure is a stressful and exhausting process after the traumatising experiences of flight. In most cases, this process is characterised by fear, uncertainty and insecurity.[51]

Firstly, an age assessment procedure can be a significant psychological burden for the individuals concerned, regardless of whether it is the first or a repetitive procedure. In most cases, the potential minors are likely to have experienced trauma and may require treatment due to their experience of flight (and the reasons for their flight).[52] This can make even a minor-sensitive interview challenging for them, as they have to report on the course of their lives and their flight in an unknown atmosphere. In a second age assessment procedure, the individuals in question must undergo this challenging process a second time.

But it's not just the minor-sensitive interview that puts a strain on those affected. A day in the clinic is also a further psychological burden. It is easy to imagine that the individuals concerned are unsure and frightened due to their experiences as refugees, the language barrier and the lack of a trusted person in the sterile clinic environment.

As part of the FAMIMOVE project, we were also told in the Awareness Raising Seminars that young people are often unable to understand why they need to carry out an age assessment — after all, it is clear to them that they are minors. This is particularly true in cases where documents are presented but not recognised.[53] The

[51] The asylum procedure as a whole is a process of uncertainty and insecurity: ECtHR 21 July 2022, 5797/17, ECLI:CE:ECHR:2022:0721JUD000579717 (Darboe and Camara versus Italy), para. 122.

[52] P. Sauer/A. Nicholson/D. Neubauer, Age determination in asylum seekers: physicians should not be implicated, European Journal of Pediatrics 2016, 299, at pp. 300 f.; M. Weinand (fn. 22), at p. 119; R. Balloff, Kinder vor dem Familiengericht, 4th ed. 2022, at p. 463; CoE, Age assessment: Council of Europe member states' policies, procedures and practices respectful of children's rights in the context of migration (2017) at p. 18 para. 80; A. Schwedler, beck-online.Großkommentar (fn. 7), Section 42a of the SGB VIII para. 2.

[53] See section IV.1.

fact that this process now has to be carried out more than once is likely even more difficult to understand and causes them further uncertainty and anxiety.

In addition, X-ray diagnostic methods impair the physical integrity of the person concerned.[54] Various international organisations have therefore called for the cessation of the use of X-ray diagnostic methods in age assessment.[55]

Another significant advantage of a binding effect would be the saving of financial and personnel resources. When carrying out a (minor-sensitive) interview, at least one employee of the competent authority is required[56] and, in the absolute majority of cases, an interpreter is also needed for translation. If there are still doubts after this, a medical examination of the person concerned is carried out. This requires qualified medical professionals, medical equipment and again an interpreter (to fulfil Article 25 para. 5 subpara. 3 lit. a of the Asylum Procedures Directive). In many countries, the (emergency) representative[57] must also give their consent. At this point, personnel, personnel costs and treatment/examination costs could be saved through a binding effect. During the FAMIMOVE Awareness Raising Seminars, we were told that there are too few specialised professionals available overall, so saving on personnel would be a great improvement. It was also reported that there is a very long waiting time in particular for interpreters. As a consequence, unqualified or untrained staff sometimes have to be used in order to ensure a quick age assessment. It was also reported that in Berlin the individuals have to wait for a particularly long time. It can take up to 8 months for the assessment to be finalised.

Moreover, the European Union is an area of mutual trust.[58] This mutual trust "obliges each of those States to consider, other than in exceptional circumstances, that all the other member states comply with EU law, including fundamental rights [...]."[59] The member states therefore also trust that procedures within the European Union are carried out in accordance with EU law. If this trust is given, then it is also trusted that the result of the age assessment — regardless of the member state — was determined in a procedure that complies with EU law.

---

[54] For details see section IV.4.

[55] Joint general comment No. 4 (2017) of the Committee on the Protection of the Rights of All Migrant Workers and Members of Their Families and No. 23 (2017) of the Committee on the Rights of the Child on State obligations regarding the human rights of children in the context of international migration in countries of origin, transit, destination and return, at 4; European Economic and Social Committee Opinion SOC/634 of 18 September 2020, at 1.12. and 4.10.

[56] At least two employees are required to maintain the four-eyes principle.

[57] In Germany, this is the youth welfare office for unaccompanied minors prior to the appointment of a guardian in accordance with Section 42a para. 3 of the SGB VIII.

[58] L. von Danwitz, Der Grundsatz des gegenseitigen Vertrauens zwischen den Mitgliedstaaten der EU. Eine wertebasierte Garantie der Einheit und Wirksamkeit des Unionsrechts, EuR 2020, 61, at pp. 72 ff.

[59] CJEU 30 April 2019, Opinion 1/17, ECLI:EU:C:2019:341 (CETA), para. 128; In a similar way in relation to the area of freedom, security and justice: CJEU 18 December 2014, Gutachten 2/13 (EMRK-Beitritt II), ECLI:EU:C:2014:2454, para. 191; CJEU 5 April 2016, joined cases C-404/15 und C-659/15 PPU (Aranyosi und Căldăraru), ECLI:EU:C:2016:140, para. 78; CJEU 25 July 2018, case C-216/18 PPU (LM), ECLI:EU:C:2018:586, para. 36.

It should be noted that Article 3 para. 2 subpara. 2 of the Dublin III Regulation cancels the principle of trust in the Dublin system for transfers.[60] However, in the absence of an explicit provision, this cannot simply be transferred to age assessment. It is important to note once more that age assessment is a factual determination, the recognition of which is unknown to the EU system. Nevertheless, from the perspective of mutual trust, the existence of a binding effect is to be welcomed in terms of legal policy.

3. Solution Approach: Interpretation of National Legislation

The solution approach of interpreting the national provisions has so far gone almost unnoticed: Possibly, a binding effect of an official/judicial age assessment could result from an interpretation in line with EU law of the respective national provisions on age assessment.[61]

If a binding effect arose from the EU Charter (in conjunction with the CRC and the Human Rights Convention), this would consequently have to be considered when interpreting the various national provisions. And if the national provisions are not open to this interpretation, they are contrary to EU law and the national legislation needs to be adapted.

In the German regulation, the term "doubt" in Section 49 para. 3 of the AufenthG and Section 42f para. 2 of the SGB VIII is suitable. If there were a binding effect, the term doubt could be interpreted to mean that there is no doubt about the age of the person concerned if they have already undergone an age assessment procedure in another EU member state.

4. Charter of Fundamental Rights of the European Union

A binding effect could arise from the EU Charter. It arises in any case if a further age assessment procedure would violate the EU Charter. A further age assessment procedure could first of all violate Article 24 paras. 1 and 2 as well as Article 3 para. 1 and Article 7 para. 1 of the EU Charter.

a) Applicability of the EU Charter

In order for there to be a violation of the EU Charter, the EU Charter would have to be applicable to the situations of age assessment. According to Article 51 para.

---

[60] L. von Danwitz, EuR 2020, 61, at p. 85.

[61] This solution approach is based on the idea of M. Weinand (fn. 22), at pp. 123 ff.

1 sentence 1 of the EU Charter, the EU Charter is only applicable when Union law is implemented. In the case of an age assessment in the context of the asylum procedure, Union law is implemented in accordance with the Asylum Procedures Directive (cf. Article 25 para. 5 of the Asylum Procedures Directive), the Return Directive, the Family Reunification Directive or in connection with the Dublin III Regulation, so that the EU Charter is applicable to related age assessments.[62]

b) Article 24 Paras. 1 and 2 of the EU Charter: The Rights of the Child

Article 24 paras. 1 and 2 of the EU Charter could provide a binding effect. Article 24 of the EU Charter is based on the CRC and must therefore be considered in conjunction with Article 3 paras. 1 and 2 of the CRC and, in the situations of age assessment of refugees, in conjunction with Articles 22 and 24 of the CRC.[63]

aa) Field of Application and Interference

Subject of the fundamental rights of Article 24 of the EU Charter are children, i.e. persons who have not yet reached the age of 18.[64] Minority is always in question when assessing age in the asylum procedure. In order to prevent children from being deprived of their specific children's rights and thus ensure comprehensive protection, Article 24 of the EU Charter must be upheld for the person concerned when assessing their age. The same applies to the rights of the CRC.

According to Article 24 para. 1 of the EU Charter in conjunction with Article 3 para. 2 of the CRC, children are entitled to the protection and care necessary for their well-being. According to Article 24 para. 2 of the EU Charter in conjunction with Article 3 para. 1 of the EU Charter, the child's best interests must be a primary consideration in all actions relating to children. This applies to measures taken by

[62] In Germany, case law and literature predominantly assume that the Asylum Procedures Directive and therefore also the EU Charter is also applicable to age assessments during provisional taking into care: BayVGH 5 July 2016, 12 CE 16.1186, ECLI:DE:BAYVGH:2016:0705.12CE16.1186.0A, BeckRS 2016, 49246 para. 22: In the case of an age assessment by the youth welfare office outside of the asylum procedure as part of provisional taking into care, the applicability of the EU Charter must be assumed in any case if this is inextricably linked to the asylum procedure; K. Tillmanns, In: Münchener Kommentar zum BGB (fn. 17), Section 42f of the SGB VIII para. 3; M. Weinand (fn. 22), at pp. 255 ff.

[63] All EU member states have ratified the UN Convention on the Rights of the Child; CJEU 27 June 2006, case C-540/03, ECLI:EU:C:2006:429 (European Parliament versus Council of the European Union), at para. 37: The CRC is an instrument for the protection of human rights and must be taken into account when applying the principles of EU law; H. Jarass, Charta der Grundrechte der EU, 4th ed. 2021, Article 24 para. 1.

[64] In line with Article 1 of the CRC, H. Jarass (fn. 63), Article 24 of the EU Charter para. 9; S. Hölscheidt, In: Meyer/Hölscheidt (eds), Charta der Grundrechte der EU, 5th ed. 2019, Article 24 of the EU Charter para. 18.

public and private institutions, in particular public authorities.[65] The meaning of the child's best interests is identical in content to the meaning of well-being in Article 24 para. 1 of the EU Charter.[66]

The interpretation of the term "well-being" or "child's best interests" is difficult due to its vagueness.[67] These are undefined legal terms that must be interpreted broadly and encompass health, material and social well-being.[68] The Committee on the Rights of the Child has issued — non-exhaustive and non-hierarchical — criteria for determining the child's best interests, which include the particular vulnerability caused by belonging to a certain group (in the case of age determination: unaccompanied minor refugees) in conjunction with Article 22 para. 1 of the CRC and the child's right to health in conjunction with Article 24 of the CRC.[69]

If an age assessment procedure is carried out a second time, the mental well-being of the (usually already traumatised) person concerned is affected. Moreover, as will be shown below, their right to health under Article 24 para. 1 of the CRC is at least at qualified risk. Article 24 para. 1 sentence 1 of the CRC even states that the contracting states recognise the right of the child to the enjoyment of the highest attainable standard of health, so that a qualified threat to the health is sufficient to affect Article 24 para. 1 of the CRC. The procedure for determining age is a stressful situation of uncertainty and insecurity for those affected after an already traumatic flight and is therefore generally not in the best interests of the child. Article 24 para. 1 and 2 of the EU Charter is interfered with.

bb) Justification

Article 52 para. 1 of the EU Charter applies to the justification of an interference with Article 24 paras. 1 and 2 of the EU Charter.[70] In particular, the principle of

---

[65] T. Kingreen, In: Calliess/Ruffert (eds), EUV/AEUV, 6th ed. 2022, Article 24 of the EU Charter para. 7; A. Thiele, In: Pechstein/Nowak/Häde (eds), Frankfurter Kommentar EUV/GRC/AEUV, 2nd ed. 2023, Article 24 of the EU Charter para. 15; H. Jarass (fn. 63), Article 24 of the EU Charter para. 15.

[66] S. Hölscheidt, In: Meyer/Hölscheidt (fn. 64), Article 24 of the EU Charter para. 22; H. Jarass (fn. 63), Article 24 of the EU Charter para. 10.

[67] S. Hölscheidt, In: Meyer/Hölscheidt (fn. 64), Article 24 of the EU Charter para. 22; J. Tobin, In: Tobin (ed), The UN-Convention on the Rights of the child. A Commentary, 2019, Article 24 of the CRC, at p. 83.

[68] A. Thiele, In: Pechstein/Nowak/Häde (fn. 65), Article 24 of the EU Charter para. 12; H. Jarass (fn. 63), Article 24 of the EU Charter para. 10; M. Weinand (fn. 22), at p. 260.

[69] CRC, General Comment No. 14, CRC/C/GC/14, 2013, paras. 52–79; S. Schmahl, Kinderrechtskonvention, 2nd ed. 2017, Article 3 of the CRC para. 11; J. Tobin, In: Tobin (fn. 67), Article 24 of the CRC, at p. 84.

[70] T. Kingreen, In: Calliess/Ruffert (fn. 65), Article 24 of the EU Charter para. 9; A. Thiele, In: Pechstein/Nowak/Häde (fn. 65), Article 24 of the EU Charter para. 21; H. Jarass (fn. 63), Article 24 of the EU Charter para. 22.

proportionality must be observed[71] and "the charges imposed must not be disproportionate to the aims pursued."[72] According to Article 24 para. 2 of the EU Charter in conjunction with Article 3 para. 1 of the CRC, the best interests of the child must be the primary consideration in all measures affecting children, i.e. when weighing up opposing aspects, the best interests of the child must be given special consideration.[73] However, the best interests of the child do not take absolute precedence; in individual cases, they may very well take second place to other interests.[74] The requirements for measures restricting Article 24 para. 2 of the EU Charter are thus significantly increased.[75]

There are two legitimate reasons for a further age assessment which could justify the interference with Article 24 of the EU Charter: (a) the avoidance of procedural delays and (b) the correct assessment as an adult or minor.

The avoidance of procedural delays, which was stated by the German legislator in the legislative materials as a reason for denying a binding effect, will be discussed here first.[76] Avoiding procedural delays is necessary on the one hand from the perspective of the child's best interests (Article 24 para. 2 of the EU Charter in conjunction with Article 3 para. 1 of the CRC)[77] and, on the other hand, Article 7 para. 1 of the EU Charter in conjunction with Article 8 para. 1 of the Human Rights Convention includes the obligation of the state and its institutions to process an asylum application quickly in order to minimise the situation of uncertainty and insecurity for the person concerned.[78]

The second age assessment would have to be suitable for achieving the legitimate reason, i.e. it would have to advance it. However, it is not clear to what extent the procedure should be delayed at all by the binding effect. If the result of an official age assessment were binding within the European Union, the data from the other authority would be adopted.[79] There would be no need to find staff and time for a lengthy personal interview and possibly a subsequent medical examination. It can take a very long time to complete an age assessment procedure due to a lack of personnel.[80] A quick data comparison, on the other hand, would provide a fast result.

---

[71] H. Jarass (fn. 63), Article 24 of the EU Charter para. 24.

[72] For the first time CJEU 11 July 1989, case 265/87, ECLI:EU:C:1989:303 (Schräder/Hauptzollamt Gronau), para. 21; this formulation is also widely used in recent case law, see for example CJEU 30 June 2016, case C-134/15, ECLI:EU:C:2016:498 (Lidl), para. 33.

[73] S. Schmahl (fn. 69), Article 3 of the CRC para. 5.

[74] S. Schmahl (fn. 69), Article 3 of the CRC para. 7; J. Tobin, In: Tobin (fn. 67), Article 24 of the CRC, at p. 75.

[75] T. Kingreen, In: Calliess/Ruffert (fn. 65), Article 24 of the EU Charter para. 9.

[76] Bundestags-Drucksache 18/6392 of 14 October 2015, at p. 20.

[77] H. Jarass (fn. 63), Article 24 of the EU Charter para. 25.

[78] ECtHR 21 July 2022, 5797/17, ECLI:CE:ECHR:2022:0721JUD000579717 (Darboe and Camara versus Italy), para. 122.

[79] To implement this, consideration could be given to storing the result of the age assessment in the European system Eurodac, together with the reasons for the result.

[80] See section V.2.

On the contrary, the age assessment would be accelerated by a binding effect (even if there were no staff shortage). This would also mean that the person concerned would be less exposed to the uncertainty of the outcome of the proceedings and the associated psychological stress. Consequently, a second age assessment is not suitable for avoiding delays in age assessments. Rather, it is itself a prolongation of age assessments.

The legitimate reason of correct categorisation as an adult or minor will now be addressed. In order for the second age assessment to be suitable, it would have to advance the legitimate reason, i.e. in this case it must provide a new insight. A differentiated examination is required here. If the authority does not know the result of the already carried out age assessment, the second age assessment is suitable for providing it with new information about the age of the person concerned. If the authority is aware of the result of the first age assessment, the suitability of this requires closer inspection.

When carrying out a second age assessment, the authority or court would basically have the same methods at its disposal that were already available for the first age assessment — possibly limited by national requirements. The weaknesses of the individual methods described above[81] naturally occur in every country. This means that the results of the new age assessment will also be inaccurate and will again only be able to cope with large deviations. It follows that a further age assessment procedure using the same method will not in itself produce a more accurate result than the initial age assessment already carried out and therefore not in itself provide any new insight.

However, a gain in knowledge could result from an overall view of the two age assessments if a different method is used. This is because different methods — e.g. (a) X-ray examination of the collarbone and (b) X-ray examination of the wrist and hand bones — can result in different age ranges.[82] Whether the different age ranges are relevant in the result is doubtful due to the inaccuracy of the different methods.[83] However, there is at least a chance that a further determination of age will promote the correct categorisation as a minor or adult and is therefore also suitable for gaining knowledge.

If the argument were to be constructed the other way around, in the sense that a new age assessment would be required by each authority precisely because of the inaccuracy of the methods, the suitability of each age assessment would have to be called into question.[84]

However, a further age assessment must also be necessary. The measure is necessary if there is no less severe, equally suitable means of achieving the objective.

[81] See section IV.

[82] L. Blahová/J. Kapounová/J. Šeba, EJTN Themis Annual Journal 2022 (fn. 15), at pp. 88 f.; Joint Research Centre, Medical Age Assessment of Juvenile Migrants (2018), at pp. 37–55.

[83] Joint Research Centre, Medical Age Assessment of Juvenile Migrants (2018), at pp. 37–55.

[84] M. Weinand (fn. 22), at p. 126.

In the absence of knowledge of the result, obtaining the result of the first age assessment would be equally suitable and also a less severe measure.[85] In this respect, the second age assessment would not be necessary.

If the authority is aware of the result of the initial age assessment, no less severe measure is apparent if an overall assessment is carried out and thus the second age assessment is required. If no overall assessment is to be carried out, recourse to the age already determined would be equally suitable and a less severe intervention.

If an overall assessment is carried out, however, the second age assessment must also be proportional, i.e. it must be proportionate to achieving the purpose (here: correct categorisation).

Firstly, it should be noted that it is of considerable importance for both the person concerned and the state that the person concerned is correctly categorised. This categorisation determines, among other things, whether certain protection obligations of the state apply, whether there is a responsibility under the Dublin III Regulation or whether family reunification of the parents can be simplified. It is also important for minors to be accommodated in a suitable environment for minors in the context of their initial reception.[86]

Having said that, it must also be recognised that a further age assessment is not particularly effective and (in most cases) offers no added value. The non-medical examinations are not very accurate and the medical methods have high standard deviations.[87] As a result, after a second age assessment, there will usually only be a second age range that does not allow a clear conclusion to whether the person is a minor or an adult.[88] In this case, on the basis of Article 25 para. 5 subpara. 1 sentence 2 of the Asylum Procedures Directive, minority would have to be assumed again.

According to Article 24 paras. 1 and 2 of the EU Charter in conjunction with Article 3 para. 1 of the CRC, the best interests of the child must be a primary consideration in all measures affecting children.[89] The special importance of the best interests of the child can already be seen from this legally stipulated, prioritised consideration. It also needs to be remembered that those affected are dually vulnerable (as minors and as refugees) and therefore require special protection, see Article 22 para. 1 of the CRC.[90]

The impairment of the child's welfare is also significant. As already shown above in section V.2., the age assessment procedure is a major burden for the minor. The age assessment represents a period of fear, uncertainty and insecurity for the person

---

[85] With regard to the transfer of personal age data, it should be noted that age data would be collected anew if it were not transferred.

[86] ECtHR 21 July 2022, 5797/17, ECLI:CE:ECHR:2022:0721JUD000579717 (Darboe and Camara versus Italy), para. 156.

[87] See section IV.4.

[88] Cf. Joint Research Centre, Medical Age Assessment of Juvenile Migrants (2018), at pp. 37–55.

[89] S. Schmahl (fn. 69), Article 3 of the CRC para. 5; T. Kingreen, In: Calliess/Ruffert (fn. 65), Article 24 of the EU Charter para. 9.

[90] S. Schmahl (fn. 69), Article 22 of the CRC para. 11: speaks of a special vulnerability.

concerned. In addition, a radiological examination also impairs the physical integrity of the person concerned.[91] As just shown, the procedure can also be (in some cases considerably) prolonged by a further determination of age — the phase of uncertainty and insecurity would be shortened with a binding effect.

There is also a risk of contradictory decisions.[92] This is a risk that is generally of a low degree, but can be very harmful if it occurs. If it becomes important, it will probably be primarily at national level. Here is a brief case to illustrate why contradictory decisions are very unfortunate: Suppose one of the few cases of different outcomes of a second age assessment occurs and the youth welfare office and the family court consider the person concerned to be an adult and do not take the person into care or appoint a guardian, but the immigration authorities determine that the person is a minor. Then the individual cannot apply for asylum. At international level, it would be conceivable that a guardianship appointed in another member state is recognised by operation of law in accordance with Article 30 of the Brussels IIter Regulation[93] and at the same time, however, the age of majority is determined in the German provisional taking into care. From the perspective of the best interests of the child, contradictory decisions must be avoided.[94]

Taking these arguments into account, in particular the low effectiveness of a further age assessment and the importance of the child's best interests, the child's best interests prevail over the interest in a further age assessment in the context of proportionality and result in the inadmissibility of a further age assessment procedure.

Carrying out a further age assessment procedure would therefore be an interference in Article 24 paras. 1 and 2 of the EU Charter, which cannot be justified. Therefore, it would be a violation of Article 24 paras. 1 and 2 of the EU Charter. Consequently, Article 24 paras. 1 and 2 of the EU Charter provides for a binding effect on the result of the first age assessment.

c) Article 3 Para. 1 of the EU Charter: Right to the Integrity of the Person

A binding effect could also arise from Article 3 para. 1 of the EU Charter. Article 3 para. 1 of the EU Charter protects the physical and mental integrity. The right to physical integrity refers to effects on the body and health in a biological-physiological sense.[95] Mental integrity refers to mental well-being, whereby

[91] See section IV.4.

[92] G. Kirchhoff, In: Schlegel/Voelzke (fn. 48), Section 42f of the SGB VIII para. 8; Bundestags-Drucksache 18/5564 of 15 July 2015, at pp. 74 ff.: for example in Brandenburg.

[93] Council Regulation (EU) 2019/1111 of 25 June 2019 on jurisdiction, the recognition and enforcement of decisions in matrimonial matters and the matters of parental responsibility, and on international child abduction (recast) (Brussels IIter Regulation).

[94] M. Weinand (fn. 22), at p. 126.

[95] S. Heselhaus, In: Pechstein/Nowak/Häde (fn. 65), Article 3 of the EU Charter para. 14; H. Jarass (fn. 63), Article 3 of the EU Charter para. 5.

interactions between mental and physical health are taken into account, i.e. it refers to impacts that have a pathological consequence — the general social well-being is not included in the field of application.[96] In general, a qualified threat is sufficient for an impairment.[97]

At this point, it should first be remembered that the (minor-sensitive) interview — despite the sensitive way it is conducted — puts psychological stress on those affected.[98] However, a pathological consequence resulting from the interview is — apart from extreme individual cases — very unlikely. In this respect, a second age assessment procedure with regard to the method of the (minor-sensitive) interview does not constitute a violation of Article 3 para. 1 of the EU Charter. The non-invasive medical methods would also not constitute a violation of Article 3 of the EU Charter due to the lack of biological-physiological influences.

However, the legal situation could be different for invasive medical methods — especially those involving X-ray diagnostics. This is due to the fact that there is an inherent radiation risk in X-ray diagnostics. This radiation risk is comparable to everyday radiation risks[99] and is in the low-dose range.[100] Nevertheless, radiation risks do exist and the possibility of damage to health as a result cannot be ruled out.[101] In particular, the long-term effects of X-ray radiation, even in the low-dose range, are still unclear.[102] It is therefore not possible to determine in advance in individual cases whether damage to health will occur.[103] This means that there tends to be a low but qualified risk to health, so that the field of protection of Article 3 para. 1 of the EU Charter is affected.[104]

If the second age assessment procedure also interferes with the field of protection of Article 3 para. 1 of the EU Charter, a parallel argumentation is used in terms of proportionality (same methods; significant impairment of the best interests of the child; hardly any added value) as in the case of Article 24 paras. 1 and 2 of the EU Charter. This would lead to the conclusion that a second age assessment procedure violates Article 3 para. 1 of the EU Charter and that there is a binding effect in this respect.

However, there would be no interference with the field of protection of Article 3 para. 1 of the EU Charter if there is informed consent of the person concerned,

---

[96] C. Calliess, In: Calliess/Ruffert (fn. 65), Article 3 of the EU Charter para. 6; S. Heselhaus, In: Pechstein/Nowak/Häde (fn. 65), Article 3 of the EU Charter para. 15.

[97] M. Borowsky, In: Meyer/Hölscheidt (fn. 64), Article 3 of the EU Charter para. 38.

[98] See section V.2.

[99] Meier/Schmeling/Loose/Vieth, Rechtsmedizin 2015, 30, at p. 30 f.

[100] M. Weinand (fn. 22), at p. 173.

[101] Joint Research Centre, Medical Age Assessment of Juvenile Migrants (2018), at pp. 22 f.; M. Weinand (fn. 22), at pp. 172 ff.; N. Meier/A. Schmeling/R. Loose/V. Vieth, Rechtsmedizin 2015, 30, at p. 33.

[102] N. Meier/A. Schmeling/R. Loose/V. Vieth, Rechtsmedizin 2015, 30, at p. 33.

[103] M. Weinand (fn. 22), at p. 174.

[104] This conclusion is shared by M. Weinand (fn. 22), at p. 258.

i.e. voluntary consent after prior information, to the radiological examination of age.[105] According to Article 25 para. 5 subpara. 3 lit. b of the Asylum Procedures Directive, the member states must ensure that the unaccompanied minor and/or their representative consent to the medical examination.

The validity of consent is a problem that should not be underestimated and is often not sufficiently considered. There are several difficulties at this point.

Firstly, the person concerned must be capable of giving consent. It could be considered that minors do not have sufficient competence to consent to a diagnostic X-ray examination and that a representative must therefore give consent.[106] It is not really possible to make a general statement, it depends on the individual.[107] The consideration that the person may have difficulties understanding the importance of consenting to an X-ray examination because of the language barrier and general socio-cultural differences might initially argue against capacity.[108]

On the other hand, the fact that the fundamental right is only slightly affected speaks in favour of capacity.[109] This is a radiation risk that is comparable to everyday radiation risks. In addition, it can be concluded from the doubts about the age of majority of the person concerned that the minor already has a certain level of mental maturity. It can therefore be assumed that the person assessed can understand the significance of consenting to the examination and is therefore capable of giving consent.

The obligation to provide information should also be briefly discussed: Although Article 25 para. 5 subpara. 3 lit. a of the Asylum Procedures Directive stipulates that the person concerned must be fully informed before consenting to the medical examination, practice shows that comprehensive information is not always provided.[110] In these cases, the consent is not informed and therefore invalid.

It is also unclear to what extent the consent of the person concerned can actually be assumed to be voluntary. Consent is voluntary if it was given in the absence of coercion and misconception (relevant errors and fraud).[111]

To begin with, Article 25 para. 5 subpara. 3 lit. a, b and c of the Asylum Procedures Directive speaks in favour of voluntariness. The person concerned is not examined without consent, the application for protection may not be rejected

[105] S. Heselhaus, In: Pechstein/Nowak/Häde (fn. 65), Article 3 of the EU Charter para. 26; H. Jarass (fn. 63), Article 24 of the EU Charter para. 9.

[106] Cf. G. Wagner, In: Münchener Kommentar zum BGB, Volume 5, 9th ed. 2023, Section 630d of the BGB para. 51.

[107] Cf. G. Wagner, In: Münchener Kommentar zum BGB (fn. 106), Section 630d of the BGB para. 51.

[108] M. Weinand (fn. 22), at p. 119; A. Aynsley-Green, Unethical age assessment, British Dental Journal 2009, 337, at p. 337.

[109] Based on G. Wagner, In: Münchener Kommentar zum BGB (fn. 106), Section 630d of the BGB para. 60.

[110] For example ECtHR 21 July 2022, 5797/17, ECLI:CE:ECHR:2022:0721JUD000579717 (Darboe and Camara versus Italy), para. 146.

[111] Thought from T. Gutmann, In: Staudinger BGB, ed. 2021, Section 630d of the BGB para. 106.

merely because of a refusal and the minor is informed of this. The minor is therefore free to choose whether or not to undergo the medical examination — a refusal must not lead automatically to negative consequences.[112]

One argument against the voluntary nature of this could be that pressure is also built up on the persons concerned by (necessarily) instructing them about their need to cooperate and the consequences of refusing to do so.[113] Firstly, the person concerned is in a relationship of subordination with the youth welfare office. Typically, the person concerned will assume that a refusal will make them appear implausible.[114] However, this idea of implausibility is an error in motive. For the error to be considered, it must refer to the legal interest concerned,[115] i.e. in this case to physical integrity. In this case, the person concerned is not mistaken about the fact that the X-ray examination poses a qualified risk to their health. Moreover, psychological pressure does not constitute a coercive effect.[116] Consequently, this error in motive is not related to physical integrity and is therefore irrelevant to the voluntariness. Voluntariness is therefore fundamentally given.

The situation would be different if the competent authority were to convey to the person concerned that they would be categorised as an adult — with all the resulting consequences — without consent and examination. In this case, the person concerned would be subjected to undue pressure and thus coercion, which would invalidate the voluntary nature of consent.[117]

Finally, there is the problem of who the minor's representative is, if a representative has to give consent.[118] As the person concerned is unaccompanied, the legal representatives are often unreachable.[119] In the event of a second age assessment, a cross-border guardianship could exist in accordance with Article 30 of the Brussels IIter Regulation. In many cases, however, this may not be the case. In Germany, the youth welfare office has an emergency right of representation for these situations in

---

[112] It must be remembered here that, in accordance with Article 25 para. 5 subpara. 4 of the Asylum Procedures Directive, the authority may also decide on age after the person concerned refused to undergo a medical examination. However, as Article 25 para. 5 subpara. 1 sentence 2 of the Asylum Procedures Directive also stipulates that, in cases of doubt, it must be assumed that the applicant is a minor and only in cases of doubt can the medical examination be carried out, the decision would necessarily have to lead to the applicant being a minor.

[113] Doubtful that consent is given without any form of pressure: P. Sauer/A. Nicholson/D. Neubauer, European Journal of Pediatrics 2016, 299, 301; M. Weinand (fn. 22), at p. 119.

[114] M. Weinand (fn. 22), at p. 119.

[115] Thought from T. Gutmann, In: Staudinger (Fn. 111), Section 630d of the BGB para. 124.

[116] Based on T. Gutmann, In: Staudinger (Fn. 111), Section 630d of the BGB para. 111.

[117] Based on BVerfG 23 March 2011, 2 BvR 882/09, BVerfGE 128, 282, 301; T. Gutmann, In: Staudinger (Fn. 111), Section 630d of the BGB para. 110.

[118] For example, in Germany: Section 42f para. 2 sentence 3 of the SGB VIII.

[119] W. Dürbeck, Unbegleitete minderjährige Flüchtlinge im Familienrecht, FamRZ 2018, 553, at p. 555; In any case, this also raises the question of the extent to which the parents are still the legal representatives, since the minor status is in question.

accordance with Section 42a para. 3 of the SGB VIII.[120] This does not solve the problem though, as we were told during the FAMIMOVE Awareness Raising Seminars: Because the youth welfare office often initiates the age assessment on the one hand and is also obliged to protect the persons concerned on the other, there is a conflict of interest. Whether a separation of personnel could provide a solution here is very doubtful, at least for smaller youth welfare offices.[121]

d) Article 7 Para. 1 of the EU Charter: Respect for Private Life

Finally, a binding effect can also be inferred from Article 7 para. 1 of the EU Charter in conjunction with Article 8 para. 1 of the Human Rights Convention and the right to respect for private life.

Article 52 para. 3 of the EU Charter stipulates that the rights of the EU Charter, which correspond to a right of the Human Rights Convention, have the same meaning and scope as the rights of the Human Rights Convention. The rights under Article 7 of the EU Charter correspond to the rights under Article 8 of the Human Rights Convention.[122]

"Private life" is an undefined legal term and cannot be conclusively defined.[123] Article 7 para. 1 of the EU Charter in conjunction with Article 8 para. 1 of the Human Rights Convention includes the obligation for the state and its institutions to process an asylum application quickly in order to minimise the situation of uncertainty and insecurity for the person concerned.[124] The CJEU has already discussed this idea of the quickest possible asylum procedure in the context of Article 8 of the Dublin III Regulation.[125] Due to the particular vulnerability of unaccompanied minors, the idea can also be applied to age assessment. At this point, reference can be made to the argument of accelerating the procedure by not having a second age assessment.[126] In addition, the right to respect for private life includes the physical and psychological integrity of a person as well as the right to personal development

[120] K. Tillmanns, In: Münchener Kommentar zum BGB (fn. 17), Section 42f of the SGB VIII para. 11.

[121] Once a representative has been found, the question arises as to why they should consent to the X-ray examination. If the refusal should not have any (reflex-like) negative consequences, but at the same time the health of the person concerned is endangered by the consent, it makes more sense not to consent. In this respect, the consent solution can be seriously questioned.

[122] Explanations relating to the Charter of Fundamental Rights, Official Journal of the European Union 2007 C 303/20.

[123] J. Pätzold, In: Karpenstein/Mayer (eds), Konvention zum Schutz der Menschenrechte und Grundfreiheiten, 3rd ed. 2022, Article 8 of the Human Rights Convention para. 5.

[124] ECtHR 21 July 2022, 5797/17, ECLI:CE:ECHR:2022:0721JUD000579717 (Darboe and Camara versus Italy), para. 122.

[125] CJEU 6 June 2013, case C-648/11, ECLI:EU:C:2013:93 (MA, BT, DA versus Secretary of State for the Home Department), NVwZ-RR 2013, 735 paras. 55 ff.

[126] See section V.4.b)bb).

and to enter into relationships with other people.[127] The qualified threat to health posed by radiological examinations is of relevance here.

Consent can also be given to interferences with Article 7 para. 1 of the EU Charter.[128] Consent to a lengthy asylum procedure is unlikely, but consent to a radiological examination will regularly be given.[129]

As with Article 24 paras. 1 and 2 of the EU Charter in the context of the justification of the interference and in particular of proportionality, the already known arguments (considerable uncertainty during an asylum procedure; same available methods; hardly any new knowledge gained; considerable impairment of the best interests of the child) lead to the conclusion that no justification is possible.

e) Summary

At this point, it can be stated that Article 24 paras. 1 and 2 of the EU Charter in conjunction with Article 3 paras. 1 and 2 of the CRC and Article 7 para. 1 of the EU Charter in conjunction with Article 8 para. 1 of the Human Rights Convention provide a binding effect within the applicability of the EU Charter. As a rule, however, there is no binding effect under Article 3 para. 1 of the EU Charter due to consent to the radiological examination.

5. Exceptions to a Binding Character

Finally, possible exceptions to the binding effect should be briefly discussed. Situations are conceivable in which a binding effect on the result of the first age assessment is not convincing. Therefore, a binding effect cannot be absolute.

On the one hand, new facts, in particular official documents, should cancel the binding effect.[130] If a new fact arises that strongly favours the age of majority, a new age assessment can be carried out, as the effectiveness of the second age assessment is significantly higher in this case. However, this only concerns the method for which there is new reliable information. Of course, this also applies if new facts arise that speak in favour of the minor.

If the age was determined without (sufficient) justification or if there is even a well-founded suspicion of arbitrariness when determining the age, a binding effect cannot be upheld either. At this point, it is not possible to determine whether the first

[127] ECtHR 21 July 2022, 5797/17, ECLI:CE:ECHR:2022:0721JUD000579717 (Darboe and Camara versus Italy), para. 123.

[128] H. Jarass (fn. 63), Article 24 of the EU Charter para. 27.

[129] See section V.4.c).

[130] The idea of the changed factual situation has also been considered by OVG Bremen 2 March 2017, 1 B 331/16, ECLI:DE:OVGHB:2017:0302.1B331.16.0A, BeckRS 2017, 104245 para. 11.

age determination was accurate, which means that the effectiveness of a second age determination is also significantly increased in this case.

Furthermore, procedural errors must be considered. At this point, however, it should be considered that formal errors (e.g. incorrect consent to the radiological examination) must not lead to a new age assessment if the factual age assessment was carried out without errors. Otherwise, the person concerned would be burdened with a new age assessment, even though there is already a correct result of an age assessment and therefore no enriching result can be achieved.

Finally, one could also consider rejecting a binding effect from the point in time at which a new method of age determination is available that is significantly more accurate and less intrusive than the existing methods.

VI. Conclusion

It has been shown that the majority of literature and practice does not assume that an initial age assessment has a binding effect. There is also no provision under European or international law that would explicitly order a binding effect. Likewise, there is no national provision in Germany that explicitly stipulates such a binding effect.

The approach of interpreting the national provisions on age determination in conformity with EU law can help: A binding effect arises from Article 24 paras 1 and 2 of the EU Charter in conjunction with Article 3 paras. 1 and 2 of the CRC and Article 7 para. 1 of the EU Charter in conjunction with Article 8 para. 1 of the Human Rights Convention. This binding effect must be incorporated in the interpretation of the national provisions.

In principle, no binding effect has arisen from Article 3 para. 1 of the EU Charter. However, it was established here that the current consent solution contains many different problems. In particular, it is unclear who — if required — fulfils the role of representative.

To clarify matters, the European legislator should also explicitly include the binding effect of an age assessment within the EU legislation.

Part III
Guardianship for Unaccompanied Minor Refugees

Guardianship of Children in the Context of Migration in Hungary

Orsolya Szeibert

I. Introduction

The focus of this study is the guardianship of unaccompanied minors in Hungary regarding real-life experiences, the implementation of children's rights and the meeting points of child protection law, family law and private international law. These special issues require an overview of the Hungarian asylum system. The Hungarian asylum regime's complexity can be attributed to several reasons. Albeit the Act No LXXX on Asylum[1] (Asylum Act) entered into force already in 2007, this Act has been amended several times, especially in last 10 years. Similarly, the implementing and "surrounding" legal area of asylum including asylum proceeding, the requirements of recognition, the different status have also been modified decisively in the last decade and these amendments affected the asylum regime deeply. It cannot be separated from the fact that the Hungarian parliament intended to promptly react to the "mass immigration" situations in the mid-2010s and manage the situations of refugees arriving in Hungary crossing the Southern Border such as the situation caused later by the refugees fleeing from Ukraine. The legal background of asylum law is thoroughly wide and fragmented. In 2015 the provisions were modified in a very short time in a huge wave and the maintenance of the "crisis situation caused by mass immigration" was criticised even at that time while pointing out the fragmented[2] legal regime concerning asylum.

In the chapter an introduction is given about the Hungarian asylum system, in particular regarding the status that may be acquired as a result of the asylum

[1] 2007. évi LXXX. törvény a menedékjogról.

[2] J. Tóth, "… A hazájukat elhagyni kényszerülők emberi jogainak és alapvető szabadságainak védelmére", Fundamentum 2015, 4, 61, at pp. 61 f.

O. Szeibert (✉)
Department of Civil Law, Faculty of Law, Eötvös Loránd University, Budapest, Hungary
e-mail: szeibert@ajk.elte.hu

S. Arnold, B. Heiderhoff (eds.), *Children in Migration and International Family Law*, https://doi.org/10.1007/978-3-031-71598-3_6

procedure, and the peculiarities of guardianship and child protection measures. It is essential to describe and analyse the consequences of the Act providing the order of "crisis situation caused by mass immigration" and a separate issue is how the children and unaccompanied minors appear in the asylum system. When the first Ukrainian refugees arrived in Hungary in late February 2022 new legal provisions were introduced. These provisions have to be discussed as well as the practical experience concerning child protection guardianship of unaccompanied minors, their age assessment, the determination of whether the unaccompanied minor is an "unaccompanied" child or not, and the possible private international law consequences of guardianship. The last section of the chapter evaluates how children's rights are implemented and exercised in real life and upon the concerning legal provisions.

II. The Outlines of the Hungarian Asylum System

1. Recognised Status According to the Asylum Act

In Hungary the main legal source of asylum is the Asylum Act which was accepted in June 2007. It stipulates the content of the asylum granted by Hungary, the criteria of recognition as a refugee, a beneficiary of subsidiary or temporary protection and a person with tolerated stay, such as the procedure aimed at expulsion ordered by the refugee authority and the recognition and the revocation thereof. The provisions of this Act shall apply to foreigners who are subject to the Dublin procedure, have submitted applications for recognition or who enjoy asylum.

The person who enjoys rights of asylum can be a refugee *(menekült),*[3] a beneficiary of subsidiary protection *(oltalmazott),*[4] a beneficiary of temporary protection *(menedékes)*[5] or a person with tolerated stay *(befogadott).*[6] These are different categories.

Hungary recognises as a refugee a foreigner who complies with the requirements stipulated by Article XIV para. 4 of the Alaptörvény (Hungarian Fundamental Law).[7] When the Asylum Act entered into force it contained the provision according to which the Hungarian Republic recognised as a refugee a foreigner who, due to racial or religious reasons, nationality, belonging to a specific social group, persecution due to political beliefs or a well-founded fear of persecution, resides outside his country of origin and does not know, or in fear of persecution does not wish to

[3] Article 6 of the Asylum Act.

[4] Article 12 of the Asylum Act.

[5] Article 19 of the Asylum Act.

[6] Article 25/A of the Asylum Act.

[7] Magyarország Alaptörvénye (25 April 2011).

use the protection of his country of origin. In 2018 the Fundamental Law was amended such as the Asylum Act.

The Seventh Amendment to the Fundamental Law introduced a new provision. Article XIV para. 1 of the Fundamental Law declares that no foreign population shall be settled in Hungary and a foreign national, not including persons who have the right to free movement and residence, may only live in the territory of Hungary under an application individually examined by the Hungarian authorities. Article XIV para. 3 of the Fundamental Law — prohibiting the expulsion or extradition of any person to a state where there is a risk that he would be sentenced to death, tortured, or subjected to other inhuman treatment or punishment — has been maintained. Article XIV para. 4 of the Fundamental Law originally contained a provision that Hungary should, upon request, grant asylum to non-Hungarian nationals who were persecuted in their country or in the country of their habitual residence for reasons of race, nationality, the membership of a particular social group, religious or political beliefs, or have a well-founded reason to fear direct persecution if they do not receive protection from their country of origin, nor from any other country. This sentence was completed by a further one in 2018. According to this further rule, a non-Hungarian national shall not be entitled to asylum if he or she arrived in the territory of Hungary through any country where he or she was not persecuted or directly threatened with persecution.

The beneficiary of subsidiary protection is granted to a foreigner who does not satisfy the criteria of recognition as a refugee but there is a risk that, in the event of his/her return to his/her country of origin, he would be exposed to serious harm and he is unable or, owing to fear of such risk, unwilling to avail himself of the protection of his country of origin. The temporary protection is granted to a foreigner who belongs to a group of displaced persons arriving in the territory of Hungary *en masse* which was recognised by the Council of the European Union as eligible for temporary protection under the procedure determined in the Temporary Protection Directive,[8] or by the Government as eligible for temporary protection as the persons belonging to the group had been forced to leave their country due to an armed conflict, civil war or ethnic clashes or the general, systematic or gross violation of human rights, in particular, torture, cruel, inhuman or degrading treatment.

In 2016 a package of acts in connection with migration was accepted and the status of a person with tolerated stay was replaced into the Asylum Act. The status of a person with tolerated stay occupies a special place in the system of statuses, since a person with such a legal status does not enjoy the right to asylum, but despite this, he is protected against deportation.[9]

[8] Council Directive 2001/55/EC of 20 July 2001 on minimum standards for giving temporary protection in the event of a mass influx of displaced persons and on measures promoting a balance of efforts between member states in receiving such persons and bearing the consequences thereof.

[9] Á. Szép, A nemzetbiztonsági okból kezdeményezett idegenrendészeti kiutasítás és a nemzetbiztonsági kockázat megállapításának kapcsolata az egyes tartózkodási jogcímek tükrében, *Iustum Aequum Salutare* 2021, 3, 39, at p. 50.

2. Asylum Procedure

Asylum procedure applied nowadays is regulated as amended by the Transitional Act (Act No. LVIII of 2020 on the transitional rules related to the end of the state of emergency and on epidemic preparedness).[10] These are interim provisions containing derogations from the rules of the Asylum Act, and must be applied until the end of 2024. The application must be submitted in the National Directorate General for Aliens Policing *(Országos Idegenrendészeti Főigazgatóság)*. The asylum authority will decide on the case and may provide refugee status or subsidiary protection. An appeal may be submitted to the court against the decision of the asylum authority. The asylum authority must examine whether the rules applicable to persons in need of special treatment are to be applied to the person seeking recognition. The refugee authority may use the assistance of a medical or psychological expert to determine whether the person seeking recognition needs special treatment. If a person seeking recognition is a minor, the refugee authority shall take action to trace the person responsible for the minor with the exception where it can be presumed on the basis of information received by the refugee authority that there is a conflict of interest between the person responsible for the minor and the minor, or where tracing the person responsible for the minor is not justified for other reasons bearing in mind the best interests of the child.[11]

3. Children in Asylum Proceedings

The asylum procedure shall be instituted upon the basis of an application for recognition submitted to the refugee authority and the person seeking recognition shall proceed in the refugee procedure in person. There is a difference between persons having limited capacity to act and those ones who do not have any capacity to act. If a minor has not reached the age of 14, he has no capacity to act according to the Act No. V of 2013 on the Hungarian Civil Code (Ptk.)[12] and if he is between the age of 14 and 18, he has a limited capacity to act if he is not incapable. (I must add that it is possible for a minor who has reached the age of 16 to enter a marriage with the permission of the public guardianship authority and in that case, he acquires full age). A person with limited legal capability shall be entitled to proceed in an asylum procedure. Upon the presentation of the application for recognition, the person seeking recognition shall appear before the refugee authority in person and if the

[10] 2020. évi LVIII. törvény a veszélyhelyzet megszűnésével összefüggő átmeneti szabályokról és a járványügyi készültségről.

[11] Government Decree 301/2007 (XI.9.) on the implementation of the Asylum Act (hereinafter Government Decree on Asylum) contains detailed rules primarily provisions and benefits granted upon reception.

[12] 2013. évi V. törvény a Polgári Törvénykönyvről.

minor is under the age of 14 and wishes to apply for recognition in person, the refugee authority shall involve his legal representative in the asylum procedure or, in the absence thereof, shall request the appointment of a guardian *ad litem*.

III. Guardianship and Child Protection Measures

1. Appointment of Child Protection Guardian

The amendments of the asylum law resulted in the better protection of unaccompanied minors. When the Asylum Act entered into force it required that if the applicant for recognition is an unaccompanied minor, the refugee authority should immediately take steps to appoint a guardian *ad litem* to represent the minor. This requirement was later mitigated with the exception that no step had to be taken if the applicant for recognition would likely reach the age of majority before the asylum authority makes its decision on the merits of the case. In 2015 a further amendment changed the minors' protection.[13] According to the modified rules if the person seeking recognition is an unaccompanied minor, the refugee authority shall, without delay, initiate the temporary placement of the child and request the guardianship authority to appoint a child protection guardian *(gyermekvédelmi gyám)*, who serves to represent the minor. The child protection guardian shall be appointed within 8 days of the arrival of the refugee authority's request. The unaccompanied minor and the refugee authority shall without delay be notified by the guardianship authority of the person of the child protection guardian appointed.

2. Refugees with Special Needs

The Government Decree on Asylum contains special provisions for persons with special needs during reception. The refugee authority must ensure separated accommodation at the reception centre for persons seeking recognition who have special needs in cases justified by their specific individual situation. The family unity must be maintained, and the child's best interests shall be a primary consideration. It requires that while being accommodated at the reception centre, food, clothing, mental hygiene and health care, attendance and education shall be provided that is advancing the child's physical, mental, emotional, and moral development, and is adequate for the child's age, health condition and other needs.

[13] Act No CXXVII. of 2015 on the establishment of the temporary security border closure and on the amendment of the laws related to migration. 2015. évi CXXVII. törvény az ideiglenes biztonsági határzár létesítésével, valamint a migrációval összefüggő törvények módosításáról.

3. Child's Placement

If the person seeking recognition is an unaccompanied minor, in accordance with the child protection legislation, he shall be placed in a child protection institution, provided that the refugee authority has determined the minor status of the child concerned. Unaccompanied minors may be placed with adult relatives if the latter undertake in writing to house, care and provide for the minor and from their personal relationship with the minor it becomes obvious that such an arrangement shall be in the interests of the unaccompanied minor seeking recognition. If a child protection accommodation is provided for the unaccompanied minor, family unity has to be maintained by keeping siblings together, taking into account their ages and degree of maturity and the accommodation may only be changed in exceptional circumstances.

Unaccompanied minors are temporarily placed. The child's temporary placement *(ideiglenes hatályú elhelyezés)* is one of the authoritative measures. It is applied in case of unaccompanied minors upon the Asylum. In case of the child's temporary placement, the child is placed at a foster parent or children's home without any delay.

4. The Significance and Scope of the Child Protection Act in "Normal" Times

In Hungary the Act No. XXXI of 1997 on the protection of children and guardianship administration (Hungarian Child Protection Act, Gyvt.)[14] regulates the child protection system, and it has decisive significance for unaccompanied minors. This Act is the first complex legal rule on the field of child protection which created an opportunity to create regulations with a unified approach and covering all areas.[15] Several aims of the child protection and the child protection system are enumerated in the Hungarian Child Protection Act. Child protection in wide sense applies to all children irrespective of the fact whether they live in their own families and whether being endangered. The solution on the field of child protection was the social work and the social assistance to be provided to the families.[16] Three layers of the care provided for the families and children are defined. The first layer is the circle of the different forms of supply belonging to the category of child welfare basic care. The aim is that the families can use these supplies voluntarily and shall have access to them nearby, close to their residence. The next layer of care is a specialised one provided to children who already live in alternative care. The third layer includes the authoritative measures which can be and simultaneously must be applied if the

[14] 1997. évi XXXI. törvény a gyermekek védelméről és a gyámügyi igazgatásról.

[15] M. Herczog, Gyermekvédelmi kézikönyv, 2001, at p. 25.

[16] G. Mattenheim, 'Preambulum', In: G. Mattenheim (ed), Kommentár a gyermekvédelmi törvényhez, 2017, at p. 21.

child's care which is needed for the child's physical, mental, emotional and moral development cannot be provided for the child upon the consent of his or her parents and this endangers the child's development. The public guardianship authority must take one of the enumerated measures in such case.

The scope of the Hungarian Child Protection Act is extensive as a main rule not only for children of Hungarian nationality residing in the territory of Hungary, and unless otherwise provided by an international treaty, those with long-term residence rights or with tolerated stay, as well as those recognised by the Hungarian authorities as refugees, having subsidiary protection or stateless minors, young for adults and their parents. The Hungarian Child Protection Act's scope extended for the foreign child applying for asylum under the age of 18 years who entered the territory of Hungary without the company of an adult responsible for his supervision on the basis of law or custom or remained without supervision following entry as long as he is not transferred under the supervision of such a person, provided that the childhood of the concerned person was determined by the asylum authority.

IV. The Consequences of the Act Providing the Order of Crisis Situation Caused by Mass Immigration

1. The Introduction of "Crisis Situation Caused by Mass Immigration"

In the mid-2010s several legal acts connected to "mass immigration" heavily affected the situation of children. The Mass Immigration Act[17] introduced a new phenomenon, the so-called "crisis situation caused by mass immigration". The Asylum Act has been completed with a new chapter to be applied in crisis situation caused by mass immigration. According to the Asylum Act a crisis situation caused by mass immigration can be declared if the number of those arriving in Hungary and seeking recognition exceeds 500 people a day as a month's average, or 700 and 50 people per day as the average of two subsequent weeks, or 800 people per day as a week's average, or the number of people staying in the transit zone in Hungary — not considering those contributing to taking care of the foreigners — exceeds 1000 people per day as a month's average, or 1500 people per day as the average of two subsequent weeks, or 1600 people per day as a week's average.

[17] 2015. évi CXL. törvény egyes törvényeknek a tömeges bevándorlás kezelésével összefüggő módosításáról.

2. A New Cause of "Crisis Situation Caused by Mass Immigration"

A further reason for the declaration of crisis situation caused by mass immigration was introduced in 2017 by the Act XX of 2017 on the amendment of certain acts relating to strengthening the procedure conducted in border surveillance areas[18] (transit zones). According to this requirement a crisis situation caused by mass immigration may be declared if a migration situation occurs that directly endangers the protection of the border of Hungary as set out in Article 2 para. 2 of the Schengen Borders Code,[19] or directly endangers the public security, public order or public health in a 60 m wide zone of the territory of Hungary measured from the border of Hungary as set out in Article 2 para. 2 of the Schengen Borders Code and the border mark or in any settlement in Hungary, in particular the outbreak of unrest or the occurrence of violent acts in the reception centre or another facility used for accommodating foreigners located within or in the outskirts of the settlement concerned.

3. The Prolonged "Crisis Situation Caused by Mass Immigration"

A crisis situation caused by mass immigration can be declared in a Government Decree on the proposal by the minister as initiated by the National Commander of the Police and the head of the refugee authority. The Government ordered the crisis situation caused by mass immigration by the Governmental Decree 41/2016. (III. 9.) on the declaration of the state of crisis due to mass migration throughout the territory of Hungary and on the rules related to the declaration, existence and termination of the state of crisis. The crisis situation caused by mass immigration has been continuously prolonged since 2016.[20] The last modifying governmental decree entered into force in March 2024, and it will lapse on 7 September 2024. Besides the continuously prolonged crisis situation caused by mass migration Hungary is a "state of danger", too.

The Tenth Amendment of the Fundamental Law of Hungary modified the Fundamental Law. While earlier the state of danger could be ordered in the case of

---

[18] 2017. évi XX. törvény a határőrizeti területen lefolytatott eljárás szigorításával kapcsolatos egyes törvények módosításáról.

[19] Regulation (EU) 2016/399 of the European Parliament and of the Council of 9 March 2016 on a Union Code on the rules governing the movement of persons across borders.

[20] The last concerning legal source is the Governmental Decree 47/2024. (III. 4.) on the amendment of the Governmental Decree 41/2016. (III. 9.) on the declaration of the state of crisis due to mass migration throughout the territory of Hungary and on the rules related to the declaration, existence and termination of the state of crisis.

a natural disaster or an industrial accident endangering life and property, according to the new rule the government can order the state of danger also in the case of an armed conflict, war or humanitarian disaster in a neighbouring country. The Tenth Amendment was accepted on 24 May 2022 and on the following day the Government Decree 180/2022. (V. 24.) on declaring a state of danger due to the armed conflict and humanitarian catastrophe in the territory of Ukraine, and in order to eliminate the consequences of these in Hungary and on a certain state of danger rules was accepted.

4. The Consequences of "Crisis Situation Caused by Mass Immigration" on the Guardianship of Children

a) The Amendment of the Hungarian Child Protection Act

In case of crisis situation caused by mass immigration the procedural rules of the Asylum Act have to be applied with exceptions enumerated in the Asylum Act as modified by the Act XX of 2017 on the amendment of certain acts relating to strengthening the procedure conducted in border surveillance areas. One of these exceptional rules affects children and their status during the asylum proceeding. According to the regularly applicable rules, if the person seeking recognition is an unaccompanied minor, the asylum authority requests the guardianship authority to appoint a child protection guardian, who will be the child's legal representative. The child protection guardian shall be appointed within 8 days of the arrival of the refugee authority's request. The unaccompanied minor and the refugee authority shall without delay be notified by the guardianship authority of the person of the child protection guardian appointed. The child is temporarily placed at the same time. These rules are applicable with exceptions in case of crisis situation caused by mass immigration. If the asylum applicant is an unaccompanied minor under 14 years of age, the competent asylum authority shall conduct the asylum procedure in accordance with the general rules, after the minor has entered the territory of Hungary. The authority shall place him temporarily without delay and, simultaneously, request the competent guardianship authority to appoint a guardian to protect and represent the minor. The guardian must be appointed within 8 days of receipt of the competent asylum authority's request. The competent guardianship authority shall notify the name of the designated child protection guardian to the unaccompanied minor and the competent asylum authority without delay.

Before the Act XX of 2017 the Hungarian Child Protection Act's scope extended for the foreign child applying for asylum under the age of 18 years who entered the territory of Hungary without the company of an adult responsible for his supervision on the basis of law or custom or remained without supervision following entry as long as he is not transferred under the supervision of such a person, provided that the childhood of the concerned person was determined by the asylum authority. The Act XX of 2017 amended the Hungarian Child Protection Act with a referral to the fact that in time of crisis situation caused by mass immigration the scope of the Hungarian Child Protection Act is not extended to minors between the age of 14 and 18 applying for asylum.

b) Difference Between Children Under the Age of 14 and Children Between the Age of 14 and 18

It has the consequence that the placement in child protection institutions is provided only for children under the age of 14. According to the official reasoning of the Act, as the asylum application must be lodged in person with the competent authority, and exclusively in the transit zone as a main rule, unaccompanied minors between the age of 14 and 18 having procedural capacity to act are not placed in child protection institution.

The application of provisions protecting children in the Governmental Decree has been restricted to children seeking recognition under the age of 14 concerning several measures in time of crisis situation caused by mass immigration. While according to the general rule, if the person seeking recognition is an unaccompanied minor, in accordance with the child protection legislation, he shall be placed in a child protection institution, provided that the refugee authority has determined the minor status of the child concerned and unaccompanied minors may be placed with adult relatives, these rules cannot be applied to minors between the age of 14 and 18. For the legal representation of an unaccompanied minor who has reached the age of 14, the asylum authority shall immediately notify the regionally competent public authority and at the same time initiate the appointment of a guardian *ad litem (eseti gyám)* for the child at the designated guardianship office.

c) Transit Zones

While the asylum application may be submitted anywhere on the territory of Hungary in "normal" times, during the crisis situation caused by mass immigration if someone arrives at the territory of Hungary may submit the application only in the transit zone. All unaccompanied minors under the age of 18 are placed in children's homes but during the crisis situation caused by mass immigration only children under the age of 14 are placed in children's homes *(gyermekotthon)*, unaccompanied minors between the age of 14 and 18 are placed in the transit zone. A further difference arises from the guardianship. In "normal" times all unaccompanied minors are under child protection guardianship, during the crisis situation caused by mass immigration unaccompanied minors under the age of 14 are under child protection guardianship, while those between 14 and 18 have guardian *ad litem*.

V. Children and Unaccompanied Minors in the Hungarian Asylum and Child Protection Legislation

1. Definitions

The Civil Code defines a child as a minor who has not reached the age of 18 (except for the case if the child marries with the authorisation of the public guardianship authority over the age of 16) and the Hungarian Child Protection Act applies the definition of the Civil Code. The Asylum Act uses the wording "minor" instead of "child". Although both the Hungarian Child Protection Act and the Asylum Act consider a minor as a child, it is a huge problem that in time of crisis situation caused by mass immigration there is a rigid difference between children under the age of 14 and between the age of 14 and 18.

The Asylum Act defines the meaning of unaccompanied minor. They are defined as a foreigner not having completed the age of 18 years who entered the territory of Hungary without the company of an adult responsible for his/her supervision based on law or custom or remained without supervision following entry as long as he is not transferred under the supervision of such a person. An unaccompanied minor is always a person who needs special treatment in the application of the Asylum Act. Besides, a vulnerable person who is found after proper individual assessment, to have special needs because of his/her individual situation needs special treatment, too. The Asylum Act mentions here, in particular, the minor such as the disabled person, pregnant woman, single parent raising a minor child and a person who has suffered from torture, rape, or any other grave form of psychological, physical, or sexual violence.

According to the Asylum Act when implementing the provisions of the present Act, the best interests and rights of the child shall be a primary consideration. A further basic principle is the unity of the family. The provisions of the Asylum Act must be applied to persons in need of special treatment with due consideration of the specific needs arising from their situation.

2. Age Assessment

The unaccompanied minor's age assessment is extremely important, primarily because the refugees including unaccompanied minors usually do not have any identification document with them. According to the experiences and research based upon surveys in the 2010s the age assessment of unaccompanied minors is not satisfying. The age assessment of children arriving in the territory of Hungary proved to be unprofessional and unfounded. When assessing the age its multidisciplinary nature is not considered and the different developmental differences between ethnic groups during puberty are ignored such as children's emotional and psychological development and their socio-cultural background.[21] A similar problem is that in most cases, the age determination is restricted to the mere observation of the unaccompanied child's physique.[22] The primary determination of age is done by a police doctor or a military doctor and only the further examination is performed by a medical expert.[23] After the primary determination of age, further investigation is only carried out if the person appearing to be a minor claims to be an adult, the other when the adult-looking foreigner claims to be a minor,[24] or if there is a doubt about the result of the first examination.[25] The age assessment examination methods used in Hungary may have even more serious consequences than before because of the continuous tightening of the asylum law.[26]

VI. Special Provisions Concerning Refugees from Ukraine

There are different provisions in the Hungarian legal order concerning Ukrainian refugees. The Government Decree No. 86/2022. (III. 7.) on rules applicable in the state of danger and related to persons recognised as eligible for temporary protection, and on derogations from the rules of Act CVI. of 2011 on public employment and on the amendment of acts related to public employment and of other acts contains regulation on the status of refugees fleeing from Ukraine.[27]

According to the Government Decree there are several persons enjoying the status of person having temporary protection *(menedékes)* when applying this Decree. Ukrainian nationals residing in Ukraine before 24 February 2022, stateless persons, and nationals of third countries other than Ukraine, who benefited from international protection or equivalent national protection in Ukraine before 24 February 2022 and family members of persons referred to in points (a) and (b),

[21] It is based upon the long-term experiences of the Helsinki Committee, A gyermekek fogvatartása Magyarországon, Helsinki Committee, 2014, 1, at p. 63, available at https://helsinki.hu/wp-content/uploads/A_gyermekek_fogvatartasa_Magyarorszagon_HUN.pdf.

[22] A gyermekek fogvatartása Magyarországon, Helsinki Committee, 2014, 1, at pp. 63 f., available at https://helsinki.hu/wp-content/uploads/A_gyermekek_fogvatartasa_Magyarorszagon_HUN.pdf.

[23] On the comparison of the international standards and the Hungarian practice, N. Takács, A kísérő nélküli kiskorú menedékkérők korának megállapítása során érvényesülő alapelvek vizsgálata, Doktori Műhelytanulmányok 2017, at pp. 371–386.

[24] M. K. Haraszti, Kísérő nélküli kiskorúak a menekültjogban és a gyermekvédelemben: árnyak a Paradicsomban, *Családi Jog*, 2014, 4, 7, at pp. 13 f.

[25] R. Kálmán, Ki vigyáz rájuk? Avagy a kísérő nélküli kiskorúak helyzete napjainkban, *Állam- és Jogtudomány* 2019, 4, 71, at pp. 83 f.

[26] See ECtHR 22 February 2024, 10940/17 and 15977/17, ECLI:CE:ECHR:2024:0222JUD001094017 (M.H. and S.B. versus Hungary).

[27] 86/2022. (III. 7.) Korm. rendelet az ideiglenes védelemre jogosultként elismert személyekkel kapcsolatos veszélyhelyzeti szabályokról, továbbá a közfoglalkoztatásról és a közfoglalkoztatáshoz kapcsolódó, valamint egyéb törvények módosításáról szóló 2011. évi CVI. törvény szabályainak eltérő alkalmazásáról.

as defined by Article 2 para. 4 of Council Implementing Decision (EU) 2022/382 of 4 March 2022 establishing the existence of a mass influx of displaced persons from Ukraine within the meaning of Article 5 of the Temporary Protection Directive, and having the effect of introducing temporary protection. Persons applying for temporary protection shall provide evidence that they fulfil at least one of the conditions above. (Hungarian nationals with permanent residence in Ukraine and arriving from Ukraine on 24 February 2022 or on a later date shall be granted all the benefits and advantages provided to beneficiaries of temporary protection unless they shall enjoy a more favourable treatment regarding to their Hungarian nationality.) The temporary protection for those who were forced to flee from Ukraine due to the armed conflict grants residence rights as long as the war lasts.

VII. Provisions and Experiences Concerning Child Protection Guardianship of Unaccompanied Minors

The experiences in connection with the guardianship of unaccompanied minors are not discussed in the Hungarian judicial literature and as the guardian, let it be child protection guardian or guardian *ad litem* is appointed by the public guardianship authority, these decisions are not followable as those are not published decisions.

The child protection guardian differs from the guardian who takes care of the child in his own household. While the guardian taking care of the child in his household has several tasks as caring for the child, administering the child's property and being the child's legal representative, the child protection guardian is a professional who does not take care of the child personally but performs the professional tasks as the administration of the child's property and the child's legal representation. Every child who is taken care of in child protection care has a child protection guardian. The child protection guardians are not only under the regular supervision of the public guardianship authority but are subject to the guardianship authority's direction. The child protection guardians are operated by the National Child Protection Special Service (*Országos Gyermekvédelmi Szakszolgálat*) and the Regional Child Protection Special Services (*Területi Gyermekvédelmi Szakszolgálatok*) and it is the responsibility of the National Child Protection Special Service to elaborate the professional programmes of the child protection guardians. It has complex monitoring competence and also employer's rights. The Social and Child Protection Directorate (*Szociális és Gyermekvédelmi Főigazgatóság*) exercises the rights concerning the maintenance of the Regional Child Protection Special Services and has further monitoring obligations concerning the child protection guardians.

In case of being represented by a child protection guardian, the child is taken care of by the staff at the children's home or the foster family and foster parent. Unaccompanied minors are placed in a children's home, currently in the István Károlyi Child Centre. The child protection guardian takes care of the guardianship for a maximum of 30 children. As the child protection guardian does not live together with the child and is obliged to exercise the guardianship over several children, they do not have close connection with each other.

The experiences related to how the guardian fulfils his tasks come from the earlier period when refugees came to Hungary across the Southern Border. According to the experiences mirrored in the Hungarian scientific literature and the reports of the Hungarian NGOs focusing and having research on the field of migration the child protection guardians appointed by the competent Regional Child Protection Special Service do not provide "active and personal"[28] connection to the concerned child. This coincided with the results of a previous research which pointed out that most child protection guardians had a passive attitude during asylum proceedings.[29]

VIII. Is the Child an "Unaccompanied" Minor?

A common difficulty is, especially concerning children arriving in Hungary from Ukraine because of the war, that the professionals cannot be sure in the case of children being escorted by adults that the adults belong to the child as a relative. The applicants seeking recognition usually arrive without documents, so it is doubtful whether the given child is the child of the adults coming with him or not, especially considering the different socio-cultural background.[30] It has been a crucial and hard task for the officials to evaluate the child's situation. Due to this lack of documents it has been a challenge to decide in a child-friendly manner and to make a decision which serves the child's best interests.

IX. Guardianship and PIL Issues

Hungary is a party of the 1996 Child Protection Convention,[31] so it is applied in Hungary on guardianship issues. It should be remarked that no published case law can be detected either on the level of judiciary nor in the decisions of the public guardianship authority. A person's legal capacity and his capacity to act must be

---

[28] B. Földváry, Az emberkereskedelem kísérő nélküli kiskorú áldozatainak azonosítása — irányelvek és a gyakorlat Magyarországon, illetve az Európai Unióban, *Geopolitikai Szemle* 2019, 3, 67, at pp. 75 f.

[29] R. Kálmán, Állam- és Jogtudomány 2019, 4, 71, at p. 77. The author refers to a comparative study (Implementation of the right of unaccompanied minors to asylum in the EU. A study comparing the situation of the 27 EU member states A study comparing the situation of the 27 EU member states) from 2012.

[30] B. Földváry, Geopolitikai Szemle 2019, 3, 67, at p. 77.

[31] Convention of 19 October 1996 on Jurisdiction, Applicable Law, Recognition, Enforcement and Co-operation in Respect of Parental Responsibility and Measures for the Protection of Children (1996 Child Protection Convention).

judged based on their personal rights according to Act No XXVIII of 2017 on Private International Law.[32] The personal right of a person is the law of the state of which he is a citizen.

Hungary is predominantly a transit country, so the private international law issues of guardianship do not emerge frequently in an articulated way for the Hungarian authorities. According to the early surveys Ukrainian refugees typically stayed only for a few days and travelled on towards Western-Europe.[33]

X. Conclusions

Besides several international and European conventions concerning persons and children as refugees the CRC[34] protects children's rights in its complexity. As the system of children's rights has to be understood and interpreted in its entirety, all pillars of the CRC are worth mentioning when discussing the rights of children as refugees. A child means every human being below the age of 18 years as a main rule (Article 1), States Parties have to respect and ensure the rights to each child without any discrimination (Article 2), all actions concerning children, whether undertaken by public or private social welfare institutions, courts of law, administrative authorities or legislative bodies, the best interests of the child shall be a primary consideration (Article 3), and every child has the inherent right to life (Article 6). Article 22 provides special further rights to children who are refugees or seek refugee status. They have a right to enjoy all rights enshrined in the CRC irrespective of the fact whether they are accompanied or unaccompanied children and they are entitled to get "appropriate protection" and "humanitarian assistance".

These children are extremely vulnerable and do have a right to child-friendly justice and a child-friendly asylum-process such as access to all forms of child-welfare benefits and child-protection measures. One of the child protection measures is the right to get support and protection from a guardian in case of need. The appointment of the guardian must be performed in a child-focused way such as the determination of the person's age and the evaluation his status. The Committee on the Rights of the Child in General Comment No. 6 (2005) dealt with the treatment of unaccompanied and separated children outside their country of origin.[35]

---

[32] 2017. évi XXVIII. törvény a nemzetközi magánjogról.

[33] A. Kyriazi, Ukrainian Refugees in Hungary: Government Measures and Discourse in the First Year of the War, available at https://papers.ssrn.com/sol3/papers.cfm?abstract_id=4313945.

[34] UN 1989 Convention on the Rights of the Child (CRC).

[35] CRC/GC/2005/6 1 September 2005.

In 2019 Hungary presented the Governmental Report[36] and the Alternative Report[37] on the CRC. The Alternative Report was elaborated on behalf of the Child Rights NGO Coalition, and it referred to the child protection and asylum consequences of "crisis situation due to mass immigration" when discussing the definition of the child.[38] The Chairperson of the Council of Europe Lanzarote Committee expressed his concern about the amendment of the asylum law as referring to the fact that unaccompanied asylum-seeking children between the age of 14 and 18 are considered as adult asylum applicants which increases their vulnerability.[39] Since 2014 the European Commission has initiated several infringement procedures against Hungary concerning its asylum legislation.[40]

In its concluding observations on the sixth periodic report of Hungary the Committee on the Rights of the Child urged the development of a national strategy to prevent and address all forms of violence against children, including asylum-seeking, refugee and migrant children, to elaborate a mechanism to facilitate and promote the complaints mechanism and to amend the asylum law. The Committee emphasised that it is necessary to repeal the amendment of the Hungarian Child Protection Act with the aim to cover all children, "including unaccompanied children aged between 14 and 18 years, in all situations, including during crises caused by mass migration".[41]

[36] Sixth periodic report submitted by Hungary under article 44 of the Convention pursuant to the simplified reporting procedure, due in 2019.

[37] Alternative Report on the UN CRC (HUNGARY) on behalf of the Child Rights NGO Coalition, 2019.

[38] Alternative Report on the UN CRC (HUNGARY) on behalf of the Child Rights NGO Coalition, 2019, at pp. 8 f.

[39] Alternative Report on the UN CRC (HUNGARY) on behalf of the Child Rights NGO Coalition, 2019, at p. 9.

[40] Alternative Report on the UN CRC (HUNGARY) on behalf of the Child Rights NGO Coalition, 2019, at p. 35.

[41] Concluding observations on the sixth periodic report of Hungary. Distr.: General 3 March 2020, at p. 11.

Guardianship and Other Protective Measures for Minor Refugees in Germany

Bettina Heiderhoff

I. Introduction

The issue of legal protection for unaccompanied minor refugees is possibly the most crucial interface between migration law, private international law and family law. Upon arrival, child-appropriate accommodation and care must be provided, the age and identity — often including the name — must be ascertained more or less simultaneously. In the following weeks a procedure under the asylum law must be initiated — which usually means that an application for asylum must be filed. Further steps are then often necessary, such as applying for family reunification. And since the minors cannot submit any applications themselves, it is essential that a guardian — or a temporary representative — is appointed for them quickly. The functionality of the legal system at this point, therefore, is a crucial issue for the protection of minors on the move.

In order to achieve the necessary speed, the appointment of a guardian is not the first step that will be taken when an unaccompanied child arrives in Germany. Rather, there are more immediate protection mechanisms that need to be put in place, and the appointment of a guardian will often happen at a later stage.

Every refugee who claims to be a child is initially provisionally taken into care. Taking children into care is the classic instrument used by youth welfare offices to protect children quickly if they are either unable to stay with their parents or have arrived in Germany alone. It only ever takes effect in the short term and is replaced by family law measures as soon as possible. The latter are decided by the family

B. Heiderhoff (✉)
Institute for German and International Family Law, Chair for Private International Law, International Civil Procedure Law and German Private Law, University of Münster, Münster, Germany
e-mail: bettina.heiderhoff@uni-muenster.de

S. Arnold, B. Heiderhoff (eds.), *Children in Migration and International Family Law*, https://doi.org/10.1007/978-3-031-71598-3_7

court, while taking children into care has the particularity that it is carried out by the youth welfare offices without a court decision.

In 2015, the SGB VIII (German Youth Welfare Act) was supplemented by new regulations that deal specifically with the taking into care of refugee minors. The so-called provisional taking into care (vorläufige Inobhutnahme) includes not only the accommodation in a facility suitable for minors, but also deals with issues such as the age assessment, the decision about the placement at the competent municipality under the Königsteiner Schlüssel (Königstein Key),[1] and even the legal representation in urgent matters.

As there is a considerable overlap between the functions of provisional taking into care by the youth welfare offices and guardianship — which will be established by court decision –, both instruments will be discussed below.

Section II. will examine who is considered to be a minor and to be unaccompanied under German law. Section III. will then describe the whole procedure that the minor goes through until a guardian is appointed. Section IV. deals with cases in which a minor refugee arrives in Germany after a guardian has been appointed in another member state and the question, how jurisdiction and recognition are handled in such cases.

II. National Law Concerning Unaccompanied Children

1. Applicable Law

a) Conflict of Laws

Whenever a foreigner arrives in Germany, it must first be asked whether the German authorities are responsible for them and which law applies to them. The responsibility for protection measures for refugees under the age of 18 is generally based on Article 6 of the 1996 Child Protection Convention.[2] However, existing protection measures may have to be taken into account.

Various other legal issues may then be of importance. It may be unclear who the child's legal parents are, whether it is validly married or even what is the legally correct name.

[1] Depending on the financial and general strength (two-thirds tax revenue and one-third population) each federal state takes a certain percentage of the refugees; see for information in English language https://www.bamf.de/EN/Themen/AsylFluechtlingsschutz/AblaufAsylverfahrens/Erstverteilung/erstverteilung-node.html.

[2] Convention of 19 October 1996 on Jurisdiction, Applicable Law, Recognition, Enforcement and Co-operation in respect of Parental Responsibility and Measures for the Protection of Children (1996 Child Protection Convention).

In the case of unaccompanied young persons, the question of the applicable law arises in particular with regard to the age of majority, so that only this one question will be examined in this contribution.

b) Applicable Law for the Age of Majority

aa) Until 2023

In Germany, until 1 January 2023, the question of when a foreign person was a underage depended on whether or not they were a refugee within the meaning of Geneva Refugee Convention.[3] This is because the question of legal capacity was based on nationality under Article 7 of the EGBGB (German Private International Law). However, under Article 12 of the Geneva Refugee Convention, the personal status of a refugee shall be governed by the law of the country of his domicile or, if he has no domicile, by the law of the country of his residence. Consequently, where the age of majority of a refugee within the meaning of the Geneva Refugee Convention had to be determined, the law of residence had to be applied instead of the law of the nationality, while in all other cases — in which there were no grounds for asylum — the Geneva Refugee Convention is inapplicable and the personal status was governed by the law of the nationality as stipulated in the former Article 7 of the EGBGB.

As it usually takes a rather long time for the competent immigration authorities to decide on refugee status, the family courts often had to determine the refugee status of the minor concerned themselves before appointing a guardian.[4]

When it turned out that an unaccompanied minor was not a refugee in the sense of the Geneva Refugee Convention, the law of the nationality was applicable, which factually meant that foreign law had to be applied in numerous cases. It then was often very difficult to determine the content of the foreign law regarding the age of majority. Some African and Asian legal systems do not provide for majority at the age of 18, but only at the age of 19 or 20.

For example, in a much noticed court case, an 18-year-old person travelled to Germany from Guinea. In such a case, the family court ought to check whether the person was a refugee, in which case German law would apply under Article 12 of the Geneva Convention and a guardian would not be appointed because the person was of legal age. If, on the contrary, the person was not a refugee Guinean law would have applied under the old Article 7 of the EGBGB and a guardian would have had to be appointed. In fact, the person involved in the case was apparently not a refugee, so that the very difficult question of when young people come of age under Guinean

---

[3] 1951 Geneva Convention relating to the Status of Refugees (Geneva Refugee Convention).

[4] S. Arnold, Der Flüchtlingsbegriff der Genfer Flüchtlingskonvention im Kontext des Internationalen Privatrechts, In: Budzikiewicz/Heiderhoff et al. (eds), Migration und IPR, 2018, 25, at pp. 25–63.

law had to be clarified. The German Federal High Court (BGH) decided that the Higher Regional Court had decided this issue without sufficient exploration of the foreign law and should not have refrained from obtaining a comprehensive expert opinion.[5]

This former legal situation was not only difficult to handle, but the results to which the legal situation led were also unsatisfactory. In short, refugees in the sense of the Geneva Refugee Convention received less protection than other young immigrants.

bb) Since 2023

In the meantime, Article 7 of the EGBGB has been amended. According to the new Article 7 para. 2 of the EGBGB, which came into force on 1 January 2023, the law of habitual residence is now always decisive for legal capacity. In the case of refugees, the general view is that simple residence is also a sufficient basis for the application of this provision, even if the standard does not expressly stipulate this.[6]

Whether a refugee is under age in the legal sense or not is therefore now almost always determined by German law. According to Section 2 of the BGB (German Civil Code) he or she must simply be under the age of 18.

2. *Taking into Care Upon Arrival*

a) Legal Framework and Purpose

In 2015 a special legal regime for the provisional taking into care of unaccompanied minors came into force. It was developed in order to combine the function of the "classical" taking into care under Section 42 of the SGB VIII (German Youth Welfare Act) with the special necessities that occur in the context of migration.

The so-called provisional taking into care (vorläufige Inobhutnahme) is regulated in Section 42a to Section 42f of the SGB VIII. It is effected by the local youth welfare office at the place where the minor first comes in contact with any administrative body — either near the border or at any other given place. The taking into care is called provisional, because, in most cases, the young people cannot stay permanently at their place of arrival, but are distributed evenly among the various municipalities in Germany according to a key (Königstein Key).

[5]BGH 7 March 2018, XII ZB 422/17, BeckRS 2018, 6043 para. 16, ECLI:DE:BGH:2018:070318BXIIZB422.17.0; OLG Hamm 21 August 2018, 12 UF 224/16, FamRZ 2019, 216, ECLI:DE:OLGHAM:2018:0821.12UF224.16.00 (based on expert opinions, the court finally assumed that also under the law of Guinea, majority is reached at the age of 18).

[6]See for instance V. Lipp, In: Münchener Kommentar zum BGB, Volume 12, ninth ed. 2024, Article 7 of the EGBGB para. 38.

At the place of arrival, however, during the provisional taking into care various important steps will be taken. During this time, it is determined how old they are, whether they have relatives in Germany, whether they are healthy and whether it is otherwise not contrary to their best interests to take them to another municipality. Only once these decisions have been made and, if applicable, the minor has been sent to the competent municipality, he or she will be taken into permanent care.

b) Practical Implementation

This system seems to work rather well in most regions of Germany. In Berlin, however, there are serious deficits in implementation. When the young people arrive in Berlin, they are initially accommodated in a dormitory. There, they can only wait until the responsible authorities have time and space for the provisional taking into care. During this waiting period, which can often last longer than 6 months, they receive food and a bed, but their age is not yet determined and they cannot go to school or apply for asylum. One can imagine how helpless and lost they must feel.

From a legal perspective, this delay can have considerable negative consequences. Primarily this is because, according to the Dublin III Regulation, it is often only possible to apply for asylum in Germany as long as the person concerned is still under 18 years old. Adults must submit the application in the member state of first entry, which is usually not Germany. Secondly, the minority at the time of the application for asylum is also decisive for the right to family reunification, as the CJEU has held several times.[7] This applies as long as the young person submits the application for family reunification within 3 months of being granted refugee status.[8]

3. Legal Representation of the Child

a) Overview

Under Section 1629 of the BGB, normally, the parents are the legal representatives of their child. If they are unable to exercise parental responsibility, a legal guardian is appointed. It should be noted, that a guardian does generally not fulfil all tasks of a parent. On the contrary, day-to-day care, e.g. in a foster family or in a group home for children, is regularly provided by persons who do not have guardianship. This explains why one guardian may take up to 50 guardianships according to section 55 of the SGB VIII.

[7] CJEU 1 August 2022, case C-273/20 and C-355/20, ECLI:EU:C:2022:617 (Bundesrepublik Deutschland); also already CJEU 12 April 2018, case C-550/16, ECLI:EU:C:2018:248 (A. and S. versus the Netherlands).

[8] CJEU 12 April 2018, case C-550/16, ECLI:EU:C:2018:248 (A. and S. versus the Netherlands) para. 61.

Before the procedure and the prerequisites of the appointment are introduced, it is worth looking at some more general problems. Appointing a guardian does not only take some time, so that a temporary legal representative can become necessary. It is also a rather difficult task to represent a minor refugee, and the asylum procedure and family reunification may require special competences. Youth welfare officers can only rarely help the child with these difficult questions, and further pressing issues may arise beyond this, for example in the event of imminent deportation.

The first problem has been solved in that the youth welfare officers can already represent the minor, at least in the most important matters, within the framework of the provisional taking into care (see below Sect. b).

The second problem is more difficult. This is, because there are not enough potential guardians with specialised knowledge of asylum law available. Instead, the youth welfare officers have to take on such a large number of guardianships that it is almost impossible to provide thorough support in individual cases. It has been much discussed whether a co-guardian can be appointed who can then contribute their specialised knowledge in the asylum proceedings, while the regular guardian is in charge for the regular tasks, e.g. education and health (see for detail Sect. III. 2. b).

As a third problem, the question of what can actually be done if the unaccompanied minor leaves the country again — or, conversely, if a minor arrives for whom a guardian has already been appointed in another member state — will be addressed in a separate part at the end of this chapter.

b) Representation During the Provisional Taking into Care

The so-called "emergency right of representation" (Notvertretungsrecht) is stipulated in Section 42a para. 3 of the SGB VIII. It allows the youth welfare office responsible for the provisional taking into care to represent the minor in necessary matters. This has the obvious advantage that the child does not remain without the possibility to act legally at all.

It should be mentioned that this "emergency right of representation" in particular covers the application for asylum or any other measure that should be taken under migration law.

However, there are doubts whether this emergency solution is sufficient. These doubts go beyond the just discussed issue of the lack of special knowledge in migration law. Rather, they concern the accumulation of partly contradictory tasks at the youth welfare office.

It was already recognised during the legislative process for the new Sections 42a ff. of the SGB VIII that the youth welfare office finds itself in a conflict of interests if, on the one hand, it is supposed to protect the young person and represent their interests, but on the other hand has to decide whether they should be taken to another municipality or whether they are already of legal age. It was suggested that this conflict of interests should be resolved by separating the different tasks in terms of personnel. Whether this is a realistic option, in particular in smaller youth welfare offices, is a valid question.

Currently, it is unclear whether this system fulfils the standards set up by the ECtHR in the Case Darboe and Camara in 2022.[9] So far, only one published German court decision has taken up this judgement. The German regional administrative court of Karlsruhe held, that a hearing conducted without the involvement of the representative of the concerned migrant, who may be under age, leads to a judicial objection to the termination of the provisional taking into care.[10]

4. Crucial Issue: Who Is Unaccompanied?

a) Unaccompanied: One Term with Three Different Meanings

Whether a minor is "unaccompanied" is initially decisive for taking them into care. For this reason, it should first be considered more thoroughly how the categorisation as unaccompanied is made in the context of the SGB VIII. The term "unaccompanied" is also used in asylum law, and in particular in European legislation such as the Dublin III Regulation. The fact that it has a different meaning there will be explained in a second point. Finally, the question of whether a minor is unaccompanied is also relevant to the appointment of a guardian under family law. Again, the meaning is different. This can be confusing, even though the term "unaccompanied" as such is not used in German family law in the context of guardianship law.

To illustrate what this means in the situation of the minor, we can imagine a brief example case.

A 12-year-old boy (M) has travelled to Germany via Sweden with an adult friend of his parents (F). Both want to apply for asylum in Europe. F looks after M reliably.

The question of whether M is unaccompanied here arises in very different contexts.

Firstly, youth welfare law becomes relevant and the question arises as to whether M needs to be taken into care.

Secondly, there is also a family law issue, which centres on whether M needs a guardian.

Thirdly, various questions relating to asylum law must be answered, including the question of where M's asylum application should be submitted. Another question may be whether M can obtain family protection with F or whether he has a right to family reunification.

All of these questions are dealt with separately below. It will then become clear, that the term "unaccompanied" is understood rather differently in all three contexts.

---

[9] ECtHR 21 July 2022, 5797/17, ECLI:CE:ECHR:2022:0721JUD000579717 (Darboe und Camara versus Italy).

[10] VG Karlsruhe 20 September 2023, 8 K 3002/23, NVwZ-RR 2024, 234, ECLI:DE:VGKARLS:2023:0920.8 K3002.23.00.

b) "Unaccompanied" in Youth Welfare Law

aa) General

The SGB VIII uses a very broad definition of when a young person is (un)-accompanied: Section 42a para. 1 sentence 2 of the SGB VIII stipulates:

A foreign child or young person is generally considered to be unaccompanied if they are not accompanied by a "Personensorgeberechtigter" (person who has parental responsibility) or "Erziehungsberechtigter" (person with parental authority).

In Section 7 para. 1 of the SGB VIII the meaning of both terms is clarified.

According to the usual interpretation under German law it is stated in Section 7 para. 1 No. 5 of the SGB VIII, that the term "Personensorgeberechtigter" comprises only persons who have parental responsibility for the child alone or jointly in accordance with the provisions of the German Civil Code. In short, it basically means the parents. In exceptional cases, the holder of personal responsibility may also be an officially appointed legal guardian who is travelling with the child.

The crucial term is "Erziehungsberechtigter" (person with parental authority). This term is not commonly used and is defined in Section 7 para. 1 No. 6 of the SGB VIII.

According to this provision, the "Erziehungsberechtigter" is not only the person with parental responsibility, but also any other person over the age of 18, insofar as they perform parental duties on the basis of an agreement with the parents, not only temporarily and not only for individual activities. This is currently understood very generously by the authorities and courts. The agreement does not need to be formalised in any way. Nor does it matter whether the person concerned is particularly suitable for taking on the responsibility. Rather, it is common for relatives, including adult siblings and friends of the parents who have taken in the child, to be regarded as legal guardians.[11] This significantly reduces the number of times a child is taken into care.

bb) Special Case: "Child Marriage"[12]

If one considers that an older brother or sister — or an older cousin — can be understood as a "Erziehungsberechtigter", then the question arises as to whether a minor travelling to Germany with their adult spouse might be accompanied by an "Erziehungsberechtigter", too. The law contains a statement on this, but it is not easy

[11] VGH München 14 October 2022, 12 BV 20.2077, BeckRS 2022, 29743, ECLI:DE:BAYVGH:2022:1014.12BV20.2077.00.

[12] While „child marriage"is a much used term, it shall be avoided here. Instead, we will speak of early or underage marriage. The term „child marriage"runs the risk of distorting reality, because early marriages usually rather involve older minors at the age 16 or 17; see for detail S. Arnold, Early Marriage in Germany — Law and Politics of Cultural Demarcation, in this volume, 161, at p. 162.

to understand. Before we take a closer look at the meaning of the respective provision, it should be briefly noted that recently published figures have shown that it is rare for early marriages between newly arrived asylum seekers to come to light. According to information from the government, since the federal "law to combat child marriages"[13] came into force in July 2017, fewer than 20 court proceedings to determine the existence or non-existence of a marriage due to the possible invalidity of a marriage on the grounds of minority have become known by the end of 2022.[14] These statistics are incomplete because they do not include marriages of minors under the age of 16. However, the extremely low number of cases shows that also the figures of early marriages between asylum seekers are not very high. This is important because it means that there is no need to enshrine simple, blanket solutions in the law.[15]

The provision in Section 7 para. 1 No. 6 of the SGB VIII should, therefore, be understood against this background. It states, this [meaning the definition of Erziehungsberechtigter] also applies if the child or young person is married.

This can be read in two ways. On the one hand, it can mean that the spouse is never the "Erziehungsberechtigter". But on the other hand, it can also mean that the adult spouse is not automatically considered an "Erziehungsberechtigter". Rather, this can only be assumed if it applies in the specific case. Of course, the underage spouse must be considered unaccompanied if the married couple does not have a good relationship and the best interests are not secured in the marriage. In addition, the parents would have to have transferred parental authority to the adult spouse.

Only this latter reading makes sense. At first glance, it does sound strange to understand a spouse as having "parental authority". But as shown, an 18-year-old sister can be the "legal guardian" of her 17-year-old brother within the meaning of the standard. And a 19-year-old cousin for his 16-year-old cousin. It would not be compatible with this if a 19-year-old cousin who is married to the 16-year-old cousin were to be excluded as a "Erziehungsberechtigter", so that she would always have to be taken into care.

Contradictions would also arise if considering a couple whose marriage is void. Firstly, it could be void even under the law of their nationality.[16] Would the older cousin then be "Erziehungsberechtigter"? And secondly, we can similarly ask this for a marriage that is valid under the law of the nationality of the spouses, however considered void under German law. Could the 19-year-old cousin now be the "Erziehungsberechtigter" at the request of the parents, while the 19-year-old man who marries a 16-year-old could not be?

---

[13] Gesetz zur Bekämpfung von Kinderehen mit Wirkung vom 22. Juli 2017 (BGBl. I, at pp. 2429 ff.), see for detail S. Arnold (fn. 12), at pp. 167 f.

[14] Bundestags-Drucksache 20/10326 of 14 February 2024.

[15] See for detail S. Arnold (fn. 12), at pp. 175 ff.

[16] The law of the nationality is applicable under Article 13 para. 1 of the German EGBGB, see for detail S. Arnold (fn. 12), at p. 164.

In conclusion, it must be said that a married child can be "accompanied" by the adult spouse. This is because the adult spouse can be "Erziehungsberechtigter". However, this is only the case if the general prerequisites (child's best interests, authorisation by parents) are fulfilled.

c) "Unaccompanied" in Family Law

aa) No Parental Responsibility

The term "unaccompanied" is not used in the provision on guardianship in the BGB. Instead, it is decisive whether the child is "not subject to parental responsibility".

Under Section 1773 of the BGB, a guardian will be appointed by the court, if a minor is not subject to parental responsibility. This is clearly the case if the parents of the child are dead. However, if the parents' whereabouts are unknown or they cannot be contacted for other reasons, the child must also be assigned a guardian. The court can (and must) then order the suspension of parental responsibility and appoint a guardian afterwards.

In many cases, the situation is less clear-cut. Children who have travelled alone often have contact with their parents, whether by telephone or the internet. Sometimes they speak to their parents every day.

bb) Guardianship and Absence of Parents

The question of whether it is possible for parents who have remained in their home country to exercise parental responsibility via the Internet or telephone has been the subject of widespread debate for many years.[17] In the meantime, the view has largely prevailed that at least in the important legal matters — above all the asylum procedure — the child cannot be adequately supported by the parents in such a situation.[18] It is therefore assumed that parental responsibility is suspended (see for detail below Sect. III. 2. a).

---

[17] See for detail A. Vitr, Inobhutnahme minderjähriger Flüchtlinge bei Kontakterhalt mit den Eltern, 2021, at pp. 105–167.

[18] See for example OLG Hamm 23 May 2023, 7 UF 67/23, BeckRS 2023, 20,715, ECLI:DE:OLGHAM:2023:0530.7UF67.23.00 paras. 31 ff.; more open apparently OLG Bamberg 10 March 2022, 7 UF 27/22, Rpfleger 2023, 165, ECLI:DE:OLGBAMB:2022:0310.7UF27.22.00.

d) "Unaccompanied" in the Asylum Proceedings

Whether the child is unaccompanied also plays an important role in the asylum procedure. In particular, for unaccompanied minors there are much more generous rules on responsibility (see Article 8 of the Dublin III Regulation).

While the definition of "unaccompanied minor" in Article 2 lit. j of the Dublin III Regulation sounds rather broad ("a minor who arrives on the territory of the Member States unaccompanied by an adult responsible for him or her, whether by law or by the practice of the Member State concerned") it does in fact only refer to persons with parental responsibility, and not to persons like F in our example case.

If we look briefly at family asylum, this also only concerns the nuclear family of spouses or parents and children. It should be mentioned that according to Section 26 para. 1 sentence 2 of the German AsylG (Asylum Act), the spouse can also receive family asylum if the marriage is considered void under German law.

e) Summary

The different readings of the term unaccompanied has considerable practical implications. This can be seen in our case example:

In accordance with Section 42a of the SGB VIII (i.e. in youth welfare law), M would not initially be taken into care. He could stay with F, who is considered the "Erziehungsberechtigter" (person with parental authority). However, under Section 1773 of the BGB (e.i. in family law), a guardian would have to be appointed for M. F is probably not eligible for this, as will be explained in more detail below.

In the asylum procedure, F and M must be treated independently. F must return to Sweden on the basis of responsibility under Article 6 of the Dublin III Regulation. M, on the other hand, can choose. He can submit the application in Germany, or he can also travel back to Sweden. However, he cannot be granted family asylum with F under any circumstances.

If M decides to stay in Germany, he will also become unaccompanied. He must then be taken into care.

It is easy to recognise that these consequences can be very hard for F and M. If one now considers that the first host country may not be Sweden, but Greece or Spain, the situation becomes even more unpleasant. One possibility to help M and F could be seen in Article 17 of the Dublin III Regulation. According to this, the member states have discretion to examine an application for international protection even if such examination is not their responsibility under the criteria laid down in this Regulation. Respect for human rights could lead to a member state having to use their discretion accordingly. However, it can hardly be said that the mere accompanying of a young person by an adult has such an effect. Otherwise, the system of the Dublin III Regulation would be undermined.

III. Appointment of a Guardian

1. Jurisdiction and Applicable Law

The international jurisdiction for the appointment of the guardian generally arises from Article 6 of the 1996 Child Protection Convention (see for detail below IV. 2.). The applicable law for the guardianship is then German law, based on Article 15 of the 1996 Child Protection Convention.[19] Thereafter, the competent court applies the lex fori.

2. Requirements and Selection of the Guardian

a) No Parental Responsibility: Suspension of Responsibility

As already explained, it must first be established that the parents cannot exercise parental responsibility themselves and that they have not effectively transferred parental authority to a person who is resident in Germany and can properly assume this task for the parents.

If one first reflects on whether the parents can exercise parental responsibility themselves, this is only conceivable if there is close contact with the parents. Minors who are alone in Germany often still have contact with their parents via the internet. In some cases, they even speak or chat with their parents on a daily basis. It could then be that the parents are still able to exercise parental responsibility themselves to such an extent that a guardian is not required in Germany. However, as a rule, this is rightly rejected.[20] With the great distance, the impossibility to meet in person, the language and culture barrier, the parents will usually be factually unable to support the child sufficiently.

Finally, if we briefly consider the situation in which the parents have transferred parental authority to a person living in Germany, we must also be extremely cautious here. It is not just a question of whether the person in question is able to exercise the respective task. Rather, it must also be examined whether the transfer of parental authority by private order was possible at all under the applicable law — and, if so, whether the transfer can also be proven. All of this may rarely be the case, but it should not simply be ignored, because parental rights must also be safeguarded in an international context.

---

[19] See BGH 20 December 2017, XII ZB 333/17, BGHZ 217, 165, ECLI:DE:BGH:2017:201217BXIIZB333.17.0; OLG Hamm 30 May 2023, 7 UF 67/23, BeckRS 2023, 20,715, ECLI:DE:OLGHAM:2023:0523.7UF67.23.0A.

[20] W. Dürbeck, Unbegleitete minderjährige Flüchtlinge im Familienrecht, FamRZ 2018, 553, at p. 555.

If the parents are alive but cannot exercise parental responsibility, the suspension of parental responsibility must be established by the court in accordance with Section 1674 of the BGB before the guardian is appointed.

b) Selection of the Guardian

It has already been mentioned that it is a major problem in Germany to find suitable people to act as guardians. According to the law, private individuals — so called "volunteer guardians" — should be prioritised. However, this "individual volunteer guardianship" is in fact rare. Relatively strict attention is paid to ensuring that the person in question really should be able to help the child in Germany, particularly in the asylum procedure. For this reason, relatives who have also travelled to Germany are not usually appointed as guardians.[21]

In the majority of cases, youth welfare officers and other professional guardians are therefore appointed. If the youth welfare office functions as guardian, there are strict provisions on the local responsibility (Section 88a of the SGB VIII). Even if the child leaves the place where it was sent to under the Königsteiner Schlüssel (see above at p. 120), the youth welfare office at this place remains responsible. If the court wants to appoint a guardian at the new place of presence of the child, this cannot be the local youth welfare office.[22] Under Section 1774 of the BGB, there are some other options, such as so-called professional guardians.

According to the BumF survey,[23] youth welfare officers were appointed as guardians in around 83% of cases in 2021. As was pointed out above, these often do not have sufficient specialised knowledge to be able to fully help the young person in difficult asylum proceedings. One might, therefore, think of appointing a co-guardian in order to ensure the competent representation of the child.

However, the German Federal Court of Justice has ruled this out in 2017 and thereby factually finished further discussion.[24] The main argument of the court was that underage refugees who come to Germany together with their parents would otherwise be in a worse position than unaccompanied refugees. Considering how different the living and legal situations of the groups being compared are, this is a weak argument. The BGH also referred to the possibility of engaging a lawyer. This is indeed possible in Germany, at least in theory, but the minor also needs a lot of

---

[21] See for more detail U. Schwarz, In: Oberloskamp/Dürbeck (eds), Vormundschaft, Pflegschaft und Beistandschaft für Minderjährige, fifth ed. 2023, § 10 paras. 117 ff.

[22] BGH 15 September 2021, XII ZB 231/21, FamRZ 2021, 1885, ECLI:DE:BGH:2021:150921BXIIZB231.21.0.

[23] https://b-umf.de/src/wp-content/uploads/2022/07/online-umfrage-komplett-final-11-07-22.pdf, at p. 62.

[24] BGH 13 September 2017, XII ZB 497/16, NJW 2017, 3520, ECLI:DE:BGH:2017:130917BXIIZB497.16.0; critically W. Schwamb, Unbegleitete minderjährige Flüchtlinge im Familienrecht- Erwiderung auf den Beitrag von Dürbeck, FamRZ 2018, 553 ff. - FamRZ 2018, 984.

support in order to find a lawyer and conclude the contract with him or her, so that, in practice, this may not be feasible.

Just looking at the figures of the cases in which the youth welfare office submits the asylum application for the young person,[25] it is clear that, at least in some federal states, there can be no connection with the individual case, but that blanket decisions are made.

It has been recognised in German doctrine that the qualification of the minor's representative in the asylum procedure is addressed in EU legislation.[26] Article 6 of the Dublin III Regulation demands that the representative "shall have the qualifications and expertise to ensure that the best interests of the minor are taken into consideration during the procedures carried out under this Regulation". And Article 25 of the Asylum Procedures Directive[27] stipulates further details about the quality of the representation.

It is regrettable that the current handling has nonetheless become entrenched.

c) Option of Provisional Guardianship

It should also be mentioned that, according to Section 1774 of the German Civil Code, it is possible to appoint the youth welfare office or a recognised guardianship association as provisional guardian. The purpose of this is to enable the judicial officer to find the most suitable guardian for the child at a later date. This option could also be used for unaccompanied minor refugees if there is hope that a volunteer guardian can still be found. As shown, however, this is rarely the case.

3. Appointment Procedure

a) Jurisdiction of the Judicial Officer (Rechtspfleger)

German law has an unfortunate weakness when it comes to functional jurisdiction. Since 1 January 2023, it is no longer the judge but the judicial officer who is responsible for appointing the guardian. The judicial officer has already before been responsible for the suspension of parental responsibility — however, as has been shown, this task is considerably more complex when it comes to unaccompanied child refugees.

[25] See J. Karpenstein/D. Rohleder, Die Situation geflüchteter junger Menschen in Deutschland, at p. 65; https://b-umf.de/material/umfrage-2021/.

[26] U. Schwarz draws attention to this, In: Oberloskamp/Dürbeck (fn. 21), § 10 para. 110.

[27] Directive 2013/32/EU of the European Parliament and of the Council of 26 June 2013 on common procedures for granting and withdrawing international protection (recast) (Asylum Procedures Directive).

Judicial officers are far less trained and practised in dealing with children than judges. The other legal difficulties involved in appointing a guardian such as checking whether the parents need to be heard or whether they may have granted an effective power of attorney for parental responsibility for an adult in Germany, are also difficult for the judicial officer to deal with. According to the presumption of some previously competent family court judges, the principles on procedural standards and hearings are therefore currently no longer consistently observed.

Nevertheless, the following is a summary of the prevailing opinion on what must lawfully be done in proceedings regarding the appointment of a guardian for a refugee minor who has travelled to Germany without their parents.

b) Participation and Hearings

Under Section 7 of the FamFG (Act on Proceedings in Family Matters and in Matters of Non-contentious Jurisdiction) a number of persons must be included into the proceedings as participants. Section 7 para. 2 No. 1 of the FamFG specifies that this applies to all persons whose rights would be directly affected by the proceedings. Looking at the appointment of a guardian this means that the child concerned must always be heard. If the parents are still alive and have parental responsibility they must be included as participants in the proceedings on the suspension of parental responsibility, as they are directly affected by this.[28] As a rule, the child must be heard in person in accordance with Section 151 No. 4, Section 159 para. 1 of the FamFG. Regarding the parents, Section 160 of the FamFG applies. According to Section 160 para. 1 of the FamFG the parents also usually need to be heard when a guardian is appointed, if even they do not have parental responsibility of the child (any more).[29] It is usually convincingly argued that they must be heard in person if there is telephone contact. However, it can be assumed that this rarely happens in practice. If necessary, an interpreter must be called in for both the child and the parents.

If contact with the parents is not possible via telephone or the Internet, it is usually assumed that there is a serious reason in the sense of Section 160 para. 3 of the FamFG and the hearing can therefore be omitted.[30] Overall, however, it must be emphasised that the current practice, in which parents are apparently not usually heard, is difficult to reconcile with the parental rights protected by the Basic Law.

---

[28] W. Dürbeck, FamRZ 2018, 553, at p. 557.

[29] B. Hoffmann, In: Gsell/Krüger/Lorenz/Reymann (eds), beck-online Großkommentar, ed. 2024, Section 1778 BGB para. 92.

[30] W. Dürbeck, FamRZ 2018, 553, at p. 558.

4. *Termination of Taking into Care and of Guardianship*

When the young refugee reaches the age of 18, the taking into care and the guardianship will be terminated. However, it is of great importance to ensure that this only happens after an appropriate age assessment and that the refugees can file against the termination without prejudice to their real age.[31]

IV. Guardianship in Cross-Border Cases

1. *Introduction*

When unaccompanied minor refugees move within the EU, the issue of a recognition of a guardianship must be considered.

On first glance, this seems very easy. The Brussels IIter Regulation[32] applies between the member states. According to Article 30 of the Brussels IIter Regulation, the guardianship is recognised by operation of law — the guardianship therefore continues in the other member states.

This is an important and helpful regulation in many cases. For example, if the ward goes on holiday in another state, either with or without the guardian, it is important that the crossing of the border does not affect the guardianship.

On closer inspection, there are considerable difficulties. After all, it is of little benefit to the child if a youth welfare officer from another country, who is already overworked and does not speak the language of the new country of residence, remains the child's guardian. Much more important than mere recognition would be the simplest possible adaptation of the guardianship, e.g. by replacing the guardian.

In the following, it will first be shown how to proceed when a minor refugee arrives in Germany for whom a guardian has already been appointed in another member state. It will then be considered whether there is room for improvement.

2. *Jurisdiction*

When it comes to jurisdiction, one needs to be more attentive. Somewhat surprisingly, the Brussels IIter Regulation does not apply. Article 11 para. 2 of the Brussels

---

[31] VG Stuttgart 24 August 2023, 7 K 3873/23, JAmt 2023, 550, ECLI:DE:VGSTUTT:2023:0824.7K3873.23.00.

[32] Council Regulation (EU) 2019/1111 of 25 June 2019 on jurisdiction, the recognition and enforcement of decisions in matrimonial matters and the matters of parental responsibility, and on international child abduction (recast) (Brussels IIter Regulation).

IIter Regulation does not cover minor refugees (“refugee children”) who only have a simple presence in Germany. This is because this provision only applies to minor refugees if they had their habitual residence in another EU member state before fleeing. This will very rarely be the case for refugees. In all other cases Article 6 of the 1996 Child Protection Convention takes precedence over the Brussels IIter Regulation.

It should be mentioned that this not a new regulation. The former Article 13 of the Brussels IIbis Regulation simply did not expressly recognise this precedence of the 1996 Child Protection Convention so that this was often overlooked. Therefore, it was clarified in the recast.

Normally, it makes no difference whether the Brussels IIter Regulation or the 1996 Child Protection Convention is applied. This is because children who have fled from a third country and do not have their habitual residence in the EU are also subject to the jurisdiction of the place of the simple presence of the child in accordance with Article 6 of the 1996 Child Protection Convention.

However, if the proceedings are pending, this makes a big difference. Under the Brussels IIter Regulation — which applies in most cases when a child moves within the EU — there is the perpetuatio fori provided for in Article 7 of the Brussels IIter Regulation. In contrast, the 1996 Child Protection Convention — which normally applies when a child moves from a third country — does not recognise perpetuatio fori.[33]

It seems difficult to ignore this exclusion of the perpetuatio fori, even if one might wish for a continuation of the proceedings. One would have to assume that perpetuatio fori represents a general principle within the EU that even prevails over the 1996 Child Protection Convention. However, that is probably going too far. Not only does it contradict the applicable written law, but it should also be remembered that the retention of perpetuatio fori was rather controversial during the reform of the Brussels IIbis Regulation.

Therefore, if the 1996 Child Protection Convention is applied, German jurisdiction ends when the child moves and the foreign court becomes competent. Continued jurisdiction would have no legal basis.

This does not mean that a guardianship that has already been established abruptly ends. As already mentioned, the guardianship is automatically recognised in accordance with the Brussels IIter Regulation. Additionally, the very basic protection stipulated in Article 14 of the 1996 Child Protection Convention also applies here.

3. Practical and Legal Difficulties and Child-Friendly Solutions

Before considering whether the current solution makes sense, let’s take a look at the actual processes. If a child enters Germany alone, the authorities cannot initially

---

[33] KG 1 August 2023, 16 UF 49/23, FamRZ 2023, 1496, ECLI:DE:KG:2023:0726.16UF49.23.00.

recognise whether he or she already has a guardian. If it is not a case of an organised entry agreed with the guardian, for example on a school trip, but the young person enters the country on their own initiative, they will be provisionally taken into care.

It can then, at least in theory, later be determined whether guardianship already exists in another member state. This will generally only be taken into consideration at all if the child states in the clearing procedure that it already has a guardian. According to the liaison judges, however, it is often not possible to verify this information. Apparently, even the liaison magistrates or central authorities responsible for communication between the member states are usually unable to verify the guardianship at all. In particular, direct communication, which is generally possible under Article 86 of the Brussels IIter Regulation seems practically difficult to perform.

Even if it is possible to contact the foreign court or the guardian, the difficulties do not end there. As shown, from a purely legal point of view, there are no major problems with jurisdiction and recognition. The guardianship could simply remain in place.

Unfortunately, in most cases, this will not protect the child enough. He or she may need the guardian in everyday life, for example for advice, for signatures at school, and certainly also in the asylum procedure. As shown, according to Article 8 of the Dublin III Regulation, the child has the right to freely choose the member state in which to file an application. However, this could be difficult with a foreign guardian. This is because the foreign guardian will rarely have enough capacity to visit the young person in Germany, usually not speak German and hardly ever know the German authorities and responsibilities.

Therefore, the courts in the child's new country of residence will often use their jurisdiction in order to terminate the guardianship. They can then appoint a new guardian or they can also find that the ward is of legal age and therefore not set up a new guardianship.

As a result, the situation of a young person with a guardian in another EU member state and without such a guardian is hardly different. During the transitional period after arrival, the young person is provisionally taken into care and later a new guardian is appointed.

Unfortunately, in this new procedure, not only will the legal requirements in the new country of residence be examined, but the factual requirements for guardianship will also have to be completely reassessed. For example, a new attempt must be made to establish contact with the parents and, above all, the age must be re-established.

The procedure of assessing the age can be very stressful for the child — not only because of the possible medical or psychological examinations, but also because the age assessment is often accompanied by fear and uncertainty. It is difficult to find solutions to this problem of repetitive investigations, as the EU system does not provide for factual findings to be recognised and it is also difficult to conceive of such a solution.[34]

The provisions on the transfer of proceedings to a court in another member state (Article 12 and 13 of the Brussels IIter Regulation) do not apply if the proceedings are not exceptionally still pending.

V. Summary

It has been shown that the German system has many elements for the protection and legal representation of unaccompanied child refugees. The youth welfare office should take them into care as soon as possible after their arrival and represent them in legal matters from then on until a guardian is appointed.

However, considerable problems have also arisen. Firstly, the youth welfare office has a conflict of interest. Secondly, the guardians often lack special knowledge in asylum law and they have to take on too many guardianships in order to have time for difficult issues. Furthermore, it can be taken into doubt whether it is sufficient for the person concerned to be deemed legally competent for the proceedings against the termination of the taking into care, if the age assessment states that they are of legal age. They then bear full responsibility for difficult court proceedings, even though they may in fact still be under the age of 18.

[34] In more detail K. Hüning, Binding effect of an age assessment, in this volume, at p. 75.

A European Approach to Cross-Border Guardianship

Bettina Heiderhoff

I. Guardianship in EU-Law: Is There Room for Improvement?

EU law only regulates some aspects of migration law — in particular concerning asylum proceedings. In the area of family law, it has so far also remained almost entirely limited to private international and procedural law. Substantive family law remains in the hands of the member states. This is for reasons of competence and is unlikely to change in the near future.

In this respect, the possibilities for EU law to directly influence guardianship practice are rather limited. However, member states are required to comply with the EU Charter — as well as the Human Rights Convention[1] and CRC[2] standards. This is not always successful, as several of the contributions in this volume make clear.

In the following, the problems will be highlighted again and the question will be asked whether the situation could be improved by the instruments of EU international family law — in this case the Brussels IIter Regulation.[3]

[1]Convention for the Protection of Human Rights and Fundamental Freedoms (Human Rights Convention).

[2]UN 1989 Convention on the Rights of the Child (CRC).

[3]Council Regulation (EU) 2019/1111 of 25 June 2019 on jurisdiction, the recognition and enforcement of decisions in matrimonial matters and the matters of parental responsibility, and on international child abduction (recast) (Brussels IIter Regulation).

B. Heiderhoff (✉)
Institute for German and International Family Law, Chair for Private International Law, International Civil Procedure Law and German Private Law, University of Münster, Münster, Germany
e-mail: bettina.heiderhoff@uni-muenster.de

S. Arnold, B. Heiderhoff (eds.), *Children in Migration and International Family Law*, https://doi.org/10.1007/978-3-031-71598-3_8

II. Protecting the Child's Best Interests by Appointing a Guardian

Guardianship for minors requires a great deal of personnel and organisation and is expensive. It is therefore understandable that there are often deficits in practical implementation. At the same time, guardianship is extremely important for the protection of unaccompanied refugee minors. This is because only guardianship can ensure that the children are legally represented and that the tasks of parental responsibility — which also include care and education — are reliably performed.[4]

It is therefore not surprising that many human rights organisations have been concerned with the practice of appointing guardians in the member states.[5] This is partly about monitoring, but it is also about working specifically to reduce staff shortages, for example. In general terms, the aim is always to improve practice.

These efforts have certainly greatly improved the situation, but there are still some general problems. When minors arrive in the EU without their parents, they are not appointed a guardian as soon as possible in every member state. As Orsolya Szeibert shows, in Hungary, for example, only *a guardian ad litem* is appointed for minors over the age of 14. This guardian has the task to conduct the asylum procedure but does not support the child in other contexts. And even in Germany, where a guardian is supposed to be appointed quickly, there are sometimes such severe staff shortages that young people have to wait months for a guardian to be appointed.

This situation is highly problematic and leads to gaps in protection that violate Article 20 of the CRC in particular. Italy is trying to fill the gaps with volunteer guardians, which is a convincing approach, but is also not easy to implement.[6]

[4]Insistent European Union Agency for Fundamental Rights, Guardianship systems for children deprived of parental care in the European Union - Summary, 2018.

[5]See for example: https://www.egnetwork.eu/; https://www.separated-children-europe-programme.org/; https://fra.europa.eu/en/publication/2022/guardianship-systems-children-update and https://fra.europa.eu/en/publication/2024/practical-tool-guardians-transnational-procedures-framework-international; http://www.europeanrights.eu/public/atti/recommendation_2190_ENG.pdf.

[6]In more detail, European Union Agency for Fundamental Rights, Guardianship systems for unaccompanied children in the European Union: developments since 2014, 2022.

III. Legal Issues at the Interface of Migration Law and Private International Law

1. Who Is Unaccompanied?

In the context of FAMIMOVE, the problems arising from the deficits of communication and harmonisation at the legal interface of migration law and private international law are of particular interest.

These are most evident in the question of which minors are categorised as "unaccompanied". This is often equated with the fact that the child is not accompanied by a parent (who has parental responsibility).[7] In private international law however, the one who has parental responsibility must be assessed in accordance with the 1996 Child Protection Convention.[8] This means that substantive national law cannot simply be applied.

Two questions are central here. Firstly, whether the parents who did not come to the EU can continue to exercise parental responsibility — for example, through communication via the Internet. And secondly, whether the parents have effectively transferred responsibility to a third person.

If the question is whether the parents still have responsibility or whether it has lapsed — e.g. due to a permanent obstacle to the exercise of this responsibility — the law of the habitual residence applies in accordance with Article 16 para. 1 of the 1996 Child Protection Convention. This means that the member state in which the minors have their habitual residence may apply its own law to this question.

However, minors are often accompanied by adults who claim that the parents have transferred responsibility to them and that they even have parental authority by operation of law under the law of the former state of residence.

According to Article 16 para. 2 of the 1996 Child Protection Convention, the law of the place where the child has its habitual residence at the time of the authorisation is decisive for the private transfer of parental responsibility by means of an "authorisation". Apparently, however, this is not always respected by all member states.

A second problem regarding authorisation, however, concerns the ability to prove the authenticity of the document that contains the authorisation. In case of an oral transfer, this is worse. Here, even careful investigation cannot always provide certainty. Member states are therefore right to be cautious. In cases of doubt, they should not recognise the parental authorisation of a third person. It should be noted that the Notaries of Europe offer a "Minors" form especially for the Ukraine through

---

[7] In more detail on the situation in Germany, B. Heiderhoff, Guardianship and other protective measures for minor refugees in Germany, in this volume, at p. 117.

[8] Convention of 19 October 1996 on Jurisdiction, Applicable Law, Recognition, Enforcement and Co-operation in respect of Parental Responsibility and Measures for the Protection of Children (1996 Child Protection Convention).

which parents can at least authorise third parties in an uncomplicated manner.[9] Unfortunately, the question of authenticity remains.

2. Guardianship and Asylum Proceedings

In migration law, there is an independent understanding of which minors are unaccompanied. The central issue here is legal representation, as unaccompanied minor refugees need a legal representative during their asylum procedure.

If — as it is the case in many member states — the youth welfare office or even a migration authority is authorised by law, this massively reduces the protection of young people. As shown above, not only is there often a lack of sufficient consideration of the young person's individual situation, but there are also conflicts of interest.[10]

However, one specific problem relating to EU law should be emphasised here. In the asylum procedure, minors have the right under the Dublin III Regulation (in particular Article 8 para. 4 of the Dublin III Regulation) to freely choose the member state in which they submit the application. This means that even after the guardian has been appointed, the minor can still decide to move on to another member state in order to apply for asylum there. In such a case, they are currently typically treated in the same way as a minor who has newly arrived from a third country. On the one hand, this "double" burden is correct and necessary for the protection of minors. However, on the other hand, it is also associated with high burdens for the minors themselves if, for example, age assessments are repeated. In conclusion, the question arises as to whether EU law could be better utilised here.

IV. Recognition of Guardianship Within the EU

1. Cross-Border Communication As Core Issue

One point that has repeatedly come to light in the context of FAMIMOVE is the currently very limited cross-border cooperation in guardianships for unaccompanied minor refugees.

However, this is not due to the legal regulations on recognising guardianship. Under Article 30 of the Brussels IIter Regulation, a guardianship established in another member state is recognised by law. The guardianship therefore continues to apply in the other member states.

---

[9] https://www.notariesofeurope.eu/en/legal-information/.

[10] In more detail on the situation in Germany, B. Heiderhoff (fn. 7), at p. 122.

Nevertheless, it must be recognised that this continued validity in the context of flight and migration is only advantageous in very few cases.

Firstly, the minors often leave the country without informing the persons in charge, and they often do not speak frankly in the country of arrival. Liaison judges reported that it was, therefore, usually not even possible to obtain information about the guardian, and it was generally said that the continuation of a guardianship was often not even considered.

Secondly, other practical impediments are high, too. Especially if, as it is currently the case in many member states, one authority is responsible for a large number of refugees and there is no personal relationship between the minor and the guardian, it is preferable if a guardian who is located in the new country of residence becomes responsible as quickly as possible.

This does not mean that recognition must completely lose its function in guardianship. It could, for example, be a great improvement, if the guardianship as such remained in place and only the guardian was replaced as soon as this seems appropriate. This could even be done under the current legal framework. Since the above mentioned important practical and legal prerequisites are missing, this does, however, not happen in practice.

There seems to be an almost complete lack of exchange of information.

2. Mutual Trust and a Pessimistic Look into the Future

Against this background, it looks like the obvious conclusion to call for more communication and transparency. In particular, minors could be registered throughout Europe and the data could be shared between all member states.

Even under the current legislation, however, a certain amount of caution must be exercised at this point. A "transparent" unaccompanied minor — whose personal data can be accessed from anywhere, might not be an ideal goal of a free EU.

This in mind, communication and mutual trust could still be immensely improved. The fact, that age assessment in particular is not recognised throughout the EU, is just one example.[11]

At a time, when the CJEU seems to be propagating a stronger binding effect of asylum status between member states, there is a feeling of encouragement to demand more mutual trust in the area of individual issues, too.[12] By improving communication it would perhaps also be possible to prevent large numbers of underage refugees from disappearing completely and their whereabouts being unknown to the authorities.

---

[11] See K. Hüning, Binding effect of an age assessment, in this volume, 75, at pp. 82 ff.

[12] See in particular CJEU 18 June 2024, case C-352/22, ECLI:EU:C:2024:521 (Generalstaatsanwaltschaft Hamm); whether this means a major shift in its jurisdiction seems still unclear.

All of this said, this chapter must end with a somewhat pessimistic outlook.

Currently, there is great concern that minors may not be granted sufficient protection under the new Pact on Migration and Asylum.[13] Articles 25 ff. of the new *Asylum and Migration Management* Regulation[14] still provides for more flexibilty on responsibility for the asylum proceedings for unaccompanied minors. However, a closer look reveals that the burden of proof often seems to lie with the minors, which is clearly unacceptable. One must also be very concerned about the age assessment and the determination whether a minor is unaccompanied.[15] The screening at the border or in the transit zone must fulfil the standards of the EU Charter and of the Human Rights Convention. Unfortunately, it must be feared that the checks at the border could become an insurmountable obstacle for many minors.

One can, therefore, only hope that the best interests of the child will continue to be paramount under the new system. In particular, a person must be considered a minor in case of doubt and unaccompanied minors must be provided with a guardian immediately and at all times.

[13] https://home-affairs.ec.europa.eu/policies/migration-and-asylum/pact-migration-and-asylum_en.

[14] Regulation (EU) 2024/1351 of the European Parliament and of the Council of 14 May 2024 on asylum and migration management, amending Regulations (EU) 2021/1147 and (EU) 2021/1060 and repealing Regulation (EU) No 604/2013 (*Asylum and Migration Management* Regulation).

[15] See https://ecre.org/wp-content/uploads/2024/05/ECRE_Comments_Asylum-and-Migration-Management-Regulation.pdf for some first critical remarks.

Part IV
Early Marriage

Early Marriages in Sweden

Ulf Maunsbach

I. Introduction

In Sweden, following recent legal developments, it is no longer possible to enter into marriages before the age of 18. The age limit is an absolute impediment to marriage under Swedish law and there is no exemption from that requirement. Another recent development in Sweden is that marriages validly concluded abroad are not recognised in Sweden if at least one of the spouses was under the age of 18 years at the time of wedding. This principle is irrespective of the spouse's connection to Sweden. Recognition of such marriages are only possible in exceptional cases when there are extraordinary reasons. Since the turn of the millennium, the Swedish legislator has moved from adhering to the principle that foreign status relationships should be respected to rather prioritising the idea that Swedish law (and thus Swedish values) should be applied in relation to early marriages, regardless of whether the issue is connected to Sweden.

I use the term "early marriage" to denote marriages between spouses if at least one of the spouses was under the age of 18 years at the time of wedding. This term seems preferable over the somewhat problematic term "child marriage" that is often used in this context. The term "child marriage" suggests inherent vulnerability and inability to grasp the implications of marriage.[1] While this may often be true, it is not universally the case, particularly with spouses aged 16 or 17. Moreover, the term can evoke images of forced marriages where the younger spouse lacks free agency.

[1] See N. Yassari/R. Michaels, Einleitung, in: Yassari/Michaels, Die Frühehe im Recht, 2021, 1, at pp. 10 ff.; D. Coester-Waltjen, Kinderehen – Neue Sonderanknüpfungen im EGBGB, IPRax 2017, 429, at p. 429; L. Möller/N. Yassari, Wenn Jugendliche heiraten: Die Minderjährigenehe aus rechtsvergleichender und international-privatrechtlicher Sicht, KJ 2017, 269, at pp. 269 ff.

U. Maunsbach (✉)
Faculty of Law, Lund University, Lund, Sweden
e-mail: ulf.maunsbach@jur.lu.se

S. Arnold, B. Heiderhoff (eds.), *Children in Migration and International Family Law*, https://doi.org/10.1007/978-3-031-71598-3_9

While early marriages may indeed involve coercion, this is not necessarily the case. At the same time, not every forced marriage is an early marriage. Terms like "minor marriage" or "marriage of minors" avoid these issues, but oversimplify matters, as the age of majority varies globally.[2]

In this chapter, I will describe in more detail the current Swedish rules regarding early marriages and the reasons raised in support of the development that led to the current legal situation. The chapter also includes a brief account of how early marriages has been handled in Swedish case-law, followed by an account of the criticism that has been raised against the current Swedish approach. The chapter concludes with a summary and conclusions.

First, however, I will briefly mention the institutional structure in Sweden, with a focus on where, and in what contexts, issues of early marriages can be raised. This is followed by a brief presentation of the sources I use as a basis for the study, with a focus on the Swedish tradition of placing great emphasis on preparatory work.

II. A Few Words About the Institutional Structure in Sweden

In Sweden, issues of early marriages can typically arise in at least three situations. (1) When a marriage is to be registered in the Swedish population registration database, (2) when a marriage becomes relevant in connection with an application for a residence permit and (3) in private law contexts when the question of the validity of a marriage may arise, for example, in connection with a custody dispute or a dispute about maintenance. The three situations illustrated take place in different institutional contexts and issues of early marriages will thus be examined by authorities and courts, whose decisions and rulings are not binding between the different deciding institutions. In other words, there is a built-in risk that similar issues will be dealt with differently, depending on when and where the issues arise.

The first situation concerns the registration of status relationships in the Swedish population registration database. That database is maintained by the Tax Authority and registration in that database is routinely carried out on the basis of an assessment of the documentation submitted by the applicant.[3] The fact that someone is registered as married in the population registration database does not mean that the question of the validity of the marriage has been decided with binding effect on other authorities, but registration as married (or unmarried) can still have practical significance for those involved, for example when it comes to questions about guardianship and/or parenthood. Actually, in many practical contexts, an extract

[2] M. Makowsky, Die „Minderjährigenehe" im deutschen IPR, RabelsZ 2019, 577, at p. 578.

[3] More information about the Swedish population registration database is available at: https://skatteverket.se/privat/folkbokforing/attvarafolkbokford/folkbokforingsdatabasen.4.3810a01c150939e893f16fe2.html.

from the Swedish population registration database (a birth certificate) is used as proof of personal status (although it does not really have legal effect).

The Tax Agency's decisions in registration matters can be reviewed after appeal. The review takes place in an administrative procedural system with three instances, where the Supreme Administrative Court (HFD) is the final instance. An example of a dispute of this kind is the case HFD 2012:17, which concerns the Swedish Tax Agency's refusal to recognise an early marriage for registration in the population registration database. The case is presented further in section "VI. Case-Law on Early Marriage" below.

The second situation in which issues of early marriages may arise is in connection with applications for residence permits, primarily when family reunification is in question.[4] An example of how a question of early marriage can arise in these situations is when someone applies for a residence permit in Sweden on the grounds that the spouse is domiciled in Sweden. The issue of early marriages may also arise as a possible impediment to obtaining a residence permit when the applicant is a child validly married abroad, that wants to be recognised as unmarried to be reunited with a parent domiciled in Sweden. These cases are handled by the Swedish Migration Agency[5] and any disputes regarding decisions in these cases are tried in a similar way as the Swedish Tax Agency's cases, i.e. in an administrative law procedure. For migration cases, however, a special procedural system applies with special courts, so-called migration courts.[6] Decisions from the Swedish Migration Agency can be appealed to one of the country's four Migration Courts, and decisions from any of these courts can ultimately be appealed to the Superior Migration Court (MIG). An example of a dispute of this kind is the case MIG 2012:4, which concerns the question of the validity of a marriage solemnised abroad as an obstacle to family reunification. The case is presented further in section "VI. Case-Law on Early Marriage" below.

The last (and third) situation in which issues of early marriages may arise is in private law disputes where marital status is important for the outcome of the case. The importance of marital status may arise as a decisive matter in several different contexts, such as divorce, parenthood, inheritance or maintenance proceedings. It is not uncommon for the question of the validity of the marriage to arise in these cases as a preliminary question. Common to all these cases is that they are tried by a general court (which in Sweden handles all private law disputes) and the process in these courts is governed by a civil procedure framework. Even in these situations, there are three instances with the Supreme Court (HD) as the last. At present, there is

---

[4]See Utlänningslag (Aliens Act) (2005:716). Chapter 5 deals with issues relating to residence permits. The current rules reflect the Swedish implementation of the Family Reunification Directive (Directive 2003/86/EC on the right to family reunification).

[5]More information about the Migration Authority can be found at: https://www.migrationsverket.se/English.html.

[6]More information about the Migration Court in Swedish language can be found at https://www.domstol.se/hitta-domstol/migrationsdomstolar/.

no case law from the HD in Sweden that specifically concerns the question of the validity of early marriages.

A common feature of status issues (such as the validity of an early marriage) is that they arise in different contexts and that they are dealt with differently by a number of different authorities. Such a situation, which may be unavoidable, undoubtedly gives rise to challenges when it comes to dealing with situations in a uniform manner, i.e. treating similar situations equally.

III. Briefly About the Sources Used as a Basis for the Study

Usually, a deeper understanding regarding how a law is and should be applied (such as regulations about early marriages) would be based on case-law. However, there are only a few relevant court decisions in Sweden where issues of early marriages have been examined. A distinctive feature of the Swedish legal system, however, is the tradition that the legislature provides extensive preparatory work, and that these are highly esteemed as a source of law and thus influential regarding how the law should be applied. In the absence of case-law, this chapter will therefore mainly be based on current preparatory work. Hence, there is reason to briefly describe the type of sources involved.

When a problem that may give rise to a need for new legislation has been identified by the Swedish Government, a special inquiry is often appointed with the task of investigating the issue. The findings are published in reports in a special series, the Statens Offentliga Utredningar (Swedish Government's official reports, SOU), which are chronologically numbered (e.g. SOU 2017:96). In cases where the inquiry is handled directly by one of the Government's ministries, these are instead published in Departementens skriftserie (Ds), also numbered chronologically (e.g. Ds 2002:54). These reports constitute an important source in the study of Swedish law, and they have been central to my work in presenting the underlying motives for the legislation on early marriage that exists in Sweden today.[7]

The investigations then form the basis for the Government's work to submit proposals to the Riksdagen (Swedish Parliament) for new legislation. These proposals are presented in bills (propositioner) that are another important source to understand how a Swedish law is intended to be applied. Government bills are also published annually in chronological order (e.g. prop. 2003/04:48).

[7]Recent reports are available electronically. See, for example: https://www.sou.gov.se/. The reports usually have relatively comprehensive summaries in English.

IV. Current Swedish Rules on Early Marriages

As mentioned, it is not possible for minors to enter into marriages in Sweden.[8] In addition, there are clear (and almost unconditional) rules for non-recognition of foreign early marriages. The age requirement is an unconditional impediment to marriage and a child is considered a child until their 18th birthday in Sweden.[9] The examination of impediments to marriage is carried out by the Tax Agency and the system is intended to guarantee that a child will not be able to enter into a marriage in Sweden. However, if there is a mistake with the result that a marriage is solemnised even though one of the spouses is a minor (for example, because of an error in the examination of impediments to marriages or because of an error committed by a marriage officiant), the marriage will still be regarded as valid, with the legal effects of a marriage. The only way to dissolve such a wrongful marriage is by divorce which, in these situations, can be possible to achieve without a reconsideration period. An action for such a divorce may be brought by either one of the spouses or by the public prosecutor.[10]

When it comes to the current Swedish regulation on the recognition of foreign marriages, the main rule is still that such marriages are recognised if they are valid in the country where the marriage took place.[11] However, there are exceptions relating to marriages that are not to be recognised, including early marriages.[12] Hence, a marriage entered into in accordance with foreign law is not recognised in Sweden if one of the spouses was under 18 years of age at the time of the marriage. The consequence of such non-recognition is that the marriage is regarded as non-existent and that none of the legal effects of the marriage are preserved. The Swedish regulation is strict, but with a limited possibility to recognise an early marriage if there are extraordinary reasons and the spouses are over 18 years of age at the time of the assessment.[13]

V. A Brief Overview of the Legal Development

The current Swedish attitude to early marriage is relatively new. Until 2004, the Swedish legal system was liberal in relation to foreign marriages. In principle, all marriages were allowed (if they were validly entered into abroad), with the only exception being that the general rule of public policy could be used to refuse

[8] Äktenskapsbalken (Marriage Code) (1987:230), Chapter 2 Section 1.

[9] Föräldrabalk (Parental Code) (1949:381), Chapter 9 Section 1.

[10] Äktenskapsbalken (1987:230), Chapter 5 Section 5.

[11] Lag om vissa internationella rättsförhållanden rörande äktenskap och förmynderskap (Act on Certain International Marriage and Guardship Relations) (1904:26), Chapter 1 Section 7.

[12] Act (1904:26), Chapter 1. Section 8a.

[13] Act (1904:26), Chapter 1. Section 8a para. 2

recognition (in exceptional cases).[14] The starting points for this position is usually attributed to the 1902 Marriage Convention[15] and the principle of nationality expressed therein. The Swedish attitude to foreign marriages has historically been characterised by a loyalty to the law of the country where the marriage took place.[16] It is evident that this approach has now changed as regards early marriages.

The process of change started in the post-war period with the initiation of extensive work on legislative reforms. In 1973, this work resulted in changes in the Swedish substantive rules regarding marriage.[17] The reform also meant that the rules in the Act (1904:26) were changed in the sense that the domicile principle had a somewhat greater impact. This changed view, which has left traces in several areas of private international law, is generally explained by the fact that Sweden during the period in question moved from being a country of emigration to becoming a country of immigration.[18] However, the principle of nationality was still retained as a general rule, but with the domicile principle as an alternative.[19]

The legislative changes introduced by the 1973 reform also meant that the scope of foreign law regarding marriages was limited and that certain impediments to marriage (mainly impediments to kinship) were to be applied under Swedish law also in situations where foreign law was otherwise applicable. However, no general ban on early marriages was introduced and it was still possible for minors to obtain an exemption to marry in Sweden.

The attitude to early marriage continued to change during the latter part of the 1970s, partly because attention was drawn to an increased number of early marriages with a foreign connection, where underage girls with a foreign background were overrepresented.[20]

An inquiry was therefore commissioned to investigate Swedish international family law. The work began in 1981 and the inquiry presented its reform proposal in 1987, in which a new approach to foreign marriages emerged. The proposals presented by the inquiry were characterised by a clear consideration of the interests of children, and it was proposed that Swedish impediments to marriages (including impediments to early marriages) should also have a greater impact in relation to foreign citizens who wanted to marry in Sweden. On the other hand, it was still considered acceptable to recognise foreign early marriages that could not have been

[14] Act (1904:26), Chapter 7. Section 4.

[15] Convention Governing Conflicts of Laws Concerning Marriage, concluded at The Hague, 12 June 1902 (now repealed), available at www.hcch.net.

[16] M. Jänterä-Jareborg, Att inte svika gifta barn är en svår balansgång, In: Jänterä-Jareborg/Brattström (eds), Vänbok till Anna Singer, 2017, at p. 198.

[17] See SOU 1972:41 and prop. 1973:32.

[18] M. Bogdan/M. Hellner, Svensk international privat- och processrätt, 9th ed. 2020, at pp. 129 f.

[19] M. Jänterä-Jareborg, Barnäktenskap i Sverige, In: Festskrift till Helge Johan Thue, 2007, at p. 311.

[20] For statistical data, see Ds 2002:54. It appears that during the 1970s there were about 300 early marriages in Sweden, of which more than 200 involved underage girls with foreign citizenship, see at pp. 50 f.

entered into in Sweden.[21] The report points out that a ban on recognising foreign early marriages would cause serious inconvenience to the spouses and their children, especially if the marriage has lasted for a long time.[22]

The 1987 proposal did not give rise to new legislation until 2004. The reason for the delay is considered to be that the issue of early marriage was less relevant during the 1990s, when the number of early marriages in Sweden decreased. The issue became politically relevant again in connection with several high-profile honour-related killings in the early 2000s.[23] The 2004 legislative reform meant a tightening of the Swedish position. It was clarified that Swedish law would always apply to marriages entered into in Sweden, with the result that Swedish impediments to marriages would always have an impact. In addition, impediments to marriage in the country of citizenship of the prospective spouses had to be taken into account if they were foreign nationals. The legislative reform also meant that the possibility for minors to obtain a permission to marry was limited to situations where there were special reasons for such an exemption to be granted.[24]

The rules were also amended regarding the issue of recognising foreign early marriages when one of the spouses had a connection to Sweden. The public policy rule in the Act (1904:26) was no longer considered sufficient to prevent the recognition of marriages that were alien to the Swedish legal system. The principle rule was still that foreign early marriages should be recognised, but when such a marriage was in conflict with Swedish impediments to marriages it would not be recognised if at least one of the spouses was a Swedish citizen or was domiciled in Sweden.[25] The purpose of the new regulation was primarily to prevent people with a connection to Sweden from being able to circumvent Swedish marriage impediments by marrying abroad.[26] However, an exception was introduced to recognise a foreign early marriage if there were special reasons for doing so. The purpose of the exception was to mitigate the negative effects of non-recognition. As an example of special reasons, the Governmental bill mentions that the spouses have lived together for a long time and that they have children together. However, it is also stated that the fact that the former minor has reached the age of adulthood does not in itself constitute a special reason for recognising an early marriage.[27]

After the law reform in 2004, the debate about early marriages and honour-based violence and oppression has continued in Sweden and voices have been raised that the regulation of early marriages must be further amended. In 2010, a new inquiry was therefore appointed to gather further knowledge about forced marriages and early marriages and to propose measures to counteract such marriages. The inquiry

[21] M. Jänterä-Jareborg (fn. 19), at pp. 312 f.

[22] See SOU 1987:18 Section 189.

[23] M. Jänterä-Jareborg (fn. 19), at pp. 314 f.

[24] See prop. 2003/04:48, at pp. 20–22; see also M. Jänterä-Jareborg (fn. 19), at p. 315.

[25] The new rule was introduced in Chapter 1 Section 8a of Act (1904:26).

[26] See prop. 2003/04:48, at pp. 24 f.

[27] See prop. 2003/04:48, at pp. 32 f.

presented its proposal in May 2012 and it led to relatively extensive legislative reforms in 2014.[28] As far as early marriages are concerned, the previous possibility of exemption for minors was removed and thus the 18-year age limit for entering into marriage in Sweden became an absolute impediment. Regarding the possibility of recognising foreign early marriages, the link to Sweden was maintained through the requirement that non-recognition of an early marriage only cover marriages where one of the spouses was a Swedish citizen or was domiciled in Sweden. On the other hand, the possibility of making exceptions was further restricted, as what had previously been special reasons now became extraordinary reasons. In addition, two new offences were introduced in Swedish criminal law, coercive early marriage and deception to travel abroad for marriage.

The development continued and it was considered that the legislative changes from 2014 had not had the intended effect. The debate in Sweden regarding the view of early marriages became even sharper. One explanation for this is the extensive migration that took place in 2015 and another is an increasingly clear focus on children's interests.[29] A new inquiry was appointed in March 2017, with the task of reviewing the Swedish regulation regarding the recognition of foreign early marriages. The inquiry presented its proposals on this issue in December 2017, which led to a bill that was adopted by the Swedish Parliament with new legislation entering into force on 1 January 2019.[30]

The new regulation meant that the connection requirement to Sweden was removed, with the result that foreign early marriages would be refused recognition in Sweden even if there was no connection to Sweden at all. One of the reasons given for the stricter rules was that it was necessary for Sweden to be able to fulfil its obligations under the CRC, which includes requirements that member states must counteract harmful practices (such as early marriages) and that these commitments cover all children in Sweden regardless of citizenship.[31] The limited possibility of recognising a foreign early marriage if there is extraordinary reasons was retained, with the addition that both spouses must be over 18 years of age when the matter is examined, in order for the exception to apply at all.

Since 2019, the current provision of the Act (1904:26) on non-recognition of foreign marriages has been amended once more (2021), but not in a way that affects the treatment of foreign early marriages. In other words, the justifications for the strict (and in principle unconditional) approach that emerges from current Swedish law are to be found in the preparatory work behind the 2004, 2014 and 2019 legislative reforms. It can be noted that the pace of change since 2004 has been

[28] SOU 2012:35 and prop. 2013/14:208. See also M. Sayed, Tvångsäktenskap och barnäktenskap – en analys av det svenska rättsläget, SvJT 2015, at p. 479.

[29] The trend towards a clear focus on children's interests is, not least, a consequence of the UN 1989 Convention on the Rights of the Child (CRC). The Convention entered into force in Sweden in 1990 and on 1 January 2020 it became Swedish law through the Act (2018:1197) on the CRC.

[30] SOU 2017:96 and prop. 2017/18:288.

[31] See, regarding the requirement to discourage harmful practices, Article 24 para. 3 of the Convention. See also SOU 2017:96, at pp. 103 f. and prop. 2017/18:288, at pp. 9 f.

intense and that the previous main rule, establishing loyalty to the law of the country where the marriage took place, has now been abandoned in favour of the domicile principle in relation to foreign early marriages. The changes presented here have been subject of criticism, which I will return to in section "VII. Criticism of the Swedish Regulation" below. Before doing so, however, I would first like to highlight two relevant rulings from Swedish courts.

VI. Case-Law on Early Marriage

As stated above, the current regulation of early marriage in Sweden is new and it is based on a legal development that began in 2004. It may also be noted that it was possible for children in Sweden to enter into marriages after permission until 2014. The fact that the rules are relatively new may be one of the reasons why there is a limited amount of case-law where the issue of early marriage is addressed. Hence, only two decisions will be presented in the following, each illustrating one of the situations I mentioned in the introduction.

The first case was decided by the HFD and concerns a request to register a marriage in the population registration database.[32] It thus illustrates the first type of situations in which issues of early marriage can arise. The case was initiated when a newlywed woman domiciled in Sweden applied to register a marriage that had taken place in Palestine according to Islamic tradition. The wedding took place 10 days before her 18th birthday. At the time of the Tax Agency's assessment, the absolute age limit had been introduced into Swedish law regarding the issue of recognition of foreign marriages when one of the spouses had a connection to Sweden (through citizenship or domicile). For that reason, the Tax Agency decided not to recognise the marriage (and thus not to register it). The Tax Agency did not consider that there were any special reasons to recognise the marriage.

The case was appealed to the Administrative Court, which found that there were special reasons (at the time, the wording had not yet been changed to extraordinary reasons) to recognise the marriage, even though the woman was a minor when the marriage was solemnised. The Tax Agency (which was the defendant in the case) appealed to the Administrative Court of Appeal, which agreed with the Administrative Court. Consequently, both courts considered that there were special reasons and they emphasised that the woman was 5 months pregnant. Both courts stressed, however, that the age limit must generally be regarded as absolute. The fact that the marriage took place in close proximity to the date of adulthood cannot, in itself, constitute a special reason. If that would be the case, the absolute age limit would lose its meaning.

The Tax Agency appealed against the judgment of the Administrative Court of Appeal to the HFD, which ruled in favour of the Tax Agency and held that the

[32] HFD 2012:17.

marriage in question should not be recognised. In its reasoning, the HFD states that the examination that the Tax Agency can carry out in connection with the registration in the population registration database must necessarily be general and focus on the information that is available to the Agency when the registration is to be made. It is not intended that the Tax Agency should conduct its own investigations into whether the conditions for registration exist. The HFD also emphasises that the routine examination carried out by the Tax Agency in these contexts is only relevant to the registration itself and that such registration is not binding on how the issue of recognition is to be assessed in other contexts.

In the present case, it was clear that the woman was a minor when the marriage took place and it was therefore right for the Tax Agency to refuse registration. According to the HFD, the fact that the woman was pregnant and that the marriage took place close to her coming of age did not constitute special reasons to recognise the marriage in order to register it in the population registration database.

The ruling illustrates how the Tax Agency is to examine the issue of early marriages in connection with registration in the population registration database and it is emphasised that this examination does not include any specific investigations into the circumstances surrounding the marriage, but that the examination must be made on the basis of the written documentation provided by the applicant. It is also apparent that registration in that database is not binding for the purposes of determining the validity of a marriage in other situations. In this context, it should be recalled that the provision in question on refusal to recognise early marriage has now been further tightened and that what were special reasons for exceptions are now extraordinary reasons.[33] One can assume that the application will be even more restrictive now that the requisite is extraordinary reasons.[34]

The second case I would like to mention illustrates the second type of situation in which the issue of early marriage can arise, namely in the context of an application for a residence permit.[35] The case was initiated when a mother applied for a residence permit in Sweden (via the embassy in Damascus) together with her daughter. The grounds for granting a residence permit were argued to be that the woman's father was domiciled in Sweden.

The Migration Authority rejected the application and the reason given was that the woman was married. As a result, she did not belong to her father's family, which meant that the special rules on family reunification in the Utlänningslag (Swedish Aliens Act) were not applicable.

The woman appealed the Migration Authority's decision to the Migration Court. She objected that it was unreasonable for her marriage to be recognised in such a way that she was regarded as married for the purposes of the examination of her

---

[33] Act (1904:26), Chapter 1 Section 8a.

[34] In connection with the most recent legislative amendment in 2019, it was clear from the Tax Authority's own data that the Authority had not concluded that exceptional circumstances existed in one single case, see SOU 2017:96, at p. 112.

[35] MIG 2012:4.

application for a residence permit. The marriage was solemnised under coercion when she was 15 years old and such a marriage would clearly be invalid under Swedish law. She also pointed out that her husband had been missing for almost a year and that there were reasons to believe that he was dead.

Despite these arguments, the Migration Court rejected the appeal on the grounds that the husband's one-year absence could not simply be taken as evidence for him to be considered deceased. Regarding the argument about the woman's young age at the time of the marriage, the Migration Court noted that there were no provisions that indicated that a marriage validly solemnised abroad should be considered invalid, when the spouses had no connection to Sweden (through citizenship or domicile). Hence, the Court concluded that the woman's marriage could not be considered invalid in connection to her application for family reunification with her father, simply because of her age at the time of the marriage.

The woman appealed to the MIG, which began by noting that it was undisputed in the case that the woman had validly married in Iraq. The Court then chose to examine the question of whether the marriage should be denied recognition on the ground that it was entered into under coercion. According to the Court, the standard of proof in this regard should not be set too high — it is sufficient that the coercion is made probable — but at the same time, a simple allegation of coercion is not sufficient. In the case, there had been no sufficiently concrete information about the existence of any coercion, only a statement that the marriage had been entered into in accordance with tradition and that the woman had no real influence of her own on the question of whether she wanted to marry. The MIG concluded that these circumstances were not sufficient to support the annulment of the marriage on the grounds that it had been entered into under coercion.

The MIG then proceeded to examine the question of the importance to be attached to the woman's young age. In this context, it should be noted that, at the time of the decision, there was no absolute prohibition on early marriage, as is the case with the current Swedish rules. Hence, it was possible to recognise foreign early marriages when the parties had no connection to Sweden. The MIG therefore examined the issue of the early marriage in question in relation to the general rule of public policy in Act (1904:26).[36] In the court's assessment of the case, it is noted that the woman would have been too young to marry under Swedish law (without special permission) but that the deviations in relation to Swedish law were not so serious that there was reason to apply the public policy exception. The woman's marriage would therefore be regarded as valid for the purposes of the Alien Act. Consequently, she could no longer be regarded as a member of her father's family and therefore not entitled to family reunification with him.

It should be underlined that the outcome of the case might have been different if the current Swedish rules — which no longer require a connection to Sweden in order to refuse recognition — had been applicable. Since the MIG's decision, the CJEU has also delivered its judgment in case C-230/21. The case before the CJEU is

[36] Act (1904:26), Chapter 4 Section 7.

based on a dispute in Belgium that is strikingly similar to the Swedish ruling just reported. In case C-230/21, the CJEU states that a minor refugee does not have to be unmarried to obtain the status of a sponsor for family reunification with his or her relatives, and the ruling thus provides for the possibility to reason in other ways than the MIG did in MIG 2012:4.

One conclusion that can be drawn from the account of the two Swedish decisions above, which were handed down around the same time, regards the importance of the context in which the issue of early marriages is raised. In the first case, an early marriage was considered invalid (mainly because the marriage was solemnised 10 days before the spouse's 18th birthday) and in the second case, an early marriage was considered valid even though the girl who had been forced to marry was only 15 years old at the time of the marriage. The question arises as to how it is possible that these diametrically different assessments were made, within the same judicial system — in both cases, the decisions of the authorities has been challenged in an administrative procedural system — even if the issues have arisen in completely different contexts. In the first case, it was emphasised that registration in the population registration database is a routine matter that does not allow for any in-depth investigation and therefore the age requirement was strictly applied. In the second case, the question was that of a residence permit, which meant that the question of age — which may appear to be the same — had to be answered in light of how the Aliens Act is intended to be applied. And then, of course, it may matter that the spouse in the first case had a connection with Sweden (through domicile) and that this amounted to a non-recognition situation under the law applicable at the time. In the second case there was no such connection and consequently no specific rule applicable in favour of non-recognition.

Although it is thus possible to explain why two courts in the same year can view the question of the validity of an early marriage so differently, it is unfortunate that the assessments are so diverging. The current situation inevitably leads to difficulties for parties in predicting whether, under Swedish law, they are married or not.

VII. Criticism of the Swedish Regulation

The criticism directed at the legal development in Sweden and the current strict attitude towards early marriage can be divided into three groups. The first is about equal treatment and is based on the fact that foreign early marriages, with the current rules, are not treated in the same way as Swedish marriages. The second group includes criticism that the current system risks leading to an increase in the number of limping legal relationships, and a third group of criticisms concerns the lack of predictability in the current system.

As regards the question of equal treatment, the criticism is based on the fact that non-recognition of a foreign marriage leads to the marriage being regarded as non-existent, with the result that it has no legal effect. The situation is different for marriages entered into in Sweden. Swedish impediments to marriages are in themselves intended to prevent early marriages (or forced marriages) from being entered into in Sweden, but it is still conceivable that mistakes are made and that such a marriage is still solemnised. Such a wrongful marriage does not become null and void but, as explained above, must be dissolved by divorce (which can take place without a reconsideration period). The important difference from non-recognition is that a divorce makes it possible to consider the legal effects of the marriage, for example in connection with the division of property and the establishment of parenthood. This discrepancy is a problem that critics argue the legislature has not paid sufficient attention to.[37] Criticism has also been expressed that the Swedish legislator's assumption, that it is always a benefit for the minor spouse that an early marriage is considered invalid, is in many cases unlikely to be true and that a decision not to recognise can be to the detriment of the person who the rules are supposed to protect (i.e. the minor spouse).[38] There has also been criticism that the lack of equal treatment in relation to early marriages may be contrary to the free movement of persons within the EU as enshrined in Article 21 of the TFEU.[39,40]

The second group of criticisms is that the number of limping marriages inevitably increases when a marriage that is valid in one country and not recognised in another. There are always negative consequences for the person affected by a limping legal relationship, and this can cause significant difficulties. Particular problems arise if children are involved, as the issue of paternity may be dealt with differently in different countries. The same applies to the possibility to enter into a new marriage, which would be possible in Sweden if the old marriage is not recognised, but at the same time means that in another country one may be regarded as a bigamist.[41]

The third (and final) group of criticisms concerns the lack of predictability that the current Swedish regulation gives rise to. Predictability is affected by the possibility of exceptions, which makes it possible to recognise a foreign early marriage if there are extraordinary reasons. It is still unclear which situations may be extraordinary, and this gives rise to uncertainty.[42] The fact that issues of early marriages arise in such different situations and are assessed by different institutions (courts and authorities) also means that it is difficult for the parties concerned to predict what applies and that people can actually be considered married in some contexts and unmarried in others. It has been suggested that this uncertainty could be cured if the spouses applied for a declaratory judgment before a competent civil court (with general jurisdiction). A judgment from such a court would probably be considered

[37] For a development of this argument, see M. Bogdan/M. Hellner (fn. 18), at pp. 166 f., and M. Jänterä-Jareborg (fn. 19), at pp. 316 f.

[38] For a further development of this argument, see M. Bogdan, Some critical comments on the new Swedish rules on non-recognition of foreign child marriages, Journal of Private International Law 2019, 247, at p. 252.

[39] Treaty of the Functioning of the European Union.

[40] M. Bogdan, JPIL 2019, 247, at p. 255; see also prop. 2017/18:288, at pp. 46-48, where the Swedish Law Council express similar criticism.

[41] M. Jänterä-Jareborg (fn. 16), at pp. 208 f.

[42] M. Jänterä-Jareborg (fn. 16) ,at p. 209 and M. Bogdan, JPIL 2019, 247, at pp. 253 f.

binding also in relation to other institutions (courts and authorities).[43] A prerequisite for such an action, however, is that there is a dispute regarding the matter (which is not the case if both spouses want the marriage to be valid) and it would thus mean that the dispute would have to be fictive in nature. Still, it would likely be possible, but the strategy has not yet been tested in practice, so the uncertainty prevails.[44] Hence, the situation in Sweden today means, as Bogdan has put it, that it becomes difficult for a person concerned to answer the seemingly obvious question of whether he or she is married with a simple yes or no.[45]

VIII. Summary and Conclusions

It can be stated that the question of whether early marriage should be valid is complicated and that the seemingly obvious answer — that a child always benefits from not being married before coming of age — is not really true in all situations. However, it is difficult to nuance the discussions on this issue. Legal developments in Sweden over the past 20 years show that it has been more politically viable to tighten the rules on early marriage than to nuance them in favour of broad-mindedness and tolerance in relation to foreign law. My personal view on the matter is that it is crucial and important that there is a possibility to make exceptions to the rule of non-recognition in individual cases and I am unsure whether the current possibility that is given, if there are exceptional reasons, is sufficient to fend off the inconveniences that the non-recognition of a foreign early marriage may lead to.

At the same time, however, it must be noted that the specific issue of early marriage does not appear to be particularly problematic in Sweden at the moment. The political discussion in Sweden nowadays is more focused on honour-based violence and oppression than about early marriages, and there are not many problems about early marriages that lead to disputes in courts. A consequence of this development is that there is a lack of case-law, which makes it difficult to evaluate the functionality of the current legal situation in Sweden, including the question of determining the precise meaning of the requirement of extraordinary reasons.

Another conclusion that becomes clear when looking at the legal development of recent years is that it is the child's interest that is in focus. In the case of early marriage, this interest is taken into account by a firm belief that children should be allowed to be children and that the life-changing decision to marry must wait until the future spouses have reached sufficient maturity. Children are simply, according to the Swedish legislator, not ready to make decisions that affect them for a long time and in ways that are difficult to foresee, before they are adults (i.e. 18 years old).

[43] M. Bogdan, JPIL 2019, 247, at p. 253.

[44] M. Bogdan/M. Hellner (fn. 18), at pp. 169 f.

[45] M. Bogdan, JPIL 2019, 247, at p. 254.

This argument is easy to endorse. In other words, it is difficult to say that you do not want children to be children and that children's interests should not be safeguarded. However, the desire to protect children must not mean forcing the authorities to take decisions that are not in the interests of the child, as can be the case with absolute and unconditional rules. There must be scope for individual exceptions, which in turn means that the authorities and courts dealing with these issues must be given the opportunity to make carefully considered decisions.

In this context, it becomes problematic that the issue of early marriages is handled by different actors in such a fragmented way. The situation is perhaps unavoidable, an inheritance dispute (which raises the question of the validity of a marriage) or a decision on a residence permit can and should not be dealt with in the same way as a question of registration in the population registration database. In other words, it is not realistic (and probably not desirable either) to centralise the assessment of the validity of early marriages in one and the same institution in order to provide the conditions for uniform and consistent decision-making. On the other hand, there is much to be gained from creating effective communication and an exchange of information between the actors involved.

Early Marriage in Germany: Law and Politics of Cultural Demarcation

Stefan Arnold

I. Introduction

This essay sheds light on the German law on early marriage, a law that is signified by symbolic politics of cultural demarcation. Today, early marriages are rare in Western European countries, but they do appear for instance within Roma and Sinti population groups.[1] Yet early marriages are still widespread, in particular in the least developed countries, Sub-Saharan Africa, South Asia, Latin America and the Caribbean, but also in the Middle East and North Africa.[2] Marriage is an institute that is deeply embedded in political and cultural backgrounds of societies.[3] The reasons for early marriage are complex and manifold.[4] Their background involves cultural and/or religious ideas of marriage and sexuality as well as political, economic and societal factors.[5] Even though early marriages are a rare phenomenon in European countries today, they have gained considerable political and public interest in recent years. Families on the move are certainly one important reason for this: Early

[1] See N. Yassari/R. Michaels, Die Frühehe im Rechtsvergleich: Praxis, Sachrecht, Kollisionsrecht, In: Yassari/Michaels (eds), Die Frühehe im Recht, 2021, 17, at p. 21.

[2] See the data by UNICEF, Global Databases, Child Marriages, last updated May 2023, available at https://data.unicef.org/wp-content/uploads/2019/10/XLS_Child-marriage-database_May-2023.xlsx.

[3] See N. Yassari/R. Michaels (fn. 1), at pp. 18 ff.

[4] See L. Möller/N. Yassari, Wenn Jugendliche heiraten: Die Minderjährigenehe aus rechtsvergleichender und international-privatrechtlicher Sicht, KJ 2017, 269, at p. 269; N. Yassari/R. Michaels, In: Yassari/Michaels (fn. 1), at pp. 21 ff.

[5] See N. Yassari/R. Michaels, In: Yassari/Michaels (fn. 1), at pp. 21 ff.

S. Arnold (✉)
Institute of International Business Law, Chair for Private Law, Philosophy of Law, and Private International Law, University of Münster, Münster, Germany
e-mail: stefan.arnold@uni-muenster.de

S. Arnold, B. Heiderhoff (eds.), *Children in Migration and International Family Law*, https://doi.org/10.1007/978-3-031-71598-3_10

marriages become visible in Europe when young spouses from countries like Syria or Afghanistan leave for Europe as a result of civil wars or political persecution.[6] Such unexpected visibility of "otherness" is a challenge to Western societies, and it seems that many Germans, for instance, feel threatened within their cultural identity and an urge to deliminate themselves from the "wrongness" of a phenomenon embedded in a very different cultural background. These feelings have heavily influenced the political and legal discourse in Germany and led to Germany's policy of strict non-recognition of early marriages in the form of the *Federal Law to combat child marriages*[7] effective from 22 July 2017 with some minor adjustments effective from 1 July 2024.[8]

In the following, I focus on the rules of German Private International Law — particularly on the German approach as regards early marriages that were concluded outside of Germany in compliance with the applicable foreign law. I use the term "early marriage" to denote a marriage where at least one of the spouses is under the age of 18 years at the time of marriage. Often, the term "child marriages" is used to denote early marriages. Yet the term "child marriage" is somewhat problematic.[9] It is true that the term generally refers to marriages which are concluded at the age of under 18 years.[10] But at the same time, the term "child" implies that the person involved is particularly vulnerable and not able to foresee the consequences of a marriage. Yet while this will often be the case, it is not necessarily so, in particular with spouses of the age of 16 or 17 years. Furthermore, the term "child marriage" might invoke images of situations where the younger spouse is forced into the marriage against their free will. Yet again, while it is possible that early marriages are at the same time forced marriages, this is not necessarily the case (and vice versa: not every forced marriage is an early marriage at the same time).[11] The terms „minor marriage" or „marriage of minors" avoid these problems, but they are misleading, since the age of maturity is not determined equally worldwide.[12]

---

[6]See also N. Dethloff, Child Brides on The Move: Legal Responses to Culture Clashes, International Journal of Law, Policy and The Family 2018, vol. 32, 302, at pp. 302–315.

[7]Gesetz zur Bekämpfung von Kinderehen mit Wirkung vom 22. Juli 2017 (BGBl. I, at pp. 2429 ff.).

[8]Gesetz zum Schutz Minderjähriger bei Auslandsehen (Gesetzesbeschluss des Deutschen Bundestages), BT-Drucksache 20/11367.

[9]N. Yassari/R. Michaels, Einleitung, In: Yassari/Michaels (fn. 1), at pp. 10 ff.; D. Coester-Waltjen, Kinderehen – Neue Sonderanknüpfungen im EGBGB, IPRax 2017, 429, at p. 429; L. Möller/N. Yassari, KJ 2017, 269, at pp. 269 ff.

[10]Cf. Bundestags-Drucksache 18/12086 of 25 April 2017, at p. 1.

[11]See N. Yassari/R. Michaels, In: Yassari/Michaels (fn. 1), at pp. 23 ff.

[12]See for instance M. Makowsky, Die „Minderjährigenehe" im deutschen IPR, RabelsZ 2019, 577, at p. 578.

II. An Overview on German Law and Politics on Early Marriages

The German law on early marriages has had a turbulent recent history from 2016 until the present day. That recent history has been written by an unfortunate interplay of many different players of the law[13] civil courts, the Constitutional Court, members of parliament and other politicians, academics and interest groups. As the law stands at the time of writing, German law follows a strict policy of non-recognition with respect to early marriages where at least one of the spouses is or was under the age of 16 at the time of the marriage. That is, of course, completely unproblematic as regards marriages concluded in Germany: Since 21 July 2017, marriages cannot be validly concluded in Germany when one of the spouses is under the age of 18 years at the time of marriage. Before that date, marriage was possible by dispense when one of the spouses was 16 or 17 years old. In practice, such marriages had been very rare.[14] German law's strict policy of non-recognition is very problematic, however, with respect to early marriages that have been validly concluded in foreign countries. The Federal Law to combat child marriages, effective since 22 July 2017, introduced Article 13 para. 3 no. 1 of the EGBGB (German Private International Law). This provision stipulates that early marriages legally concluded in foreign countries are invalid without individual case-by-case examination when one of the spouses was under the age of 16 at the time of marriage. When one of the spouses was 16 or 17 years old at the time of marriage, the marriage is merely subject to annulment according to Article 13 para. 3 no. 2 of the EGBGB. Article 13 para. 3 no. 1 of the EGBGB has been declared unconstitutional by the Constitutional Court, but it was still to be applied at the time of writing and will continue to be applied with minimal adaptions from 1 July 2024 on.[15]

[13] See on this development from a theoretical perspective and on the term „players of the law": S. Arnold, The Chain Novel and Its Normative Fine Structure in Civil Law and Common Law: Dworkin, Brandom and Law's Normativity, In: Bersier-Ladavac/Bezemek/Schauer (eds), Common Law – Civil Law: The Great Divide, 2021, 29–50, https://doi.org/10.1007/978-3-030-87718-7.

[14] For details see M. Martinek, Minderjährigenehen im nationalen und internationalen Familienrecht, 2023, at p. 47; L. Möller/N. Yassari, KJ 2017, 269, at p. 281; I. Plich, Rechtliche Aspekte von Minderjährigenehen – Die gesetzliche Neuregelung, RPsych 2017, 299, at p. 300.

[15] For details see below (VI.).

III. Early Marriages in Germany Before 22 July 2017

1. Ordre Public*: Just and Flexible Solutions Through Individual Case-by-Case Examinations*

Before 22 July 2017, there were no specific provisions as regards early marriages within German Private International Law. The applicable law for the conclusion of a marriage was determined by Article 13 of the EGBGB: According to Article 13 para. 1 of the EGBGB, the requirements for the marriage of foreign nationals are determined by the law of the state of the respective fiancé or fiancée. Thus, in principle, marriages of spouses under the age of 18 concluded abroad could be valid according to foreign norms in case the applicable foreign norms enabled minors to marry. But that was merely the "point of departure" for the law in action, of course: Courts solved early marriage cases with the help of the general clause of the *ordre public* contained in Article 6 of the EGBGB[16] according to which a legal provision of another state must not be applied if its application leads to a result that is manifestly incompatible with fundamental principles of German Law — in particular with fundamental rights. Therefore, it was decisive whether or not the individual early marriage at play would lead to manifestly incompatible results. The present — not the past — was the relevant time for assessing that question.[17] The age of the spouses at the time of marriage was merely a factor weighing in.[18] For instance, courts have regarded marriages concluded under twelve years as a violation of the *ordre public.*[19] Marriages concluded at the age of 14 and 15 years have been treated differently by the courts who have taken particular care to consider the individual circumstances of each case.[20] The applicability of the *ordre public*-clause opened a certain leeway for the courts, allowing them to administer justice on a case-by-case basis by considering various crucial criteria. These included the domestic relevance (*hinreichender Inlandsbezug*), the individual physical and mental maturity of the spouse at the time of marriage and at the time of the decision, the duration of the marital relationship, whether the spouses wanted to pursue their marriage, and

[16]"Eine Rechtsnorm eines anderen Staates ist nicht anzuwenden, wenn ihre Anwendung zu einem Ergebnis führt, das mit wesentlichen Grundsätzen des deutschen Rechts offensichtlich unvereinbar ist. Sie ist insbesondere nicht anzuwenden, wenn die Anwendung mit den Grundrechten unvereinbar ist."

[17]L. Möller/N. Yassari, KJ 2017, 269, at p. 277.

[18]N. Dethloff, International Journal of Law, Policy and The Family, 2018, vol. 32, 302, at pp. 307 f.

[19]See for instance OLG Zweibrücken, FamRZ 2001, 920; OLG Köln, FamRZ 1997, 1240; AG Fürth (Odenwald), BeckRS 2019, 22704, ECLI:DE:OLGHE:2019:0111.5UF172.18.0A, paras. 18 ff.

[20]See for instance for the age of 14 years: no violation of the ordre public: AG Tübingen, ZfJ 1992, 48; OLG Frankfurt, BeckRS 2019, 3941 paras. 22 ff.; violation of the ordre public: KG, NJOZ 2012, 165; AG Wuppertal, BeckRS 2016, 135247 paras. 39 ff.; 15 years: no violation of the ordre public: KG, FamRZ 1990, 45; 15 years: violation of the ordre public: AG Offenbach, FamRZ 2010, 1561.

whether children were born as a result of the marriage.[21] At the same time, courts considered the consequences of the application of Article 6 of the EGBGB — particularly the emergence of limping marriages and the consequences for those involved.[22] Thus, Article 6 of the EGBGB enabled carefully balancing decisions aimed at restoring justice between the parties involved — particularly the spouse who was a child at the time of marriage, but also any potential children born from the marriage.[23]

2. *The Eminent Case of the OLG Bamberg*

One of the courts‘ decisions on early marriage and *ordre public* — a decision by the Higher Regional Court (OLG) Bamberg[24] — resulted in fundamental changes of the well-established legal practice: The court's decision led to a fierce public and political debate which finally resulted in the Federal Law to combat child marriages and Germany's strict policy of non-recognition as regards marriages where one of the spouse was under the age of 16 years at the time of marriage. The OLG Bamberg's decision was also the cause for the Federal Court of Justice's referral in November 2017 to the Constitutional Court for a preliminary ruling on the compatibility of the law reform with the German constitution,[25] the following decision of the German Constitutional Court and the recent "Law for the Protection of Minors in Foreign Marriages" (effective from 1 July 2024 on).[26]

The case of the OLG Bamberg concerned a marriage between a 15-year old wife and her 21-year old husband (both from Syria). The husband was born on 1 January 1994, the wife was born on 1 January 2001. Both were Syrians of Sunni faith and related as cousins. The marriage was concluded on 10 February 2015 at a Sharia court in Syria. Due to the Syrian civil war, the couple fled together to Germany, where they arrived in August 2015. Shortly after their arrival — namely in September 2015 – , the local youth authority took custody of the wife, placed her in a youth help facility for unaccompanied refugee minors. The official guardianship had separated the wife from her husband and only allowed contact on an hourly basis accompanied by a third party. The OLG Bamberg overturned this contact arrangement in the appeal proceedings. It did not explicitly deny a violation of the *ordre public*.[27] It held that, even if there were a violation, the marriage would only be

[21] M. Martinek (fn. 14), at pp. 92 ff. and p. 364.

[22] M. Martinek (fn. 14), at pp. 105 ff. and p. 364; L. Möller/N. Yassari, KJ 2017, 269, at pp. 277 ff.

[23] N. Dethloff, International Journal of Law, Policy and The Family, 2018, vol. 32, 302, at pp. 307 f.

[24] OLG Bamberg, BeckRS 2016, 9621, ECLI:DE:OLGBAMB:2016:0512.2UF58.16.0A.

[25] BGH, NJOZ 2019, 43, ECLI:DE:BGH:2018:141118BXIIZB292.16.0.

[26] Gesetz zum Schutz Minderjähriger bei Auslandsehen (Gesetzesbeschluss des Deutschen Bundestages), BT-Drucksache 20/11367.

[27] See also L. Möller/N. Yassari, KJ 2017, 269, at pp. 279 ff.

revocable, since neither Syrian nor German Law regarded the marriage as invalid. The municipal youth welfare office (*Stadtjugendamt*) had therefore no authority to regulate the contact period of the spouses.[28] The ruling of the OLG Bamberg did not imply that early marriages are generally considered valid. Instead, it focused on the specific case at hand and aimed to administer justice, particularly in the best interests of the wife.[29]

3. The Aftermath: The Discourse on the OLG Bamberg's Decision and the Proposal of Law Reform

Legal scholars discussed the OLG Bamberg's decision in a balanced and predominantly approving manner.[30] From a constitutional law perspective, no reform was necessary in order to protect children from early marriages.[31] Yet the decision was also publicly debated by politicians and interest groups who sweepingly criticised the ruling and the underlying legal framework as violating fundamental morals as well as human and women's rights. At this stage, in retrospective, political ideology rather than legal and constitutional thinking dominated the public debate. For instance, Susanne Schröter argued in a talk with Benedikt Schulz: „Do marriages validly concluded under foreign jurisdiction have legal effect here or do they violate the fundamentals of the German legal and moral order? I answer this question with: Yes indeed, they violate the ordre public! Even though there might be good reasons in individual cases to recognise these marriages, we would open floodgates if we accept morals prevailing in Syria or other countries."[32] Or Chantal Louis (from the journal *Emma*) wrote: "Even though child marriages violate our social values, we

[28] OLG Bamberg, BeckRS 2016, 9621, ECLI:DE:OLGBAMB:2016:0512.2UF58.16.0A.

[29] M. Martinek (fn. 14), at pp. 112 ff.

[30] See for instance P. Mankowski, Anmerkung zu OLG Bamberg 12 May 2016, 2 UF 58/16, FamRZ 2016, 1274, at p. 1275: "eine sehr sorgfältig und eingehend begründete Entscheidung"; S. Arnold, Die Entwicklung der Rechtsprechung zum Internationalen Privatrecht, GPR 2017, 29, at p. 35.

[31] For further analysis see F. Schulte-Rudzio, Minderjährigenehen in Deutschland, 2020, at pp. 267 ff.

[32] Susanne Schröter im Gespräch mit Benedikt Schulz https://www.deutschlandfunk.de/urteil-von-bamberg-bayerisches-gericht-erklaert-kinderehe.886.de.html?dram:article_id=357185. German original text: "Und da kommt dann natürlich das Moment zum Tragen, ob diese Ehen und die im Ausland geschlossenen Werte und Normen, ob die bei uns eben Bestand haben sollen oder ob sie gegen den 'ordre public' verstoßen. Das heißt gegen die Werte und Rechtsnormen, die bei uns gelten. Und da würde ich relativ klar sagen: Ja, das tun sie. Wir können – obwohl das im Einzelfall vielleicht gute Gründe gibt, so etwas dann auch anzuerkennen –, wir können grundsätzlich nicht Tür und Tor öffnen für die Anerkennung von Normen, die vielleicht in Syrien oder anderen Ländern gelten, aber bei uns auch einfach gegen die guten Sitten verstoßen."

recognise them. This is truly horrifying."[33] The ideologically laden discussion was heard by important political players, such as the then member of Parliament Stephan Harbarth.[34] The conservative and social democrat groups in the German parliament proposed a "law to combat child marriage" in April 2017. The law proposal explicitly referred to the decision of the OLG Bamberg and expressed its concerns about the compatibility with the best interests of the child.[35] The proposal suggested that marriages should not be recognised if at least one of the spouses was under the age of sixteen years at the time of marriage, regardless of whether the marriage is deemed legal under the applicable foreign law and irrespective of the current age of the spouses. Legal scholars and interest groups raised objections against the lawfulness of the proposal.[36]

IV. Early Marriages in Germany After 22 July 2017: Rigid Solutions Outside the *Ordre Public* at the Expense of Individual Justice

The Federal Law to combat child marriages passed the German parliament in July 2017. Since 22 July 2017, early marriages are regulated by specific provisions so that courts can no longer apply the flexible *ordre public* clause, but are rather bound by very specific provisions. The "point of departure" is still Article 13 para. 1 of the EGBGB, according to which the requirements for the marriage of foreign nationals are determined by the law of the state to which the respective fiancé or fiancée belongs. But rather than Article 6 of the EGBGB it is now Article 13 para. 3 of the EGBGB that determines the law in action: According to Article 13 para. 3 no. 1 of the EGBGB, marriages concluded under foreign law are invalid if at least one partner was under the age of 16 at the time of marriage. If one person was 16 or 17 years old at the time of marriage, the marriage is not invalid, but subject to annulation by a court decision according to Article 13 para. 3 no. 2 of the EGBGB. Thus, Article 13 para. 3 of the EGBGB prevents courts to make avail of the flexible ordre public

[33] https://www.emma.de/artikel/deuts-333561; German original text: "Selbst wenn die Kinderehe gegen unsere gesellschaftlichen Werte verstößt, erkennen wir sie trotzdem an. Das [ist] ungeheuerlich."

[34] See M. Klatt, Über die personelle und inhaltliche Verzahnung von Politik und Verfassungsrecht, JuWissBlog no. 3/2020, https://www.juwiss.de/3-2020.

[35] BT-Drucks. 18/12086, at pp. 14 ff.

[36] See for instance J. Antomo, Verbot von Kinderehen?, ZRP 2017, 79; Statements by the German Association of Women Lawyers [Deutscher Juristinnenbund], 18 April 2017, German Institute for Human Rights [Deutsches Institut für Menschenrechte], 16 May 2017, German Lawyers Association [Deutscher Anwaltsverein], 1 February 2017, German Notary Association [Deutscher Notarverein], 22 February 2017 and the German Children's Charity Foundation [Deutsches Kinderhilfswerk], 17 February 2017.

rule in Article 6 of the EGBGB.[37] The legislator intended to create legal clarity and to protect the minors involved.[38] Article 229 Section 44 para. 4 of the EGBGB makes an exception to the rule in Article 13 para. 3 no. 1 of the EGBGB: Article 13 para. 3 sentence 1 of the EGBGB does not apply if, firstly, the minor spouse was born before 22 July 1999, or, secondly, the marriage was valid under foreign law, performed until the age of majority of the minor partner and neither spouse had his or her habitual residence in Germany from the time of the marriage until the age of majority of the minor spouse.[39] Legal scientists expressed their doubts whether the law's rules are compatible with basic rights guaranteed by the German constitution as well as mobility rights protected by European primary law.[40]

V. The Federal Court's Submission of a Pending Case and the Constitutional Court's Decision from 1 February 2024

1. The Federal Court's Submission to the Constitutional Court

Following the critiques of the legal scientific community, the Federal Court of Justice (BGH) (Twelfth Civil Senate) submitted a pending case in November 2017 to the Constitutional Court for a preliminary ruling on the compatibility of the law reform with the German constitution.[41] The pending case was the OLG Bamberg's

[37] See also J. Basedow, Gesellschaftliche Akzeptanz und internationales Familienrecht, FamRZ 2019, 1833, at p. 1837.

[38] BT-Drucks 18/12086, at p. 1.

[39] For a more detailed interpretation see M. Andrae, Zur Anwendung von Art. 13 Abs. 3 Nr. 2 EGBGB unter Beachtung von Sinn und Zweck des Gesetzes zur Bekämpfung von Kinderehen (Art. 13 Abs. 3 Nr. 2 EGBGB), IPRax 2021, 522, at pp. 524 f.

[40] For critical evaluations of the law see for instance C. Hornung, Internationales Privatrecht zwischen Wertneutralität und Politik, 2021, at pp. 273 ff.; J. Antomo, ZRP 2017, 79, at p. 82; J. Bongartz, Zur gebotenen rechtlichen Behandlung von Ehen unter Beteiligung Minderjähriger, NZFam 2017, 541, at p. 546; D. Coester-Waltjen, IPRax 2017, 429, at p. 436; M. Coester, Kinderehen in Deutschland, FamRZ 2017, 77; N. Dethloff, International Journal of Law, Policy and The Family, 2018, vol. 32, 302; B. Frie, Drum prüfe, wer sich ewig bindet... – Zum Entwurf eines Gesetzes zur Bekämpfung von Kinderehen, FamRB 2017, 232, at p. 238; R. Hüßtege, Das Verbot der Kinderehe nach neuem Recht aus kollisionsrechtlicher Sicht, FamRZ 2017, 1374, at p. 1380; L. Möller/N. Yassari, KJ 2017, 279, at pp. 281 ff.; R. Kemper, Neues aus dem Abstammungsrecht, FamRB 2017, 438, at pp. 442 ff.; P. Reuß, Das Verbot von ‚Kinderehen, FamRZ 2019, 1, at pp. 5 f.; D. Schwab, Die verbotene Kinderehe, FamRZ 2017, 1369, at pp. 1373 ff.; a minority of scholars approved of the law, see S. Lentz, Islamisches Recht vor deutschen Familiengerichten, FuR 2017, 597, at p. 601; C. Majer, Das Gesetz zur Bekämpfung von Kinderehen, NZFam 2017, 537, at pp. 538 ff.; R. Opris, Ausländische Ehen im deutschen Recht im Lichte des Gesetzesentwurfs zur Bekämpfung von Kinderehen, ZErb 2017, 158, at pp. 162 ff.; M. Payandeh, Im Ausland geschlossene Minderjährigenehen, JuS 2023, 1170, at pp. 1170 f.

[41] BGH, NJOZ 2019, 43, ECLI:DE:BGH:2018:141118BXIIZB292.16.0.

case of the two Syrian spouses mentioned above. The Senate was convinced that the nullity of early marriages violates the right to family life under Article 6 para. 1 of the GG (Basic Law) and the best interests of the child protected as part of the "general personality right" (Allgemeines Persönlichkeitsrecht [APR]) under Article 2 para. 1 in connection with Article 1 para. 1 of the GG (Protection of and respect towards the personal development). The Senate argued that every minor benefits from the general principle that the state is obliged to act only in his or her best interest. According to the court, nullity of marriage without case-by-case assessment ignores a child's human dignity and his or her right to personal development. The BGH also argued that the law violates Article 20 para. 3 of the GG because of its retroactive effects and Article 3 para. 1 of the GG (Equality of Treatment) since the transitional rule of Article 229 Section 44 para. 1 of the EGBGB sets out a different treatment of domestic and foreign marriages. The Senate could not find any objective justification for this differentiation.[42] The Senate abundantly referred to opinions of legal scholars.[43] It also outlined the case law of the Constitutional Court with regard to the interpretation of fundamental rights[44] and expounded the intentions of the Federal Law to combat child marriages.[45] The legal community acclaimed the preliminary ruling as a chance to reverse "a product of hastily political activism".[46]

2. The Constitutional Court's Decision from 1 February 2024: Violation of the German Basic Law: Yet Only in a Very Restrictive Sense

The Constitutional Court's decision illustrates how law and politics are interwoven. It also shows that players of the law can participate in legal discourse and development in different positions over time: One panel member of the Constitutional Court's senate was Stephan Harbarth, a former politician and important force behind the Federal Law to combat child marriages. His participation was contested, of course. But in an order from 5 December 2019, the Constitutional Court had held that Harbarth was not disqualified from serving as a judge in the Constitutional

[42] BGH, NJOZ 2019, 43, ECLI:DE:BGH:2018:141118BXIIZB292.16.0.

[43] Just see Ibid., para. 68 regarding the violation of Article 6 para. 1 of the GG (Basic Law): "[. . .] ist nach Überzeugung des Senats mit Art. 6 Abs. 1 GG unvereinbar [. . .]".

[44] Ibid., paras. 69, 74, 77, 82.

[45] Ibid., paras. 61–62, 64.

[46] M. Löhnig, Anmerkung zu BGH, NZFam 2019, 72, at p. 73 ("Produkt unbedachten politischen Aktionismus"); see also B. Heiderhoff, "Möge diesem Gesetz kein langes Leben beschieden sein!": das Kinderehengesetz vor dem BVerfG, Verfassungsblog, 17 December 2018, https://verfassungsblog.de/moege-diesem-gesetz-kein-langes-leben-beschieden-sein-das-kinderehengesetz-vor-dem-bverfg/; J. Antomo, Verdruss mit Ansage – BGH legt dem BVerfG das Kinderehengesetz vor, LTO 21.12.2018, https://www.lto.de/recht/hintergruende/h/kinderehen-gesetz-vorlage-bgh-bverfg-harbath-befangenheit/.

proceedings — despite his deep involvement as a politician and member of parliament in the legislative process.[47]

a) The Constitutional Court's General Backing of the German Legislator's Strict Non-Recognition Approach

The decision enforced the German strict non-recognition approach as regards marriages concluded abroad when one of the spouses was under the age of 16 years at the time of marriage. It is true that the Constitutional Court held that Article 13 para. 3 no. 1 of the EGBGB violates the basic law of freedom to marriage (Article 6 para. 1 of the GG) as far as the exceptions of Article 229 Section 44 para. 4 of the EGBGB do not apply. Yet the Court's decision left ample room for the legislator to further pursue the policy of strict non-recognition. The court acknowledged that Article 6 para. 1 of the GG protects marital partnerships established outside of Germany and also covers limping marriages. Yet according to the Constitutional Court, marital partnerships concluded on the basis of foreign law are not necessarily within the scope of Article 6 para. 1 of the GG, if such partnerships are not compatible with the Basic Law's idea of marriage and family, thus violating fundamental constitutional structures. The Constitutional Court explicitly held that the legislator was acting in its capacity by setting a minimum age for the recognition of marriages concluded abroad and that the legislator could regard such marriages as void.

According to the Constitutional Court, the legislator was even pursuing legitimate objectives and Article 13 para. 3 no. 1 of the EGBGB was suitable and necessary to achieve these goals. The legitimate goals are (in the court's perspective): protection of minors and legal certainty. As regards the protection of minors, the court argued that children under the age of 16 are regularly not able to assess the consequences of entering into a marriage due to their development. For the Constitutional Court, the legislator's purpose contributes to the international outlawing of early marriages and is in line with the efforts of the United Nations to counter early marriage and forced marriage worldwide. The court invoked several legal sources of International Law (Article 16 para. 1 of the Universal Declaration of Human Rights, Article 23 no. 3 of the International Covenant on Civil and Political Rights,[48] Article 10 no. 1 of the International Covenant on Economic, Social and Cultural Rights,[49] Article 16 para. 1 and 2 of the Convention on the Elimination of All Forms of Discrimination against

[47] BVerfG, NJW 2020, 1577. See on that critically M. Klatt, Über die personelle und inhaltliche Verzahnung von Politik und Verfassungsrecht, JuWissBlog no. 3/2020, https://www.juwiss.de/3-2020; J. Antomo, Kinderehen in Karlsruhe, NJW 2023, 1474, at p. 1475; J. Basedow, FamRZ 2019, 1833, at p. 1837.

[48] "No marriage shall be entered into without the free and full consent of the intending spouses."

[49] "Marriage must be entered into with the free consent of the intending spouses."

Women[50]) and the recommendation of the UN's *Committee on the Rights of the Child* according to which a minimum age of 18 years for entering into marriage is recommended.[51] The court argued that it was legitimate in light of the constitution's decision for international cooperation, if German laws aimed to protect minors worldwide suffering under the practice of early marriage. The court held the aim of legal certainty to be equally legitimate.

According to the Constitutional Court, Article 13 para. 3 no. 1 of the EGBGB was suitable in the constitutional sense for achieving these purposes (protection of minors and legal certainty). Since the marriage is void from a German perspective, spouses under the age of 16 years could be protected from the consequences of the marriage. The non-recognition of marriage could therefore — according to the court — restore the spouse's freedom of self-determination. At the same time, the voidness of the marriage can contribute to the minor's protection of endangerments resulting from further marital cohabitation. The court brushed aside the legal practice which separates the spouses only in cases where the cohabitation endangers the best interests of the child: the court felt that it was still possible for the law to further protect the child, since the legal possibilities of guardians are enlarged.

The court did not agree that the norm is unsuitable in the constitutional sense because it abolishes sensible case-by-case examinations: It rather reasoned that standardised norms are a legitimate way to protect minors. The court also argued that the norm was not unsuitable to prevent early marriages concluded abroad in the future as regards the idea of a general prevention. The legislator's assumption that Article 13 para. 3 no. 1 of the EGBGB will raise international awareness of early marriage as a harmful practice was — according to the Constitutional Court — sufficiently based on the international legal provisions that also apply to early marriages. It remains a complete mystery, of course, which basis these provisions might provide for a highly speculative and doubtful assumption as regards possible future factual effects of Article 13 para. 3 no. 1of the EGBGB.

As regards legal certainty, the court felt that Article 13 para. 3 no. 1 of the EGBGB served that purpose, since the rule was less vague than the general *ordre public* provision. The court acknowledged that age assessment is a major practical obstacle, in particular as regards refugees. Yet despite that fact, the norm was not unsuitable with respect to the enhancement of legal certainty in the Court's

[50]"States Parties shall take all appropriate measures to eliminate discrimination against women in all matters relating to marriage and family relations and in particular shall ensure, on a basis of equality of men and women: (a) The same right to enter into marriage;

(b) The same right freely to choose a spouse and to enter into marriage only with their free and full consent."

[51]CRC, General comment No. 4: Adolescent Health and Development in the Convention on the Rights of the Child, UN Doc. CRC/GC/2003/4 (1 July 2003), para. 16 and General comment No. 20 on the implementation of the rights of the child during adolescence, UN Doc. CRC/C/GC/20 (6 December 2016), para. 40.

reasoning.[52] At the same token, according to the court, the norm was not unsuitable — despite the missing of express provisions on the legal consequences of non-recognition. The Court considered the alternative of separate judicial status proceedings in which the non-recognition (or recognition) of the foreign marriage would be assessed with effect for and against everyone.[53] Yet, according to the court, strict non-recognition without exception and individual assessment were more effective to protect the minors. The Court did not, of course, rely on any empirical evidence to support that proposition. The court also considered a rule comparable to Article 6 of the EGBGB that would abstractly specify only those constellations in which minors needed protection from the dangers of early marriage. But the court argued that it was uncertain whether or not such a rule would burden the minors less. The court also considered a rule according to which the marriage would not be void, but subject to annulment by a court decision — as is the case with marriage of spouses with the age of 16 or 17 at the time of marriage (Article 13 para. 3 no. 2 of the EGBGB). But according to the court, if the marriage was valid (even if subject to annulation), detriments for the minors could result and the aim of internationally outlawing child marriage would be less efficiently fulfilled.

b) The Two Constitutional Shortcomings of the Law According to the Constitutional Court and the Ongoing Applicability of Article 13 Para. 3 no. 1 of the EGBGB

Despite the Court's general approval of the strict non-recognition approach, it could not close its eyes to the most obvious shortcomings of the Law. Thus, the Court held Article 13 para. 3 no. 1 of the EGBGB to be not proportionate in the narrow sense, since there are no follow-up rules as regards the consequences of the invalidity and insufficient possibilities to effectively continue the marriage domestically after reaching the age of majority. The lack of rules on the consequences are particularly important in the eyes of the court in cases where the spouses had already been living together as spouses before moving to Germany.

Problems arise with respect to the marital relationship, maintenance, inheritance, divorce, marriage, parentage and paternal care (as regards children born out of the marriage).[54] This inevitably leads to difficult problems and can detriment the very persons the legislator aimed to protect. There was one notable exception to the legislator's refusal of problem solving: Section 26 para. 1 of the AsylG (Asylum Law) determines that the spouse of a minor at the time of marriage can be granted

[52] Critically on the Constitutional Court's reasoning in this respect D. Coester-Waltjen, Non-Recognition of "Child Marriages" Concluded Abroad and Constitutional Standards, IPRax 2023, 350, at p. 354.

[53] On that sensible alternative see for instance J. Antomo, ZRP 2017, 79, at p. 81.

[54] For further analysis regarding the consequences of an invalid marriage see M. Martinek (fn. 14), at pp. 186 ff.

family asylum even if the marriage is invalid under German law. With respect to maintenance law, it is particularly evident that the law significantly worsened the minor spouse's position. The Court identified an important common good that might justify the disadvantages: protection of minors. It pointed out that early marriage regularly restricts the education and economic development opportunities of the women concerned and increases the likelihood of early, frequent and high-risk pregnancies. Also, the second aim — legal certainty — was regarded as a concern of some importance. Weighing the disadvantages against the legislator's aims, the Court regarded Article 13 para. 3 no. 1 of the EGBGB as not proportionate in the narrow sense. Yet the Court also emphasised that this was not due to the abstract character of Article 13 para. 3 no. 1 of the EGBGB and the fact that it precludes a case-by-case examination. The Court explicitly confirmed that the legislator was free to create regulations concerning the protection of minors and the best interests of the child without the requirement of a case-by-case examination.[55] The Court dismissed many opinions by experts and youth councils in this respect as well as the predominating opinion in legal science.

The two shortcomings the court acknowledged as leading to the law's unconstitutionality were: There are — with the exception of family asylum — no special rules as regards the consequences of non-recognition and there is no possibility to live the marriage as a valid marriage in Germany after the age of majority. Only for these reasons, Article 13 para. 3 no. 1 of the EGBGB is not compatible with Article 6 of the GG — except as regards cases falling under Article 229 Section 44 para. 4 of the EGBGB. Yet the Court declared Article 13 para. 3 no. 1 of the EGBGB still to be applied until 30 June 2024 — since the legislator had several possibilities to restore the law's compatibility with the Basic Law.

VI. German Law Since 1 July 2024: Ongoing Symbolic Contempt of Early Marriages at the Expense of the Best Interests of the Persons Worthy of Protection

1. Overview

In May 2024, the German government (*Bundesregierung*) proposed a Draft Law as a reaction to the Constitutional Court's decision. The new rules entered into force on 1 July 2024. It has been prepared rather hastily. The law's title „Law for the Protection of Minors in Foreign Marriages"[56] is a clear misnomer.[57] The legislator

[55] See also M. Payandeh, JuS 2023, 1170, at p. 1172.

[56] Gesetz zum Schutz Minderjähriger bei Auslandsehen (Gesetzesbeschluss des Deutschen Bundestages), BT-Drucksache 20/11367.

[57] B. Heiderhoff, Männer- statt Minderjährigenschutz, Verfassungsblog, 15 September 2024, https://verfassungsblog.de/manner-statt-minderjahrigenschutz/.

aims to minimally remedy the two constitutional defects of Article 13 para. 3 no. 1 of the EGBGB according to the Constitutional Court's decision.

2. Article 13 Para. 3 EGBGB Remains Unchanged

The legislator accepted the Court's invitation for a minimal change of the law. Article 13 para. 3 no. 2 of the EGBGB remains unchanged: Where one of the spouses was 16 or 17 years old at the time of marriage, the marriage is valid, but it can be annihilated by a court decision. And crucially, also Article 13 para. 3 no. 1 of the EGBGB remains equally unchanged: A marriage is still invalid if one of the spouses was under the age of 16 at the time of marriage – without any individual assessment of the case at hand. Even if the marriage was validly concluded abroad in accordance with the applicable law, it is invalid *ex lege* in German perspective. The government emphasised the preventive policy of the law: It argues that any case-by-case solution would express less clearly the outlawing of early marriages and could be misunderstood in the sense that early marriages might be legally acceptable under certain circumstances.[58]

3. Minimal Changes

a) Maintenance Claims of the Spouse Who Was Under the Age of 16 at the Time of Marriage

According to the Constitutional Court, the law must mitigate the negative consequences of the invalidity. Firstly, in particular, maintenance claims in favour of the spouse who was a minor at the time of marriage are necessary. That major setback is tackled by the new law that introduces maintenance claims of the person who was under the age of 16 at the time of the marriage against the other spouse, Section 1305 para. 1 of the BGB (German Civil Code). The law regulates the according application of existing statutory provisions on marital and post-marital maintenance claims. The person who was under the age of 16 at the time of the marriage is not obliged to pay maintenance.

58 Draft Law for the Protection of Minors in Foreign Marriages, at p. 7 (https://www.bmj.de/SharedDocs/Downloads/DE/Gesetzgebung/RefE/RefE_Schutz_Minderjaehrige_Auslandsehen.pdf?__blob=publicationFile&v=6,).

b) The Spouses' Possibility to Marry Again on the Basis of a Self-Determined Decision

The law also aims to remedy the second constitutional *lacuna* of the law (according to the Constitutional Court): The lack of a possibility to live the marriage as a valid marriage in Germany after the minor has reached the age of maturity. According to the Constitutional Court, Article 13 para. 3 of the EGBGB violates the freedom to marry because there was no provision that enables the minor to enter into the marriage on the basis of a now self-determined decision.[59] The court explicitly added that the possibility to remarry the same partner in Germany after the age of maturity is not enough: The invalidity of the marriage (in German perspective) amounts to a serious obstacle for the freedom to marry. In particular, the spouses will not be able to obtain a „certificate of no impediment to marriage" (*Ehefähigkeitszeugnis,* Section 1309 of the BGB) in their home countries; after all, they are already validly married in the perspective of these countries. The Constitutional Court had also argued that it is problematic that the effects of the new marriage would only apply from the time of the new current marriage. This could be disadvantagous for the spouse who was minor at the time of the first marriage. And the Constitutional Court also pointed out that the need to remarry will not be readily understandable by the spouses, since they are already married under the law of their country of origin (possibly for a long time) and they might feel married in their home country. With this background, it is more than astonishing that the draft law only installs the possibility to validate the invalid marriage by marrying again — at least without having to obtain a certificate of no impediment to marriage (Section 1305 para. 3 sentence 2 of the BGB).

4. *Critique*

a) General Considerations

It is highly unfortunate that the 2024 legislature missed the opportunity to correct the 2017 law reform. There are, of course, valid concerns with respect to the compatibility of German law with European law.[60] What is more, the pre-2017 case-by-case approach allowed for sensible solutions tailored to individual cases and could accommodate the best interests of the persons involved — particularly the best

[59] BVerfG, NJW 2023, 1494, para. 125, ECLI:DE:BVerfG:2023:ls20230201.1bvl000718.

[60] See F. Schulte-Rudzio (fn. 31), at pp. 365–408; Deutscher Rat für IPR (German Council for Private International Law), Stellungnahme zum Referentenentwurf eines Gesetzes zum Schutze Minderjähriger bei Auslandsehen, 22 April 2024, at pp. 23, 27, https://www.bmj.de/SharedDocs/Downloads/DE/Gesetzgebung/Stellungnahmen/2024/0422_Schutz_Minderjaehriger_Auslandsehen_Dt-Rat-IPR.pdf?__blob=publicationFile&v=3.

interests of the spouse who was minor at the time of marriage.[61] This approach aligned well with the obligation stemming from Article 12 of the CRC[62] to examine the individual maturity and autonomy of children concerned.[63] It is hardly convincing that German law now relies on the age at the time of marriage as decisive key criterion for recognition.[64] The age at the time of marriage should, of course, be decisive for the question of whether or not persons should be able to legally marry. But once the marriage has been concluded and persons have factually lived the marriage — possibly for several years – , the age at the time of marriage becomes increasingly less relevant over time. Classifying a marriage as invalid or valid (or as annullable) solely relying on the fact whether the person was 15 or 16 at the time of marriage after the couple has already been living as a married couple for a while seems arbitrary.[65] The best interests of the spouse who was minor at the time of marriage can only be assessed sensibly with reference to the age and situation at the time of recognition. Once the marriage has been concluded and lived as matters of fact, these facts cannot miraculously be conjured away.[66]

b) Outlawing Early Marriages: Symbolism Rather Than Combatting Early Marriages

The government argues that the law serves the best interests of the minor. Yet it does so at best in a very strange and abstract sense: The new law — just like the law reform 2017 and the Constitutional Court's reasoning — rests on an abstract hope as regards factual developments in the future: It is the hope that non-recognition of early marriages in Germany as a clear signpost of outlawing early marriage will lead to future reduction of early marriages worldwide, thereby protecting future children abroad from early marriage. It may seem honourable that players of the law want to take a firm stand against early and forced marriage. Yet the hope that non-recognition in Germany will have any effect whatsoever on the practice of

[61] See N. Dethloff, International Journal of Law, Policy and The Family, 2018, vol. 32, 302, at p. 309 (underlining the importance to keep fighting against forced marriages at the same time); Deutscher Rat für IPR (fn. 60), at p. 31.

[62] UN 1989 Convention on the Rights of the Child (CRC).

[63] Such an obligation can also be derived from Article 8 of the Human Rights Convention (Convention for the Protection of Human Rights and Fundamental Freedoms) or Article 12 para. 2 of the Geneva Refugee Convention (1951 Geneva Convention relating to the Status of Refugees); see N. Yassari/R. Michaels, In: Yassari/Michaels (fn. 1), at p. 68.

[64] Deutscher Rat für IPR (fn. 60), at p. 6.

[65] Deutscher Rat für IPR (fn. 60), at p. 6.

[66] Even other European countries that decided on the non-recognition approach at least implemented rules to prohibit following problems regarding children of the spouses, see N. Yassari/R. Michaels, In: Yassari/Michaels (fn. 1), at p. 82 with further references and at p. 84.

early marriages in other countries far away from Germany seems to be an illusion.[67] There are many cultural, economic, religious and societal reasons why early marriages take place.[68] Germany's policy of non-recognition will hardly be known in the relevant countries and, even if it were, that knowledge would not change the practice of early marriage. Of course, this is also a factual assumption and, for lack of sufficient statistical data, the reader may decide which assumption seems more likely to her.[69] What remains as the teleological foundation of German law seems to be a mere display of symbolism: the outlawing of a practice abroad that conflicts with European or German values. Such symbolic demarcation may have its place in the realm of politics, yet it is highly problematic in the realm of law. The price for this symbolism is paid by the individuals who were victims of the practices the symbolism aims to reject.[70]

c) Outlawing Early Marriages: Injustice Towards Those in Need of Protection

Even if we shared the legislator's hope, non-recognition as a signpost of outlawing early marriages comes at a very high price: such outlawing is unjust with respect to the persons worthy of protection. The law manifestly worsens the legal situation and violates the interests of the persons who were minor at the time of marriage.[71] Such harm is particularly significant in the international context and with regard to the typical case of younger women married to older men: Young women who have been abandoned will often worsen their social status and not be able to marry again; they may also be forced to give up their children already born out of the (not recognised) marriage.[72] The draft does not regulate any advisory or informatory support for the spouse, which is harsh as regards the massive consequences of non-recognition.[73]

---

[67] See as well M. Coester, FamRZ 2017, 77, at p. 79 and see the feedback received for the report of the federal ministry of justice concerning the law from 2017, Bundesministerium der Justiz, Evaluierung des Gesetzes zur Bekämpfung von Kinderehen, at p. 14, https://www.bmj.de/SharedDocs/Downloads/DE/Gesetzgebung/Evaluierung/Evaluierung_Gesetz_Kinderehen_Gesamtbericht.pdf?__blob=publicationFile&v=3.

[68] See N. Yassari/R. Michaels, In: Yassari/Michaels (fn. 1), at pp. 23-36 for further analysis.

[69] See also the report of the Bundesministerium der Justiz (fn. 67), at p. 14; in the Netherlands it was found that European laws regarding early marriages are mostly unknown to foreigners, Rutten / Smits van Waesberghe et al., Verboden huwelijken (No. 130) 133, at p. 153.

[70] See also the experiences in other countries such as the Netherlands or Denmark, see Rutten / Smits van Waesberghe et al., Verboden huwelijken (No. 130), 132, at p. 177; Røde Kors, Anmodning om dispensationsadgang for adskillelse af asylansøger – par, hvor den ene ægtefælle er mindreårig og parret har børn (3 March 2016), www.ft.dk/samling/20151/almdel/uui/spm/694/svar/1333857/1648844.pdf.

[71] C. Budzikiewicz/B. Heiderhoff, Das Gesetz zum Schutz Minderjähriger bei Auslandsehen - Ergänzungen zur Stellungnahme zum Referentenentwurf des Bundesministeriums der Justiz aufgrund des Regierungsentwurfes v. 14. 5. 2024, FamRZ 2024, 918, at p. 919.

[72] Deutscher Rat für IPR (fn. 60), at p. 11.

[73] See Deutsches Institut für Jugendhilfe und Familienrecht e.V. (DIJuF), Hinweise zum Referentenentwurf des Bundesministeriums der Justiz vom 19. April 2024, at p. 2.

Maintenance claims according to German substantive law, Section 1305 para. 2 of the BGB may somewhat soften the negative effects on the (then) minor spouse. In that respect, the new law improves upon the situation.[74] Yet clearly, material maintenance claims are not enough. Firstly, it is by no means certain that German maintenance law will be the applicable substantive law:[75] Conflict of laws rules may in certain instances lead to the application of foreign substantial maintenance law, in particular in cases where minors have their habitual residence abroad (Article 3 lit. a of the Maintenance Regulation[76]). The foreign maintenance law might not provide for sufficient maintenance claims, since the preliminary requirement of a valid marriage is to be determined according to German private international law — leading to a negative answer. Private international law would be challenged and could at best apply justice-related instruments in order to solve these situations. These instruments (such as "*Normenmangel*" [gap in norms]) are inherently uncertain in their application. Furthermore, there are disadvantages for the younger spouse beyond maintenance:[77] She has no legal right to inheritance, and no right to share in the assets of the deceased under inheritance law. In the event of separation, she has no rights to the household items and the home (cf. Sections 1361a f. of the BGB). The remedy of marriage envisaged by the law of 2024 is equally problematic. Often, the spouses will feel legally married — which they are in their home country's perspective.[78] It is not convincing that implied confirmation is not considered enough.[79] Such implied confirmation of persons who have already reached maturity should in principle be understood as a free expression of self-determination. The denial of implied confirmation is paternalistic since the spouses have, after all, reached the age of maturity.[80] Furthermore, the couple will often not be aware that they need to marry again for their marriage to become valid in German perspective.[81] Even in cases where the couple does know that Germany does not accept their marriage, a new marriage will often not materialise. That is particularly true in cases

---

[74] See Deutsches Institut für Jugendhilfe und Familienrecht e.V. (fn. 73), at p. 3.

[75] See also Deutscher Rat für IPR (fn. 60), at pp. 22 f.

[76] Council Regulation (EC) No 4/2009 of 18 December 2008 on jurisdiction, applicable law, recognition and enforcement of decisions and cooperation in matters relating to maintenance obligations (Maintenance Regulation).

[77] For details see Deutscher Rat für IPR (fn. 60), at pp. 17 and 23–27.

[78] See also L. Möller/N. Yassari, KJ 2017, 269, at pp. 282 ff.; D. Coester-Waltjen, IPRax 2023, 350, at p. 358.

[79] Deutscher Rat für IPR (fn. 60), at p.14.

[80] Deutscher Rat für IPR (fn. 60), at p. 14; D. Coester-Waltjen, Stellungnahme der wissenschaftlichen Vereinigung für Familienrecht zum Referentenentwurf des Bundesministeriums der Justiz, at p. 11, https://www.bmj.de/SharedDocs/Downloads/DE/Gesetzgebung/Stellungnahmen/2024/0421_Schutz_Minderjaehriger_Auslandsehen_wiss-V-Familienrecht.pdf?__blob=publicationFile&v=2.

[81] D. Coester-Waltjen, IPRax 2023, 350, at p. 358.

where the spouse who was minor at the time of (first) marriage wants to marry in order to enjoy the legal benefits of marriage and where marriage is objectively advantageous for her. The other spouse may simply deny to marry again — feeling or knowing that the marriage would benefit his spouse while at the same time being disadvantageous for himself. This shows, how non-recognition significantly improves the legal position of the older spouse concerned.[82] The older spouse is free to leave his younger partner and marry another person without having to divorce his spouse first.[83] Once a new marriage has been effectuated, remarrying the "old" spouse to validate the invalid underage marriage is not possible anymore. Thus, the new law allows the older spouse to grant or deprive the younger partner of the advantages of an effective marriage. He can also keep the common marital home in the case of separation, and he is not automatically the legal father of a child born out of the partnership — which is convenient in order to avoid maintenance claims of the child.

d) Legal Uncertainty

Non-recognition also creates legal uncertainty at the cost of the spouses and their children:[84] Often, the spouses are not aware that their marriage is not recognised. The law offers no clear or convincing solutions as regards parentage and paternal care: Children born out of the (invalid) marriage will regularly be without a father. Parentage through marriage cannot be established. Parentage through recognition is unlikely since the man already assumes to be the father as a consequence of a valid marriage. Where the father does indeed know that his marriage is not recognised in Germany, he might simply opt against marrying again in order to avoid maintenance claims. His paternal pride might be satisfied sufficiently by the knowledge that his paternity is beyond doubt in the perspective of the country of marriage. Sometimes there might even be no legal custodian of the child at all, in particular where the mother is still minor.[85] At the same time, non-recognition does not overcome the difficulties in finding out at what age the marriage was concluded.[86]

[82] B. Heiderhoff, Verfassungsblog (fn. 57); Deutscher Rat für IPR (fn. 60), at p. 15.

[83] Some fear this might even encourage the older spouse to marry another person for residency status purposes, see N. Yassari/R. Michaels, In: Yassari/Michaels (fn. 1), at p. 90; M. Bogdan, Some Critical Comments on the New Swedish Rules on Non-recognition of Foreign Child Marriages, JPIL 2019, 247, at p. 252; C. v. Bar / P. Mankowski, Internationales Privatrecht Band II: Besonderer Teil, 2nd ed. 2019, Section 4 para. 87; R. Hüßtege, FamRZ 2017, 1374, at p. 1377; D. Coester-Waltjen, IPRax 2017, 429, at p. 435.

[84] D. Coester-Waltjen, IPRax 2023, 350, at p. 358.

[85] B. Heiderhoff, Verfassungsblog (fn. 57).

[86] N. Yassari/R. Michaels, In: Yassari/Michaels (fn. 1), at p. 76.

e) Alternative Solutions Respecting Justice and the Best Interests of the Persons Worthy of Protection

Since the new law will undergo evaluation in three years, and due to the chance of another constitutional review, there remains hope for the law's future evolution for the better. History, foreign experiences and scientists have developed alternative solutions that respect the best interests of the child, enable just solutions and do not resort to symbolic politics at the expense of the most vulnerable persons.[87] Some authors have suggested a "partial invalidity"-approach.[88] The idea of that approach is that the invalidity of the marriage is only provided to the extent that it favours the minor. The adult spouse would remain fully responsible, while the spouse who was underage at the time of the marriage would not suffer any detriment, but merely reap the advantages as a result of the marriage. Second, one might regard marriages where one of the spouses was under the age of 16 at the time of marriage as valid, but subject to annulment — as it is the case for early marriages of 16 and 17 years old spouses.[89] This solution would increase legal certainty and enable courts to safeguard the best interests of the protectworthy persons.[90] A third way consists in the return to the law's status quo ante 2017. This would enable courts to decide individual cases on the basis of a careful analysis of the individual circumstances and to deliver sensible and just solutions.[91] Contrary to public and political reception, the case law and practice reports never supported the hypothesis that the status quo ante 2017 promoted early marriages or produced unjust or unacceptable outcomes.[92]

[87] M. Coester, FamRZ 2017, 77, at p. 80; L. Möller/N. Yassari, KJ 2017, 269; F. Schulte-Rudzio (fn. 31), at p. 419; B. Heiderhoff, IPRax 2017, 160, at p. 161; M. Martinek (fn. 14), at p. 377; P. Reuß, FamRZ 2019, 1; B. Gausing/C. Wittebol, Die Wirksamkeit von im Ausland geschlossenen Minderjährigenehen, DÖV 2018, 41; N. Dethloff, International Journal of Law, Policy and The Family, 2018, vol. 32, 302; C. Hornung (fn. 40), at pp. 275 ff.

[88] B. Heiderhoff, Verfassungsblog (fn. 57); Deutscher Rat für IPR (fn. 60), at p. 29 f.; K. Duden, Zur Unwirksamkeit der Frühehe in Deutschland. Differenzierte Anwendung des Art. 13 Abs. 3 Nr. 1 of the EGBGB, In: Yassari/Michaels (fn. 1), at pp. 629 ff.

[89] F. Schulte-Rudzio (fn. 31), at p.419; D. Coester-Waltjen, IPRax 2023, 350, at pp. 358 ff.; C. Hornung (fn. 40), at pp. 268 ff.; M. Coester, FamRZ 2017, 77, at p. 80.

[90] See J. Antomo, ZRP 2017, 79, at p. 81.

[91] M. Coester, FamRZ 2017, 77, at p. 80; L. Möller/N. Yassari, KJ 2017, 269, at pp. 282 ff.; A. Dutta, Anmerkung zu BGH 14 November 2018, XII ZB 292/16, FamRZ 2019, 189; P. Reuß, FamRZ 2019, 1, at pp. 9 ff.; for a differing view see M. Weller/C. Thomale/I. Hategan/J. Werner, Das Gesetz zur Bekämpfung von Kinderehen, FamRZ 2018, 1289, at p. 1294, but see also A. Erbarth, Unwirksamkeit einer Minderjährigenehe, FamRB 2018, 338, at p. 340; A. Dutta, Anmerkung zu AG Kassel 7 March 2018, 524 F 3451/17 E1, FamRZ 2018, 1150, at p. 1151.

[92] Deutscher Rat für IPR (fn. 60), at p. 28.

VII. Final Remarks

The positive law is in a pitiful state in Germany since 2017. The political debate and the law's ressort to a merely symbolic outlawing of early marriages abroad have significantly worsened the position of the persons worthy of protection. The new law as of 1 July 2024 does not significantly improve upon the status quo since 2017. The German Constitutional Court as well as the legislator failed to fully appreciate the difference between early marriages and forced marriages.[93] Too many players of the law have resorted to political symbolism rather than pragmatic problem solving. Neither the Constitutional Court's decision nor the legislator's actions managed to put rationality and justice at the center of the discourse. The new law reform achieves only little improvement with respect to maintenance claims. Yet, neither does it provide for information or counseling of the protectworthy persons involved nor does it install individual procedures for checking the actual needs of the individuals who need protection. The law's development bitterly illustrates the potential detrimental power of symbolic law making. This ongoing development is interesting in the perspective of Jacques Rancière's idea of the "political". In his thoughts on social order, Rancière focuses on issues of visibility of subjects and "sayability" of ideas. From his point of view, the crucial question of "the *political*" is *who* is even capable and able to participate in discourses.[94] The articulations of those excluded from the political domain may be perceived as groans or cries, but constitute nothing more than "incomprehensible noise" (*das Unvernehmen – la mésentente*).[95] German Law increasingly excludes the persons concerned from the discourse — in particular, young woman who were under the age of 16 at the time of marriage: Their interests are neglected as well as the interest of the children born out of the marriages.[96] The advocacy of their interests and moral values is rather suppressed than made perceptible in public discourse. One very likely effect of the law reform is that early marriages will remain even more in the dark: factually lived but not in view of society and without the legal protective shield that marriage would provide in particular for the factually weaker spouse — in many cases young women. Uncomfortable court decisions which would transport the actual needs and interests of the persons to the public discourse — such as the OLG Bamberg's 2017 decision — are becoming less likely while politicians may content themselves with the cozy feeling of having demonstrated the moral superiority of German Law.

---

[93] Differentiating between the two: Deutscher Rat für IPR (fn. 60), at p. 6.

[94] See C. Hornung (fn. 40), at p. 301.

[95] J. Rancière, Ten Theses on Politics, Thesis no. 8, English translation by Bowlby and Panagia, In: Theory & Event 2001, vol. 5 issue 3; S. Krasmann, In: v. Bröckling/Feustel (eds), Das Politische denken - Zeitgenössische Positionen, 3rd ed. 2012, 77, at p. 78 ff. with further references.

[96] C. Hornung (fn. 40), at p. 271.

Early Marriages in Austria: Private International Law and Ordre Public Assessment

Martina Melcher

I. Introduction

As an immigration country, Austria hosts a rising number of refugees and other people with foreign nationalities. The determination of their marital status often requires the application of foreign law. In this context, the Austrian authorities must also deal with complex questions regarding early marriages.[1] An "early marriage" involves at least one spouse who has not yet turned 18 at the date of marriage.[2] Often, also the term 'child marriage' is used. Yet the term "child marriage" is problematic:[3] it suggests that the spouses involved are vulnerable and unable to understand the implications of marriage. But this is not necessarily the case, especially with 16- or 17-years old partners. At the same time, the term "child marriage" evokes images of forced marriages where the younger spouse is forced into the marriage without any autonomy. Of course, early marriages may involve coercion,

[1] A statistical survey regarding the number of early marriages in Austria does not exist. See the request of parliamentary delegates from 26 March 2021, 1460/A(E) XXVII. GP (legislative period), and from 29 June 2023, 15441/J XXVII. GP. However, recently a study regarding forced marriages involving minors and young adults has been published: B. Haller/V. Eberhardt/A.Hasenauer, Zwangsheirat in Österreich (2023), edited by Österreichischer Integrationsfonds, available at: https://www.integrationsfonds.at/fileadmin/user_upload/OEIF-Forschungsbericht-Zwangsheirat.pdf.

[2] See also Highest Administrative Court (VwGH) 3 July 2020, Ra 2020/14/0006, ECLI:AT:VWGH:2020:RA2020140006.L00.

[3] See N. Yassari/R. Michaels, Einleitung, in: N. Yassari/R. Michaels, Die Frühehe im Recht, 2021, 1, 10 et seq.; D. Coester-Waltjen, IPRax 2017, 429, at p. 429; L. Möller/N. Yassari, KJ 2017, 269, at p. 269 et seq.

M. Melcher (✉)
Institute for Private Law, Foreign and International Private Law, University of Graz, Graz, Austria
e-mail: martina.melcher@uni-graz.at

S. Arnold, B. Heiderhoff (eds.), *Children in Migration and International Family Law*, https://doi.org/10.1007/978-3-031-71598-3_11

yet not every early marriage is a forced marriage at the same time. The terms 'minor marriage' or 'marriage of minors' avoid these problems. Still, "early marriage" seems preferable, since the age of majority varies globally.[4]

A lower or no minimum age for marriage and/or generous exceptions in the foreigners' countries of origin[5] may allow them to get married already at a very young age. Before Austrian authorities the (preliminary) question of a valid marriage arises, for example, with regard to filiation and parental responsibilities, maintenance and divorce, succession or proceedings regarding the legal representation of minors. Most often, however, the question comes up in the context of family reunification and asylum proceedings.[6] As a family member, a spouse may apply for the issue of a visa pursuant to Section 26 of the FPG (Immigration Police Act) and Section 35 of the AsylG 2005 (Asylum Law Act) to follow their husband or wife, who is a recognised refugee and entitled to asylum in Austria. If both spouses are already in Austria, according to Section 34 of the AsylG 2005 a request to be granted asylum based on the asylum decision regarding their spouse must be granted under certain conditions. If the spouses got married while at least one of them was still a minor, the validity and legal existence of the marriage is often questioned.

In most cases an early marriage is already "imported" from abroad (i.e. the marriage took place in another country and both or at least one spouse takes up residence in Austria). However, this issue may also come up with a view to marriages of foreign nationals in Austria.

Whether such early marriages are to be regarded as valid in Austria depends on two aspects[7]: First, the marriage must have been concluded in accordance with the applicable law. In this regard, a private international law assessment in accordance with Sections 16 and 17 of the IPRG (Private International Law Act) is required to determine the applicable (substantive) law (see section II. below). Second, if the marriage is governed by foreign substantive law, its application need not violate the Austrian *ordre public* (see section III. below).

---

[4] M. Makowsky, RabelsZ 2019, 577, at p. 578.

[5] For a comparative overview see P. Mankowski, In: Staudinger, BGB, 2011, Art 13 of the EGBGB paras. 196–201.

[6] As regards residence permits, Section 46 and Section 2 para. 1 no. 9 of the NAG (Settlement and Residence Act) requires spouses to be at least 21 years old to benefit from the rules on family reunion.

[7] For this two-step assessment see also VwGH 10 June 2021, Ro 2021/18/0001, ECLI:AT:VWGH:2021:RO2021180001.J00.

II. Determination of the Applicable Substantive Law

1. Recognition of Judgments, Private International Law and Mere Acceptance

In general, the status of a person may be the result of a judicial (or administrative) decision or created by the applicable substantive law without authoritative interference. In the first case (e.g. the marital status is based on a divorce decree), the laws on procedural recognition apply (e.g. Article 21 of the Brussels IIbis Regulation[8] or Article 30 of the Brussels IIter Regulation[9]; Sections 97–100 of the AußStrG (Non-Contentious Proceedings Act). As a rule, however, a marriage is not based on a court decision; at most, such recognition would only be possible if there is a foreign declaratory judgment on the existence of a marriage.[10]

If it is a question of status that is not based on a court decision, private international law rules apply. The validity of the status is therefore determined by the applicable law in accordance with the relevant private international law rules, which — in case of a marriage — are Sections 16 and 17 of the IPRG (see subsection 2).

The recognition of the validity of a status acquired abroad *without* recourse to the relevant domestic reference rules (Verweisungsnormen), i.e. the acceptance of status, is being discussed *de lege ferenda*,[11] but not yet part of Austrian (domestic) private international law rules. However, an EU law shaped practice of this method can already be found regarding the name of a person and the status of a company.[12] Similarly, Article 12 para. 2 of the Geneva Refugee Convention[13] and Article

---

[8]Regulation (EC) 2201/2003 of 27 November 2003 concerning jurisdiction and the recognition and enforcement of judgments in matrimonial matters and the matters of parental responsibility.

[9]Council Regulation (EU) 2019/1111 of 25 June 2019 on jurisdiction, the recognition and enforcement of decisions in matrimonial matters and the matters of parental responsibility, and on international child abduction (recast).

[10]Cf. however the recent tendency in the Austrian judiciary to recognise the filiation status that has been established abroad and put down in a foreign birth certificate: BG (district court) NN (Tyrol), 21 November 2019, 2 FAM 54/19z. The judgment itself was not published, but a summary can be found in M. Nademleinsky, Anerkennung ukrainischer Leihmutterschaft, EF-Z 2020, at pp. 45 ff. For more details see F. Heindler/M. Melcher, Recognition of a status acquired abroad: Austria, CDT 2022, 1148, at pp. 1150 ff.

[11]See, for example, B. Lurger, Der freie Verkehr von öffentlichen Urkunden im europäischen kollisionsrechtlichen System, In: FS Posch, 2011, 409, at p. 418; R. Wagner, Anerkennung im Ausland begründeter Statusverhältnisse – neue Wege? StAZ 2012, 133.

[12]B. Lurger/M. Melcher, Handbuch Internationales Privatrecht, 2nd ed. 2021, paras. 8/8 ff.; F. Heindler/M. Melcher, CDT 2022, 1148, at pp. 1160 ff.

[13]Convention Relating to the Status of Refugees of 28 July 1951. See also F. Jault-Seseke, Minderjährigenehe und IPRG, In: Heindler (ed), Festschrift 40 Jahre IPRG, 2020, 233, at p. 237.

12 para. 2 of the Status of Stateless Persons Convention[14] appear to be methodologically based on the mere acceptance of the status.

2. *Section 17 of the IPRG as a Central Legal Rule*

a) Age as Part of the Substantive Marriage Requirements

To determine the law applicable to a marriage with a cross-border element, Sections 16 and 17 of the IPRG apply. Section 16 of the IPRG governs the form of the act of marriage („gesamter äußerer Ablauf des Eheschließungsaktes") including the consequences of a breach and the possibility of a remedy.[15] These issues usually do not provide any particular difficulties with regard to early marriages.

In contrast, Section 17 of the IPRG governs the substantive marriage requirements, such as certain consent requirements[16] (e.g. admissibility of a proxy, consent of the legal representative) and impediments to marriage. Also, the permissible age of each fiancé[17] (marriageability) is one of the substantive requirements that is determined in accordance with Section 17 of the IPRG, irrespective of whether the marriage is concluded in Austria or abroad. It is also of no relevance if the age of the fiancé(e)s is part of the broader concept of the capacity to marry or an individual requirement in the applicable substantive law.

b) Personal Statute as Connecting Factor

Whether the fiancé(e)s fulfil(ed) the substantive requirements for marriage is to be assessed separately for each of them in accordance with their "personal statute" (Personalstatut) at the time of the marriage.[18]

Generally, the personal statute of a person is the law of the nationality of this person according to Section 9 para. 1 of the IPRG.[19] For example, the personal statute of an Austrian is Austrian (substantive) law. As Section 9 para. 1 of the IPRG contains a global reference (Gesamtverweisung, as stipulated in Section 5 of the IPRG), references from a foreign law back to Austrian (substantive) law or forward to another legal system must be respected.

---

[14] Convention Relating to the Status of Stateless Persons of 28 July 1954.

[15] M. Neumayr in KBB, 7th ed. 2023, Section 16 of the IPRG para. 3; B. Verschraegen, In: Rummel/Lukas/Geroldinger (eds), ABGB, 4th ed. 2023, Section 16 of the IPRG paras. 2 ff.

[16] OGH (Supreme Court) 29 October 1998, 2 Ob 267/98y, ECLI:AT:OGH0002:1998:0020OB00267.98Y.1029.000.

[17] OGH 10 April 1997, 6 Ob 2275/96v, ECLI:AT:OGH0002:1997:E45962.

[18] In detail: B. Lurger/M. Melcher (fn. 12), paras. 2/61 ff.

[19] For a comprehensive discussion of Section 9 of the IPRG see K. Huber, In: Laimer (ed), ABGB Praxiskommentar, 2023, Section 9 of the IPRG.

In case of multiple nationalities, the "effective" nationality, which is the one with the strongest connection to the person, counts. Various factors can be used to determine the effective nationality, such as the place of (habitual) residence, social and economic relationships, or mother tongue.[20] For example, if a person with Greek and German nationality was born in Greece but lived her whole life in Germany, German law qualifies as her personal statute. Pursuant to Section 9 para. 1 sentence 2 of the IPRG, the Austrian nationality is always decisive for Austrians with multiple nationalities, irrespective of the effective nationality.

Due to the primacy of international Conventions (Section 53 of the IPRG), the personal status of refugees governed by the Geneva Refugee Convention must be assessed in accordance with Article 12 of the Geneva Refugee Convention.[21] Article 12 para. 1 of the Geneva Refugee Convention applies if their personal status is to be determined in view of a current event, such as an upcoming marriage as a refugee. In this case, the substantive law at their domicile or, in the absence of such, at their current residence is applicable.[22] "Rights previously acquired by a refugee and dependent on personal status, more particularly rights attaching to marriage, shall be respected" pursuant to Article 12 para. 2 of the Geneva Refugee Convention. A marriage validly concluded in the country of origin must therefore deemed to be effective also from an Austrian perspective. However, this "acceptance" is subject to a public policy exception.[23] For refugees who are not refugees governed by the Geneva Refugee Convention and beneficiaries of subsidiary protection,[24] the law of the country of residence and, subsidiarily, the law of the habitual residence, including any referrals and further referrals shall apply as the personal statute (Section 9 para. 3 of the IPRG).

c) Individual Assessment of Each Personal Status

The compliance with the personal statute must be checked for each of the fiancé(e)s/spouses individually. Hence, different substantive rules may apply to the spouses. It

---

[20] B. Verschraegen, In: Rummel/Lukas/Geroldinger (fn. 15), Section 9 of the IPRG para. 56.

[21] Similarly R. Lukits, Mehrehen und Familiennachzug, iFamZ 2017, 261, at p. 261; P. Mankowski, Die Reaktion des Internationalen Privatrechts auf neue Erscheinungsformen der Migration, IPRax 2017, 40, at p. 41. Article 12 of the Status of Stateless Persons Convention is modelled after Article 12 of the Geneva Refugee Convention. The assessment of the personal status of stateless persons is therefore based on similar rules. Subsidiarily, Section 9 para. 2 of the IPRG applies and points to the law at the habitual place of residence. In the case of (simple) residence only, the strongest connection must be determined in accordance with Section 1 para. 1 of the IPRG (see M. Neumayr, In: KBB (fn. 15), Section 9 of the IPRG para. 3).

[22] See also OGH 26 June 2018, 10 Ob 40/18g, ECLI:AT:OGH0002:2019:E122462.

[23] R. Lukits, iFamZ 2017, 261, at p. 262 with further references.

[24] See thereto Directive 2011/95/EU of 13 December 2011 on standards for the qualification of third-country nationals or stateless persons as beneficiaries of international protection, for a uniform status for refugees or for persons eligible for subsidiary protection, and for the content of the protection granted (recast).

is possible, that one may be allowed to marry at the age of 15 whereas the other must be at least 21 years old.

The individual assessment of each personal statute pursuant to Section 17 para. 1 of the IPRG means that a materially valid marriage comes into being only if both fiancées cumulatively fulfil the respective marriage requirements of their own personal statute. The marriage of an Austrian citizen concluded before the age of 16 can be rendered void in accordance with Sections 1, 22 of the EheG (Marriage Act) — even if it was validly concluded abroad in accordance with the *lex loci*. Conversely, a marriage concluded abroad with an Austrian of legal age is valid from an Austrian perspective, even if the latter would not yet be capable of marriage according to the laws at the place of marriage or the personal statute of the other fiancée[25] or if the other spouse would not be capable of marriage if Austrian law were applicable. The capacity to marry is usually qualified as a unilateral impediment to marriage.[26]

It also follows from Section 17 para. 1 of the IPRG that the Austrian minimum age for marriage does not apply in the case of (purely) foreign personal statutes of the fiancé(e)s. It is sufficient that the capacity to marry is given in accordance with the foreign personal statutes — even if the marriage takes place in Austria.

d) Legal Consequences

The law applicable according to Section 17 para. 1 of the IPRG also determines the legal consequences of any violation of the substantive marriage requirements, including, but not limited to voidability and the right to contest.[27] If only the personal statute of one spouse has been violated, the legal consequence of the violation is determined by that personal statute. If — in case of different nationalities — both personal statutes have been violated, the legal consequences provided for by each personal statute have to be compared. Generally, the principle of the stricter law applies, i.e. the more unfavourable effect on marriage is decisive.[28] If the personal statute of one spouse requires the nullity of the marriage (*ex tunc* effect) and the other personal statute only provides for the marriage to be repealed (*ex nunc* effect), the first prevails and the marriage must be declared null and void.

---

[25] OGH 10 April 1997, 6 Ob 2275/96v, ECLI:AT:OGH0002:1997:E45962.

[26] M. Nademleinsky/M. Neumayr, Internationales Familienrecht, 3rd ed. 2022, para. 2.14 and para. 2.19.

[27] RIS-Justiz RS0077152, ECLI:AT:OGH0002:1994:RS007715; RIS-Justiz RS0077156, ECLI:AT:OGH0002:1989:RS0077156; M. Nademleinsky/M. Neumayr (fn. 26), para. 2.29.

[28] RIS-Justiz RS0077156, ECLI:AT:OGH0002:1989:RS0077156; M. Neumayr, In: KBB (fn. 15), Section 17 of the IPRG para. 1.

III. Early Marriage as a Violation of the Austrian *Ordre Public*?

1. The Austrian Ordre Public *Rule*

The Austrian *ordre public* is stipulated in Section 6 of the IPRG:[29] "A provision of foreign law shall not be applied when its application would lead to a result irreconcilable with the basic tenets of the Austrian legal order. In its place, if necessary, the corresponding provision of Austrian law shall apply."[30]

It should be applied in the most restrictive way only.[31] References to the Austrian *ordre public* must be an exception reserved for insupportable violations of fundamental values. In principle, foreign law remains applicable even if it deviates from Austrian substantive law to some extent. Moreover, not foreign law as such, but rather its *application* in the individual situation must result in an insupportable violation of fundamental values and principles at the time of the decision. The specific extent of the required connection to Austria also has an impact on the balancing to be carried out as part of the public policy test: The greater the extent and significance of the domestic connection, the more likely results deviating from domestic law will be rejected (spatial relativity).[32] In other words, the intensity of the connection to Austria and the intensity of the violation of fundamental values form a "flexible system" (bewegliches System).[33]

2. Assessment and Balancing of Values

The prohibition of early marriage (or "child marriage" as it is called by the courts) is one of the fundamental values of the Austrian legal system.[34] However, this does not mean that all marriages in which at least one spouse is not yet 18 years old violate the Austrian *ordre public* as stipulated in Section 6 of the IPRG.

As regards marriages involving spouses who are or have been 16 years or older at the time of the marriage, an exception in Austrian substantive law prevents a

---

[29] For a thorough overview in English see B. Verschraegen/F. Heindler, Austria, In: Meyer (ed), Public Policy and Private International Law, 2022, at pp. 48 ff.

[30] Translation by E. Palmer, The Austrian Codification of Conflicts Law, The American Journal of Comparative Law 1980, 197, at p. 223.

[31] See also B. Verschraegen/F. Heindler, In: Meyer (fn. 29), 3-007.

[32] OGH 12 October 2011, 3 Ob 186/11s, ECLI:AT:OGH0002:2011:0030OB00186.11S.1012.000; and OGH 29 January 2019, 2 Ob 170/18s, ECLI:AT:OGH0002:2021:E124086.

[33] OGH 29 January 2019, 2 Ob 170/18s, ECLI:AT:OGH0002:2021:E124086.

[34] OGH 13 September 2000, 4 Ob 199/00v, ECLI:AT:OGH0002:2000:E59176; B. Verschraegen, In: Rummel/Lukas/Geroldinger (fn. 15), Section 6 of the IPRG para. 13.

successful reference to the *ordre public*.[35] Pursuant to Section 1 para. 1 of the EheG, men and women are generally deemed capable of marriage by the law only if they are at least 18 years old and have sufficient decision-making capacity in accordance with Section 24 para. 2 of the ABGB (Austrian Civil Code).[36] Exceptionally however, a person may apply to be declared capable of marriage from the age of 16 (see Section 1 para. 2 of the EheG).[37] It must therefore be assumed that any marriage involving one person who was only 16 years old at the time of the marriage is not — in general — contrary to the Austrian *ordre public* as (even) Austrian law exceptionally allows 16-year-olds to get married. Although Austrian substantive law does not allow *two* minors to marry each other, given that at least one spouse must be an adult, it may still be assumed that such a marriage would not violate the Austrian *ordre public* as 16-year-olds may be declared to be capable of marriage in principle. In August 2024, the then-government of Austria announced a draft legislation which would allow only persons who are at least 18 years old (without exceptions) to get married.[38] However, to this author's knowledge, no such legislation has been passed in August-October 2024; probably due to the national election which took place at the end of September 2024.

If one or both of the spouses are younger than 16 years at the time of the conclusion of the marriage, a violation of the Austrian *ordre public* is more likely, but still cannot automatically be assumed.[39] The fact that a foreign law allows marriages at an earlier age than Austrian substantive law is not sufficient *per se* to set such a marriage aside. Other aspects must be considered during an assessment, in particular the preservation of the free will of the minor(s) including the lack of pressure or constraint and the protection from exploitation, their individual age and maturity, the intensity of the connection to Austria and, in case of an already existing marriage, its shape, intensity and duration.[40]

In this respect, firstly, it should be highlighted that the prohibition of early marriage (also) serves to ensure the free (marriage) will of each fiancé(e).[41] Hence, the actual preservation of the free will of the fiancé(es) regarding the conclusion of

---

[35] See already M. Melcher, (Un-)Wirksamkeit von Kinderehen in Österreich, EF-Z 2018, 104, at p. 105.

[36] As amended by the second ErwSchG (Adult Protection Act). If a marriage has been concluded before 1 July 2018, Sections 1–3 of the EheG apply in their prior version (i.e. without the latest amendment). As regards the marriable age, no significant modification took place. The term "capacity to marry" (Ehefähigkeit) is now based on two aspects: majority (Volljährigkeit) as well as the capacity to decide (Entscheidungsfähigkeit).

[37] Additional requirements that are stipulated by Section 1 para. 2 of the EheG are that the underage fiancé(e) is sufficiently mature for this marriage and that the other fiancé(e) is at least 18 years old.

[38] https://www.derstandard.at/story/3000000232987/regierung-einigt-sich-heirat-ausnahmslos-erst-ab-18-jahren; https://orf.at/stories/3366973/.

[39] Similarly, VwGH 16 February 2021, Ra 2020/19/0153, ECLI:AT:VWGH:2021:RA2020190153.L00; doubting also B. Verschraegen, In: Rummel/Lukas/Geroldinger (fn. 15), Section 17 of the IPRG para. 6.

[40] See also B. Verschraegen/F. Heindler, In: Meyer (fn. 29), 3-043.

[41] On this link see also VwGH 3 July 2020, Ra 2020/14/0006, ECLI:AT:VWGH:2020:RA2020140006.L00.

the marriage (i.e. self-determined decision, no coercion) must be a central element in an individual assessment.[42] Pressure and coercion from third parties (parents, relatives) tend to play a greater role in early marriages than in marriages of adults.[43] Therefore, particular attention must be paid to the existence of any terms or conditions associated with the conclusion of the marriage.[44] If the free will of the fiancé(es) is impaired, an early marriage would violate the Austrian *ordre public*.

Secondly, the individual age of the fiancé(es) at the time of the marriage must be taken into consideration. While the marriage of a 15 years and 9 months old bride, whose free will and maturity have been ascertained, might not necessarily violate the Austrian *ordre public*, the marriage of a 12-year-old will certainly violate the Austrian *ordre public*; except if the marriage is assessed after the minor turned 18 (or at least 16[45]) and wants to hold on to the marriage (see below).[46] In essence: The lower the age at marriage, the more likely a violation of the fundamental values becomes.[47] In order to draw a line, one might look to the general capacity to contract and act. In this regard, the age of 14 (legal maturity, Mündigkeit) is an important mark in Austrian law.[48] Moreover, it should be noted that in Austria, sexual relations with persons who have not yet reached the age of 14 are prohibited under criminal law (Section 206 of the StGB (Austrian Criminal Code)). In this vein, the prohibition of early marriage is intended to protect the (personal) rights of children and minors and also to protect them from exploitation and unauthorised obligations of any kind. Hence, 14 years should also be considered as an (unwavering) red line regarding the assessment of early marriages. Between 14 and 16 years an individual assessment should be made.

Thirdly, a strong connection to Austria would justify less leniency as regards the age. In this regard, it can be assumed that marriages concluded in Austria, in which (at least) one of the foreign nationals is not even 16 years old, violate the Austrian *ordre public*. Given the extremely strong domestic connection, already a slight deviation from the Austrian minimum age is sufficient.[49] A similar assessment

[42] See also VwGH 3 July 2020, Ra 2020/14/0006, ECLI:AT:VWGH:2020:RA2020140006.L00.

[43] Similarly, M. Coester, Die rechtliche Behandlung von im Ausland geschlossenen Kinderehen, StAZ 2016, 257, at p. 258. Regarding the prohibition of a forced marriage in Austria see Section 106a of the Austrian Criminal Code.

[44] See also VwGH 3 July 2020, Ra 2020/14/0006, ECLI:AT:VWGH:2020:RA2020140006.L00.

[45] See B. Verschraegen/F. Heindler, In: Meyer (fn. 29), 3-044.

[46] But cf. older decisions of the BVwG (Federal Administrative Court) from 1 March 2018, W239 2169600-1, ECLI:AT:BVWG:2018:W239.2169600.1.00; from 8 March 2018, W243 2182039-1, ECLI:AT:BVWG:2018:W243.2182039.1.00, and from 22 May 2019, W1442217648-1, ECLI: AT:BVWG:2019:W144.2217648.1.00.

[47] M. Nademleinsky/M. Neumayr (fn. 26), para. 2.15 consider a marriage where one of the spouses is significantly younger than 16 years to violate Austrian public policy.

[48] Cf. M. Nademleinsky/M. Neumayr (fn. 26), para. 2.15 ("14 years is too young").

[49] See also K. Siehr, Die Frühehe in Österreich, In: Yassari/Michaels (eds), Die Frühehe im Recht, 2021, 551, at p. 565; B. Heiderhoff, Das autonome IPR in familienrechtlichen Fragen, IPRax 2017, 160, at p. 161.

should take place regarding situations in which there is a comparably strong domestic connection (e.g. habitual residence of one (or even) both spouses in Austria or Austrian nationality of (one of) the spouses at the time of marriage), even if the marriage took place in another country and in accordance with its law.

Finally, the assessment must differentiate between a marriage that is to be concluded and a marriage that already exists in accordance with a foreign law. Similarly, its duration and shape (i.e. marriage solely on paper versus family relationship and personal contact) must be taken into account. The freedom to marry (Article 12 of the Human Rights Convention[50]) and the protection of marriage and family life (Article 8 of the Human Rights Convention), which is also expressed in the principle of *favour matrimonii*, are also part of the fundamental values of Austrian law[51] and thus have to be balanced against the prohibition of early marriage. As a rule, the spouses rely on the validity of the marriage, which is also associated with essential rights (and obligations), such as maintenance and inheritance rights. Hence, some restraint is required if a marriage that is actually "lived" and supported by the spouses is evaluated to be rendered invalid.

Without doubt, the cases which are most complex to assess are the cases, where (at least) one of the spouses is still a minor at the time of the assessment in Austria and where there was no (or almost no) connection to Austria at the time the marriage was concluded.[52] Taking all the above mentioned aspects and the specific circumstances (i.e. interest of the minor, free will/lack of coercion, personal maturity, intensity and quality of the marriage) into consideration, it must be determined individually on a case-by-case basis whether the result of the application of the foreign law on marital capacity violates fundamental values in Austria and whether the domestic legal system is therefore required to correct an intolerable situation.[53] The general (abstract) admissibility of a early marriage under the law applicable is not subject of the examination or of any relevance for the individual assessment.[54] The most important factors must always be the best interests and well-being of the child or minor and their protection from exploitation and illegal obligations.[55]

[50] Convention for the Protection of Human Rights and Fundamental Freedoms (Human Rights Convention).

[51] OGH 13 September 2000, 4 Ob 199/00v, ECLI:AT:OGH0002:2000:E59176; B. Verschraegen, In: Rummel/Lukas/Geroldinger (fn. 15), Section 6 of the IPRG para. 13.

[52] Cf. OLG Bamberg 12 May 2016, 2 UF 58/16, FamRZ 2016, at p. 1270, ECLI:DE:OLGBAMB:2016:0512.2UF58.16.0A.

[53] See already M. Melcher, EF-Z 2018, 104, at p. 106. Now similarly, B. Verschraegen, In: Rummel/Lukas/Geroldinger (fn. 15), Section 6 of the IPRG para. 27. Cf. also the arguments in OLG Bamberg 12 May 2016, 2 UF 58/16, ECLI:DE:OLGBAMB:2016:0512.2UF58.16.0A.

[54] OGH 28 February 2011, 9 Ob 34/10f, ECLI:AT:OGH0002:2011:0090OB00034.10F.0228.000; M. Nademleinsky, Die neue EU-Unterhaltsverordnung samt dem neuen Haager Unterhaltsprotokoll, EF-Z 2011, 103; R. Fucik, Neues zur Unterhaltsdurchsetzung im Ausland, iFamZ 2011, at p. 180. Also VwGH 3 July 2020, Ra 2020/14/0006, ECLI:AT:VWGH:2020:RA2020140006.L00, regarding the legal possibility of 13-year-old girls to marry (if they are deemed mature enough) in accordance with Syrian law.

[55] Similarly, VwGH 3 July 2020, Ra 2020/14/0006, ECLI:AT:VWGH:2020:RA2020140006.L00.

(Former) Early marriages where one or both spouses were younger than 16 years at the time of the conclusion of the marriage, but turned 18 since, have to be assessed differently. If it is supported by the once-minor, now-adult spouse, the marriage shall in principle be deemed valid.[56] Although, the Austrian Supreme Court (OGH) did not take a posterior consent of the wife into consideration when assessing a *talaq* divorce,[57] this must not necessarily be reflected in the assessment of early marriages. The *ordre public* violation associated with a *talaq* divorce is mostly based on the principle of non-discrimination, whereas the prohibition of early marriages serves primarily to protect the free will of the future spouses. Moreover, Austrian marriage law allows the lack of marriage capacity at the time of the marriage to heal, if the spouse indicates that he/she wants to remain married once they reach an age where they would have been legally capable to marry (Section 22 para. 2 of the EheG).

Thus, at least in the cases in which the spouses are already 18 years or older at the time of the assessment and want to uphold their marriage, courts should not find an *ordre public* violation — even if one of the spouses was significantly younger than 16 years at the time of the marriage.[58] After all, it is not (primarily) the fact that a marriage was concluded between minors that is relevant for the assessment, but the result of the application of the foreign law at the moment of assessment.[59] In case of a marriage that is actually lived and wanted by both spouses, this aspect should be taken into account even if the spouses are still minors (i.e. between 16 and 18 years old), although the actual age and maturity of the minor at the time of the marriage must be of considerably greater importance. In this regard, also the quality and genuineness of an official (judicial or administrative) assessment of the maturity of the minor regarding the marriage should be taken into consideration.[60]

---

[56] See also BVerfG (German Constitutional Court) 1 February 2023, 1 BvL 7/18, ECLI:DE:BVerfG:2023:ls20230201.1bvl000718.

[57] OGH 21 January 2019, 7 Ob 10/08h, iFamZ 2008, 169, ECLI:AT:OGH0002:2008:0070OB00010.08H.0207.000; OGH 28 June 2007, 3 Ob 130/07z, EF-Z 2008, 24 (M. Nademleinsky), ECLI:AT:OGH0002:2007:0030OB00130.07Z.0628.000.

[58] See already M. Melcher, EF-Z 2018, 104, at p. 105. Now, also BVwG, 19 October 2023, W144 2219524-3/5E, ECLI:AT:BVWG:2023:W144.2219524.3.00, referring to VwGH 10 June 2021, Ro 2021/18/0001, ECLI:AT:VWGH:2021:RO2021180001.J00; similarly, BVwG 15 December 2022, W159 2255626-1/6E, ECLI:AT:BVWG:2022:W159.2255626.1.00, and BVwG 22 September 2022 W123 2253745-1/2E, ECLI:AT:BVWG:2022:W123.2253745.1.00 (the women were 15 years old at the time of marriage). See also BVwG 4 March 2024, W239 2271853/1/6E, ECLI:AT:BVWG:2024:W239.2271853.1.00 (the wife was 14 years and 7 months at the time of marriage).

[59] Similarly, B. Verschraegen/F. Heindler, In: Meyer (fn. 29), 3-044; to this effect VwGH 3 July 2020, Ra 2020/14/0006, ECLI:AT:VWGH:2020:RA2020140006.L00.

[60] See also VwGH 3 July 2020, Ra 2020/14/0006, ECLI:AT:VWGH:2020:RA2020140006.L00; B. Verschraegen, In: Rummel/Lukas/Geroldinger (fn. 15), Section 6 of the IPRG para. 26.

3. *Legal Consequences*

a) Application of Austrian Substantive Law

If the application of the foreign law (i.e. its more lenient age restrictions) violates the Austrian *ordre public*, it need not be applied. In these cases, the legal fate of the marriage must be addressed. It could be considered as non-marriage ("Nichtehe"), as voidable marriage (*ex tunc* effect, "nichtige Ehe") or as a marriage that may be set aside (*ex nunc* effect, "aufhebbare Ehe"). Pursuant to Section 6 para. 2 of the IPRG, Austrian substantive law is to be applied instead of the foreign law[61] — whether its legal consequences are more lenient or stricter than the foreign statute had it hypothetically been breached.

The same approach is also favoured if the minimum marriage age in the applicable foreign law was undercut by an exceptional provision only, for example, marriage at the age of 13 with the consent of the legal representative.[62] In contrast, a strict perspective would require the application of the (other) foreign legal rules, including the minimum age of marriage and the legal consequences of a violation, because only the application of the exceptional provision would be contrary to the Austrian *ordre public*. However, if the legal consequences provided for under the foreign law for a breach of the minimum marriage age are also applied to a marriage that is to be regarded as valid from the perspective of this foreign law, this is probably a misguided consideration.[63] The standard of review and the legal consequences should always be based on the same substantive law, especially given that the legal consequence (as stipulated by the foreign statute) must (again) be tested against the Austrian *ordre public*.

b) "Voidability" of the Marriage?

Pursuant to Section 22 para. 1 of the EheG, a marriage is null and void if one of the spouses was not (legally) capable of marriage at the time of the marriage and does not indicate that they wish to continue the marriage when they become (legally) capable of marriage and the grounds for annulment (i.e. setting aside the marriage, see Section 35 of the EheG) do not apply.[64]

In prior versions, Section 22 of the EheG only addressed the legal incapacity (Geschäftsunfähigkeit) of a spouse. The lack of the capacity to marry

---

[61] Similarly, B. Verschraegen/F. Heindler, In: Meyer (fn. 29), 3-043.

[62] See already M. Melcher, EF-Z 2018, 104, at p. 106. But cf. OLG Bamberg 12 May 2016, 2 UF 58/16, FamRZ 2016, 1270, ECLI:DE:OLGBAMB:2016:0512.2UF58.16.0A.

[63] Similarly P. Mankowski, Anmerkung zu OLG Bamberg 12 May 2016, 2 UF 58/16, FamRZ 2016, 1274, at p. 1276.

[64] As regards marriages involving spouses who are younger than 14 years old, Kissich suggests to treat such marriages as non-marriages (Nichtehen), see S. Kissich, In: Klang (ed), ABGB, 3rd ed. 2016, Section 1 of the EheG para. 39.

(marriageability [Eheunfähigkeit, fehlende Ehemündigkeit]) did not entail any particular legal consequences.[65] In practice, the civil registry office procedure prevented any marriage of an Austrian minor under the age of 16, so that a regulation of the legal consequences must have seemed redundant. Accordingly, the sanction or legal consequence provided by Section 22 para. 1 of the EheG, namely voidability, should also be applied to early marriages that violate the Austrian *ordre public* and have been concluded before 30 June 2018.[66]

In accordance with the current case law, a marriage must be declared null and void in separate proceedings.[67] It does not become invalid until the respective judgment becomes final but the judgment has a retrospective effect (*ex tunc* effect).[68] However, pursuant to Section 28 para. 1 of the EheG only the spouses can apply for such a declaration of nullity. Apparently, the legislator did not see a public interest in authorising the public prosecutor's office to do so.[69] This reasoning is not very convincing with regard to cases in which one of the spouses was not capable of marriage due to his/her age. It would seem rather unfortunate and unconvincing if the public prosecutor's office — based on sufficient public interest — were able to bring an action for annulment pursuant to Section 28 para. 2 of the EheG if the prohibition of polygamy was violated (Section 24 of the EheG) or if the marriage was concluded between very close relatives (Section 25 of the EheG), but not regarding the marriage of a 14-year-old or even an 8-year-old. More likely, the restriction of the right to bring an action to the spouses that was introduced by the 2nd Adult Protection Act aimed at situations where an adult spouse lacked the capacity to decide. This interpretation is sustained by the prior content of Section 22 of the EheG which was limited to such cases.

In this respect, I would suggest a teleological interpretation which limits the reference in Section 28 para. 1 of the EheG to cases involving spouses who are at least 16 years old.[70] Otherwise, a marriage involving at least one spouse under the age of 16, which violates Section 1 para. 1 of the EheG cannot be declared null and void against the will of the spouses, unless the well-being of the child is endangered and the legal representative of the child (e.g. a parent or the Youth Welfare Office (KJHT) demands such a declaration. This also requires a teleological interpretation that limits Section 174 of the ABGB to 16- and 17-year-old minors. This provision assigns the full legal rights and obligations regarding their personal circumstances

---

[65] F. Kerschner/K. Sagerer-Forić/T. Schoditsch, Familienrecht, 7th ed. 2020, para. 2/17.

[66] Similarly M. Nademleinsky/M. Neumayr (fn. 26), para. 2.15.

[67] See for example OGH 31 August 2010, 5 Ob 143/10f, iFamZ 2011, 32, ECLI:AT:OGH0002:2010:0050OB00143.10F.0831.000.

[68] M. Hinteregger, Familienrecht, 8th ed, 2017, at p. 34; H. Koziol/R. Welser/A. Kletečka, Bürgerliches Recht I, 14th ed. 2014, para. 1461.

[69] Ministerial proposal 222, 25th legislative period, comments 52.

[70] See already M. Melcher, EF-Z 2018, 104, at pp. 106 ff.; also M. Neumayr, In: Schoditsch (ed), EheG Section 28 para. 2.

(persönliche Verhältnisse) to married minors who are seen for these purposes by the law as adults.

Furthermore, the minor, who is as worthy of protection as a spouse acting in good faith, should be able to choose the application of the — more favourable (e.g. regarding maintenance) — legal consequences of a divorce instead of the consequences of annulment.[71]

IV. Conclusion

Contrary to the situation in Germany, where the issue of early marriage has been the subject of an intense political and academic debate — following the judgment of the Bamberg Higher Regional court,[72] the (now outdated) German legislation and the respective decision of the German Bundesverfassungsgericht — a more intense debate is missing in Austria.[73] Unfortunately, to my knowledge, also the Austrian Supreme Court has never had to deal with the validity of early marriages so far. Hence, an assessment from the highest civil law court in Austria is still to be awaited. In contrast, however, the Highest Administrative Court in Austria (VwGH) has already had several opportunities in the past few years to address questions regarding early marriages in the context of asylum and family reunion cases.[74] Only a few years ago, administrative courts tended to see a violation of the Austrian *ordre public* if at least one of the spouses was younger than 16 years old at the time of the conclusion of the marriage, no matter the current age of the spouses and the duration of their marriage.[75] Now, due to the influence of the most recent decisions of the Highest Administrative Court in Austria, early marriages are no longer deemed to violate the Austrian *ordre public* if both spouses are adults at the time of the

[71] M. Hinteregger (fn. 68), at p. 38.

[72] Decision from 12 May 2016, 2 UF 58/16, FamRZ 2016, 1270, ECLI:DE:OLGBAMB:2016:0512.2UF58.16.0A. See thereto J. Antomo, Kinderehen, ordre public und Gesetzesreform, NJW 2016, 3558, at p. 3560; B. Heiderhoff, IPRax 2017, 160, at p. 161; P. Mankowski, Anmerkung zu OLG Bamberg 12 May 2016, 2 UF 58/16, FamRZ 2016, 1274, at p. 1275. Critically M. Andrae, Flüchtlinge und Kinderehen, NZFam 2017, 923, at pp. 927 ff.

[73] However, see media coverage, for example, Ö1 Journal Panorama "Ehebett statt Klassenzimmer – Von Kinderbräuten und Zwangsehen", 23 October 2017, http://oe1.orf.at/programm/20171023/493021 or "Teufelskreis Kinderehe", 6 November 2016, http://derstandard.at/2000047041974/Teufelskreis-Kinderehe. Also, individual political motions have been made: Request for respective statistical investigations from November 2016 (1889/A(E) 25. GP) und from 19 June 2017 (2261/A(E) 25. GP) as well as a request for a minimum marriage age of 18 without exceptions, http://derstandard.at/2000062103261/Karmasin-will-Eheschliessung-erst-ab-18.

[74] For an overview see C. Pascher/A. Utz-Ferner, Parameter für die Beurteilung der Rechtskonformität von Kinder- und Minderjährigenehen, iFamZ 2022, 56.

[75] See BVwG 8 October 2018, W175 2183104-1/2E, ECLI:AT:BVWG:2018:W175.2183104.1.00; BVwG 15 January 2018, W240 2164625-1/2E, ECLI:AT:BVWG:2018:W240.2164625.1.00; BVwG 7 September 2018, W212 2147807-1, ECLI:AT:BVWG:2018:W212.2147807.1.00.

assessment and want to uphold their marriage and no coercion or lack of will at the time of the conclusion of the marriage can be found.[76] This development improves the legal certainty for couples and is to be welcomed.

Altogether, the lack of specific legislation on early marriages and of a more intense debate may be not so bad at all. Explicit legislation, i.e. a particular legal act, is not necessary and would probably not improve the situation. What is more important is a careful, individual, and conscious analysis of all relevant aspects of the situation. In this regard, Section 17 of the IPRG and the *ordre public* exception seem to form a well-balanced system which allows an adequate assessment of early marriages. The VwGH has repeatedly elaborated on the relevant criteria, so that lower instances may follow this blueprint. In contrast, the codification of a certain age, namely 18 years, as an intervention standard in international cases should be viewed rather critically.[77] Although such a codification would send a clear signal against early marriage and ensures legal clarity, it does so at the expense of fairness in individual cases and therefore possibly also at the expense of the child's welfare. The age of the engaged couple at the time of the marriage is *prima facie* the only criterion. Handling this issue with the help of the domestic *ordre public* instead places higher demands on authorities and courts but allows appropriate consideration of the special circumstances of the individual case and the consideration of different, age-independent criteria.

However, legislative action should be taken regarding certain aspects. In particular, only marriages between adults (i.e. persons who are at least 18 years old) should be allowed by Austrian substantive law and any declaration of marriageability at a lower age should be abolished.[78] The legitimising function of marriage hardly exists anymore. Unmarried relationships are socially accepted. Unmarried children are (largely) legally equal to married children. Even the apparent contradiction to the generally desired strengthening of the self-determination of minors (including consent to medical treatment, making a will)[79] does not constitute a sufficient reason in view of the lack of need for marriage and the considerable legal commitment associated with marriage. Since religious or traditional unions create *de facto* undesirable, marriage-like situations and comparable (social) obligations without a

---

[76] See BVwG, 19 October 2023, W144 2219524-3/5E, ECLI:AT:BVWG:2023:W144.2219524.3.00, referring to VwGH 10 June 2021, Ro 2021/18/0001, ECLI:AT:VWGH:2021:RO2021180001.J01; similarly, BVwG 15 December 2022, W159 2255626-1, ECLI:AT:BVWG:2022:W159.2255626.1.00, and BVwG 22 September 2022 W123 2253745-1, ECLI:AT:BVWG:2022:W123.2253745.1.00; BVwG 4 March 2024, W239 2271853/1/6E, ECLI:AT:BVWG:2024:W239.2271853.1.00.

[77] See also S. Gössl, Das Gesetz zur Bekämpfung von Kinderehen – eine politische Reaktion auf die Flüchtlingskrise, In: Friedrichs/Gössl/Hoven/Steinbicker (eds), Migration. Gesellschaftliches Zusammenleben im Wandel, 2018, 19, at pp. 35 ff. Cf. BVerfG 1 February 2023, 1 BvL 7/18, ECLI:DE:BVerfG:2023:ls20230201.1bvl000718.

[78] Already M. Melcher, EF-Z 2018, 104, at p. 107. Similarly S. Kissich, In: Klang (fn. 64), Section 1 of the EheG para. 43. For more recent political developments (August 2024) see above.

[79] Similarly D. Coester-Waltjen, Kinderehen – Neue Sonderanknüpfungen im EGBGB, IPRax 2017, 429, at p. 430.

legal marriage bond,[80] such unions should also be prohibited for minors. Unfortunately though, any governmental efforts have been postponed so far.[81]

Furthermore, in case of an early marriage which violates the Austrian *ordre public* or does not respect the minimum age for marriage in accordance with (the applicable) Austrian substantive law, the public prosecutor's office should be granted an express right for action. Although such a right can probably also be deduced from Section 28 para. 1 of the EheG by teleological interpretation (see above), an explicit and clear regulation would offer more legal certainty.

Finally, the legislator should explicitly address the legal consequences of a prohibited early marriage. An *ex tunc* annulment might not always provide an adequate answer, in particular regarding maintenance and succession law as well as filiation issues.[82] Given that the protection of the minor is the underlying objective of the prohibition of early marriage, this objective should also shape the legal consequences. To treat such a marriage as if it had never existed might not be the most favourable option for the affected minor.

[80] Critically also J. Antomo, NJW 2016, at p. 3558.

[81] See S. Karmasin from 2017, https://orf.at/v2/stories/2400746/2400763/; Reply (3965/AB) from the Ministry of Justice from 23 December 2020 regarding a parliamentary request (3959/J (XXVII. GP) and Reply (8345/AB from the Ministry of Social Affairs, Health and Consumer Protection, from 10 January 2022 regarding a parliamentary request (8514/J (XXVII.GP). For more recent political developments (August 2024) see above.

[82] For some alternatives see for example D. Coester-Waltjen, Die "Kinderehen"-Entscheidung des Bundesverfassungsgerichts: Welche Schlussfolgerungen ergeben sich für das internationale Eheschließungsrecht? RabelsZ 2023, 766, at pp. 777 ff.

Early Marriage: A European Perspective

Stefan Arnold

I. Introduction

Even though early marriages are rarely concluded in Western European countries, they have become increasingly visible in recent years, in particular in the context of migration and families on the move. As the chapters of Ulf Maunsbach, Stefan Arnold and Martina Melcher in this book show, European countries need to answer difficult questions with respect to early marriages: How should European legal systems treat early marriages? Under which circumstances can marriages be valid in the perspective of European legal systems? How can the best interests of the person who was minor at the time of marriage be ensured? Which institutions or rules ensure justice between the spouses, but also with respect to other persons involved, particularly children born out of early marriages? The following lines cannot develop fully fledged solutions. Yet, they try to point out some important aspects that should bear relevance to the problem. They are mainly based on a brief comparative evaluation of the German, Swedish and Austrian experience.[1] A note on terminology: Sometimes, the terms "child marriage" or "marriage by minors" are used to denote early marriages. However, for the reasons expounded in the chapters on early marriage in Sweden, Austria and Germany, the term "early marriage" is preferable and will be used in the following lines to denote marriages where at least one of the spouses is under the age of 18 years at the time of marriage.

[1] For further comparative studies see N. Yassari/R. Michaels, Die Frühehe im Rechtsvergleich: Praxis, Sachrecht, Kollisionsrecht, In: Yassari/Michaels (eds), Die Frühehe im Recht, 2021, 17, at pp. 21 ff.

S. Arnold (✉)
Institute of International Business Law, Chair for Private Law, Philosophy of Law, and Private International Law, University of Münster, Münster, Germany
e-mail: stefan.arnold@uni-muenster.de

S. Arnold, B. Heiderhoff (eds.), *Children in Migration and International Family Law*, https://doi.org/10.1007/978-3-031-71598-3_12

II. Comparative Evaluation: Sweden, Austria and Germany

A comparative evaluation of the law relating to early marriages is difficult since case-law on early marriages exists, but is relatively rare. At the same time, there can be different institutional settings or framings of early marriages: asylum matters, family or inheritance matters and — as the Swedish example shows — registration in population registration databases. The chapters on early marriage in Sweden, Austria and Germany illustrated different answers to the problems of early marriage.

First, it is somewhat surprising that the three countries differ with respect to the minimum age for marriage: In Sweden and Germany, no one can enter into marriages before the age of 18 anymore. In Austria, in exceptional cases it is still possible to marry from the age of 16 years on if the other spouse is at least 18 years old. As Martina Melcher has shown, there seem to be no convincing policy reasons for such exceptions any more. The Swedish and German approach seems preferable in this respect.[2]

Second, the most pressing issue is the recognition of early marriages validly concluded abroad. It is this topic that the current debate centres around. Here, the countries also remarkably differ. Politics entered the realm of law in Sweden and Germany and led to strict non-recognition solutions at the cost of the persons worthy of protection. As *Ulf Maunsbach* has shown, early marriages validly concluded abroad are, in principle, not recognised under Swedish Law. Germany follows a similarly strict approach, but only for marriages where one of the spouses was under 16 at the time of marriage. In both countries, non-recognition means, in principle, that the marriage has no legal effects whatsoever. In Germany, the spouse who was minor at the time of marriage is at least awarded maintenance claims since 1 July 2024. German Law does not allow for the marriage to be healed by implied confirmation. Rather, the spouses need to marry again. It is interesting to note that political actors in both countries invoked national obligations derived from international law — particularly the UN Convention on the Rights of the Child, which obligates member states to counteract harmful practices such as early marriages. Both countries have exceptions to their rule of non-recognition. Swedish Law includes an exception in the form of a general clause, allowing recognition for "extraordinary reasons" in cases where the spouses are over 18 years of age at the time of assessment.[3] However, institutional settings play a significant role in the application of this exception: In the context of requests to register a marriage in the population registration database, it is highly unlikely that the exception will ever be applied, as the Swedish Tax Agency bases its decision on written documentation without specific investigations into the circumstances surrounding the marriage.[4] Germany, on the other hand, has detailed rules regarding exceptions: The first significant exception in German Law is that the non-recognition principle does not

[2] See M. Melcher, in this book.

[3] See U. Maunsbach, in this book.

[4] See U. Maunsbach, in this book.

apply if the spouse was not under 16 years old, but rather 16 or 17 years old at the time of marriage. Such marriages are merely subject to annulment. Another exception exists even for marriages involving a spouse under 16, if the minor spouse was born before 22 July 1999, or if the marriage took place before the minor reached the age of majority and neither spouse had their habitual residence in Germany from the time of the marriage until the minor spouse reached adulthood. Despite these exceptions, the strict non-recognition approach in Swedish and German Law is very problematic for systematic and normative reasons.

Austrian Law offers a compelling alternative perspective. As Martina Melcher has shown, the legal realm in Austria was relatively untouched by heated political debates. Austria maintains a flexible approach that allows institutions to administer justice through careful case-by-case analysis: The recognition of early marriages is governed by the general ordre public clause and depends on an individual assessment of the specific case. Since Austria permits 16- and 17-year-olds to marry in exceptional cases, a violation of the ordre public is generally denied in cases where the spouses were 16 or 17 years old at the time of marriage. If one of the spouses was under 16 at the time of marriage, a violation of the ordre public is possible, depending on a careful case-by-case analysis. Courts consider the preservation of the minor's free will, their age and maturity. Generally, there is no ordre public violation in cases where the spouses wish to maintain their marriage and are 18 years or older at the time of assessment, irrespective of their age at the time of marriage.

The development in Sweden and Germany is deeply connected with political developments: Swedish Law followed a liberal and flexible public policy approach until 2004. Yet following political discussions, a 2004 law reform denied recognition of early marriages concluded abroad in certain cases. After further political debates in the context of migration, the new Swedish Law entered into force in 2019: non-recognition now covered any early marriages irrespective of the connection to Sweden. In Germany, the political influence on the law of early marriages is remarkably similar: Germany followed a flexible approach before 21 July 2017. The solutions were based on the ordre public-clause and resembled the sensible case-by-case approach akin to that which still prevails in Austria. Yet following fierce political debates, since 22 July 2017, German Law follows the aforementioned strict policy of non-recognition. The law was declared unconstitutional by the Constitutional Court, but it was nevertheless applied until 30 June 2024. From 1 July 2024 onwards, it is applied with only minimal adaptations. The Swedish and German examples vividly illustrate that the justice function of the law can be seriously endangered if day-to-day politics intrude into the realm of law.

III. Policy Recommendations

As regards marriages entered into in European countries, a strict age limit of 18 years — as is the case in Germany and Sweden — seems clearly preferable. There is no practical need to allow for exceptions.

Much more problematic is the recognition of early marriages validly concluded abroad. Here, the law must in particular protect the spouse who was minor at the time of marriage — even if the spouse is now (at least) 18 years old. At the same time, the best interests of the children born out of the marriage deserve protection. European solutions should refrain from symbolic law making at the expense of the persons concerned — as is the case in particular in Germany.[5] The problems are complex and the individual circumstances can vary immensely. The Austrian case-by-case approach seems recommendable here. A policy of strict non-recognition — as in Sweden and Germany — is not advisable. The relevant time for the assessment of the best interests of the persons worthy of protection should be the time of recognition — not the time of marriage:[6] Even if the best interests of a 15 year-old in the year 2020 advised against marriage back then, the best interests of the now 19 year-old person are violated by non-recognition of the marriage if the 19 year-old has been living in that marriage for four years and might have children together with her husband. European solutions cannot ignore the fact that early marriages that have been validly concluded abroad may have been effectively lived for a possibly long time. Non-recognition cannot change the facts retrospectively. It is furthermore highly doubtful (if not illusory) that non-recognition will add to the prevention of early marriages in foreign countries in the future. There is no statistical evidence that would support that supposition. At the same time, non-recognition can violate the best interests of the most vulnerable persons involved, in particular the best interests of young women.[7] The Danish experience illustrates how disastrous the consequences can be: Inger Støjberg, the then Minister of Immigration and Integration, had ordered the separation of couples who had fled to Denmark with a partner under the age of 18 in February 2016. The aim was to protect the underage spouse from the (supposedly) forced partnership, as the "Deutscher Rat für IPR" (German Council for PIL) points out:[8] The "Deutscher Rat für IPR" reports that 23 women were forcibly separated from their partners — without consideration of children or pregnancy.[9] The consequences for the young women were devastating according to an investigation report of December 2020.[10] Furthermore, non-recognition generally rather favours the older male spouse in the typical instance of younger women

[5] C. Hornung, Internationales Privatrecht zwischen Wertneutralität und Politik, 2021, at p. 275.

[6] C. Hornung (fn. 5), at p. 277.

[7] B. Heiderhoff, Männer- statt Minderjährigenschutz, Verfassungsblog, 15 September 2024, https://verfassungsblog.de/manner-statt-minderjahrigenschutz/.

[8] Deutscher Rat für IPR (German Council for Private International Law), Stellungnahme zum Referentenentwurf eines Gesetzes zum Schutze Minderjähriger bei Auslandsehen, 22 April 2024, at p. 7, https://www.bmj.de/SharedDocs/Downloads/DE/Gesetzgebung/Stellungnahmen/2024/0422_Schutz_Minderjaehriger_Auslandsehen_Dt-Rat-IPR.pdf?__blob=publicationFile&v=3.

[9] Deutscher Rat für IPR, (fn. 8), at pp. 7 ff.

[10] Deutscher Rat für IPR, (fn. 8), at p. 7 with reference to https://www.justitsministeriet.dk/wp-content/uploads/2020/12/Instrukskommissionen-Bind-1-kapitel-1-7.pdf.

marrying older men.[11] If non-recognition is opted for, European solutions should at least foresee that the marriage can be healed by implied confirmation.[12] Since the problems, needs and individual circumstances vary a lot, an individual case-by-case analysis is preferable for any European solutions.[13] Specific rules can be harmful with respect to those who need protection, as the German and Swedish examples show. The German and Swedish laws prior to specific regulations (starting 2004 in Sweden, 2017 in Germany) enabled courts and authorities to solve individual cases so that the best interest principle could be adhered to and justice could be administered. Such a case-by-case approach is still possible in Austria. The Austrian solution is preferable, even though clarifying provisions as regards the consequences of non-recognition would be desirable.[14]

If European legislators want to regulate early marriage, they should refrain from symbolic law-making at the expense of the persons involved. Rather, the legislators should tackle the real problems at hand. It would be desirable to find solutions that could help to lift early marriages from the dark into the open and to provide legal institutions with the means to protect the factually weaker spouse.[15] One important aspect might be that the persons involved — in particular the spouse who was under the age of 18 years at the time of marriage — lack information and counselling. Thus, special laws should install information duties and counselling options for the persons involved — in particular in favour of young women.[16] Also, European solutions might aim at the obligatory registration of early marriages concluded abroad. Instead of non-recognition, one might also consider solutions where early marriages are valid, but subject to annulment in court or administrative proceedings — as is the case for marriages where one of the spouses was 16 or 17 years old at the time of wedding in Germany. Such solutions might also enable legal institutions to provide justice in individual cases.[17]

---

[11] B. Heiderhoff, Verfassungsblog (fn. 7); Deutscher Rat für IPR, (fn. 8), at p. 10.

[12] With special criticism towards the German provisions T. Pfeiffer, Konkrete Normenkontrollvorlage zur Nichtigkeit von Kinderehen, LMK 2019, 415153.

[13] K. Duden, Zur Unwirksamkeit der Frühehe in Deutschland, In: Yassari/Michaels (fn. 1), 629, at pp. 657 ff.

[14] M. Melcher, Early marriage in Austria, in this volume, 183, at pp. 183 ff.

[15] Deutscher Rat für IPR, (fn. 8), at pp. 19 ff.

[16] R. Michaels, Der Gesetzgeber ist zu weit gegangen, Verfassungsblog, 3 April 2023, https://verfassungsblog.de/der-gesetzgeber-ist-zu-weit-gegangen/, emphasises the need to respect the autonomy of the persons involved as far as possible.

[17] There is no room for distrust in this context, as M. Gebauer, Zur sogenannten Wertneutralität des klassischen IPR, In: Gebauer/Huber (eds), Politisches Kollisionsrecht, 2021, 35, at p. 71 points out.

Part V
Kafāla

Beyond Kafāla: How Parentless Children Are Placed in New Homes in Muslim Jurisdictions

Nadjma Yassari

I. Introduction

This chapter explores the legal options in Muslim jurisdictions for the placement of parentless children in new homes. One option is adoption, but there are also various other arrangements under which a child can be cared for by new caretakers. Premodern Islamic law considers the concept of adoption (tabannī) to be forbidden, in particular for the unwanted legal effects it would confer on the adopted person, effects that are confined otherwise to parent-child relations resulting from legitimate procreation by a married couple. Accordingly, any legal structure that allows the transfer of one person's name (ism) to another person not related to by blood, that establishes intestate inheritance rights not based on legitimate biological descent, or that instigates marriage impediments between persons other than blood relatives and in-laws, is considered to infringe upon the basic principle governing filiation (nasab).[1] The prohibition of tabannī in premodern Islamic law, however different the ways and approaches, has survived in the modern nation states of Muslim jurisdictions. Today we can observe that the safeguarding of children without proper caretakers is a notable objective in many Muslim jurisdictions, leading to the development of a variety of devices for the placement of parentless children in

[1] On (the prohibition of) adoption (tabannī) in traditional Islamic law, see generally F. Kutty, Islamic "Adoptions": Kafalah, Raadah, Istilhaq and the Best Interests of the Child, In: Ballard et al. (eds), The Intercountry Adoption Debate, 2015, 526, at p. 539; for a bibliography on adoption in Islam, see D. Powers, Adoption, Oxford Bibliographies – Islamic Studies 2016, available at https://doi.org/10.1093/obo/9780195390155-0226; A. al-Azhary Sonbol, Adoption in Islamic Society: A Historical Survey, In: Warnock Fernea (ed), Children in the Muslim Middle East, 1995, at pp. 45–67; A. R. Naqvi, Adoption in Muslim Law, Islamic Studies 1980, at pp. 283–302.

N. Yassari (✉)
Swiss Institute of Comparative Law, Lausanne, Switzerland
e-mail: nadjma.yassari@isdc-dfjp.unil.ch

S. Arnold, B. Heiderhoff (eds.), *Children in Migration and International Family Law*, https://doi.org/10.1007/978-3-031-71598-3_13

new homes. As has been argued elsewhere, these can act as functional equivalents to adoption if one focuses on the three key elements that characterise adoption in the modern world, i.e., the best interests of the child, the transfer of parental care and authority, and the endurance of the bond.[2] In this chapter, the picture shall be expanded by bringing in additional types of arrangements that Muslim jurisdictions have conceived of to protect and care for parentless children, going beyond the question of equivalence to show the variety of concepts and values that have influenced the respective legislatures.[3]

Alternative care arrangements have become operative in all Muslim jurisdictions in order to protect and care for left-behind children whose parents have abandoned them, died, or been stripped of their parental rights because of their deficiencies as parents. While the legal implications of the respective device may vary, as do their labels and practical relevance, they have led to the creation of familial communities based on social bonds, and thus these devices have connected persons who share neither a legal nor a biological lineage. With due respect to the differences in each jurisdiction, four categories of (alternative) caretaking arrangements can be broadly distinguished: the complete incorporation of a child into a new family (section "II. The Complete Incorporation of a Child Into a New Family"), wide-ranging incorporation (section "III. Legal Arrangements Allowing for the Wide-Ranging Incorporation of a Child Into a New Home"), structures for the temporary care of abandoned or orphaned children (section "IV. Temporary Caretaking of a Child") and finally, jurisdictions where the caretaking operates on an informal basis, with little or no state supervision or intervention (section "V. No Formalised Legal Framework for the Accommodation of Parentless Children").

II. The Complete Incorporation of a Child Into a New Family

Tunisia is currently the only country that has regulated an institution called tabannī.[4] According to Tunisian Law no. 58-27 of 4 March 1958,[5] a child can be placed in a new home and awarded a status equal to that of a legitimate biological child. Tabannī under Tunisian law creates a parent-child relationship that displays all the legal effects of what can be called "full" adoption, including parental care and authority, reciprocal inheritance rights, and the right to carry the adoptive parent's surname.

---

[2] See N. Yassari, Adding by Choice: Adoption and Functional Equivalents in Islamic and Middle Eastern Law, AJCL 2015, 927, at pp. 941 f.

[3] The article will focus on the legal foundations of such arrangements and refer to further literature, in particular regarding the various countries' practices, in the footnotes.

[4] Adoption was also permissible in Somalia, but its practice today is very uncertain, see N. Yassari, AJCL 2015, 927, at pp. 947 f.

[5] Law no. 58-27 Regarding Official Guardianship, Kafala and Adoption [qānūn yataʿallaq bi-l-wilāya al-ʿumūmiyya wa-l-kafāla wa-l-tabannī] of 4 March 1958, Official Gazette no. 19 of 7 March 1958, amended by Law no. 59-69 of 19 June 1959, Official Gazette no. 34 of 23-26 June 1959.

Law no. 58-27 contains a total of 17 articles. Section 3 of the law, entitled tabannī (in French: adoption) regulates, in ten articles (Articles 8-17 of the Law no. 58-27), the framework within which a child can be adopted. According to Article 9 of the Law no. 58-27, the adopter must be an adult of either sex who is legally competent, of good character and sound mind and body, and capable of attending to the needs of the adopted child. The person must be married, but the court can dispense with this requirement in the best interests of the child on a case-to-case basis for a widowed or divorced applicant. There must also be an age difference of at least 15 years between the child and the adopter. Orphaned minors as well as minors of known and unknown filiation, with or without living parents, are eligible for adoption. The law thus allows the children of a divorced or widowed person to be adopted by that person's new spouse, in which case the age difference requirement does not apply. A minor is a person under the age of 18 years. The adoption is established by court order.[6]

Article 15 of the Law no. 58-27 states that the adopted child has the same rights and is under the same obligations as a legitimate child (al-ibn al-sharʿī), but without enumerating these rights and duties explicitly. It makes a notable exception with regard to the transfer of the surname of the adopter(s) to the child. Article 14 of the Law no. 58-27 explicitly mentions that the adopted child takes the surname of the adopter and that the child's first name can also be changed.[7] This is to be seen as a safeguard, because under premodern Islamic law, one of the issues that led ultimately to the prohibition of adoption was the fear that adoption, and thus the transfer of names, would endanger the genealogy of the child. Interestingly, Law no. 58-27 contains no provision on the revocation of an adoption, and Article 16 of the Law no. 58-27 regulates only the revocation of the adopter's custody rights (ḥaḍāna). Initially, the Tunisian courts therefore assumed that adoptions could not be revoked,[8] but this trend has been corrected by the judicature of the Tunisian Court of Cassation. In its decision of March 1993, the Court of Cassation held that adoptions are revocable by court order in exceptional cases if the best interests of the child so demand.[9] As regards the family of origin, all legal relations are severed except for the marriage obstacle of a blood relationship, to prevent incestuous unions.[10]

[6] Article 13 of the Law no. 58-27.

[7] Articles 14, 15 of the Law no. 58-27.

[8] Court of First Instance of Tunis, decision no. 57554 of 17 April 1978, cited in B. Ben Hadj Yahia, La révocation de l'adoption en droit tunisien, Revue tunisienne de droit 1979, 83, at p. 96.

[9] Tun. Court of Cassation, decision no. 29577 of 23 March 1993, cited in I. Bejaoui Attar, L'intérêt de l'enfant fondement de l'adoption en droit tunisien, Actualités juridiques tunisiennes (special issue: L'enfant en droit privé) 2003, 79, at p. 100.

[10] Article 15 para. 3 of the Law no. 58-27.

III. Legal Arrangements Allowing for the Wide-Ranging Incorporation of a Child Into a New Home

Some jurisdictions — without resorting to the Arabic term tabannī — have developed legal arrangements allowing for a far-reaching incorporation of a child into a new home. The Iranian sarparastī, the Iraqi ḍamm and the Algerian kafāla fall into this category.

The Iranian sarparastī and the Iraqi ḍamm are regulated outside the respective family law codes in a separate code, while the Algerian kafāla is regulated in the comprehensive Family Law Code.

1. Iran

In 1975 the Iranian legislature regulated, for the first time, the placement of parentless children in new homes.[11] The 1975 Act on the Protection of Children without a Guardian introduced a legal institution, termed sarparastī, the holder of which is a sarparast.[12] The Act was replaced in 2013 by the Act on the Protection of Uncared-for (bī-sarparast) and Poorly Cared-for (bad-sarparast) Children and Adolescents (CPA 2013).[13] While the 1975 Act focussed on the permanent placement of children in new homes, the CPA 2013 regulates both permanent and temporary integration of a minor into a new family, as it addresses both *uncared-for* and *poorly cared-for* children. Interestingly, the CPA 2013 uses not only the term sarparastī but also, synonymously, the Farsi term for adoption, "farzand khāndigī".[14]

The CPA 2013 came into force in October 2013 and consists of 36 articles. According to Articles 3-6 of the CPA 2013, Iranian couples married for over five years (with or without children) as well as single women — a category including both never-married women as well as widows and divorcees — are eligible to be a sarparast provided that one of them is over thirty years old. Single women can only

---

[11] On the CPA of 2013, see the country report on Iran, N. Yassari, Iran, In: Yassari/Möller/Najm (eds), Filiation and the Protection of Parentless Children: Towards a Social Definition of the Family in Muslim Jurisdictions, 2019, at pp. 67–102; N. Yassari, AJCL 2015, at pp. 927–962; M. Dambach/J. Wöllenstein-Tripathi (eds), La kafalah: analyse préliminaire de pratiques nationales et transfrontières, Service Social International 2020, at pp. 32–38 (La république islamique de l'Iran).

[12] Family Protection Act [qānūn-i ḥimāyat az kūdakān bidūn-i sarparast] of 20 March 1975, Official Gazette no. 8819 of 20 April 1975 (CPA 1975).

[13] Family Protection Act [qānūn-i ḥimāyat az kūdakān va nūjavānān bī sarparast va bad sarparast] of 2 October 2013, Official Gazette no. 19997 of 28 October 2013 (CPA 2013).

[14] Articles 26 and 35 of the CPA 2013. Equally, some court decisions use the term "farzand khāndigī" in the heading of their decisions, whereas the actual text of the decision sticks to the word "sarparastī". Decisions on file with author.

apply for the sarparastī of a girl.[15] The applicants must be of good reputation and morality, mature, physically and mentally fit, and factually and financially capable of caring for and educating a child.[16]

Minors whose parents cannot be identified or who are deceased are eligible for permanent caretaking.[17] For purposes of the law, a minor is a person who has not reached the age of puberty.[18] The child is initially placed in the care of the potential parents for a six-month trial period under the supervision of the youth welfare office.[19] During this period, the sarparastī is subject to strict conditions and regular monitoring by state authorities. Once this period has expired and the personal relationship has been consolidated, the final sarparastī order is pronounced by the court, and full parental care and authority are transferred to the sarparast.[20] The sarparast must care for, educate, and maintain the child as their own.[21] The court will award the sarparast a general mandate under a guardianship device called qaymūmat,[22] which vests in the sarparast's financial authority to manage the child's assets and obliges them to provide for the child financially. To ensure the financial security of the child, the court will only render final judgement on the sarparastī once the sarparasts have transferred assets to the child.[23] In practice, this is often done by having an irrevocable last will notarised in which the child is bequeathed up to one-third of the estate. Also, the sarparast must purchase a life insurance policy in favour of the child in order to ensure the financing of all costs arising from the care, upbringing, and education of the adopted child, in the event of their death.[24] Finally, the sarparastī of a parentless child may be revoked by order of the court if the best interests of the child so require, or if the sarparast and the adult child have reached an agreement.[25]

---

[15] Article 5 lit. c of the CPA 2013.

[16] Article 6 of the CPA 2013.

[17] Article 8 of the CPA 2013; children whose parents are still alive can only be placed in a new family temporarily.

[18] That is, nine lunar years for girls and fifteen lunar years for boys, Article 1210 note 1 of the Iranian Civil Code. Children who have reached the age of puberty but are under the age of sixteen are also eligible if the court finds them lacking of mental maturity (Article 9 of the CPA 2013).

[19] Article 11 of the CPA 2013.

[20] Article 13 of the CPA 2013.

[21] Article 17 of the CPA 2013.

[22] Article 16 of the CPA 2013.

[23] Articles 14 and 15 of the CPA 2013.

[24] Article 15 of the CPA 2013.

[25] Article 25 of the CPA 2013.

2. Iraq

Iraq has a long history of statutes dedicated to the placement of children in new homes. The first law that related to the permanent integration of a child into a new family, entitled the Act on Juveniles, was enacted in 1955,[26] even before Tunisia legalised adoption.[27] This Act was amended several times and dates in its current form to 1983. The Juvenile Welfare Act of 1983 (JWA)[28] introduced a legal institution called ḍamm, which can be translated as "attachment" or "annexation". It permits spouses to jointly apply to "attach" a minor to their family provided this is in the best interests of the child (Articles 39 and 42 of the JWA).

According to Article 30 of the JWA, a married couple can jointly apply for ḍamm. They must be of good character, of sound mind, and capable of raising and providing for the child. Only orphan minors and minors of unknown descent (Article 39 of the JWA) are eligible for ḍamm. Article 3 of the JWA explicitly defines the term ṣaghīr (minor) used in Article 39 as a person who has not reached the age of nine, whereas the age of majority under the Iraqi Civil Code is 18 years.[29] As in Iranian law, Iraqi law also provides for an initial probationary period of six months, during which the applicants look after the child under the supervision of the court (Article 40 of the JWA) before a final decision is rendered.

The effects of ḍamm are far-reaching. The attached child is treated the same as a legitimate biological child. Custody and guardianship are transferred to the new parents.[30] The caretakers are subject to maintenance obligations: for a son, until he is able to support himself; for a daughter, until she marries.[31] On the other hand, the caretaker is entitled to state social welfare, and the woman can be granted maternity leave if the child is under the age of four.[32] The JWA also provides for a compulsory, irrevocable bequest in favour of the child, amounting to up to one-third of each parent's estate.[33] As regards minors of unknown descent, the new caretaker can acknowledge their filiation to the child, thereby creating a (fictitious) parent-child

[26] Act on Juveniles [qānūn al-aḥdāth], Law no. 44 of 1955, Official Gazette no. 3603 of 20 April 1955.

[27] On Iraqi ḍamm, see the country report on Iraq, H. Al-Dabbagh, Iraq, In: Yassari/Möller/Najm (fn. 11), at pp. 103–133; K. Dilger, Die Adoption im modernen Orient – ein Beitrag zu den hiyal im islamischen Recht, Recht van de Islam 1988, at pp. 44–66; M. Dambach/J. Wöllenstein-Tripathi (fn. 11), Service Social International 2020, at pp. 38–42 (L'Iraq).

[28] Juvenile Welfare Act [qānūn riʿāyat al-aḥdāth], Law no. 76 of 1983, Official Gazette no. 2951 of 1 August 1983 (JWA).

[29] Article 106 of the Iraqi Civil Code.

[30] See K. Dilger (fn. 27), at p. 51; H. Al-Dabbagh, Iraq, In: Yassari/Möller/Najm (fn. 11), 103, at pp. 127 ff.

[31] Article 43 para. 1 of the JWA.

[32] H. Al-Dabbagh, Iraq, In: Yassari/Möller/Najm (fn. 11), 103, at p. 127.

[33] Article 43 para. 2 of the JWA.

relationship with all its legal effects, including the transfer of their surname.[34] This does not apply to orphans whose parents were known, whose filiation and genealogy are not permitted to be tampered with by a change of name.[35]

3. Algeria

Finally, one needs to pay attention to the Algerian kafāla.[36] While the term kafāla is known in the European literature, where it is often assumed to encompass a unitary legal figure in all Muslim jurisdictions, the term is used only in the Maghreb countries of North Africa, such as Algeria, Morocco, Libya, Sudan, Egypt and Tunisia, to denote a care-taking arrangement. While the regulations in each state differ to a variable degree, these jurisdictions generally understand kafāla to be the placement of a child in a new home. In other Muslim jurisdictions, however, in particular in the Gulf states, kafāla is an institution stemming from the law of obligations that denotes a surety or guarantee.[37] From that fundament, in the context of family law, kafāla has become the vehicle to describe the commitment of one person in favour of another person, to the benefit of both.[38]

Further, even if the terminology kafāla for the institution, kāfil for the person undertaking kafāla, and makfūl for the child—seems to suggest that the same legal structure applies in all Maghreb states, in the area of child law the term kafāla is not understood uniformly in North Africa, either. The following section explores the Algerian version of kafāla,[39] as its implementation is wider than its Tunisian and Moroccan counterparts, which are treated under subsequent headings.

[34] Article 44 of the JWA; the acknowledgement must be done in accordance with Article 52 of the Iraqi Code of Personal Status.

[35] H. Al-Dabbagh, Iraq, In: Yassari/Möller/Najm (fn. 11), 103, at p. 128.

[36] On Algerian kafāla, see the country report on Algeria, M. Guénon, Algeria, In: Yassari/Möller/Najm (fn. 11), at pp. 45–65; see also N. Younsi Haddad, La kafala en droit algérien, Revue algérienne des sciences juridiques, politiques et économiques 1999, at pp. 7–42; A. Bencheneb, La formation du lien de kafala et les silences législatifs, Communication à la journée d'étude AEFAB/LADH: L'enfant et le droit, June 1989, Revue algérienne des sciences juridiques, politiques et économiques 1991, at pp. 47–53; N. Saadi, L'institution de la kafala en Algérie et sa perception par le système juridique français, Revue internationale de droit comparé 2014, 99, at pp. 103–116; N. Ait Zaï, La kafāla en droit algérien, In: Bleuchot (ed), Les institutions traditionnelles dans le monde arabe, 1996, at pp. 95–105, available at https://doi.org/10.4000/books.iremam.267.

[37] See Y. Linant de Bellefonds, Kafāla, In: Bearman (ed), Encyclopaedia of Islam New Edition Online (EI-2 English), 2012, available at https://doi.org/10.1163/1573-3912_islam_COM_0415; T. Oubrou, La kafala et la sharia, Droit de la famille, revue mensuelle Lexisnexis 2009, 10, at p. 14; U. M. Assim/J. Sloth-Nielsen, Islamic kafalah as an alternative care option for children deprived of a family environment, African Human Rights Law Journal 2014, 322, at p. 329.

[38] U. M. Assim/J. Sloth-Nielsen, African Human Rights Law Journal 2014, 322, at p. 329.

[39] Articles 116-125 of the Law no. 84-11 on Family Law [qānūn yataḍammanu qānūn al-usra] of 9 June 1984, Official Gazette no. 24 of 6 June 1984 (FLC).

Algerian law explicitly prohibits tabannī.[40] This prohibition mirrors the Islamic rejection of tabannī, which is an instrument that may create artificially what cannot be created but by biology, a legal fiction that cannot confer the effects of nasab. Instead, the legislature enacted the institution of kafāla (in French: recueil légal) in statutory form in 1976 by incorporating it into the newly enacted Code of Public Health.[41] Regarding abandoned children, Article 256 of the code stated that "the public assistance service must endeavour to find, before any other option, a family in which the child can enjoy the same living conditions as a child within his or her own family". It continued to state that the commitment "to take in a child deprived of a family, to raise and to educate him or her, is enshrined in a kafala deed, drawn up in accordance with the procedures set out in family legislation."[42] In 1984, said code was repealed, and kafāla was incorporated into the newly enacted Algerian Family Law Code (FLC) that dedicated nine articles to kafāla (Articles 116-125 of the FLC). None of the articles have been amended since its enactment. Additionally, a decree was promulgated in 1971 regulating the transfer of surnames. This decree has been reformed, once in 1992 and again in 2020.[43]

Article 116 of the FLC defines kafāla as "a commitment to take voluntary responsibility for the care, education and protection of a minor child, in the same way as a father would for his son".[44] The age of majority is set, by Article 40 of the Algerian Civil Code, at 19 years. Thus any person under that age can become a makfūl. In the French version of Article 117 of the FLC, the child has to give its consent to the kafāla if they still have a mother and a father. The Arabic version of the article, however, can be read such that the parents of a minor child must consent

[40] Article 46 of the FLC.

[41] Ordinance no. 76-79 on the Code of Public Health [Ordonnance portant code de la santé publique] of 23 October 1976, Official Gazette no. 101 of 19 December 1976 (French version); cf. A. Bencheneb, Revue algérienne des sciences juridiques, politiques et économiques 1991, 47, at pp. 49 f.

[42] The Code of Public Health was enacted in the specific context of providing help to single mothers. Abandoned children were handed over to the public assistance service and placed under its guardianship. Their mothers lost their rights, and the children could be placed in kafāla with another family, see L. Pruvost, Intégration familiale de l'enfant sans généalogie en Algérie et en Tunisie: kafāla ou adoption, In: Recueil d'articles offert à Maurice Borrmans par ses collègues et amis, 1996, 155, at p. 170.

[43] Decree no. 71-157 Regarding the Change of the Name [marsūm yataʿallaq bi-taghyīr al-laqab] of 3 June 1971, Official Gazette no. 47 of 11 June 1971, as amended by Decree no. 92-24 of 13 January 1992, Official Gazette no. 5 of 22 January 1992 and Decree no. 20-223 of 8 August 2020, Official Gazette no. 47 of 11 August 2020.

[44] Because of this wording, some scholars assume that only a male can be a kāfil; cf. N. Ait Zai, Les droits de l'enfant en Algérie, Rapport Alternatif, 2005, p. 24 f., available at https://archive.crin.org/sites/default/files/images/docs/resources/treaties/crc.40/Algeria_ngo_report.pdf; A. Bencheneb, Revue algérienne des sciences juridiques, politiques et économiques 1991, 47, at p. 50.

to the kafāla if they are still alive. And this seems to be the more accurate reading, as a child below the age of majority is legally incompetent.[45]

Article 118 of the FLC gives the conditions for a person to become a kāfil, Articles 119, 120 those for becoming a makfūl. Accordingly, the kāfil must be Muslim, of integrity, and capable of supervising and protecting the child. Children of both known and unknown descent are eligible for kafāla, but a child of known descent must keep their filiation of origin (nasab), while the child of unknown descent is subject to Article 64 of the Algerian Code of Civil Status,[46] which points to the regulation of names to be given to children. It states that the civil servant is to give children of unknown descent a first name (ism) and that the child is to be identified by a sequence of first names, the last of which would figure as surname (laqab).[47] A decree was enacted in 1971 and amended in 1992 (and most recently in 2020) that explicitly allows a makfūl of unknown descent (i.e., whose father is unknown) to take the surname of his kāfil.[48] This provision was the outcome of lengthy debates that had culminated in 1991 in the issuance of a series of fatwas by Sheikh Hamani of the Conseil supérieur islamique (a counsel that later was renamed as the Haute conseil islamique algérien).[49] One of these fatwas justified the transfer of the name of the kāfil to the makfūl as long as it was not done with intent to confer inheritance rights on the makfūl or to introduce a marriage obstacle between the kāfil and the makfūl, both of which are considered to infringe upon Islamic law.[50]

As regards parental authority, the kafāla arrangement confers upon the kāfil both the custody[51] and the legal guardianship (wilāya) of the child.[52] In other words, an Algerian kafāla transfers full parental authority to the kāfil, who is entitled to manage

---

[45] Cf. N. Younsi Haddad, Revue algérienne des sciences juridiques, politiques et économiques 1999, 7, at p. 17; similarly M. Boulenouar Azzemou, Recueil légal (kafala) et droit(s) positif(s), Droit de la famille, revue mensuelle Lexisnexis 2009, 17, at pp. 18 f.

[46] Ordinance no. 70-20 Regarding Civil Status [amr yataʿallaq al-ḥāla al-madaniyya] of 19 February 1970, Official Gazette no. 21 of 27 February 1970.

[47] On the formation of Arab names, see J. Sublet, Le voile du nom, Essai sur le nom propre arabe, 1991.

[48] See D. Dendani, Droit de filiation: adoption et kafala, Revue algérienne des sciences juridiques, économiques et politiques 1993, 779, at p. 789. If the child has a (known) mother, the mother must give her consent to the transfer of name, cf. Article 1 alinéa 2 of the Decree no. 71-157 in its current version.

[49] L. Pruvost (fn. 42), at p. 174.

[50] Y. Bettahar, La construction sociale de la parentalité: l'exemple de l'Algérie, L'Année du Maghreb 2005-2006, 155, at p. 163.

[51] Article 16 of the FLC. In Tunisia, the kāfil is only awarded the custody of the child (Articles 3, 5 of the Law no. 58-27); the same applies to Morocco (Article 22 of the Dahir no. 1-02-172 Promulgating the Law on Foster Care for Abandoned Children [qānūn yataʿallaq bi-kafālat al-aṭfāl al-muhmalīn] of 13 June 2002, Official Gazette no. 5031 of 19 August 2002).

[52] Article 121 of the FLC: the wilāya qānūniyya is transferred to the kāfil; see also N. Younsi Haddad, Revue algérienne des sciences juridiques, politiques et économiques 1999, 7, at pp. 24 f. On wilāya, see L.-M. Möller, An Enduring Relic: Family Law Reform and the Inflexibility of Wilāya, AJCL 2015, at pp. 893–925.

the assets of the makfūl, including property received by an inheritance, bequest or gift, with due consideration to the best interests of the child.[53] Because the kāfil is given wilāya, his parental authority is all-embracing. Only in cases involving greater financial commitments (the purchase or sale of immovables, for example) must the kāfil address the court.[54] Finally, Article 123 of the FLC explicitly points to the possibility of the kāfil bequeathing to the makfūl up to one-third of his estate by last will.

Interestingly, the Algerian Family Law Code does not entail provisions on the termination of the kafāla. Some scholars hold that there is no specific reason for this silence, and that Algerian kafāla evidently ends with the majority of the makfūl.[55] But, and as has been argued elsewhere, there is ground to argue otherwise,[56] in particular considering the very vague ways in which the law contemplates the revocation of a kafāla. A last point, and one that differentiates an Algerian kafāla from its Moroccan or Tunisian counterparts, is the regulation in Article 125 of the FLC regarding the death of the kāfil. Accordingly, upon the death of the kāfil the kafāla is transferred to the heirs of the kāfil, which suggests that the makfūl belongs to the family of his kāfil.[57]

As a result, an Algerian kafāla has broad effects: it confers full parental authority on the kāfil, who is both custodian and guardian of the child; a child of unknown descent may take the kāfil's name; and the law recommends conferring upon the child, by last will, up to one-third of the kāfil's estate.

IV. Temporary Caretaking of a Child

The third category encompasses jurisdictions that acknowledge the need to care for parentless children but that have conceived of temporary placements in order to overcome shortfalls in care, either because the parents are unfit or have died, or because the child has been abandoned. The terms used to denote these devices vary. In Morocco and Tunisia, the institution under which children are temporarily placed in new homes is also called kafāla. In the United Arab Emirates, the term is riʿāyat al-aṭfāl majhūlī al-nasab, and in Jordan and Saudi Arabia this care arrangement is called iḥtiḍān. The following sections describe Tunisian and Moroccan kafāla, as

[53] Article 122 of the FLC.

[54] N. Younsi Haddad, Revue algérienne des sciences juridiques, politiques et économiques 1999, 7, at p. 27.

[55] See, e.g., N. Saadi, Revue internationale de droit comparé 2014, 99, at p. 114; M.-C. Le Boursicot, La Kafâla ou recueil légal des mineurs en droit musulman: une adoption sans filiation, Droit et cultures 2010, para. 36, available at http://droitcultures.revues.org/2138.

[56] N. Yassari, AJCL 2015, 927, at pp. 952–954.

[57] See L. Pruvost (fn. 42), at p. 175.

well as the Emirati riʿāyat al-aṭfāl, as examples of these alternative care-taking arrangements.

1. Tunisian Kafāla

In Tunisia, the norms related to kafāla — a total of five articles (Articles 3–7) — are incorporated into Law no. 58-27 of 4 March 1958, next to the regulation on tabannī, demarking their different natures and uses.[58]

Article 3 of the Law no. 58-27 defines kafāla as a contract or agreement (ʻaqd) by which a person of full age and legal capacity takes charge of a minor. The kāfil can, however, also be a welfare organization. The French version of the article reads slightly differently, for it states that it is an act (acte) by which a person or organization takes charge of a minor child and assumes custody and attends to its needs.[59] There are no further requirements articulated with regard to the kāfil, and in particular there is no reference to either party's religion. The makfūl is to be a minor (i.e., a person under the age of 18) of known or unknown descent.[60]

The kafāla contract must be drawn before a notary and comes about between the kāfil on one hand and the father and mother of the minor on the other, or one of them if the other is unknown or deceased, or failing this, the public guardian. The kafāla deed must furthermore be approved by the provisional judge.[61]

Article 5 regulates the rights and duties of the kāfil by referring to Articles 54 ff. of the Tunisian Code of Personal Status (CPS). Articles 54-67 of the CPS regulate (only) custody (ḥaḍāna). Article 5 further emphasises that the kāfil's civil liability for the makfūl's acts equals that of fathers and mothers towards their (legitimate, biological) children. This is to make up for the custodian not having such a duty, which normally does reside with the guardian of a minor. This shows that, in contrast to an Algerian kafāla, in Tunisia the kāfil does not become the guardian of the makfūl.[62] Article 6 of the Law 58-27 emphasises that the makfūl keeps their filiation of origin and all rights arising from it, in particular their original name and inheritance rights towards their biological family.[63] Finally, Article 7 of the Law 58-27 sets the end of kafāla upon the makfūl reaching the age of majority. This is a notable

[58] On Tunisian kafāla see country report S. Ben Achour, Tunisia, In: Yassari/Möller/Najm (fn. 11), 325, at pp. 344 ff.

[59] "Article 3. - La tutelle officieuse est l'acte par lequel une personne majeure jouissant de la pleine capacité civile, ou un organisme d'assistance, prend à sa charge un enfant mineur dont il assure la garde et subvient à ses besoins."

[60] Articles 3 and 4 of the Law no. 58-27.

[61] Article 4 of the Law no. 58-27.

[62] See also L. Pruvost (fn. 42), at p. 173.

[63] This article, as Pruvost notes, seems to overlook that the makfūl more often than not is an abandoned child of unknown descent, with no name nor any aspiration to inherit one day, L. Pruvost (fn. 42), at p. 173.

difference to a Tunisian tabannī, which persists after majority.[64] A Tunisian kafāla however can end early if the kāfil, the parents of the makfūl or the public prosecutor so requests. The decision is for the court, with due consideration of the best interests of the child.

2. Moroccan Kafāla

A Moroccan kafāla is very similar to its Tunisian counterpart, although the Moroccan legislature has regulated it much more extensively, dedicating an entire act, Dahir no. 1-02-172 of 2002 Promulgating the Law on Foster Care for Abandoned Children, consisting of 32 articles,[65] to kafāla while explicitly prohibiting tabannī.[66] Article 2 of the Dahir no. 1-02-172 of 2002 is quite explicit. It states that a kafāla is "the commitment to take responsibility for the protection, education and maintenance of an abandoned child in the same way as a father would for his child." A Moroccan kafāla does not give rise to a right to filiation or inheritance.

Abandoned children are eligible for a Moroccan kafāla. An abandoned child is defined as a minor born of unknown parents or of a known mother who have/has abandoned the child of their/her own free will, or as an orphaned child or a child whose parents are unable to provide for the child's needs or who do not have legal means of support, or who are of bad conduct, particularly when they have been deprived of their guardianship.

The kāfil must be Muslim, married, and of the age of majority. They must be morally and socially sound and have sufficient financial resources to provide for the child. A Muslim single woman who meets these conditions may also apply for a kafāla.[67] Generally, priority is given to childless couples, but as long as all children can benefit equally from the means available to the family, having children does not constitute an obstacle.

The kāfil is under a duty to maintain, care for and protect the child and to ensure that the child is brought up in a healthy environment while providing for their basic needs until the age of majority. If the makfūl is a girl, the duty to maintain her financially continues until she marries.[68] As under Tunisian law, the kāfil is civilly

---

[64] Article 7 of the Law no. 58-27.

[65] Dahir no. 1-02-172 of 2002; for a thorough analysis of the Dahir, see J. Bargach, Adoption and Wardship (Kafāla) in Morocco, Recht van de Islam 2001, 77, at pp. 83-86.

[66] Article 149 of the Law no. 70.03 on the Family Code [qānūn bi-mathābat mudawwanat al-usra] of 3 February 2004, Official Gazette no. 5184 of 5 February 2004 (Mudawwana). On Moroccan kafāla, see K. E. Hoffman, Morocco, In: Yassari/Möller/Najm (fn. 11), at pp. 231–266; J. Bargach, Orphans of Islam: Family, Abandonment, and Secret Adoption in Morocco, 2002; M. Dambach/J. Wöllenstein-Tripathi (fn. 11), Service Social International 2020, at pp. 48 ff.

[67] Article 9 para. 2 of the Dahir no. 1-02-172 of 2002.

[68] Article 22 of the Dahir no. 1-02-172 of 2002.

liable for the actions of the child in their care.[69] At the same time, the kāfil benefits from state allowances and social benefits allocated to parents for their children. The kāfil is not awarded guardianship, however. Accordingly, financial matters, including gifts or bequests in favour of the child, must be submitted to the guardianship court, which ensures that the necessary contract is drawn and that the child's rights are protected.[70] The kāfil may leave Morocco with the makfūl, to settle permanently abroad, subject to the authorization of the guardianship court if it is deemed to be in the interests of all parties.[71]

Articles 25-29 of the Dahir no. 1-02-172 of 2002 regulate the revocation of the kafāla. Generally, the kafāla ends automatically when the child reaches majority, which is 18 years of age,[72] or it can end if the kāfil dies or becomes incapable of assuming his responsibilities.[73] If the kāfil parents divorce, the court can order the kafāla to be transferred to one spouse. Also, the biological parents of the makfūl may petition the court for the return of the child if the reason for depriving them of their supervision has fallen away.

3. *United Arab Emirates*

The Emirati Federal Foster Care Act of 2012[74] introduced an institution called riʿāyat al-aṭfāl majhūlī al-nasab that makes children of unknown filiation eligible for care arrangements.[75] The Act sets a minimum age for different applicants: married

[69] Ibid.

[70] Article 23 of the Dahir no. 1-02-172 of 2002.

[71] Article 24 of the Dahir 1-02-172 of 2002. This did however pose a concern for the Moroccan state. Circulaire no. 40 S/2 of 12 September 2012 of the Ministry of Justice therefore requested that the authorities should be very cautious with foreign applicants residing outside of Morocco. The circulaire states: "[...] Although the provisions of article 24 of law n° 15-01 allow kafils to leave the national territory with the abandoned child to reside permanently abroad, this is not without raising a number of difficulties, particularly with regard to monitoring the situation of the child, the subject of the kafala, outside the national territory. This is because how can the extent of the kafil's compliance with its legal obligations be monitored?" It continues that "while the legislator's intention, through the provisions on kafala, is essentially to protect the best interests of the Moroccan child, the preservation of these interests requires, in accordance with the spirit and philosophy of the kafala regime for abandoned children, that kafala be granted only to applicants who are habitually resident on national territory."

[72] Except for the unmarried girl or a physically and financially disabled child, Article 25 of the Dahir no. 1-02-172 of 2002.

[73] Article 25 of the Dahir 1-02-172 of 2002.

[74] Federal Law no. 1/2012 on the Care for Children of Unknown Filiation [qānūn ittiḥādī fī sha'n riʿāyat al-aṭfāl majhūlī al-nasab] of 24 May 2012, Official Gazette no. 537 of 7 June 2012 (Foster Care Act).

[75] See the country report on the United Arab Emirates, L.-M. Möller, United Arab Emirates, In: Yassari/Möller/Najm (fn. 11), at pp. 351–372.

applicants must be 25 years old, single women applying for riʿāyat at least 30. This Act only applies to foundlings, i.e., to children of unknown descent found in the United Arab Emirates. The essence of this arrangement is visible in the terminology applied to the parties: the caretaker, who can be a married couple or a single woman, is labelled "al-usra al-ḥāḍina", i.e., a family entrusted with custody, or, for the single woman, "al-ḥāḍina", i.e., a custodian.[76] In the same vein, the caretaker's main duty is to raise and see to the healthy upbringing of the child, provide for medical, psychological, social, and educational care, uphold the child's best interests, protect them from abuse or neglect, and provide them with a sound (Islamic) religious education.[77] Thus, similar to the Tunisian kafāla, the caretakers receive only custody of the child. The competent authorities must be notified of any major change in residence or other circumstances and are owed an annual report on the child's health. There is no requirement of erecting a will in favour of the child or of making any financial provisions in their favour.

Because only foundlings and orphans are eligible for riʿāyat, by the time the children are accommodated in their new home, they will already have received names at the orphanage,[78] and thus they are not permitted to bear the name of the caretakers. Finally, the legal relationship ends (at the latest) automatically when the child comes of age.

We can thus see that these devices and arrangements allow abandoned children to live in families for a certain period of time. Accordingly, caretakers are only awarded custody while guardianship remains with the court or the relevant state agency, which thereby retains oversight authority.

V. No Formalised Legal Framework for the Accommodation of Parentless Children

In some countries, the legislature has not or has only poorly conceived of a formalised system by which to see to the care of parentless children. Among these countries are Pakistan and Lebanon.[79]

[76] Article 1 of the Foster Care Act; L.-M. Möller, United Arab Emirates, In: Yassari/Möller/Najm (fn. 11), 351, at p. 364. See also the similar terminology used in Jordan, where the caretaking arrangement is called usra al-badīla aw al-ḥāḍina, D. Engelcke, Jordan, In: Yassari/Möller/Najm (fn. 11), 135, at pp. 137 f.

[77] L.-M. Möller, United Arab Emirates, In: Yassari/Möller/Najm (fn. 11), 351, at p. 367.

[78] L.-M. Möller, United Arab Emirates, In: Yassari/Möller/Najm (fn. 11), 351, at p. 369, pointing to Article 3 para. 5 of the Executive Regulations to the Act, which points out that to avoid discrimination, the name should not contain any indication of the unknown origin of the child.

[79] This is also true for Syria; see L.-M. Möller, Kindschaftsrecht und elterliche Sorge in Syrien: Eine rechtsvergleichende Einordnung, In: Schneider/Elliesie/Tellenbach (eds), Migration und Heimatrecht: Herausforderungen muslimisch geprägter Zuwanderung nach Deutschland, 2022, at pp. 81–92.

Lebanese Islamic law prohibits tabannī. However, Lebanese statutory law lacks concrete regulations on the alternative care of parentless children.[80] For children of known descent but with unfit parents, issues related to custody and guardianship can be brought before religious courts.[81] Statutory law does not, however, contain clear provisions for the care of foundlings, orphans, or of children born out of wedlock, who, in cases requiring immediate action, would come under the supervision of the civil juvenile courts.[82] But in practice, informal care alternatives have evolved based on customary and social practices and on cultural norms. Children are often accommodated in their own extended families or taken care of in private, often faith-based, residential care institutions without a court order.[83] There is also the practice of what are known as "secret adoptions", which are accomplished for example through an acknowledgement of filiation by the parents-to-be or through the registration of a new-born child under their name, often with the consent of the biological mother.[84] Interestingly, one practice in Lebanon is an unofficial form of caretaking, also labelled kafāla, by which it is understood that a person (the kāfil) undertakes to provide for a child (usually an orphan) financially for living and education expenses. The child does not live with the kāfil but rather with members of the kāfil's family or is raised in (private) residential care institutions.[85] This kind of support is more of a sponsorship than actual personal care-taking. In the big picture, the Lebanese system of child protections lacks state policies and oversight over alternative care for parentless children.

The situation is similar in Pakistan,[86] where adoption is forbidden and alternative care arrangements are not officially recognised, and there are instead informal arrangements by which a child can be cared for by a childless couple. These are informal accommodations based on the mutual consent of the biological and the care-giving parents that more often than not are not endorsed by a court order.[87] Children are often placed in the care of their own relatives, but orphans and foundlings can be taken care of by unrelated couples. A care arrangement can also

[80] See the country report on Lebanon, M.-C. Najm/M. Mehanna/L. Karamé, Lebanon, In: Yassari/Möller/Najm (fn. 11), at pp. 165–203.

[81] M.-C. Najm/M. Mehanna/L. Karamé, Lebanon, In: Yassari/Möller/Najm (fn. 11), 165, at p. 186.

[82] For the procedure before the Juvenile Courts, see M.-C. Najm/M. Mehanna/L. Karamé, Lebanon, In: Yassari/Möller/Najm (fn. 11), 165, at pp. 189–191.

[83] M.-C. Najm/M. Mehanna/L. Karamé, Lebanon, In: Yassari/Möller/Najm (fn. 11), 165, at pp. 186 f.

[84] M.-C. Najm/M. Mehanna/L. Karamé, Lebanon, In: Yassari/Möller/Najm (fn. 11), 165, at pp. 186 f.

[85] M.-C. Najm/M. Mehanna/L. Karamé, Lebanon, In: Yassari/Möller/Najm (fn. 11), 165, at pp. 196 f.

[86] See the country report on Pakistan, A. Shahid/I. A. Khan, Pakistan, In: Yassari/Möller/Najm (fn. 11), at pp. 267–298; L. Carroll, Adoption in Pakistani law: Repercussions in U.-K. immigration law: A critique of David Pearl and Werner Menski, Muslim Family Law, 3rd ed. 1998, The Islamic Quarterly 2001, at pp. 161–172.

[87] A. Shahid/I. A. Khan, Pakistan, In: Yassari/Möller/Najm (fn. 11), 267, at p. 288.

come about within the framework of the Guardians and Wards Act of 1890, whereby the potential foster family will be awarded guardianship and custody through a court order. The child is thereby placed in the care of a competent family by judicial decree while the child's knowledge of his or her filiation is assured.

VI. Conclusion and Summary

All the Muslim jurisdictions reviewed in the present discussion have devised arrangements for alternative caretaking of parentless children, ranging from the child's full incorporation as a family member entrusted with full rights and duties (as under a Tunisian tabannī) to a loose bond of sponsorship intended, at a minimum, to attend to a child's financial needs (as in Lebanon). These devices and arrangements differ in the density of provisions by which they are codified or in the actual codes they have been incorporated into. All the countries have been careful with their terminology, avoiding the term tabannī and using other terms to refer to their particular arrangements. This shows how these states have dealt with the prohibition of tabannī while finding ways to accommodate children in new homes.

Tunisia is the only country to have regulated and accepted tabannī, i.e., the complete incorporation of a child into a new family. The parent-child relationship created by Tunisian Law no. 58-27 of 4 March 1958 displays all the legal effects of adoption, including the creation of parental care and authority, reciprocal inheritance rights, and the right to carry the adoptive parent's surname.

Iran and Iraq have instituted legal arrangements with wide-ranging effects while taking care to regulate them outside their respective main family law code, providing for them instead in separate or seemingly unrelated legislative acts to dampen the impression that they actually have accommodated the effects of adoption in their legal systems. The effects of either country's arrangements are subject to fairly detailed regulation, including the transfer of full parental care and authority (i.e., custody or ḥaḍāna and guardianship or wilāya), the legal representation of the child without state interference, the new caretaker's duty to provide financial support beyond the caretaker's death (mostly through the erection of an irrevocable will and the right of the child to carry the caretaker's family name). The same applies to a great extent to Algerian kafāla. As a result, enduring social bonds of family are being created to accommodate children in new families both socially as well as legally.

But as exemplified by Emirati law, other arrangements have also been devised to provide for the temporary caretaking of parentless children. These kinds of devices only award to new caretakers the custody of a child while the court or other competent authority retains guardianship and oversight authority. In some jurisdictions, the child may take the caretaker's surname, in particular when the child is of unknown descent. As regards financial rights, none of these temporary arrangements provides for a compulsory will or any financial provision in favour of the child to be demanded as a precondition for the child's placement with the caretaker. Most importantly, the legal relationship ends (at the latest) automatically with the child coming of age.

Finally, there are countries that have not designed any formalised legal framework for the placement of parentless children in new homes. In Lebanon, foundlings, orphans, and children of unfit caretakers mostly come under the care of extended family without a court order, or they enter private residential care institutions. Secret "adoptions" are also practiced. In Pakistan, orphans, children born out of wedlock, and other destitute children are provided for through various legislative and institutional measures, but these measures are broad, and there is room for improvement.

Kafāla in France

Fabienne Jault-Seseke

I. Introduction

Within the FAMIMOVE project, it has been observed that the EU member states adopt very different approaches in handling and recognising kafālas.[1] The project has focused mainly on three member states, Belgium, France and the Netherlands.[2] The situation in France is particularly interesting because of its strong links with Morocco and Algeria, where kafāla is widely accepted but differs slightly.[3]

It is quite common for people of Moroccan or Algerian nationality living in France to be given responsibility for a child born in their country of origin through a kafāla. This is quite often an intra-family kafāla. The child is entrusted to an uncle, aunt or grandparent, or even to an older brother or sister. The aim of kafāla is either to make up for the absence of parents, or to offer the child better living conditions, or even a better education. The kāfil is then a close relative of the child. In other cases, kafāla serves as a substitute for adoption, which is prohibited in both Morocco and Algeria. In this case, the child may be entrusted to a parent who has no particular ties with Morocco or Algeria but who can take care of him or her. Before the 2001 French Act on intercountry adoption,[4] it was not uncommon for French case law to allow a kafāla to be treated as an adoption. This is not the case anymore (section "II.

[1] A round table on kafāla was organised in Paris in December 2023.

[2] To go further, see the study published by the International Social Service (ISS) in 2021, Kafalah - Preliminary analysis of national and cross-border practices (hereinafter ISS Report).

[3] On the various approaches, see supra N. Yassari, Beyond kafāla: How parentless children are placed in new homes in Muslim jurisdictions, in this volume, at p. 207.

[4] Loi 2001-111 of 6 February 2001 relative à l'adoption internationale.

F. Jault-Seseke (✉)
Faculty of Law and Political Science, Laboratory DANTE, University of Paris Saclay, Versailles Saint-Quentin-en-Yvelines, France
e-mail: fabienne.jault-seseke@uvsq.fr

S. Arnold, B. Heiderhoff (eds.), *Children in Migration and International Family Law*, https://doi.org/10.1007/978-3-031-71598-3_14

Kafāla Is Not an Adoption"). Therefore, it is necessary to find another qualification. In the framework of the 1996 Child Protection Convention,[5] kafāla has been qualified as a placement. The French and Moroccan Central authorities follow the procedure given by Article 33 of the 1996 Child Protection Convention (section "III. Kafāla, a Placement in the Meaning of the 1996 Child Protection Convention"). Regarding kafālas outside of the scope of this convention, the framework is less clear (section "IV. Kafāla, Out of the 1996 Child Protection Convention"). Dealing with migration issues, administrative courts take a case-by-case approach (section "V. Kafāla and Migration Issues").

II. Kafāla Is Not an Adoption

Before 2001, it was not uncommon for French case law to allow a kafāla to be treated as an adoption.[6] Since 2001, Article 370-3 para. 2 of the CC (French Civil Code) states that "the adoption of a foreign minor may not be granted if the minor's personal law prohibits this institution, unless the minor was born and habitually resides in France".[7] The objective of this provision adopted by the 2001 Law on intercountry adoption is to limit child trafficking, to respect the sovereignty of states that prohibit adoption and to comply with the requirements of the 1993 Child Adoption Convention[8] ratified by France in 1998.[9] This provision confirms the position of the French government expressed in a circular, which refuses to classify a kafāla as an adoption.[10] In the early years of implementation, some courts have ruled that if a kafāla cannot be classified as a full adoption, it can still be classified as a simple adoption.

In accordance with Article 370-3 of the CC, in two decisions of principle dated 10 May 2006, the Court of Cassation affirmed that kafāla is not equivalent to adoption.[11] The solution was repeated in a case where a child entrusted to French parents by the authorities in his country of origin (Algeria) had been definitively and irrevocably abandoned in Algeria.[12] It was then clear that the child would remain in France. For some, it would have been justified to set aside any rigid approach and

[5]Convention of 19 October 1996 on Jurisdiction, Applicable Law, Recognition, Enforcement and Co-operation in respect of Parental Responsibility and Measures for the Protection of Children (1996 Child Protection Convention).

[6]Court of cassation 10 May 1995, n° 93-17.634.

[7]Loi 2001-111 of 6 February 2001 on intercountry adoption.

[8]Convention of 29 May 1993 on Protection of Children and Co-operation in Respect of Intercountry Adoption (1993 Child Adoption Convention).

[9]Article 4 of the 1993 Child Adoption Convention stipulates that adoptions may only take place if the competent authorities of the State of origin have established that the child is adoptable.

[10]Circular of the Minister of Justice, 16 February 1999, on intercountry adoption.

[11]Court of cassation 10 May 2006, n° 06-15.264.

[12]Court of cassation 9 July 2008, n° 07-20.279.

consider the best interests of the child to pronounce an adoption.[13] This was not the choice made by the Court who later received the support of the European Court of Human Rights (ECtHR) in the case Harroudj.[14]

Given that kafāla cannot be classified as either an adoption or even a placement with a view to adoption, the question of its classification remained. Surprisingly, the case law in civil matters is not numerous. Decisions relating to kafāla mainly come from the administrative courts and concern the granting of a visa or the benefit of family reunification.[15] The civil courts mainly deal with kafāla when it comes to knowing whether the kafāla can be qualified as fosterage within the meaning of Article 21-12 of the CC, which allows the French foster parent to apply for French nationality for the child after 3 years.[16] There are only very few rulings dealing with the nature of the kafāla as a child protection measure. Because of its special nature, kafāla should not be reduced to a delegation of parental responsibility or a guardianship measure.[17] The notion of legal foster care ("recueil legal"), which would best correspond to kafāla, has no meaning in French law, where foster care ("recueil") is a fact.[18] Therefore, kafāla should be recognised as such.[19] However, in various cases, it is necessary for practical reasons to find a concept within the French legal system that corresponds to kafāla. Adaptation is needed. In some cases where the kāfil applied for exequatur of the kafāla, the result was that the judge qualified it as a delegation of parental authority.[20] The repetition of this solution as well as the lack of more case law can be explained by the publication in 2014 of a circular on the legal effects of kafāla in France.[21] This circular of the Minister of Justice, despite its lack of binding effect, is the framework for the recognition of kafāla in France. It states that a kafāla can be recognised in France and has the effect of a delegation of parental responsibility or of a guardianship. The choice between the two concepts depends on the child's situation. For children, who are orphans or have no known parentage, the circular retains the classification as guardianship. Where parentage has been established and one of the parents is alive, the proposed qualification is delegation of parental responsibility.

[13] M. Farge, Comment accueillir les "kafālas" musulmanes?, Droit de la famille, 2008, para. 133.

[14] ECtHR 4 October 2012, 43631/09, ECLI:CE:ECHR:2012:1004JUD004363109 (Harroudj versus France).

[15] See IV.

[16] See below, at p. 236.

[17] See F. Marchadier on Court of appeal Limoges 25 January 2011, RG n° 08/01139, Revue critique de droit international privé 2011, 686, at p. 686, and the references.

[18] On the terminology see the circular of 22 October 2014 mentioning an opinion of a terminology committee published the 5 December 2013 who suggested to translate kafāla by "recueil legal".

[19] For example, Court of appeal Paris, 27 March 2008, n° 06/17327.

[20] Court of appeal Paris, 9 June 2011, n° 10/18164; Court of appeal Toulouse 23 June 2015, RG n° 14/00886 excluding the guardianship to retain the delegation of parental authority. Court of appeal Dijon 21 may 2015 n° RG 14/01330.

[21] Circular of 22 October 2014 on the legal effects of kafāla in France.

Surprisingly, this circular does not address the role given to the Central Authorities by Article 33 of the 1996 Child Protection Convention.

III. Kafāla, a Placement in the Meaning of the 1996 Child Protection Convention

The 1996 Child Protection Convention has been ratified by 54 states including all EU member states. Morocco has been a contracting state since 1 December 2002. Morocco is the only contracting state where kafālas are issued. Therefore, the 1996 Child Protection Convention only applies to Moroccan kafālas.[22] It would be desirable for other states with kafāla arrangements to ratify the 1996 Child Protection Convention. In this respect, the European Council, when authorising France to negotiate a bilateral agreement with Algeria on family law, suggested that efforts be made to ensure that Algeria became a party to the various Hague Conventions.[23]

Article 3 lit. e of the 1996 Child Protection Convention provides that the kafāla is comparable to the placement of the child in a foster family or in institutional care and is covered by the Convention. And with regard to the placement of children (including kafāla), Article 33 of the 1996 Child Protection Convention establishes a compulsory consultation procedure between the contracting states concerned when a child is to be placed in another contracting state. For a time, the Moroccan authorities seemed reluctant to implement Article 33 of the 1996 Child Protection Convention: in 2012, the Moroccan Minister of Justice adopted a circular banning international kafāla.[24] But the dual nationality of many kāfils made its implementation illusory.

According to Article 33 of the 1996 Child Protection Convention, the competent authority shall transmit a report on the child together with the reasons for the proposed placement or provision of care to the Central Authority or other competent authority in the requested state. The decision of placement or the provision of care by way of kafāla may be made only after such Central Authority or other competent authority of the requested state has consented to the placement or provision of care, taking into account the child's best interests.

At the global scale, there is little awareness of the existence or the applicability of Article 33 of the 1996 Child Protection Convention.[25] But France consistently

---

[22] See Practical Handbook on the Operation of the 1996 Hague Child Protection Convention (The Hague: HCCH, 2014), at p. 30.

[23] Council Decision (EU) 2024/592 of 23 January 2024 empowering France to negotiate a bilateral agreement with Algeria concerning judicial cooperation in civil matters related to family law.

[24] Circular n° 40 S/2, 14 September 2012.

[25] See the responses to the 2023 Questionnaire on the 1996 Child Protection Convention, at pp. 109-121 (see in particular, responses from Switzerland (at p. 111), France (at p. 119) and Norway (at p. 120)), https://assets.hcch.net/docs/79105a67-45d6-47ed-8ca5-2def687cf130.pdf.

applies Article 33 of the 1996 Child Protection Convention. Of course, the French Central Authority should be contacted by the Moroccan one.

The scheme of cooperation is the following. The kāfil submits his request for the establishment of the kafāla to the Moroccan family court. The court informs the Moroccan Central Authority. The French Central Authority receives the request for cooperation, the birth certificate, the abandonment judgment[26] and a social report from the Moroccan Central Authority. After this, the French Central Authority contacts the social services of the kāfil's habitual residence. A social investigation of the kāfil follows. It can show that the kāfil had a fraudulent conduct (by paying the mother for example). Article L 221-3 al. 4 of the Code de l'action sociale et des familles (Social welfare and Families Code) states that the child welfare service responds as quickly as possible to requests for cooperation from a Central Authority. After receiving the social report, the French Central Authority issues an opinion to the Moroccan Central Authority. An unfavorable opinion is binding. The decision of the Central Authority, which is in fact a decision of the Minister of Justice, may be appealed to the administrative courts.[27]

The French Central authority is confronted with many kafāla requests coming from Morocco. Their numbers are growing every year. In 2023, 143 Moroccan kafāla cases under the 1996 Child Protection Convention have been registered. This number should not mask the other cases where the cooperation mechanism is not implemented. Sometimes the kāfil contacts the social services directly to receive a suitability report. This is the wrong way. The report will not be sufficient to obtain the kafāla. The information has to be exchanged through the Central Authorities as underlined in Article 34 of the 1996 Child Protection Convention.

Kafāla placements that fall under the scope of the 1996 Child Protection Convention are recognised by operation of law in France if the procedure of Article 33 of the 1996 Child Protection Convention has been respected. Kafāla is then recognised as such. An adaptation, however, is necessary to determine the rights and duties of the kāfil on the French territory. As said above, the kafāla will produce the effect of delegation of parental authority or of guardianship. Moreover, the recognition concerns civil law effects and is not systematically followed by the possibility for the child to legally reside in an EU member state.[28] There is a gap between the civil status and the migration status. There is no communication between the Ministry of Justice (Central Authority) and the Ministry of Home Affairs. However, if the cooperation mechanism leads to the pronouncement of the kafāla, it seems difficult to identify the reason that would justify a visa refusal.

---

[26] According to Moroccan Law, only abandoned children are eligible to kafāla. See ISS Report (fn. 2), at p. 51.

[27] See for example Paris Administrative Court 2 February 2024, n° 2207163. In this case, the applicant was successful. The judge found that the decision of the French Central Authority adopted in 2021 was mainly based on the fact that in 2017 the applicant has been refused approval for adoption. In this way, the judge reviews the reasons for the decision.

[28] See IV.

The implementation of the cooperation mechanism of Article 33 in the 1996 Child Protection Convention is to be welcomed. It ensures that the measure taken respects fundamental rights, with dual control by the host country and the country of origin. The system is similar to the one implemented by the 1993 Child Adoption Convention which establishes a system of cooperation between authorities in both countries in order to ensure that intercountry adoption is in the best interests of the child and to eliminate abuses.

However, it has been observed that some Moroccan judges are not familiar with the 1996 Child Protection Convention system. Some Moroccan kafāla judgments where the kāfil is living in France are issued without the implication of the Central Authorities. It is therefore important to raise awareness of the convention in the legal community. It is also important to inform the kāfils of the existence of the Convention mechanism so that they can draw the judge's attention to the need to involve the Central Authorities.

IV. Kafāla, Out of the 1996 Child Protection Convention

If the country of origin is not a contracting state to the 1996 Child Protection Convention — this is the case namely of Algeria — or if the kafāla placements is a private arrangement or a kafāla adoulaire,[29] the cooperation mechanism of Article 33 of the 1996 Child Protection Convention does not apply. Indeed the 1996 Child Protection Convention only applies to a decision taken by an authority, i.e. in the context of a kafāla to judicial kafāla. Moreover, it must be considered that Article 33 of the 1996 Child Protection Convention only applies to the situation of a cross-border kafāla, i.e. if the kāfil does not reside in the country of origin of the child. Therefore, Article 33 of the 1996 Child Protection Convention does not apply to every Moroccan judicial kafāla that has a link with France (or with another contracting state). For example, if a child was entrusted to his uncle who lived in Morocco and moved to France only after the decision, Article 33 of the 1996 Child Protection Convention is not relevant. It becomes relevant only if the uncle decides to be joined by the makfūl. But in this case, Article 33 of the 1996 Child Protection Convention seems to be disregarded.

When kafāla is out of the scope of the 1996 Child Protection Convention, it is possible to obtain the recognition of the kafāla in France. As stated by the 2014 circular of the Minister of Justice, a judicial kafāla like any decision relating to the status of a person is automatically recognised on French territory, without any particular formality, provided that its international legality is not contested. The

[29] See 8th Meeting of the Special Commission on the Practical Operation of the 1980 Child Abduction Convention and the 1996 Child Protection Convention, Conclusions and Recommendations 2023, para. 84. See also, ECtHR 16 December 2014, 52265/10, ECLI:CE:ECHR:2014:1216JUD005226510 (Chbihi Loudoudi and others versus Belgium).

Franco-Moroccan Convention on Mutual Legal Assistance, Enforceability of Judgments and Extradition of 5 October 1957 and the Franco-Algerian Convention on Enforceability and Extradition of 27 August 1964 are relevant. They state that the Moroccan or Algerian decisions have res judicata in France if they meet various conditions (international jurisdiction of the court, regularity of the proceedings, enforceability of the decision, no conflict with French public policy or with a decision rendered in France). Therefore, it is not necessary to apply for the exequatur of the court decision granting kafāla. But exequatur is still possible. The kāfil may request it for practical reasons: an exequatur ruling makes it easier for him to prove his relationship with the child. As already seen, the kāfil is likely to ask the exequatur court to qualify the kafāla as a French measure of protection.

Regarding private arrangements, they are not recognised as such. They have to be confirmed or approved by a measure taken by an authority (homologation). The homologation decision can be recognised, but a distinction is to be made. If the homologation has merely attested the formal legality of the deed, exequatur may be refused. If the homologation has enabled the child's interests to be taken into account, exequatur is to be granted.[30]

There are no recent judgments refusing the recognition of kafāla as a measure of child care. The requests for exequatur are decreasing. It is likely an effect of the 2014 circular ascertaining the principle of recognition. Now most often in front of the French authorities the kāfils produce only the decision to ask for different rights (social benefits, . . .). There is therefore a risk that practices will vary depending on the authority involved. Some will be strict and ask for details that are complicated to give, some will be lax and agree to give effect to a kafāla that does not necessarily respect fundamental rights. In this framework, there is no place for the control of the Central Authorities. There is then a risk that the kafāla has been established without assessing the best interests of the child and without assessing the suitability of the kāfil. This also makes it difficult to check that the principles of the CRC,[31] such as the principle of subsidiarity, are being respected.[32]

However, it must be said that once the child has settled in France, it is difficult to pretend that the kafāla does not exist. We are back to the policy of "fait accompli", which makes questions of private international law concerning children very complicated as demonstrated by the tricky issue of surrogacy.

When the kafāla is recognised as such and the child is living in France with her or his kāfil, there is still place for the application of the 1996 Child Protection Convention, given that then the child has his or her habitual residence in France. It follows from Article 14 of the 1996 Child Protection Convention[33] that a French

[30] See the 2014 Circular (fn. 21).

[31] UN 1989 Convention on the Rights of the Child (CRC).

[32] On the principle, see ISS Report (fn. 2), especially at p. 133.

[33] This article reads as follows "The measures taken in application of Articles 5 to 10 remain in force according to their terms, even if a change of circumstances has eliminated the basis upon which

judge, whose jurisdiction derives from Article 7 of the Brussels IIter Regulation,[34] has the possibility to issue a child protection measure according to the French Law.[35] This possibility will make the monitoring of the child protection easier. A French authority will have to apply French Law and French concepts.

Beside the civil effects, the main issues regarding the kafāla concern the entry and stay in France for the makfūl.

V. Kafāla and Migration Issues

At national level, but also at international level, civil law rules do not interfere with migration law rules.[36] So, in theory, even if the kafāla has been recognised following cooperation between the French and Moroccan Central Authorities, the authorities responsible for issuing visas or family reunification authorizations remain free to assess the situation. This is even more the case when the kafāla has been established outside the framework set up by the 1996 Child Protection Convention.

There are no provision on the kafāla in the CESEDA (Code of entry and the residence of foreigners and right of asylum).[37] The framework is given by the case law, with an exception regarding the family reunification for Algerians. The case law concerns the issuance of a visa and the family reunification. There is no issue with residence permits. Indeed, in France, a child under the age of 18 does not need a residence permit.

In a first stage, kafāla, since it does not create any parent-child relationship, did not give the child any particular right to access French territory.[38] This statement can still be found on the Ministry of the Interior website.[39] But the growing importance

jurisdiction was founded, so long as the authorities which have jurisdiction under the Convention have not modified, replaced or terminated such measures".

[34]Council Regulation (EU) 2019/1111 of 25 June 2019 on jurisdiction, the recognition and enforcement of decisions in matrimonial matters and the matters of parental responsibility, and on international child abduction (recast).

[35]For an example of the application of Brussels IIbis regulation, see Court of appeal Limoges 25 January 2011, Revue critique de droit international privé 2011, 686, at p. 686. See also Court of appeal Paris 25 September 2018, RG 16/22118, arriving at the very curious conclusion that the Brussels IIbis Regulation precluded recognition of the Algerian decision on the grounds that the Algerian court lacked jurisdiction, since the child was in France at the date of the decision.

[36]The 1996 Child Protection Convention does not apply to "decisions on the right of asylum and on immigration" (Article 4 lit. j).

[37]The title in French is "Code de l'entrée et du séjour des étrangers et du droit d'asile".

[38]See for example Conseil d'État 29 December 2006, n° 284467; 9 February 2007, n° 296173; 18 April 2008, n°303765; and of 27 June 2008, n° 291561 and Conseil d'État 30 July 2003, n° 223327, ECLI:FR:CECHS:2003:223327.20030730 (Agbane) (family reunification).

[39]https://www.immigration.interieur.gouv.fr/Immigration/L-immigration-familiale/Focus-sur-la-kafala. But the site puts it into perspective by mentioning both the Franco-Algerian agreement and administrative case law.

of fundamental rights, and in particular the right to respect for private and family life, has changed the situation. The change can also be explained by the fact that kafāla can no longer be seen as adoption. For as long as kafālas granted in the child's interest could be described as adoption, the makfūl's entry and residence were viewed through the prism of the rules specific to adoption.

By now the administrative courts take a case-by-case approach following guidelines that are the same for granting family reunification or issuing a visa.

Family reunification with the kāfil may be admitted even if the CESEDA contains a restrictive list of beneficiaries of family reunification, which does not include a makfūl.[40]

First, for Algerians, family reunification is provided for by the Franco-Algerian agreement of 1968. Children under the age of 18, for whom the Algerian citizen is legally responsible by virtue of a decision by the Algerian judicial authority in the child's best interests, may benefit from family reunification.[41] Nevertheless, the condition relating to the "best interests of the child" may limit access to the territory.[42] For example, according to a ministerial circular, if there are parents or siblings present in Algeria, the planned establishment in France could only be considered to be in the child's best interests if it was justified by particular circumstances, such as the parents' inability to provide for the child's basic material and emotional needs, it being specified that socio-economic considerations were not sufficient.[43]

Since 2010, the Conseil d'Etat (Council of State) considers that an application for family reunification based on the Franco-Algerian agreement and aimed at enabling a child to join an Algerian national in France, who is responsible for him or her by virtue of a decision by the Algerian judicial authority, may no longer, as a general rule, be refused on the grounds that it would be in the child's interest to remain in Algeria with his or her parents or other family members.[44] The administrative authority may still reject the application on the grounds listed in Article 4 of the Franco-Algerian Agreement, in particular on the grounds that the conditions for receiving the child in France would be contrary to the child's interests, taking into account, in particular, the resources and housing conditions of the holder of parental authority.[45]

State liability of the state may be invoked when the refusal to reunify a family disproportionately infringes the right to private and family life. Thus in 2016, the Conseil d'Etat ordered the French State to pay compensation to a kāfil and his wife, as well as to their makfūls: the rejection of their application for family reunification

[40] CESEDA, Articles L. 434-2 and L. 434-3.

[41] Title II of the Protocol annexed to the rider of 22 December 1985 to the Franco-Algerian agreement of 27 December 1968.

[42] Administrative Court of appeal Bordeaux, 4 November 2008, n° 06BX01112.

[43] Circular Ministry of Home Affairs 27 October 2005.

[44] Conseil d'Etat 1 December 2010, n° 328063.

[45] Ibid.

was deemed illegal. The amount of compensation intended to repair the non-material loss suffered by the kāfil and his wife as a result of not being able, for twelve years, to bring up the children entrusted to them by the Algerian judicial authorities (in this case their nephew and niece) was assessed at 10,000 euros. The prejudice suffered by the makfūls as a result of being deprived of the opportunity to be brought up by their uncle and aunt was assessed at 15,000 euros each.[46]

Secondly, and out of the scope of the Franco-Algerian agreement, in principle, family reunification is not available to the makfūl in the absence of a parent-child relationship with the kāfil.[47] Nevertheless, the Conseil d'Etat specified that it is the responsibility of the administrative authority, under the control of the judge, to ensure that a decision to refuse family reunification, in the case of children entrusted to kafāla, does not disproportionately affect the exercise of the right to a normal family life.[48] More recently, it has been stated that it is in the child's best interests to live with the person who, by virtue of a court decision having legal effect in France, has parental authority over him or her. This principle first set out regarding the visa also applies to family reunification based on the provisions of the CESEDA.[49]

If the authorization of family reunification has been given, the authority asked for the visa cannot refuse it on the ground of the best interests of the child. It cannot invoke a risk of misuse of the family reunification and visa procedure for migration purposes, given that the applicant has reached, or is about to reach, the age of 18.[50]

There is no specific visa for the makfūl. He or she has to apply for a visitor visa. The competent authorities (consular authorities) have to take the best interests of the child into consideration. They consult the social services in France. The kāfils have to prove that they have accommodation in France and have sufficient financial resources. The sole argument that education is better in France than in the country of origin is not sufficient.

There are numerous appeals against visa refusal decisions. From 2004, the Conseil d'État ruled that, in certain specific cases, refusing a visa to a makfūl entrusted to a French national could disproportionately infringe the makfūl's right to private and family life (violation of Article 8 of the Human Rights Convention[51]) or disregard the child's best interests (violation of Article 3 para. 1 of the CRC).[52] This is the case, in particular, when the child has been abandoned and has no family ties in his or her country of origin, or when he or she no longer has a family that can materially take care of him or her, and when, at the same time, the kāfils cannot have

[46] Conseil d'Etat 6 April 2016, n° 378338, ECLI:FR:CECHR:2016:378338.20160406.

[47] See recently Administrative Court of appeal Paris 5 December 2022, 210A02008.

[48] Conseil d'Etat 24 March 2004, n° 220434.

[49] For example, Administrative Court of appeal Marseille, 6 October 2015, n° 15MA01180.

[50] For example, Conseil d'Etat 28 February 2008, n° 296908.

[51] Convention for the Protection of Human Rights and Fundamental Freedoms (Human Rights Convention).

[52] Conseil d'Etat 17 December 2004, n° 242192; 5 December 2005, n° 267953.

children and their situation, both personal and professional, does not allow them to envisage regular stays in the makfūl's country of origin.[53]

Later, in 2009, the Conseil d'État made the general assertion, based on the CRC, that "in principle, it is in a child's interest to live with the person who, by virtue of a court decision that has legal effect in France, has parental authority over him or her".[54] Thus, according to the Supreme Court, "where a visa [...] is applied for with a view to enabling a child to join a French or foreign national who has been delegated parental authority [...], the visa may not, as a general rule [...] be refused on the grounds that it would be in the child's best interests to remain with his or her parents or other family members". The Conseil d'État added that the fact that the delegation of parental authority was intended to enable the minor to settle permanently in France could not be construed as a misuse of the purpose of the visa or of the international adoption procedure. This case law is consistent.[55]

The result of this case law is a reversal of the burden of proof: the authorities must demonstrate that it is in the child's best interests to remain in his or her country. However, this case law always concerns judicial kafālas. It does not apply to unregistered or notarial kafālas (kafālas adoulaires).[56] For the latter, since they do not concern orphans or children whose parents are unable to exercise parental authority, their effects on the transfer of parental authority are variable. There is no presumption that living with the kāfil will be in the child's best interests. Therefore, the kāfil has to establish that this the case. The proof is not impossible so that there is no prohibition to give effect to a notarial kafāla.

The presumption set out by the Supreme Court and scrupulously reiterated by the lower courts does not mean that a visa must always be issued to the makfūl. Other conditions may prevent this: the visa may be refused on the grounds that the material conditions (resources and accommodation) for receiving the child in France are not sufficient, so that it is not in the child's best interests to live in France. But the argument that migration laws are being circumvented is not valid. For example, the circumstances that the kafāla concerns a child aged 17 and confers the responsibility to the grandparents living in France cannot lead to the conclusion that the kafāla circumvents the migration rules and they do not justify the visa's refusal.[57]

Once in France, the makfūl should be able to obtain a travel document that will enable him or her to travel, even though there is no legal provision for this. The solution is based on consideration of the child's best interests.[58]

---

[53]Respectively, Conseil d'Etat 16 January 2006, n° 274934; 17 February 2010, n° 319818; Conseil d'Etat 17 December 2004, n° 242192; 5 December 2005, n° 267953; Conseil d'Etat 29 December 2006, n° 284467; 9 November 2007, n° 296173; 28 December 2007 n° 303956.

[54]Conseil d'Etat 9 December 2009, n° 305031, case "Sekpon".

[55]Conseil d'Etat 22 October 2010, n° 33035; 30 March 2011, n° 334553; 19 April 2011, n° 332231 and n° 336681.

[56]Conseil d'Etat 22 October 2010, n° 321645, ECLI:FR:CESSR:2010:321645.20101022; 22 February 2013, n° 330211, ECLI:FR:CESSR:2013:330211.20130222.

[57]Conseil d'Etat 19 December 2007, n° 297417.

[58]Conseil d'Etat 3 October 2012, n° 351906, ECLI:FR:CESSR:2012:351906.20121003.

It is interesting to note that the Courts often invoke the child's best interests or the right to family life, but never mention the principle of subsidiarity enshrined in the CRC.[59] The balance between this principle and the child's best interests after the kafāla has been pronounced will lead to the recognition of the kafāla and its effects. In doing so, it is as if only the authorities in the country of origin were bound by the principle of subsidiarity. The FAMIMOVE project roundtable in Paris was the occasion to address the role of the consular authorities: they are aware of the principle of subsidiarity and refuse the visa when there is still a parent in the country of origin that can take care of the child with the help of the kāfil. All difficulties will end if the makfūl acquires French nationality. The acquisition of the French nationality is possible when the kāfil is French. It will open the door to adoption, given that the new national law of the child will then be the French one.[60] Article 21-12 para. 2 of the CC, amended in 2016, provides that a child may claim French nationality, by simple declaration, "if he or she has been taken in by court order and raised by a person of French nationality for at least three years, or if he or she has been entrusted to the child welfare service", as well as "if he or she has been taken in in France and raised in conditions that have enabled him or her to receive a French education for at least five years [...]". The first hypothesis covers judicial kafālas, whereas the second could concern adoulaire or notarial kafālas. The homologation decision or even the French decision of exequatur can be seen as a court order requested in the first hypothesis.[61] There are many refusals to register declarations of nationality made for children taken in through a kafāla. Finally, it is at this stage that the French court exercises its control over the kafāla. Essentially, the French court checks that the foreign authority has ensured that the kafāla does not contravene public order and is in the child's best interests.[62]

In conclusion, although kafāla is not an adoption, it would be desirable for it to be regulated in a similar way to ensure respect for the fundamental rights of the various

[59] The principle itself is controversial: L. Martínez Mora/H. Baker/E. Harang, The 1993 Hague Intercountry Adoption Convention and subsidiarity: is the subsidiarity principle still "fit for purpose"?, In: A Commitment to Private International Law: essays in honour of Hans van Loon, 2013, at pp. 346–351.

[60] F. Jault-Seseke/S. Corneloup/S. Barbou des Places, Droit de la nationalité et des étrangers, 2015, especially para. 198, stating that this is a kind of circumvention of the prohibition on the adoption of children of prohibitive personal status. But it is a legal circumvention that was, moreover, a decisive factor in the assessment of the conformity of Article 370-3 para. 2 of the CC with the Human Rights Convention (See ECtHR 4 October 2012, 43631/09, ECLI:CE:ECHR:2012:1004JUD004363109 (Harroudj versus France)). Cf. Court of cassation, 4 December 2013, n° 12-26.161, ECLI:FR: CCASS:2013:C101387.

[61] Respectively Court of appeal Douai 6 July 2023, n° 20/04748; Court of appeal Paris 1 June 2021 n° 19/17654.

[62] For example, Court of appeal Douai 6 July 2023, n° 20/04748.

people involved. The mechanism put in place by Article 33 of the 1996 Child Protection Convention provides this framework. In cases not covered by this provision, it would be useful to give more information on the ins and outs of kafāla. In this respect, the initiative taken by the Greater Lyon Metropolitan Area to organise this information is to be welcomed.[63]

[63] See ISS Report (fn. 2), especially at p. 148.

Kafāla in the Netherlands

María Mayela Celis Aguilar

I. Introduction[1]

Within the framework of the FAMIMOVE project, it has been observed that the Netherlands is one of the most advanced states in handling and recognising kafālas, having acquired significant expertise in this area. Most of the kafālas handled by the Netherlands originate from Morocco.

By way of background, it should be noted that before the year 2013 the Netherlands treated kafālas either as adoptions or as foster care measures.[2] Following a letter of 5 February 2013 issued by the Dutch Ministry of Justice and addressed to the relevant Dutch institutions, this practice was amended and kafālas are no longer treated as adoptions. This is in stark contrast to practices existing in other partner states of the FAMIMOVE project, which continue to forward kafāla applications to the adoption authorities or have not acquired any expertise in this area. With some caution, it could be stated that kafālas are often treated similar to foster care measures in the Netherlands.[3]

---

[1] The author would like to thank Hans van Loon (former Secretary General of the Hague Conference on Private International Law [HCCH]) and Prof. Susan Rutten for their comments. All errors are the sole responsibility of the author.

[2] See Werkinstructie SUA, WI 2023/9 Pleegkinderenbeleid, at pp. 4 f., available at https://puc.overheid.nl/ind/doc/PUC_1315180_1/1/. This policy is also referred to in the case law of the administrative Dutch courts, see Rechtbank Den Haag 12 June 2015, ECLI:NL:RBDHA:2015:6791.

[3] Case commentary I. Rebbik, Kafalah and the right to reside in the Netherlands, CUREDI Database CUREDI089NL003 (forthcoming).

M. M. Celis Aguilar (✉)
Assistant Professor, Faculty of Law, Maastricht University, Maastricht, Netherlands
e-mail: mayela.celisaguilar@maastrichtuniversity.nl

S. Arnold, B. Heiderhoff (eds.), *Children in Migration and International Family Law*, https://doi.org/10.1007/978-3-031-71598-3_15

Surprisingly, the event that triggered the change in policy was not prompted by the Netherlands but by Morocco. Indeed, the Ministry of Justice and Liberties of Morocco issued circular No. 40 S/2 dated 26 September 2012 in which it explained the position of Morocco regarding abandoned children and kafāla.[4] Subsequently, a meeting was held between a magistrate of the Moroccan Embassy and Dutch officials in which the circular and the position of Morocco were further clarified. In particular, it was stressed that adoptions are prohibited under Moroccan law.

As regards the domestic legal framework, the Netherlands has adopted implementing legislation concerning the 1996 Child Protection Convention[5] as well as the Brussels IIter Regulation.[6] This legislation is entitled *Uitvoeringswet internationale kinderbescherming* (International Child Protection Implementation Act) and will be considered below. The Netherlands consistently applies the above-mentioned implementing legislation (in particular, Articles 10 and 11) coupled with Article 33 of the 1996 Child Protection Convention when assessing kafālas.

This chapter seeks to provide information about the legal framework and the manner in which kafālas are handled in the Netherlands. As such, kafāla is an unknown legal institution in the Netherlands and other (European) countries. This poses difficulties, some of which will be discussed in this chapter.

This chapter will begin with some remarks on the legal framework and on the case law on Kafāla in the Netherlands. It will then analyse developments regarding the conversion of kafalas to adoptions. Afterwards the interface between Kafāla and Dutch migration law will be investigated. The contribution ends with some concerns about kafālas and a conclusion.

Given that kafāla is at the intersection of both migration and family law, it is a crucial topic within the context of the FAMIMOVE project and some of its findings will be included under every heading but keeping in mind the sensitive nature of the reports.[7]

[4] This circular is available in its entirety on the Dutch Government website, together with a Dutch translation. This circular is also available in other government websites such as Switzerland and Non-Profit Organisations, see https://www.bj.admin.ch/dam/data/bj/gesellschaft/adoption/herkunftslaender/ld-marokko-rundschreiben-justizminister-f.pdf; https://puc.overheid.nl/PUC/Handlers/DownloadBijlage.ashx?pucid=PUC_1315180_1_1&bestand=WI_2023-9_Bijlage_Marokko__Circulaire_nr._40_S_2_van_Ministerie_van_Justitie_en_Vrijheden_van_Ma....pdf&bestandsnaam=WI+2023-9+Bijlage+Marokko_+Circulaire+nr.+40+S_2+van+Ministerie+van+Justitie+en+Vrijheden+van+Ma..pdf.

[5] Convention of 19 October 1996 on Jurisdiction, Applicable Law, Recognition, Enforcement and Co-operation in respect of Parental Responsibility and Measures for the Protection of Children.

[6] Council Regulation (EU) 2019/1111 of 25 June 2019 on jurisdiction, the recognition and enforcement of decisions in matrimonial matters and the matters of parental responsibility, and on international child abduction.

[7] The reports resulting from FAMIMOVE (incl. the meeting on kafāla) are classified as sensitive information and thus cannot be shared with the public.

II. Kafāla in the Netherlands

Kafāla is a child protection measure of legal systems based on or influenced by Sharia law. The International Social Service (ISS) has published a very useful study entitled Kafalah - Preliminary analysis of national and cross-border practices.[8] This study is a key document to disseminate knowledge of this institution and good practices.

This section will analyse the relevant international instruments, the Dutch implementing law and Dutch case law on this topic.

1. Legal Framework

a) CRC and the 1996 Child Protection Convention

There are two main international instruments that make an express reference to kafāla, and which provide the basis upon which kafālas are dealt with in the Netherlands: the CRC[9] and the 1996 Child Protection Convention.

The CRC is one of the most successful human rights conventions ever concluded with 196 parties, including all EU member states.

At the outset, it should be noted that the CRC has several articles that oblige states to maintain and support children's family environment and relationships. In this regard, Professor John Tobin specifically mentions Articles 5, 7, 8, 18 and 27 of the CRC. Prof. Tobin also mentions Article 10 regarding facilitating reunification following family separation and Article 9 with respect to not separating children from their families unless this is in the best interests of the child.[10] In addition, Article 11 of the CRC provides that measures must be taken to combat the illicit transfer and non-return of children abroad.

According to Article 20 of the CRC, kafāla is an alternative form of care for children deprived — temporarily or permanently — of their family environment. A principle that is at the very heart of Article 20 is the need to pay due regard to the desirability of continuity in a child's upbringing and to the child's ethnic, religious, cultural and linguistic background.[11] While the principle of continuity has not been defined, academics have favoured a broad interpretation. According to this

---

[8] See in general, International Social Service (ISS), Kafalah: Preliminary analysis of national and cross-border practices, 2020 (hereinafter 'ISS Kafalah study').

[9] UN 1989 Convention on the Rights of the Child.

[10] J. Tobin, In: Tobin (ed), The UN-Convention on the Rights of the Child. A Commentary, 2019, Article 20 of the CRC, at p. 727.

[11] The lack of absolute clarity of this provision (in particular, the terms "continuity" and "upbringing") has been analysed in N. Cantwell/A. Holzscheiter, Article 20, Children deprived of their family environment, In: Liefaard/Sloth-Nielsen (eds), A commentary on the United Nations Convention on the Rights of the Child, at pp. 59–63.

interpretation, "continuity" would extend to "every aspect of the child's former living arrangements, including education and proximity to family and friends".[12] This approach would seem to be also in line with the UN Guidelines for the Alternative Care of Children.[13]

Indeed, Article 20 of the CRC should not be read in a void but in conjunction with the above-mentioned articles of the CRC and its Preamble. In particular, the principle of continuity is overarching as it applies to all forms of alternative care, including kafāla and adoption.

In this regard, it is worth noting that Dutch authorities have taken into account the principle of subsidiarity when considering kafālas. The principle of subsidiarity[14] is enshrined in Article 21 of the CRC and concerns inter-country adoption.[15] While the principle of continuity does not equal the principle of subsidiarity, it shares some of its elements.

Undoubtedly, the principle of subsidiarity has been controversial and has given rise to much debate.[16] Whether this principle is applicable to kafālas is a broader discussion that will not be analysed in this contribution. In any case, it is clear that when considering kafālas due regard should be paid to the applicability of the principle of continuity.

The second international instrument that will be mentioned is the 1996 Child Protection Convention, which has been ratified by 54 states including all EU member states.[17] Both the Netherlands and Morocco are contracting states to this treaty.

Article 3 lit. e of the 1996 Child Protection Convention provides that among the measures of protection referred to in Article 1 of the said Convention are "the placement of the child in a foster family or in institutional care, or the provision of care by *kafala* or an analogous institution" (our emphasis).

Moreover, Article 33 of the 1996 Child Protection Convention establishes a compulsory consultation procedure for the placement of children (incl. kafāla) by one State party in another State party. This chapter only deals with judicial kafāla

[12] J. Tobin, In: Tobin (fn. 10), Article 20 of the CRC, at pp. 753 f.

[13] See UN Guidelines for the Alternative Care of Children, A/RES/64/142, 24 February 2010, at pp. 2, 4, 21 f.

[14] For a definition of the subsidiarity principle, see Hague Conference on Private International Law (ed), The Implementation and Operation of the 1993 Hague Intercountry Adoption Convention: Guide to Good Practice. Guide No. 1, para. 47, at p. 29.

[15] P. Alston/N. Cantwell,/J. Tobin, In: Tobin (ed), at pp. 795 f.

[16] L. Martínez Mora/H. Baker/E. Harang, The 1993 Hague Intercountry Adoption Convention and subsidiarity: is the subsidiarity principle still "fit for purpose"?, In: The Permanent Bureau of the Hague Conference on Private International Law (ed), A Commitment to Private International Law. Essays in honour of Hans van Loon, at pp. 346–351.

[17] The 1993 Hague Convention on Protection of Children and International Cooperation in Respect of Intercountry Adoption (1993 Child Adoption Convention) is not applicable because kafālas are not adoptions as they do not "create a permanent parent-child relationship" (see Art 2 para. 1 of the 1993 Child Adoption Convention), and in addition, those states that grant kafālas are not a party to the 1993 Child Adoption Convention.

placements[18] by an authority (as a result, it does not include kafāla placements made under a private arrangement).[19] According to this chapter, the competent authority shall transmit a report on the child together with the reasons for the proposed placement or provision of care to the Central Authority or other Competent Authority in the requested state. The decision of placement or the provision of care by way of kafāla may be made only after such Central Authority or other competent authority of the requested state has consented to the placement or provision of care, taking into account the child's best interests.

At the global scale, there is little awareness of the existence or the applicability of Article 33 of the 1996 Child Protection Convention.[20] As previously indicated, the Netherlands is one of the few states that consistently applies Article 33 of the1996 Child Protection Convention.

The need to improve the current state of affairs was recognised at the 2023 meeting of the Special Commission on the practical operation on this Convention. As a result, a conclusion was adopted to establish a working group to develop: (a) a model form for cooperation under Article 33; and (b) a guide on the operation of Article 33.[21] These developments are very much welcome.

b) Dutch Implementing Legislation

The discussion and the efforts to understand kafāla are growing worldwide, including in the Netherlands.

As previously indicated, increasing awareness of the meaning and the requirements of kafāla (and what it is not) began in 2013 in the Netherlands after receiving the circular No. 40 S/2 issued by the Ministry of Justice and Freedoms of Morocco and the ensuing bilateral meeting.

According to the FAMIMOVE findings, Dutch authorities (both administrative and judicial) are mainly confronted with kafāla requests coming from Morocco. While there are no exact numbers, it is estimated that the Dutch Central Authority under the 1996 Child Protection Convention (i.e. the Ministry of Justice and Security) deals with four requests per year. This number does not reflect all requests for the recognition of kafālas received by Dutch authorities but only those received

[18] It is evident that kafāla is a placement. See Hague Conference on Private International Law (ed), Practical Handbook on the Operation of the 1996 Hague Child Protection Convention, at p. 30.

[19] See Conclusions and Recommendations of the 18th meeting of the Special Commission in October 2023, No. 84. See also, ECtHR 16 December 2014, 52265/10, ECLI:CE:ECHR:2014:1216JUD005226510 (Chbihi Loudoudi et Autres c. Belgique).

[20] See the Compilation of responses received to the October 2022 Questionnaire on the Practical Operation of the 1996 Child Protection Convention, pp. 109–121 (see in particular, responses from Switzerland (at p. 111), France (at p. 119) and Norway [at p. 120]), https://assets.hcch.net/docs/79105a67-45d6-47ed-8ca5-2def687cf130.pdf.

[21] This conclusion was approved by the Council on General Affairs and Policy of the Hague Conference on Private International law in 2024 (Conclusion & Decision No. 26).

by the Dutch Central Authority under Article 33 of the 1996 Child Protection Convention. The case law that has been studied in this contribution also refers to kafālas from Afghanistan, Algeria and Sudan, as will be mentioned below.

When it comes to recognising kafāla placements in the Netherlands, two distinct situations may be considered: Kafāla placements that fall under the scope of the 1996 Child Protection Convention and those that do not. While the former are recognised by operation of law in the Netherlands — provided Article 33 of the 1996 Child Protection Convention is respected —, the latter are generally not recognised and a guardian is assigned to the children.[22] This distinction has been made clear by the case law and the findings of FAMIMOVE.

We have previously alluded to the International Child Protection Implementation Act,[23] which implements both the 1996 Child Protection Convention and the Brussels IIter Regulation. However, this Act does not apply to all kafāla cases because not all states that grant kafālas are a party to the 1996 Child Protection Convention. In the case of the Netherlands, it only applies to Moroccan kafālas.

Furthermore, a third category of kafāla placements also seems to emerge: a kafāla placement that falls within the scope of Article 33 of the 1996 Child Protection Convention but fails to meet its requirements. As a result, the Central Authority faces a "*fait accompli*" as the child is often already in the Netherlands. The question then arises whether the requirements could be remedied if that would be in the best interests of the child, in particular if the child has been in the care of the kāfils for a significant period of time. In practice, however, in such situations the kāfils request an adoption under Dutch law particularly if they have taken care of the child for over a year (see the section "III. Conversion of Kafālas to Adoptions").

Unlike other countries (e.g. France), the Netherlands has not concluded any bilateral agreements on mutual recognition that would allow the recognition of kafālas with states not party to the 1996 Child Protection Convention.

aa) Kafālas That Fall Under the Scope of the 1996 Child Protection Convention

The International Child Protection Implementation Act applies only to kafāla placements that fall within the scope of Article 33 of the 1996 Child Protection

[22] See Rechtbank Noord-Nederland 28 September 2023, ECLI:NL:RBNNE:2023:5531 where an Algerian kafāla was not recognised and a guardian was appointed (i.e. Stichting Leger des Heils Jeugdbescherming & Reclassering te Groningen). The reasoning of the court is not conclusive however, because the fact that Algeria is not a party to the 1996 Child Protection Convention is, contrary to what the court says, not by itself a reason not to recognise the kafāla. Before the 1996 Child Protection Convention came into force for the Netherlands, a kafāla could be recognised under Dutch private international law, see Rechtbank 's-Gravenhage 13 April 2012, ECLI:NL:RBSGR:2012:7671 (indicating that in order to recognise the kafāla three factors should be considered: the jurisdiction of the court, due process considerations and the public policy).

[23] Implementation Act International Child Protection of 16 February 2006.

Convention. The Dutch Implementation Act specifies the conditions for placements of Dutch children abroad (Article 9) and the placements of foreign children in the Netherlands (Article 10). Only the second category will be examined in this contribution as this chapter deals with incoming applications.[24]

Given their relevance, an (unofficial) English translation of the relevant articles of the Dutch Implementation Act is included below (our emphasis):

Article 10

1. In case of *placement of a child from another State in the Netherlands or provision of care to such a child in a foster family or in an institution in the Netherlands* pursuant to Article 33 of the Convention or Article 82 of the Regulation, the consent or approval referred to in the said articles shall be given by the central authority referred to in Article 4 para. 1.
2. The consent or approval referred to in para. 1 shall be given only after the central authority referred to in Article 4 para. 1, has received from the competent authority of the child's State of origin *a reasoned request accompanied by a report concerning the child, and after it has received the following documents*, which it shall transmit to the competent authority of the child's State of origin:

   a. a written statement from the persons or institution with which the placement or provision of care is to take place, showing their consent or approval;
   b. if requested, a report showing the suitability of the foster parent to provide foster care to the child;
   c. if applicable, documents showing that the child has or will obtain a permit to enter the Netherlands and, with a view to the placement or provision of care, has or will obtain a right of residence in the Netherlands.

Article 10 of the Implementation Act specifies the requirements that must be fulfilled in order to process and grant a request for a placement of a child in the Netherlands pursuant to Article 33 of the 1996 Child Protection Convention, including a kafāla placement, and Article 82 of the Brussels IIter Regulation.

This mandatory consultation and the need for a report of the child that must accompany the request is in conformity with Article 33 of the1996 Child Protection Convention.[25] However, there are a few distinct features regarding Article 10 of the Dutch Implementation Act. First, it requires a written statement of approval or consent from the persons or institutions with which the placement of the child will take place. Secondly, if requested, a report showing the suitability of the foster parent must be submitted and thirdly, if applicable, the document showing that the child will obtain a permission to enter the Netherlands for that purpose. All these

[24] M. J. C. Koens/A. P. M. J. Vonken, Personen- en familierecht, IPR en mensenrechten 2022, at p. 3703.

[25] See also the Conclusions and Recommendations (fn. 19), No. 82.

documents are to be transmitted to the Competent Authority of the State of origin of the child.

Furthermore, the Dutch Implementation Act also indicates the consequences of not complying with the conditions set out in Article 10 of the Implementation Act.

Article 11

1. If the *requirements of Article 10 are not observed*, the public prosecutor or the Central Authority *may* request the Juvenile court to entrust a certified institution referred to in Article 1.1 of the Jeugdwet (Youth Act) with the provisional guardianship of the child. This request can also be made by the child protection council. Unless the Juvenile court has determined a longer period of expiration of the provisional guardianship, the council shall apply to the court within six weeks of the decision on the provisional guardianship in order to obtain a provision for the custody of the minor. Article 241 paras. 4 and 5, as well as Article 306 lit. a of Book 1 of the Civil Code shall apply mutatis mutandis. Article 813 para. 2 of the Code of Civil Procedure shall apply mutatis mutandis.
2. The provisional guardianship ends, subject to earlier termination, at the time when either the guardianship of the child, or his placement with other persons or another institution, commences, or his return to the country of origin is arranged.
3. The expenses incurred by the guardianship institution for the benefit of the child shall be borne by the person with whom the child has been placed in violation of Article 10. Articles 8.2.1 to 8.2.7 of the Jeugdwet shall apply mutatis mutandis.

As stated above, Article 11 of the Implementation Act imposes a sanction if the conditions of Article 10 are not fulfilled.[26] This consists of the possibility that the placement may not be recognised (which is implicit in Article 11)[27] and that therefore, the authorities may file a request for a provisional guardianship of the child if he or she is in the Netherlands. In such cases, and given that the child is already in the Netherlands, this is of the utmost importance. This can be requested by the public prosecutor or the Central Authority to the Children's Court.

[26] M. J. C. Koens/A. P. M. J. Vonken (fn. 24), at p. 3705.

[27] See for example the following case where the request was not considered because a report of the child was not provided: Rechtbank Den Haag 15 February 2016, ECLI:NL:RBDHA:2016:2105.

bb) Kafālas That Do Not Fall Under the Scope of the 1996 Child Protection Convention

If the kafāla is not recognised under the 1996 Child Protection Convention, then the Child Care and Protection Board will investigate the case and request the Dutch court to take a guardianship measure.[28] Subsequently, it is possible for the kāfils to request an adoption provided there is permission from the Dutch Ministry of Justice (see more information below). In such cases, consideration is given to whether there is family life in accordance with Article 8 of the Human Rights Convention.[29,30]

c) General Safeguards: When Civil Law Meets Migration

In order to bring children to the Netherlands from abroad, it is of the utmost importance to follow procedures that establish the necessary safeguards and ensure that the measure is in the best interests of the child. This is not only limited to migration laws. Domestic legislation that is civil in nature — in this case, family law (*Personen- en familierecht*) — also establishes procedures for the migration of children from one State to another and is necessarily coupled to specific migration legislation.

In the case of inter-country adoption, the *Wet opneming buitenlandse kinderen ter adoptie* (Placing foreign children for adoption act — WOBKA) is of crucial importance. The WOBKA applies when the child is a foreign national and will be adopted in the Netherlands. In the case of a placement in a foster family or institutional care or under a kafāla regime, the Dutch implementation legislation of the 1996 Child Protection Convention establishes the mechanism to bring children from abroad for this purpose (incl. kafāla), as indicated above. In these matters both civil law and migration law are inextricably linked and must be studied in conjunction, which is one of the purposes of the FAMIMOVE project.

2. *Kafāla in the Case Law*

The Dutch case law on kafāla is scant. It should be noted that not all the case law on kafāla has been published and thus our brief study is by no means comprehensive

[28] A case in which an Algerian kafāla could not be recognised by operation of law, the court ordered a guardianship measure in favour of *Stichting Leger des Heils Jeugdbescherming & Reclassering te Groningen*. See Rechtbank Noord-Nederland, 28 November 2023, ECLI:NL:RBNNE:2023:5531.

[29] Convention for the Protection of Human Rights and Fundamental Freedoms (Human Rights Convention).

[30] See for example, Rechtbank Den Haag 12 June 2015, ECLI:NL:RBDHA:2015:6791.

and only reflects the case law that is accessible through the courts' judgments database.[31]

Generally, the case law does not deal with the recognition of kafālas but concentrates on adoption, custody or migration matters. There is a distinction made between case law pertaining to the civil courts (*Civiel recht; Personen- en familierecht*) and case law pertaining to the administrative courts (*Bestuursrecht; Vreemdelingenrecht*). Our focus will primarily be the case law pertaining to the civil courts.

There are 19 cases published by the civil courts on kafāla. Of those cases, 12 have been resolved after the entry into force of the 1996 Child Protection Convention in the Netherlands (i.e. 1 May 2011) and are within the temporal scope of this Convention.[32] These cases relate to kafālas granted in Morocco (nine cases),[33] Afghanistan (one case),[34] Algeria (one case)[35] and Sudan (one case).[36]

The most experienced civil court in dealing with kafāla requests in the Netherlands is by far the Court of The Hague (with eight cases). It is then followed with one case each by the courts of East-Brabant, Gelderland, North-the Netherlands and Rotterdam.

With regard to migration courts, there are only five cases published, most of which have been resolved by the Court of The Hague (with the exception of one, which was dealt with by the *Raad van State* [Council of State]).

The majority of cases relate to abandoned children. In some cases, it is noted that the parent(s) of the children have very likely been given fictitious names in the civil

---

[31] The database is available at https://uitspraken.rechtspraak.nl/.

[32] One case was resolved in 2012 — after the entry into force of the Convention for the Netherlands — , but the kafāla was granted in 2009 and thus it was outside the scope of the 1996 Child Protection Convention. See Rechtbank 's-Gravenhage 13 April 2012, ECLI:NL:RBSGR:2012: 7671.

[33] Rechtbank Den Haag, 25 May 2022, ECLI:NL:RBDHA:2022:5076; Rechtbank Den Haag, 29 March 2021, ECLI:NL:RBDHA:2021:3639; Rechtbank Gelderland, 27 November 2017, ECLI:NL:RBGEL:2017:6903; Rechtbank Den Haag 10 September 2014, ECLI:NL: RBDHA:2014:12138; Rechtbank Den Haag 26 February 2014, ECLI:NL:RBDHA:2014:4525; Rechtbank Den Haag 08 January 2014, ECLI:NL:RBDHA:2014:1679; Rechtbank Den Haag 28 August 2013, ECLI:NL:RBDHA:2013:11319; Rechtbank Den Haag 12 June 2013, ECLI:NL: RBDHA:2013:6946; Rechtbank Oost-Brabant, 27 February 2013, ECLI:NL:RBOBR:2013: BZ2677.

[34] Rechtbank Rotterdam 11 March 2024, ECLI:NL:RBROT:2024:2263.

[35] Rechtbank Noord-Nederland, 28 November 2023, ECLI:NL:RBNNE:2023:5531.

[36] Rechtbank Den Haag 7 August 2013, ECLI:NL:RBDHA:2013:11124.

status record.[37] In at least one case, this fact has complicated the registration of the child in the Netherlands.[38]

In the literature, reference has been made to the practice in some Muslim countries of giving fictitious names to the "parents" of (what previously was referred to as) "bastards" or abandoned children. In addition, academics have studied the background and the difficulties that this entails, which require choosing a fictitious name from a roster of names.[39] This occurs even if the name of the father is known to the mother. Such practice requires the State to keep a secret that no one can break and goes counter to the right of children to know their origin.

Indeed, the stigma that is placed on children born out of wedlock (and their mothers) and the silence of the Moroccan Family Code on their status is "deafening"; according to academics, only the Moroccan kafāla law of 2002 deals with their status and only with respect to guardianship.[40]

Finally, it should be noted that Article 7 of the CRC refers to the right of the child "[. . .] as far as possible, the right to know, and be cared for by his or her parents." Although there is no absolute certainty as to what the meaning of "as far as possible" is, academics have indicated that the intent of this article is that if it is *possible* to determine the identity of the parents, a child has a right to know that information, unless it is against his or her best interests.[41]

III. Conversion of Kafālas to Adoptions

While it is clear that kafāla is not an adoption given its different legal nature, it shares some of its psychological and social functions.[42]

In practice, kafālas and adoption proceedings are often intertwined in the Netherlands. A study of the case law shows that often kāfils request an adoption after the makfūl has stayed for a period of a year in the Netherlands. Alternatively, when the

[37] Rechtbank Den Haag 29 March 2021, ECLI:NL:RBDHA:2021:3639; Rechtbank Gelderland 27 November 2017, ECLI:NL:RBGEL:2017:6903; Rechtbank Den Haag 12 June 2013, ECLI:NL:RBDHA:2013:6946; Rechtbank Den Haag 26 February 2014, ECLI:NL:RBDHA:2014:4525; Rechtbank Den Haag 10 September 2014, ECLI:NL:RBDHA:2014:12138; Rechtbank Den Haag 28 August 2013, ECLI:NL:RBDHA:2013:11319; Rechtbank Den Haag 7 August 2013, ECLI:NL:RBDHA:2013:11124.

[38] Rechtbank Den Haag 7 August 2013, ECLI:NL:RBDHA:2013:11124.

[39] J. Bargach, Orphans of Islam: Family, Abandonment, and Secret Adoption in Morocco, 2002, at pp. 116–120.

[40] K. E. Hoffman, Chapter 9, Morocco, In: Yassari/Möller/Najm (eds), Filiation and the Protection of Parentless Children: Towards a Social Definition of the Family in Muslim Jurisdictions, 2019, at pp. 246 f. https://doi.org/10.1007/978-94-6265-311-5.

[41] See J. Tobin/F. Seow, In: Tobin (fn. 10), Article 7 of the CRC, at pp. 261 f.

[42] Remark by L. Martínez Mora, In: ISS Kafalah study (fn. 8), at p. 134.

kafāla placement has been rejected, the claimants often request an adoption. In this regard, makfūls may be adopted in the Netherlands if certain conditions are fulfilled.

The kāfils' impetus to convert the kafāla into an adoption may be understandable. This is so in particular, when the child has stayed for a longer period of time in the Netherlands and in the case of abandoned children. In many of these cases, the adoption has been granted by Dutch courts.[43]

Indeed, kafāla is not considered the most protective measure according to Dutch law.[44] One may think for example of inheritance rights, tax and social benefits, as well as migration status. The regulation of these matters sharply differs between adoptive and foster children — including children under kafāla care — , granting less benefits and rights to the latter.[45]

However, early 2024 the court of Rotterdam was very stringent in its approach and refused to grant an adoption when all the applicable rules had been breached and the child still had parents in Afghanistan. Because it was unclear that the biological parents had expressly consented to the adoption, among other matters, the court denied the adoption as it was not in the best interests of the child. This was so even if this ruling was against the advice of the Child Protection Council in favour of the adoption and indeed, the court reproached the Council for taking such a stand.[46]

That being said, given concerns about the manner in which intercountry adoptions had been authorised in the past in the Netherlands, in particular after irregularities and abuses came to the surface years later, an official committee ("Commissie Joustra") was established in 2021 by the Dutch government. The Committee's objective was to investigate how adoptions were conducted from 1967 to 1998 and focused mainly on Bangladesh, Brazil, Colombia, Indonesia and Sri Lanka. For the last two states, the existence of baby farms and child trafficking was even established. This Committee issued a report entitled *Rapport Commissie onderzoek interlandelijke adoptie* (Report of the intercountry adoption fact-finding

[43] In many of these cases there was a "declaration of approval in principle" of the adoption (*beginseltoestemming*) issued by the Ministry of Justice (see below): Rechtbank Den Haag 29 March 2021, ECLI:NL:RBDHA:2021:3639; Rechtbank Gelderland 27 November 2017, ECLI:NL:RBGEL:2017:6903; Rechtbank Den Haag 08 January 2014, ECLI:NL: RBDHA:2014:1679 ; Rechtbank Den Haag 26 February 2014, ECLI:NL:RBDHA:2014:4525; Rechtbank Den Haag 10 September 2014, ECLI:NL:RBDHA:2014:12138; Rechtbank Den Haag 28 August 2013, ECLI:NL:RBDHA:2013:11319; Rechtbank Den Haag 07 August 2013, ECLI: NL:RBDHA:2013:11124.

[44] See S. Rutten, De erkenning van de kafala in het IPR en het vreemdelingenrecht, Tijdschrift voor Familie, Jeugdrecht, No. 12, 2007, at. p. 306.

[45] S.F.M. Wortmann/J. van Duijvendijk-Brand, Personen- en familierecht, 2021, at pp. 245 f.

[46] Rechtbank Rotterdam, 11 March 2024, ECLI:NL:RBROT:2024:2263.

committee).[47] The Committee's results[48] were widely broadcasted by Dutch and foreign news media and aroused public attention and outcry.[49]

As a result, intercountry adoptions were suspended from February 2021 to November 2022. This occurred even though the 1993 Child Adoption Convention has applied to the Netherlands since 1998. Adoptions were subsequently resumed but only with a handful of countries (Bulgaria, Hungary, Lesotho, Taiwan, Thailand, the Philippines, Portugal and South Africa).[50] It is important to clarify that Morocco is not a party to the 1993 Child Adoption Convention because, as we mentioned, according to its law adoptions are prohibited.

Considering that, the handling of intercountry adoptions is quite politically charged and given the existing concerns, one may only wonder whether this topic could influence or cast a shadow on the treatment of kafālas in the Netherlands.[51] In this regard, the FAMIMOVE findings have shown that Dutch authorities are concerned that kafālas are often used to circumvent adoption procedures. This is particularly so when there has been contact between the kāfils and the makfūl's family in advance (which is prohibited in adoption proceedings — except when it takes place within the family — , see Article 29 of the 1993 Child Adoption Convention) and because the kāfils often request an adoption in the Netherlands after a kafāla has been granted abroad.

[47] Commissie onderzoek interlandelijke adoptie, "Rapport Commissie onderzoek interlandelijke adoptie", February 2021, available at https://www.rijksoverheid.nl/documenten/rapporten/2021/02/08/tk-bijlage-coia-rapport; For a critical review of this report regarding its findings for the period extending beyond 1998, see H. van Loon, Blinde vlek Commissie Joustra voor Adoptieverdrag, Nederlands JuristenBlad, 19 March 2012 (11) at pp. 842–846.

[48] An English summary of this report (fn. 47) is available at pp. 139–142.

[49] Voorlopig geen nieuwe adopties uit het buitenland, *NOS*, 8 February 2021, https://nos.nl/artikel/2367782-voorlopig-geen-nieuwe-adopties-uit-het-buitenland. The controversy continued in the years following the report; see Nieuwe regels adoptie geven geen garantie op waterdicht system, *NOS*, 3 April 2024, https://nos.nl/nieuwsuur/artikel/2515360-nieuwe-regels-adoptie-geven-geen-garantie-op-waterdicht-systeem.

[50] See Het adopteren van een kind uit de Filipijnen, Hongarije, Lesotho, Taiwan, Thailand en Zuid-Afrika blijft mogelijk, 2 November 2022, https://www.rijksoverheid.nl/onderwerpen/adoptie/nieuws/2022/11/02/adoptie-mogelijk-uit-zes-geselecteerde-landen. After the submission of this chapter, the Dutch government halted intercountry adoptions with immediate effect. As a result, as of 21 May 2024, new intercountry adoptions are no longer possible in the Netherlands and the intercountry adoption system will be phased out. More information about the consequences and the phasing out of the system will likely be available in the fall of 2024. See https://www.rijksoverheid.nl/actueel/nieuws/2024/05/21/per-direct-geen-nieuwe-interlandelijke-adopties.

[51] See for example, Rechtbank Den Haag 07 July 2023, ECLI:NL:RBDHA:2023:10143 (the child had resided seven years with family of the sponsor in Morocco where she goes to school but that sole fact does not constitute family law between the sponsor and the child, even if it is argued that the sponsor's family cannot longer take care of the child).

In this regard, it should be noted that the Netherlands only contemplates full/ plenary adoption,[52] an institution that in principle runs counter to Sharia law as it severs the links with the biological parents.

When granting or rejecting an adoption, courts have invoked Articles 1:227 and 1:228 of the Dutch Civil Code, as well as the WOBKA.

Among the requirements set out by the Dutch Civil Code and referred to in the case law are the following: that the child be taken care of by the prospective adoptive parents for a year (Article 1:228 lit. f)). Moreover, there must be approval for the adoption by the parents or institution in charge [Article 1:228 lit. d]). Article 10:105 of the Dutch Civil Code provides that this approval be governed by the law of the nationality of the child (which is usually Moroccan law).

A crucial requirement of the WOBKA is the *beginseltoestemming* ("declaration of approval in principle"), which is given by the Dutch Ministry of Justice. Article 2 of the WOBKA indicates the following (an unofficial English translation):

> The adoption in the Netherlands of a foreign child for the purpose of adoption shall be permitted only if prior written notification has been obtained from Our Minister that Our Minister in principle grants permission for such adoption.

In the case law, courts sometimes make explicit reference to the WOBKA or just indicate whether the "declaration of approval in principle" has been complied with or not.

In one case, the lack of declaration was excused given that authorities were working on an immigration policy for children placed in a kafāla.[53] Indeed, one court has indicated that such a requirement could be set aside if rejecting the adoption would be very damaging to the child and contrary to his or her best interests.[54]

In one case, the Ministry of Justice refused to issue the "declaration of approval in principle" because the requested adoption did not comply, among other provisions, with the WOBKA and this was challenged before the administrative court. The administrative court suggested to the Ministry of Justice to consider granting a permit on the basis of Article 33 of the 1996 Child Protection Convention. In that case, it was stressed that a kafāla was not an adoption and the court summarised the policy developments in this regard.[55]

In this regard, a correlation may be found with the case of Harroudj versus France[56] decided by the European Court of Human Rights (ECtHR). In Harroudj versus France, the ECtHR found no violation of Article 8 of the Human Rights

[52] A.J.M. Nuytinck, Personen- en familierecht, relatievermogensrecht en erfrecht, 2021, at pp. 235–237.

[53] Rechtbank Den Haag 8 January 2014, ECLI:NL:RBDHA:2014:1679.

[54] Rechtbank Den Haag 12 June 2013, ECLI:NL:RBDHA:2013:6946.

[55] See Rechtsbank Den Haag 12 June 2015, ECLI:NL:RBDHA:2015:6791.

[56] Application no. 43631/09, 4 October 2012.

Convention when the French courts denied the application made by a French woman for the full adoption of a child who had been placed with her by way of a kafāla. The French courts referred to the French conflict of law rules, which point to the law of nationality, which prohibits adoption. In particular, it held that the legal distinction between kafāla and adoption had been acknowledged by the CRC, and the 1993 Child Adoption Convention and 1996 Child Protection Convention. Moreover, the child could inherit by way of a will, and after five years in foster care a child may acquire French nationality and could then be adopted by the kāfil (who in this case was a French national as required by the legislation).

In addition, and as indicated by Hans van Loon, this case shows that Private International Law rules "may inform the human rights norm, here article 8 [Human Rights Convention], so that it will be applied with due regard to a person's cultural identity and its evolution over time".[57]

IV. Kafāla and Dutch Migration Law

In migration matters, the applicable instrument — among others — is the *Vreemdelingencirculaire* 2000 (B) (Aliens Circular 2000 (B).[58] In this circular, a distinction is made between kafāla placements that fall within the scope of the 1996 Child Protection Convention and those that do not.

In accordance with sections B8 and B9 of the Vreemdelingencirculaire, a residence permit (on permanent or temporary basis) is granted on the basis of *humanitarian grounds* to placements made under the 1996 Child Protection Convention. In this circular, this particular ground is referred to as "*plaatsing in een pleeggezin of instelling in Nederland op grond van het Haags Kinderbeschermingsverdrag 1996*" (Placement in a foster family or institution in the Netherlands under the 1996 Hague Convention on the Protection of Children).

In contrast, B.7 *Gezinsmigratie* (family migration) — Section 3.7 of the Vreemdelingencirculaire is applicable to *foreign foster children* in general, that is those who do not fall under the 1996 Child Protection Convention. Section 3.7 further distinguishes children who do not have a family life with the foster parents in the country of origin (Section 3.7.1) and those who do (Section 3.7.2), with the latter category having a likelier chance to get a residence permit.

Among the requirements for the first category is that the foster child does not have an acceptable future in the Country of origin (*geen aanvaardbare toekomst*), meaning that the child cannot be cared for by blood or by affinity relatives (3.7.1.1.). For

[57] H. van Loon, Chapter 26.2 Cultural identities: *Wagner v. Luxembourg*, In: Horatia Muir Watt et al. (eds), Global Private International Law, Adjudication Without Frontiers, 2019, at pp. 535 f.

[58] Available at https://wetten.overheid.nl/BWBR0012289/2024-04-27. The Aliens Circular implements the Vreemdelingenwet 2000 (Aliens Act 2000) and the Vreemdelingenbesluit 2000 (Aliens Decision 2000).

the second category, the requirement is that the child belonged to the foster family — and still does — and the child was cared for and raised by the foster parents for at least one year because the child's own parents died or were unable to care for the child (3.7.2.1.).

Moreover, in the case of *intercountry adoption*, B.7 *Gezinsmigratie* - Section 3.6 of the Vreemdelingencirculaire applies. In this section, the "declaration of approval in principle" under WOBKA is featured prominently.

In practice and according to the FAMIMOVE findings, when confronted with a kafāla placement that falls under the 1996 Child Protection Convention, the Dutch Central Authority contacts the Dutch migration authorities to make sure that a residence permit on humanitarian grounds is granted to the makfūl.

Furthermore, the FAMIMOVE findings point to a concern of migration authorities when the kāfils travel with the child to the Netherlands and develop a family life in the Netherlands (as opposed to the country of origin as stated in the Vreemdelingencirculaire). This situation makes it complicated for the migration authorities. Sometimes the child travels with a tourist visa and then stays (*faux touriste*).

V. Concerns About Kafālas

According to the FAMIMOVE findings, one of main concerns about dealing with kafālas in the Netherlands is that it is often used as a way to circumvent adoption and migrations laws. In particular, it is worrisome that kāfils are able to establish contact with the children in advance without proper procedures being put in place.

In one particular case, it had been established that the kāfils had deliberately chosen to apply for a kafāla because it was less burdensome and less expensive than applying for an adoption in the Netherlands. However, the situation on the ground because of the rise of the Taliban made their stay untenable. As a result, they had to return to the Netherlands before the planned one year of residence in order to build a family life with the child in Afghanistan.[59]

Other concerns according to FAMIMMOVE findings are that kāfils are not aware of the procedures established by the 1996 Child Protection Convention and that applications are often unfounded or lack adequate documentation.

Another concern is the deficient protection of mothers in states where it is prohibited to have sex outside the marriage and to give birth to children out of wedlock. In such cases, mothers are forced to give up their children as both mothers and children are stigmatised.[60] As a result, the child may then be placed under a kafāla regime and separated from the mother, giving rise to issues when the child settles in the Netherlands.

[59] Rechtbank Rotterdam 11 March 2024, ECLI:NL:RBROT:2024:2263.

[60] J. Bargach (fn. 39), at pp. 34–39.

Admittedly, not all of these concerns could be addressed or solved by existing Private International Law instruments. Nevertheless, some concerns may be tackled by increasing awareness of Article 33 of the 1996 Child Protection Convention and by entering and carrying out projects such as FAMIMOVE, in order to build bridges between migration law and international family law and disseminate crucial information.

VI. Conclusion

The policy of the Netherlands with regard to the recognition of kafālas is generally coherent and in line with the relevant international instruments applicable in this field. However, there are concerns about the use of kafāla to circumvent adoption and immigration policies and regulations. It has been noted that in practice kāfils usually request an adoption when the makfūl has stayed over one year in the Netherlands. These requests are examined by the Dutch courts with great caution, in particular, consideration is given if the rules established in the Dutch Civil Code and the WOBKA have been complied with. Obtaining the declaration of approval in principle (*beginseltoestemming*) issued by the Dutch Ministry of Justice is of great importance for the adoption to be granted. Finally, the Dutch discussions about adoption in the Netherlands may colour or influence the perception about kafāla, given the frequency in which adoptions are requested by kāfils. In this regard, it should be noted that after the submission of this chapter, the Dutch government halted intercountry adoptions with immediate effect as per 21 May 2024.

Kafāla in Belgium: Private International Law as an Essential Tool to Establish Migration Law Consequences?

Leontine Bruijnen

I. Introduction

How can a kafāla be characterised and recognised in Belgium?[1] Should it be converted into an adoption? Or is a kafāla equal to foster care? The entry into force of the 1996 Child Protection Convention in Belgium on 1 September 2014 clarified that a kafāla should be characterised as a child protection measure under Article 3 lit. e of the 1996 Child Protection Convention.[2] Based on Article 23 of the Convention, a kafāla should automatically be recognised as such in Belgium when the procedure of Article 33 has been followed. However, the entry into force of the 1996 Child Protection Convention did not solve all issues related to a kafāla. The fact that a kafāla should be recognised in Belgium does not mean that a kafāla can automatically have migration law consequences.[3] Moreover, the 1996 Child Protection Convention only covers the recognition of a Moroccan judicial kafāla because

[1] As explained in Nadjma Yassari's contribution, Beyond kafāla: How parentless children are placed in new homes in Muslim jurisdictions, in this volume, at p. 207, kafāla is a form of guardianship under Islamic law. The term kafāla is mainly used in North African countries to describe the transfer of the care of a child, also called makfūl, from the biological parents to another person or persons called the kāfil or kāfils. A kafāla does not create any ties of filiation between the makfūl and the kāfil(s).

[2] Convention of 19 October 1996 on Jurisdiction, Applicable Law, Recognition, Enforcement and Co-operation in respect of Parental Responsibility and Measures for the Protection of Children (1996 Child Protection Convention).

[3] Article 4 lit. j of the 1996 Child Protection Convention clarifies that the Convention does not apply to decisions on the right of asylum and on immigration.

L. Bruijnen (✉)
Institute for Private International Law, Ghent University, Ghent, Belgium

Law and Development Research Group, University of Antwerp, Antwerp, Belgium
e-mail: Leontine.Bruijnen@uantwerpen.be

S. Arnold, B. Heiderhoff (eds.), *Children in Migration and International Family Law*, https://doi.org/10.1007/978-3-031-71598-3_16

Morocco is the only country where a kafāla can be established that has ratified the Convention.[4] The recognition of a kafāla established in another state, for example Algeria, is not covered by the Convention. Nevertheless, the entry into force of the 1996 Child Protection Convention has provided much needed clarity on the recognition of a Moroccan judicial kafāla in Belgium.[5] Another aspect not governed by the Convention is the intra-EU recognition (of the migration law consequences) of a kafāla. This concerns, for example, the situation where the kāfil and makfūl lived in one member state where the kafāla is converted into foster care and a residence right is obtained, and then move to Belgium.[6] One may question whether the right to free movement requires the recognition of the migration law consequences of the kafāla in another member state. This chapter will focus on the recognition of a kafāla in Belgium and, in particular, on the migration law consequences of a kafāla. The relevant legal framework will be explained and for illustrative purposes, Belgian family and migration case law will be discussed.

At the Belgian national level, the Council for Alien Law Litigation (hereafter Council) deals with migration cases. The Council's competence is twofold.[7] First, the Council has full competence in appeals lodged against the decisions of the Office of the Commissioner General for Refugees and Stateless persons (CGRS). This concerns asylum and subsidiary protection cases.[8] In these cases, the Council may confirm the challenged decision but also modify it. Second, the Council can act as an annulment judge with regard to other appeals.[9] This second competence includes appeals against the decisions of the Immigration Office (Dienst

[4]HCCH, Status Table, available at https://www.hcch.net/en/instruments/conventions/status-table/?cid=70. A distinction should be made between the judicial kafāla established by a court and the notarial kafāla. In Morocco, the notarial kafāla is also called an *adoulaire* kafāla. Article 23 of the Convention only covers the recognition of a judicial kafāla.

[5]In some judgments before the entry into force of the 1996 Child Protection Convention, Belgian courts refer to the Convention's recognition regime and the fact that, unfortunately, the Convention cannot yet be applied. See for example the judgment of the Brussels juvenile court of 16 February 2010, Revue trimestrielle de droit familial 2011, 147, at pp. 147–152; and the judgment of the Brussels juvenile court of 19 May 2010, Revue trimestrielle de droit familial 2012, 384, at pp. 384–390.

[6]This chapter will discuss the intra-EU recognition of the migration law consequences of a kafāla. However, it is beyond the scope of this chapter to discuss the intra-EU recognition of the private international law recognition of the kafāla. The author's doctoral thesis concerns the recognition of a kafāla for family and migration law purposes in Belgium and Germany. In her thesis, she discusses the intra-EU recognition of a kafāla from both perspectives.

[7]Article 39/1, § 1 of the Vreemdelingenwet (Belgian Aliens Act). The official title in Dutch of the Aliens Act is "Wet betreffende de toegang tot het grondgebied, het verblijf, de vestiging en de verwijdering van vreemdelingen". This chapter discusses the case law of the Council during the period from 1 January 2010 to 30 June 2021. This case law was analysed by the author as part of her doctoral thesis on the recognition of a kafāla for family and migration law purposes in Belgium. This case study includes 62 judgments of the Council.

[8]Article 39/2, § 1 of the Vreemdelingenwet.

[9]Article 39/2, § 2 of the Vreemdelingenwet.

Vreemdelingenzaken).[10] The examined case law on kafāla mainly relates to this annulment competence. The competence of the Council as an annulment judge is not a full competence.[11] In these cases, the Council will conduct only a marginal review and will not assess the facts. The Council may evaluate the reasoning of the Immigration Office based on the information in the file and the principles of reasonableness and required clarity. The Council can only review the contested decision against the legal rules invoked.[12] Consequently, the Council cannot assess the recognition of a kafāla on its own initiative.

The Council's case law will be discussed for illustrative purposes in section III. on the migration law consequences of a kafāla and in section IV. on the intra-EU recognition of the migration law consequences of a kafāla. Before addressing these two aspects, the next section will outline the Belgian private international law framework relating to the recognition of a kafāla.

II. How Is a Kafāla Recognised in Belgium?

As mentioned in the introduction, the 1996 Child Protection Convention applies to the recognition of a Moroccan kafāla in Belgium. The (correct) application of this Convention was not possible for a long time because the Convention did not enter into force in Belgium until 2014, and because of the non-existence of a central authority in Belgium until 2018. The Antwerp court of appeal brought this last point to the attention in its judgment of 16 May 2017. The Antwerp court points out that the Belgian legislature has not yet appointed a central authority as required by the 1996 Child Protection Convention. As a result, the procedure of Article 33 of the Convention cannot be followed and the Belgian Wetboek van Internationaal Privaatrecht (Belgian Code of Private International Law or WIPR) applies.[13] It was not until 2018 that the Federal Government Department of Justice (FOD Justitie) was appointed as competent central authority and the cooperation procedure between central authorities under Article 33 of the 1996 Child Protection Convention could be used for a Moroccan judicial kafāla.[14]

---

[10] L. Denys, Overzicht van het Vreemdelingenrecht, 4th ed. 2019, at p. 993.

[11] L. Denys (fn. 10), at p. 993. However, when there is a risk that the treatment violates the prohibition of torture of Article 3 of the Convention for the Protection of Human Rights and Fundamental Freedoms of 4 November 1950 (Human Rights Convention), the Council is obliged to handle the case with full competence.

[12] L. Denys (fn. 10), at pp. 994–996.

[13] Court of appeal Antwerp 16 May 2017, tijdschrift@ipr.be 2017(3), at pp. 15 f.

[14] Act of 26 November 2018, Official Gazette of 24 December 2018; and J. Verhellen and P. Wautelet, The Treatment of Diversity in Family Law in Belgium: Between Acknowledgment and Indifference, In: Yassari and Foblets (eds), Normativity and Diversity in Family Law 2022, at pp. 227–253.

If the recognition regime of the 1996 Child Protection Convention cannot be applied, for example because it concerns an Algerian kafāla, the WIPR will be applicable. If the kafāla is established in a judgment, the general recognition rule of Article 22 of the WIPR applies, which determines that a foreign judgment is automatically recognised in Belgium. Article 25 of the WIPR lists the grounds for refusal of recognition, which includes the refusal ground that the consequence of recognition is contrary to public policy.[15]

If a kafāla is not established in a judgment but in an authentic instrument, such as a notarial kafāla, the general recognition regime for authentic instruments under Article 27 of the WIPR applies. One difference with the recognition regime for a judgment under Article 22 is that Article 27 leads to a conflict of laws test. To recognise the authentic instrument, its validity has to be established in accordance with the law applicable according to the WIPR. Article 35 of the WIPR stipulates that the 1996 Child Protection Convention governs all situations regarding parental responsibility. Therefore, the conflict of laws test will lead to the application of Article 16 para. 2 of the 1996 Child Protection Convention. Article 16 para. 2 governs the applicable law regarding the attribution of parental responsibility by an agreement or a unilateral act, without the intervention of a judicial or administrative authority. The applicable law is the law of the State of the child's habitual residence at the time when the agreement or unilateral act takes effect. For example, if the kafāla is established in Algeria, Algerian law applies and will determine whether the authentic instrument is valid and can be recognised.[16] Besides the conflict of laws test, Article 27 of the WIPR requires that the recognition of the authentic instrument establishing the kafāla does not lead to an evasion of the law under Article 18 of the WIPR or a violation of the public policy under Article 21 of the WIPR.

III. What Are the Migration Law Consequences of a Kafāla?

The question on how to recognise a kafāla is not only important to determine the family law consequences of the kafāla, such as whether the makfūl can have the surname of the kāfil or whether the kafāla changes the inheritance status of the makfūl, but also to determine the migration law consequences of the kafāla. For example, how a kafāla is recognised affects whether family reunification between the makfūl and kāfil(s) can take place,[17] as well as whether the kāfil(s) can represent

[15] For an example of the application of this recognition regime to an Algerian kafāla, see the judgment of the court of first instance Liege (Huy department) 12 July 2021, tijdschrift@ipr.be 2022(2), at pp. 112–115.

[16] Article 16 para. 2 of the 1996 Child Protection Convention governs the establishment of parental responsibility. The exercise of parental responsibility falls under Article 17 of the Convention.

[17] See section 0.

the makfūl in migration law proceedings.[18] Belgian migration case law shows that the makfūl applies, inter alia, for a residence right on the basis of family reunification, as an unaccompanied minor, and on humanitarian grounds.[19] Below, the possible qualification of a makfūl as an unaccompanied minor and the determination of what constitutes a durable solution for a makfūl as unaccompanied minor are elaborated. Thereafter, the possibility of family reunification between the makfūl and the kāfil(s) will be addressed.

1. Durable Solution for a Makfūl as an Unaccompanied Minor

At the Belgian national level, the definition of an unaccompanied minor is laid down in Article 61/14, 1° of the Vreemdelingenwet (Belgian Aliens Act) and Article 5 of the Voogdijwet (Belgian Guardianship Act).[20] Based on these articles, an unaccompanied minor is not a national of a member state of the European Economic Area, is under 18 years and not accompanied by a person who exercises parental authority or guardianship over him/her in accordance with Article 35 of the WIPR.[21] Moreover, the minor has applied for international protection or does not meet the conditions for entry and residence in Belgium. Thus, if a minor enters Belgium with a valid visa, he/she is not considered an unaccompanied minor.[22] A Belgian authority has to notify the Guardianship Service (Dienst Voogdij) and the Immigration Office if it is aware of the presence of an unaccompanied minor at the border or on the Belgian territory. The Guardianship Service investigates whether the child can be qualified as an unaccompanied minor and can appoint a guardian.[23] Based on the examined migration case law, the Belgian awareness raising seminar organised in the framework of the FAMIMOVE project and the transnational roundtable on kafāla in Paris,

[18] Regarding the representation of the makfūl, see, for example, the judgments of the Council for Alien Law Litigation of 19 March 2015 (141 295), 29 September 2015 (153 472) and 21 September 2020 (241 270).

[19] See for example the connected judgments of the Council for Alien Law Litigation of 5 September 2017 (191 454) and 7 April 2020 (234 943).

[20] The official title in Dutch of the Guardianship Act is "Programmawet (I) (art. 479) - Titel XIII - Hoofdstuk VI: Voogdij over niet-begeleide minderjarige vreemdelingen".

[21] As mentioned before, Article 35 of the WIPR stipulates that the 1996 Child Protection Convention governs all situations regarding parental responsibility. The definition of Article 61/14, 1° of the Vreemdelingenwet is based on Article 2 lit. f of the Council Directive 2003/86/EC of 22 September 2003 on the right to family reunification (Family Reunification Directive). It is beyond the scope of this chapter to discuss the difference between the definition of unaccompanied minor in Article 61/14 of the Vreemdelingenwet and Article 2 lit. f of the Family Reunification Directive.

[22] P. Pede and E. Delwiche, Hoofdstuk 5. De specifieke voogdij voor niet-begeleide minderjarige vreemdelingen, In: Desmet, Verhellen and Bouckaert (eds), Rechten van niet-begeleide minderjarige vreemdelingen in België 2019, at p. 114.

[23] Articles 6 and 8 of the Voogdijwet. The appointment of a guardian is an administrative decision.

which was also part of the FAMIMOVE project, it appears that a makfūl is often considered an unaccompanied minor, even if the makfūl accompanies his/her kāfil who has a residence right in Belgium.

When a child is qualified as unaccompanied, a durable solution should be found. This can include family reunification in the State of residence of the parents, return to the State of origin or the State where the minor has an authorised stay, or stay in Belgium.[24] Article 61/14, 2° of the Vreemdelingenwet does not refer to private international law to determine what constitutes a durable solution for the unaccompanied minor. Consequently, it is unclear whether the kafāla has to be recognised in the Belgian legal order to be considered a durable solution. The examined migration case law, which is discussed below, does not clarify this.[25]

In the judgment of 26 October 2015, for example, there was discussion about the durable solution for an abandoned makfūl in a Moroccan kafāla.[26] In this case, the migration authorities argued that the kafāla is not binding on the Belgian authorities and does not confer a residence right to the makfūl. If the kāfil wants to take care of the makfūl, this can also be done by providing financial support in Morocco. The Council does not share this view. Even if a kafāla cannot be converted into an adoption under Belgian law and therefore the migration authorities do not grant a residence permit for the makfūl based on adoption, it must be ensured that there are sufficient safeguards for the child in the country of origin. This did not happen. Based on the Moroccan kafāla judgment, the kāfil was in charge of the makfūl. The makfūl first lived with the kāfil's mother in Morocco. However, the mother of the kāfil moved to Belgium. Consequently, there are no ties anymore with Morocco. In this case, the durable solution for the makfūl is to stay with the kāfil in Belgium.

Another example regarding the discussion on a durable solution for the makfūl is the judgment of 9 April 2018. Despite the fact that the kāfil is the makfūl's aunt and that the makfūl arrived in Belgium with his mother, a guardian was appointed because the Guardianship Service found that the Moroccan kafāla had no legal value in Belgium.[27] The Council supports the view that a durable solution for the minor does not lie in Belgium since there is a strong presumption of planned migration to Belgium in this case. In addition, the special residence regime for unaccompanied minors does not apply to residence for economic reasons, better education or to live with a family member.[28]

It is not illogical that the case law does not address whether the recognition of the kafāla is a condition for considering it a durable solution for the makfūl to reside with the kāfil(s) in Belgium. Indeed, the recognition of the kafāla should already be

[24] Article 61/14, 2° of the Vreemdelingenwet.

[25] See for example Council for Alien Law Litigation 26 October 2015 (155 326); Council for Alien Law Litigation 9 April 2018 (202 127); Council for Alien Law Litigation 27 June 2018 (206 055); and Council for Alien Law Litigation 19 November 2020 (244 421).

[26] Council for Alien Law Litigation 26 October 2015 (155 326).

[27] The judgment does not clarify whether this concerns a judicial or *adoulaire* kafāla.

[28] Council for Alien Law Litigation 9 April 2018 (202 127).

examined to assess whether a child is unaccompanied. A kafāla that is not recognised in this regard is unlikely to be recognised to determine what constitutes a durable solution. However, despite the non-recognition of the kafāla based on private international law, the kafāla can be given factual effect pursuant to Article 29 of the WIPR.[29] This enables the existence of a non-recognised kafāla to be taken into account when determining a durable solution for the child.

As mentioned before, it is debatable whether the recognition of the kafāla is necessary for making a decision on what constitutes a durable solution. One situation in which it is deemed necessary to assess whether there is a valid kafāla is when examining whether the durable solution for the child lies in the country of origin. This can be illustrated by the judgment of 11 September 2020 concerning a Moroccan kafāla. The makfūl came to Belgium with one of the kāfils. Seven years after his arrival, a request for a guardian and residence as an unaccompanied minor were made. A guardian was appointed. Regarding the request for a residence right as unaccompanied minor, the Guardianship Service has to examine whether the durable solution for the makfūl lies with the kāfil in Belgium or with the kāfil living in Morocco.[30] It can be argued that in this context, it matters whether a valid kafāla has been established in Morocco and whether the kāfil can legally care for the child in Morocco. A return to Morocco can only be seen as a durable solution for the makfūl if this is the case.

The examined migration case law reveals that a tension may arise when, on the one hand, the recognition of a kafāla is not assessed and taken into account to determine whether a makfūl is an unaccompanied minor and, on the other hand, the kafāla is taken into account to find a durable solution for the makfūl. If the kafāla is recognised and taken into account to determine whether a makfūl is an unaccompanied minor, it would mean that the makfūl is accompanied by the kāfil(s).[31] The case law shows that the recognition of a kafāla is not always examined. Nevertheless, the kafāla is taken into account when determining a durable solution for the makfūl. Indeed, staying with the kāfil in Belgium can be considered a durable solution.

The private international law framework set out in section II. demonstrates that a kafāla established in a country other than Morocco, and not only the judicial kafāla but also the notarial kafāla, can be recognised in Belgium. To determine whether a makfūl is accompanied by a person exercising parental responsibility, it is relevant to

---

[29] Based on Article 29 of the WIPR, the existence of a foreign judgment or authentic instrument can be considered to be evidence without verification of the conditions for recognition.

[30] Council for Alien Law Litigation 11 September 2020 (240 738).

[31] It is noteworthy that the manual for guardians of the Guardianship Service states that the Guardianship Service should examine the validity of the kafāla. If the kafāla is valid, no guardian should be appointed for the unaccompanied minor. This seems to contradict what is happening in the case law. One possible explanation could be that the kāfil(s) cannot sufficiently prove that he/she is the legal guardian of the child. See for the manual: Federale Overheidsdienst Justitie – Dienst Voogdij, Handboek voor voogden: Boek 1: Dienst Voogdij en opdracht van de voogd, 2022, available at https://justitie.belgium.be/nl/themas/kinderen_en_jongeren/niet_begeleide_minderjarige_vreemdeling_nbmv/handboek_voor_voogden.

apply the private international law framework. One possible explanation that the kāfils pursue to have the makfūl qualify as an unaccompanied minor and thus not have the kafāla recognised is that otherwise it is not possible or very difficult to obtain a residence right for the makfūl. By invoking the special procedure for unaccompanied minors and considering the residence with the kāfil as a durable solution, it is still possible for the kāfil and makfūl to reside and exercise their family life together in Belgium. Moreover, providing the makfūl a right of residence may be in the makfūl's best interests under Article 3 of the CRC[32] and consistent with his/her right to family reunification under Article 10 of the CRC.

2. Family Reunification as Other Family Member

The case law examined also includes examples in which the makfūl requests a residence right based on family reunification. If one of the kāfils has the nationality of an EU member state and has exercised his/her right to free movement, the application will fall under the Citizenship Directive.[33] The application of this Directive and the influence of the right to free movement on a request for family reunification in a kafāla case is illustrated in the judgment "SM versus Entry Clearance Officer" of the Court of Justice of the European Union (hereafter CJEU). This case concerns the request for family reunification between a makfūl in an Algerian judicial kafāla and her kāfil of French nationality residing in the United Kingdom. The CJEU held that the makfūl does not fall within the concept of 'direct descendant' under Article 2 para. 2 of the Citizenship Directive because the kafāla does not create any parent-child relationship between the kāfil and makfūl. Therefore, the makfūl does not have an independent right to residence. However, entry and residence as 'other family member' under Article 3 para. 2 lit. a of the Citizenship Directive should be facilitated to the makfūl who leads a genuine family life with the kāfil and who is dependent on the kāfil. The right to respect for family life and the principle of the best interests of the child require this. Furthermore, a balanced and reasonable assessment of all the circumstances of the case should be made.[34]

The question can be raised whether the recognition of the kafāla based on a member state's private international law is a necessary condition to qualify as 'other family member' under Article 3 para. 2 lit. a of the Citizenship Directive.[35] As will

[32] UN 1989 Convention on the Rights of the Child (CRC).

[33] Directive 2004/38/EC of the European Parliament and of the Council of 29 April 2004 on the right of citizens of the Union and their family members to move and reside freely within the territory of the Member States.

[34] CJEU 26 March 2019, case C-129/18, ECLI:EU:C:2019:248 (SM versus Entry Clearance Officer, UK Visa Section).

[35] In the "SM" judgment, the CJEU ruled that the concept of family member under Article 2 para. 2 Citizenship Directive should be interpreted autonomously. The CJEU did not clarify this for the

be illustrated by the case law below, the examined Belgian migration case law does not provide an univocal answer to this question.

In the two connected judgments of 18 February 2021, a makfūl in an Algerian notarial kafāla requested family reunification with his sister-in-law who is also his kāfil. She is Dutch and resides in Belgium. The brother of the makfūl is the other kāfil. The question arises whether the makfūl qualifies as other family member under Article 47/1, 2° of the Vreemdelingenwet. This article, which governs family reunification between an EU citizen and his/her other family members, requires that the makfūl is dependent on the sponsor in the country of origin or is part of the sponsor's family. The Council for Alien Law Litigation finds that the applicant has not shown that the Algerian kafāla relates to legal guardianship. Moreover, the submitted foster care declaration is not sufficient to prove this. Thus, according to the Council, the kafāla does not prove that the makfūl is part of the sponsor's family or dependent on the kāfils.[36] As a result, the request for annulment of the decisions of the Immigration Office is unfounded. In these judgments, the recognition of the kafāla under private international law is not examined to determine whether the makfūl is a family member of the kāfil for family reunification purposes. Instead, the Council seems to give its own interpretation to the term 'other family member'. In this context, the Council does not clarify the role of private international law and whether recognition based on the WIPR is necessary to qualify as other family member.

The recognition of a kafāla based on private international law is not addressed in the two connected judgments of 18 February 2021. The Council focuses on whether a dependency relationship existed between the makfūl and the kāfils in the country of origin. It follows from the "SM" judgment that the dependency relationship is a condition for family reunification between the makfūl and kāfil(s). However, there is only a narrow margin to deny entry and residence for a makfūl in an Algerian kafāla.[37] The Council also examines, as required by the "SM" judgment, what the best interests of the child are and whether the right to family life has been violated. This analysis could have been more comprehensive. For example, it is unknown how

---

concept of other family member. CJEU 26 March 2019, case C-129/18, ECLI:EU:C:2019:248 (SM versus Entry Clearance Officer, UK Visa Section), para. 40. In the "Minister for Justice and Equality (Ressortissant de pays tiers cousin d'un citoyen de l'Union)" judgment, the CJEU indicated that the concept of other family member refers "to persons who have a relationship of dependence with that citizen, based on close and stable personal ties, forged within the same household, in the context of a shared domestic life going beyond a mere temporary cohabitation entered into for reasons of pure convenience". However, the CJEU did not clarify whether the private international law recognition of the family relationship is necessary. CJEU 15 September 2022, case C-22/21, ECLI:EU:C:2022:683 (Minister for Justice and Equality (Ressortissant de pays tiers cousin d'un citoyen de l'Union)).

[36] Council for Alien Law Litigation 18 February 2021 (249 344); and Council for Alien Law Litigation 18 February 2021 (249 345).

[37] Since the legal consequences of an Algerian notarial and judicial kafāla are the same, it can be argued that the "SM" judgment, which dealt with a judicial kafāla, also applies to the notarial kafāla in the two connected judgments of 18 February 2021.

long the kafāla has been in existence and whether the kāfils and makfūl have a family life together. The Council does not motivate why it deviates from the principle of the "SM" judgment that entry and residence in principle should be granted to the makfūl.

Unlike the two connected judgments of 18 February 2021, the judgment of 7 April 2020 illustrates the application of the CJEU judgment "SM" at the Belgian level. The judgment of 7 April 2020 concerns an application for family reunification as other family member of a Moroccan makfūl. The kāfils have Italian and Moroccan nationality. After the kafāla was established, the kāfils and makfūl lived in Italy. In Italy, the makfūl had a residence permit as a family member of an Italian citizen. Moreover, the Italian court appointed the kāfils as the makfūl's full guardian and co-guardian. After living together in Italy, they moved to Belgium. Here, they first applied for a residence permit for the makfūl based on humanitarian grounds pursuant to Article 9bis of the Vreemdelingenwet and then based on family reunification pursuant to Article 47/1, 2° of the Vreemdelingenwet.

In this case, the migration authorities argued that the makfūl could not be considered a family member. The documents submitted demonstrated that there is a relationship between a guardian and his ward and not a family relationship within the meaning of the Citizenship Directive. According to the kāfils, family reunification under the Citizenship Directive is not limited to a specific composition such as blood family or the nuclear family. Moreover, the Vreemdelingenwet does not define what a family is. The only requirement for family reunification is that the other family member is dependent or part of the household of the Union citizen.[38]

The Council rules that the migration authorities did not give sufficient reasons why the makfūl is not a family member within the meaning of the Citizenship Directive. The migration authorities failed to make a balanced and reasonable assessment of all the current and relevant circumstances of the case, taking into account the various interests, as required by the "SM" judgment. Moreover, the migration authorities did not interpret Article 47/1, 2° Vreemdelingenwet in accordance with the "SM" judgment. Therefore, the Council annuls the decision of the Immigration Office.[39]

The judgment of 7 April 2020 is an example where the Council (rightly) follows the CJEU's approach that a makfūl falls under the concept other family member. Like in the case before the CJEU, the private international law recognition of the kafāla is not part of the discussion and therefore its role remains unclear. The Council's reasoning leads to the conclusion that despite the absence of the examination of the recognition of the kafāla, the makfūl is considered a (other) family member and can enter and reside in Belgium. Since the private international law recognition of the kafāla is not examined and taken into account, the kafāla may have different effects for different legal issues. The same kafāla may be recognised

[38] This is also specified in Article 47/3 of the Vreemdelingenwet.

[39] Council for Alien Law Litigation 7 April 2020 (234 943). This judgment is connected to Council for Alien Law Litigation 5 September 2017 (191 454); and Council for Alien Law Litigation 5 September 2017 (191 455).

differently for family law purposes, such as the change of the makfūl's surname, since here the recognition under private international law is assessed and taken into account. When the kafāla is recognised differently for migration law purposes than for family law purposes, it can lead to a limping legal situation and legal uncertainty. The existence of such a limping legal situation is not desirable and demonstrates the importance of aligning the recognition of a kafāla for migration law purposes and family law purposes. One way to achieve more alignment is to use private international law as a guiding tool in both areas. Consequently, the concept of other family member under Article 3 para. 2 lit. a of the Citizenship Directive should also take into account the recognition of kafāla based on a member state's private international law.

3. How Can EU Principles Influence the Migration Law Consequences of a Kafāla?

In the "SM versus Entry Clearance Officer" case, only the kāfils moved within the EU. The question can be raised whether the right of free movement also affects the recognition and the migration law consequences of a kafāla if the makfūl resided with the kāfils in one member state and then moved to Belgium. This scenario will be made more concrete based on the judgment of the Council for Alien Law Litigation of 25 June 2015, which concerns a Moroccan kafāla. The kāfils requested family reunification with the makfūl as their direct descendant in Belgium. It can be deduced from the facts that the kāfils lived in Spain before coming to Belgium. However, the migration authorities and Council do not address whether the makfūl also lived in Spain and if so, what kind of residence right the makfūl had there and how the kafāla was recognised there.[40]

One may wonder why the recognition of the kafāla in Spain is relevant in Belgium and thus should have been addressed by the migration authorities and Council. Only if the makfūl has been granted a long-term residence status in Spain, which gives the makfūl an independent residence status, should this be respected in Belgium. Regarding other types of residence rights, Belgium does not have to grant the same residence status as Spain.[41] However, the judgment of 25 June 2015 concerns family reunification and this is a derived residence right

[40] Council for Alien Law Litigation 25 June 2015 (148 503).

[41] The conditions for the long-term resident status are laid down in the Council Directive 2003/109/EC of 25 November 2003 concerning the status of third-country nationals who are long-term residents (Long-Term Residence Directive). In principle, the status can be granted when the makfūl has resided in Spain for five years. As Goldner Lang notes, Article 14 of this Directive gives the impression that once the makfūl obtained the long-term resident status, he/she must be granted a residence right in another member state. However, the Directive gives some discretion to member states, so this cannot be stated with certainty. For a more detailed explanation see I. Goldner Lang, Intra-EU Mobility of EU Citizens and Third-Country Nationals: Where EU Free Movement and

from the kāfils who are Union citizens. Since this case concerns family reunification with EU citizens, the conditions for a residence permit in Spain and Belgium are based on the Citizenship Directive.[42] The implementation of this Directive in Spain and Belgium may differ. However, for both, the interpretation of the CJEU is decisive. Based on the "SM" judgment, this means that in both countries the makfūl should be qualified as other family member.[43]

The principle of the right to free movement does not mean that because the makfūl had a certain residence right in one EU member state, the makfūl must also be granted this residence right in another EU member state. Strictly speaking, the makfūl as a third-country national cannot invoke the right to free movement, as opposed to the kāfil, who has the nationality of an EU member state and is therefore a Union citizen. The makfūl can only derive rights from the kāfil's right to freedom of movement.[44] If the makfūl has acquired the nationality of a member state, he/she becomes a Union citizen and can therefore invoke the right to free movement. This could be the case, for example, if an Algerian makfūl moves to France, acquires French nationality and then wants to move to Belgium together with his/her kāfils. In this situation, the makfūl does not have to rely on family reunification with the kāfils to reside in Belgium but can invoke his/her right to free movement.

IV. Conclusion

The central question in this chapter was whether private international law is an essential tool to establish migration law consequences in a kafāla case. The chapter aimed to answer this question by first explaining the Belgian private international law framework on kafāla. Regarding the recognition of a Moroccan judicial kafāla, the 1996 Child Protection Convention has provided clarity. However, this does not mean that a kafāla falling outside the scope of the Convention cannot be recognised in Belgium. The general recognition rules in the WIPR offer a solution here.

How this private international framework can play a role in determining the migration law consequences of a kafāla in Belgium, in particular for an unaccompanied minor and for family reunification, was also discussed. This showed that the private international law framework should be taken into account to determine whether a makfūl can be considered an unaccompanied minor. Regarding family reunification as other family member under Article 3 para. 2 lit. a of the Citizenship

Migration Policies Intersect or Disconnect?, In: De Bruycker and Tsourdi (eds), Research Handbook on EU Migration and Asylum Law, 2022, at pp. 106–108.

[42] I. Goldner Lang, In: De Bruycker and Tsourdi (fn. 41), at pp. 105 f.; and L. Della Torre and T. de Lange, The 'importance of staying put': third country nationals' limited intra-EU mobility rights, Journal of Ethnic and Migration Studies 2018, 1409, at pp. 1409–1424.

[43] This was addressed in paragraph III. 2.

[44] L. Della Torre and T. de Lange, Journal of Ethnic and Migration Studies 2018, 1409, at pp. 1413 f.

Directive, the role of private international law has not (yet) been clearly established. It was submitted that recognition based on a member state's private international law should be a condition so that the recognition of a kafāla for migration and family law consequences are more aligned. Depending on the migration law consequence, it can thus be concluded that private international law cannot be ignored.

Principles to Ensure a Cross-Border Kafāla Placement Is in the Best Interests of the Child

Giovanna Ricciardi and Jeannette Wöllenstein-Tripathi

I. Introduction

The protection of the rights of children has been at the heart of the International Social Services (ISS) mission since its inception a century ago.[1] Regarding the protection of children placed in kafāla, in 2017 ISS embarked on a research journey that led to the publication of a first-of-a-kind study on national and cross-border kafāla practices[2] in December 2020 with the overall aim to contribute to a better understanding of this unique child protection measure, its origins, characteristics and legal effects. For ISS and in line with other invaluable contributions in this book,[3] such understanding is the *conditio sine qua non* for any discussion on the recognition and enforcement of kafāla in a civil or common law system. Way too often, the debates on kafāla are dominated by Western perspectives assimilating kafāla to child protection measures such as adoption, guardianship, and/or foster care.

The fascination and complexity with kafāla lie indeed in the fact that due to its recognition in various international conventions, it is a topic situated at the intersection of international human rights law and private international law, especially when involving a cross-border element. In its ISS' Kafalah study and based on the analyses of over twenty State contexts, ISS calls for a greater respect of the rights of the

[1] See for information on the work and team of the ISS https://iss-ssi.org/.

[2] See Kafalah: 'Preliminary analysis of national and cross-border practices' (hereinafter 'ISS Kafalah study'). International Social Service. December 2020. Available in English (https://www.iss-ssi.org/storage/2023/03/ISS_Kafalah_ENG.pdf) and French (https://www.iss-ssi.org/storage/2023/03/ISS_Kafalah_FRA.pdf).

[3] See for detail N. Yassari, Beyond kafāla: How parentless children are placed in new homes in Muslim jurisdictions, in this volume, at p. 207.

G. Ricciardi (✉) · J. Wöllenstein-Tripathi
International Social Service (ISS), Geneva, Switzerland
e-mail: giovanna.ricciardi@iss-ssi.org; Jeannette.Woellenstein@iss-ssi.org

S. Arnold, B. Heiderhoff (eds.), *Children in Migration and International Family Law*, https://doi.org/10.1007/978-3-031-71598-3_17

makfūl child and reflects on possible avenues for solutions to address current challenges at national and cross-border levels to ensure that kafāla remains a protection measure respectful of children's rights.

DEFINITIONS & TERMS

When discussing kafāla, it is important to first clarify definitions and terms used.

The uniqueness of kafāla lies in its religious origins. For a comprehensive understanding of the different religious and legal sources of Sharia, it is therefore important to study the genesis of Sharia law and adopt a historical lens of its evolution throughout time and transformation into contemporary law in different jurisdictions. Kafāla etymologically means, "taking care", "sponsoring someone", and "responding on behalf of someone", hence it reflects the moral duty to protect children in need as prescribed by the Quran.[4] It is generally defined as "the commitment to voluntarily care for a person (kāfil) for the education and protection of a child as would a father do for his son (makfūl).[5]

Due to different evolutions in contemporary law, this all-encompassing term 'kafāla' covers today a variety of different situations (i.e. intra-family placements, judicial and notarial[6] decisions, informal arrangements)[7] and can occur under a local term (i.e *Ithidan* in Jordan, *sarparasti* in Iran). While it appears to have certain common characteristics,[8] it presents very diverse facets throughout different legislations.[9] Additionally, there is great variety in the form it can take. In many contexts, kafāla remains the (only) family-based care option available to children deprived of parental care (i.e. Algeria, Jordan, Morocco). However, some States have mixed systems that recognise not only kafāla but also placements in a foster care and/or adoption (i.e. Indonesia, Malaysia, Tunisia). In other States, other categories of kafāla or analogous measures exist; these are measures that establish child-parent relationships or forms of sponsorship for children living in institutional care (i.e. Egypt, Lebanon, Pakistan).[10]

(continued)

[4] See ISS' Kafalah study, at p. 14.

[5] See Code de la Famille algérien [*Algerian Family Code*], law no. 84 – 11 of 9 June 1984, Article 123, https://www.refworld.org/docid/5e55403b4.html.

[6] Also called kafāla 'adoulaire' in certain contexts.

[7] ISS' Kafalah study, at p. 17.

[8] The non-severance of birth filiation ties and the preservation of the child's civil status; the legal timeframe of the kafāla placement when the child reaches the age of majority; the non-granting of inheritance rights; and the possibility for revocation.

[9] See for detail N. Yassari, Beyond kafāla: How parentless children are placed in new homes in Muslim jurisdictions, in this volume, at p. 207.

[10] See ISS' Kafalah study, at pp. 22 ff. for further details on each country-context.

At the cross-border level, there are typically three different scenarios for a kafāla placement.[11]

1) The first refers to a national kafāla measure that acquires a cross-border nature following, for example, the change of the habitual residence of the parties involved (relocation of the family, etc.).

2) The second scenario concerns a kafāla arrangement that has been of a cross-border nature since its inception as its implementation is intended to take place in a State different from the one that issued the protection measure.

3) The third and last scenario could also concern an informal arrangement following an agreement, unilateral act, or testament entrusting a person living in another State with the care of the child. This is typically the case where the child is placed abroad with relatives or friends at the initiative of the birth parents or even the child, without the public authorities being involved.

II. Principles

The present contribution aims at highlighting principles as well as recommended practice that are drawn from the mentioned ISS' Kafalah study to guide States in ensuring a cross-border kafāla placement is in the best interests of a child. These principles stem from ISS' conviction that, from a child rights perspective, both public international and private international law provisions need to inform approaches concerning cross-border kafāla. This joint approach is based on ISS' long-standing casework experience in working daily and across the globe on complex cross-border child protection cases. Indeed, while the adoption and circulation of a decision concerning the cross-border kafāla placement falls within the scope of application of the 1996 Child Protection Convention[12] as the key legal instrument, its premises need to be combined with international standards applicable to any alternative care measure for a child deprived of parental care.[13] For ISS, adopting this joint approach would specifically aim at: ensuring the continuity of the child's situation across borders; respecting the rights conferred by the measure without distorting it; ensuring the legal security of the child; andrespecting the child's fundamental human rights (right to access their origins, right to participate in any

[11] See ISS' Kafalah study, at p. 127.

[12] Convention of 19 October 1996 on Jurisdiction, Applicable Law, Recognition, Enforcement and Co-operation in Respect of Parental Responsibility and Measures for the Protection of Children, available at: https://www.hcch.net/en/instruments/conventions/full-text/?cid=70.

[13] This refers in particular to Articles 20, 3 of the UN 1989 Convention on the Rights of the Child (hereinafter 'CRC'), available at https://www.ohchr.org/en/instruments-mechanisms/instruments/convention-rights-child, and the UN Guidelines for the Alternative Care of Children (hereinafter 'UN Alternative Care Guidelines'), available at https://www.alternativecareguidelines.org/Home/tabid/2372/language/en-GB/Default.aspx.

decision concerning their life, etc.). To achieve these objectives, it is crucial to improve the treatment of cross-border kafāla placements by implementing concrete actions and measures both in the State whose legislation is based on or influenced by Sharia law (hereinafter 'states of origin') and in the State concerned by the recognition and enforcement of a kafāla placement (hereinafter 'receiving State').[14]

Principle 1: Ensuring the genuine necessity of a kafāla placement for a child.

The recognition and enforcement of a kafāla placement in another State require consideration for the exact circumstances under which this protection measure was adopted in the State of origin. This entails considering both the existing practices within the overall child protection system as well as the individual case.

Trying to understand kafāla through a siloed or isolated lens does not allow for informed decisions based on a child's best interests. As for any child protection measure, kafāla is to be seen as a solution for a child deprived of parental care within an integrated child protection system whose aim is to ensure continuity and permanency for the child. Further, a series of transversal aspects are needed for a well-functioning child protection and alternative care system[15] that responds to children who need protection and care after all prevention efforts to maintain or reintegrate the child in(to) their family have failed. Family breakdown and separation are often the result of a multitude of factors, which are individual to each situation. To cope with this, a legal framework and a national policy should be based on three levels of prevention ensuring available and accessible basic services to all families, specialised services to families in vulnerable situations, and a robust gatekeeping mechanism that helps prevent unnecessary family separations.[16] At the individual level, based on the existing prevention system in place, it is crucial to understand whether it is or was truly necessary to place the child into kafāla (principle of necessity).[17]

[14] Concrete suggestions and existing promising practices in this context can be consulted in detail in the ISS' Kafalah study (see for instance Technical notes on national and cross-border kafāla, at pp. 98 ff. and at pp. 174 ff.).

[15] Legal and policy framework, governance and coordination structures, a continuum of services, minimum standards and oversight mechanisms, human, financial and infrastructure resources, mechanisms for child participation and community engagement, data collection and monitoring (see UNICEF, 2021: https://www.unicef.org/media/110871/file/1.%20the%20unicef%20child%20protection%20systems%20strengthening%20approach.pdf).

[16] *Level 1* aims at guaranteeing access to basic services (health, education, etc.) by all families and *level 2* should be aimed at providing specialised services to vulnerable families (single mothers, families with special needs children, etc.). *Level 3* promotes family reintegration as an objective to be achieved, provided that it is possible, adequately prepared and monitored. Further, a robust gatekeeping mechanism is necessary to prevent unnecessary family separations. Such a mechanism should systematically determine a child's placement after considering family support and other services, and to decide from the available range of options, which is the alternative care option that best corresponds to the child's individual situation. See Moving Forward Handbook (2012), available at https://bettercarenetwork.org/sites/default/files/Moving-Forward-implementing-the-guidelines-for-web.pdf.

[17] Principle of necessity – major pillar of the UN Alternative Care Guidelines. See Moving Forward Handbook (2012), at p. 23.

As shown in the ISS' Kafalah study, the reality in many States of origin that foresee kafāla is that child protection systems in place are at a nascent stage and present a variety of complexities. The latter are for instance often characterised by a lack of formal procedures as well as adequate human and financial resources. Further, family law provisions are frequently influenced by a prevailing inequality of rights when it comes to matters of parentage and parental responsibility, and stigma over extra-marital relationships and, as a result, children born out of wedlock. It is therefore not surprising that little focus is currently placed in many contexts on avoiding a child's separation from their family through effective prevention measures and concrete family strengthening efforts.

Recommended practice:

- Approaches as to recognition and enforcement need to be nuanced and require a thorough understanding of the kafāla system and the related practices in place as well as the concrete circumstances of the individual situation in question.
- It needs to be considered that child protection systems in many States of origin are not (yet) fully compliant with international standards, which possibly has an impact on any kafāla decision made. Current systems require further strengthening through, *inter alia*, public awareness raising, capacity building of professionals, consolidation of the status of social workers and psychologists, improved intersectoral and interdisciplinary coordination, adequate budget allocation, effective data collection, preservation, and analysis mechanisms.

Principle 2: Ensuring minimum safeguards in kafāla placement processes.

The alternative care system must provide for a range of options that are chosen according to the child's individual needs, circumstances, and wishes. To determine whether a kafāla placement is based on best interests' considerations, it is key to ensure that minimum safeguards are respected in the placement process (principle of suitability).[18] The receiving State should hence verify the procedural steps that led to the decision to place the child within its national context or abroad in another legislation (for example, evidence of the necessary consent, authentication of the required documents). It is not a matter of questioning the merit of the decision, but rather making sure that substantial and procedural safeguards have been respected.

For any formal family-based care placement, including in the form of kafāla, the following crucial steps should be ensured as per applicable international standards:[19]

Determining the suitability of a kafāla based on a thorough process (systematic judicial and administrative procedures with psycho-social, legal, and medical assessments undertaken by qualified professionals).

---

[18] The suitability principle, another major pillar of the UN Alternative Care Guidelines. This principle dictates that the most suitable forms of care must be provided under conditions that "promote the child's full and harmonious development" (preamble of the CRC). See Moving Forward Handbook (2012), at p. 23.

[19] Several key provisions of the CRC (Articles 3, 9, 12, 20) and the UN Alternative Care Guidelines.

Consent and active participation of all parties involved must be freely provided and be the result of a genuine and informed choice by the child, the child's birth parents or the child's legal guardian, in light of viable alternatives offered to them.

Evaluation of kāfil candidates' suitability to care must be guided by the best interests of the child and the existence of well-defined criteria for the selection of a potential family for the child, as well as a thorough psychosocial assessment of that family.

Matching must be made by a professional, interdisciplinary, and independent team who can assess whether the profile of the candidates corresponds best to the specific needs of the child.

Final placement decision by a judicial or administrative authority. The preparation of and support for the child and the family before and during the placement are also essential steps in a successful placement.

Monitoring, follow-up and support must be ensured for each placement by a specific entity/authority composed of professionals from various fields and by offering specialised services. Supervision of the kafāla system must take the form of an effective complaint mechanism, and the costs involved in the procedure must also be monitored. In addition, regular follow-up must be ensured, to be able to address complex situations such as kafāla breakdowns or support during a search for origins process.

Data collection, preservation and analysis mechanisms must exist to be able to determine children's needs and adapt laws and policies accordingly. Disaggregated data should be gathered especially in relation to vulnerable families and children, children separated or at risk of being separated from their families, and children in care. This is also key to ensure the child's right to identity and guarantee future opportunities for search for origins. Ideally, data should be centralised, managed, and supervised by the State. Specific rules on access to data should be set down, taking into consideration the potential impact of the disclosure of information on the child requesting access to it.

In the extensive study of different States of origin both through a legal and practical implementation lens, ISS found that there is a prevalence of informal arrangements in the context of kafāla, which escape any form of regulation and monitoring by public authorities, and that can put children at extreme risk of rights violations. The study also emphasises the absence of data collected on the number of children who benefit from a kafāla at the national and cross-border levels, the profile of children, and the type of placements in question. This makes it difficult to determine the extent of these situations and identify children's real needs. In relation to the existing legislations, some countries have a limited legal framework that remains silent on the implementation of certain key steps such as obtaining consent from birth parents, matching by a competent and independent body, and preparation of the child, and the kāfil applicants. Other aspects that are rarely foreseen by the law are the regulation of costs related to the placement, the prevention and responses to placement breakdowns, the provision of leaving care (e.g. once the child reaches the age of majority or their independence) or the right to access one's origins. Finally, certain key safeguards such as the assessment of the child and of the applicants, a regular follow-up and review of the placement, as well as adequate monitoring of the quality of the placement are often not implemented in practice.

When it comes to a cross-border kafāla placement, the above-listed safeguards should equally be implemented. The complexity lies, however, in the fact that currently most States of origin concerned do not have a clear internal approach to processing cross-border kafāla placements from a legal, political, and practical standpoint, which can lead to heterogeneous practices among involved professionals (judiciary for instance), and to practices such as "forum shopping" (choice of the most convenient authority). A lack of consistency in the approach may equally lead to the emergence of illicit practices such as circumventing procedural safeguards in place, and involving undue sums of money and intermediaries whose work methods may be described as unethical. Lastly, as demonstrated in most of the countries examined in the ISS' Kafalah study, supervision and/or follow up of cross-border placements is not provided for by many legislations in force. The State of origin is often limited to providing authorisation to travel or exit from its own territory.

Recommended practice:

- There is a need to strengthen kafāla systems and ensure formal decision-making processes and effective monitoring mechanisms, at national and cross-border levels.
- Ensuring the implementation of the procedural steps of a cross-border placement is a States' shared responsibility and can be achieved through various means.[20]
- Any State should adopt a clear position and standards on cross-border kafāla consisting of clarifying, and if necessary, adapting, applicable standards related to recognising and enforcing a national or cross-border kafāla placement. This would also allow the identification of stakeholders involved and clarify their respective roles and responsibilities.
- Professionals involved require further capacity building on some of these key safeguards for the child. This is also crucial to ensure common understandings and harmonised practices among professionals.

Principle 3: A cross-border kafāla placement shall be considered only after domestic solutions were explored.

For any alternative care option, it is of utmost importance to ensure the child's continuity with their upbringing and background, primarily in their national context (principle of double subsidiarity).[21] In case the child cannot remain within their birth family, national placements should first be explored. If after thorough examination this is not a valid solution for the child, a cross-border placement can be considered.

[20] See further Principles 5, 6 and 8.

[21] The principle of double subsidiarity is enshrined in the CRC, as well as in the UN Alternative Care Guidelines and a well-established principle in the field of intercountry adoption (see 1993 Child Adoption Convention, available at https://www.hcch.net/en/instruments/conventions/full-text/?cid=69). The first level of the principle of subsidiarity relates to efforts conducted to keep the child within their birth or extended family prior to considering any other placement with other caregivers (see also above principle 1).

On a general note, placements with the child's extended family or close friends of the family known to the child should always be prioritised over a placement with caregivers with whom the child has no pre-established relationship.[22]

As highlighted in the ISS' Kafalah study,[23] some professionals dealing with these cases have however the tendency to turn to cross-border solutions for the child prior effectively considering any national solution. Based on ISS' practical experience, a lack of a profound understanding of the international standards governing the issuing of a child's protection measure, as well as the general belief that the child will have a better future abroad are among the reasons for the generally observed preference given to cross-border placements.

Recommended practice:

- Any final decision on whether to adopt a national or cross-border protection measure cannot but be considered on a case-by-case basis.
- All efforts to find solutions to maintain the child within their birth and/or extended family in the State of origin need to be documented and information therein made available for the receiving State dealing with the recognition and enforcement of the protection measure as well as for the child in search for their origins.
- General awareness raising on the principle of double subsidiarity and its benefits for the concerned child is needed both aimed at professionals working in the State of origin as well as the receiving State.

Principle 4: Determining the nature of the cross-border kafāla placement and the applicable law instrument.

Cross-border scenarios require the receiving States to respond differently, depending on the circumstances under which the kafāla placement took place. For instance, for those cases that come to light as pure national placements — and hence are not subject to uniform private international law rules on jurisdiction — the application of the recognition mechanism provided for by the 1996 Child Protection Convention might be precluded. Private international law rules of the receiving State may apply to such situations. Conversely, for the kafāla placements that have a cross-border element since its inception, the application of the 1996 Child Protection Convention is mandatory among the Contracting States. Finally, unless approved by an authority or embedded in a court decision, kafāla placements that result from private arrangements cannot benefit from the application of the 1996 Child Protection Convention.[24] Indeed, these kinds of placements may pose the child at a risk

[22] The placement of the child in their extended family or close friends of the family known to the former is known as 'kinship care' and expressly defined by the UN Alternative Care Guidelines, para. 29.

[23] See ISS' Kafalah study, at pp. 133 and 177.

[24] See Conclusions and Recommendations, 8th Special Commission on the practical operation of the 1980 Child Abduction Convention and the 1996 Child Protection Convention, para. 87, available at https://assets.hcch.net/docs/5b48f412-6979-4dc1-b4c1-782fe0d5cfa7.pdf.

given the lack of basic safeguards as above-mentioned,[25] including the right to access to the territory and residence permit for the child.

As emphasised in the ISS' Kafalah study, the absence of uniformed approaches concerning the applicable legal instrument aimed at recognising and enforcing the cross-border kafāla can result in a variety of possible outcomes potentially placing the child in a situation of legal uncertainty.

Recommended practice:

- The legal instruments applicable will need to be determined on a case-by-case basis, considering the exact nature of the cross-border placement.
- Further awareness-raising is needed among professionals in both States of origin and receiving States on the adoption of a case-by-case approach depending on the nature of the cross-border placement.
- A coordinated approach among receiving States is of essence when dealing with the recognition and enforcement of cross-border placements to grant the children involved the same rights and safeguards independently from the State in which they will be placed.

Principle 5: Respecting the co-operation mechanism under Article 33 of the 1996 Child Protection Convention.

The co-operation mechanism laid down in Article 33 of the 1996 Child Protection Convention should always take place prior to deciding to place a makfūl child in another Contracting State. According to this mechanism, the competent authority of the State of origin of the child is obliged to consult with the Central Authority or other competent authority of the receiving State where the said measure will be implemented. When consulting with the latter, the State of origin transmits a report on the child together with the reasons for the proposed placement. Following the consent of the receiving State, and only in this circumstance, the State of origin is allowed to proceed with the cross-border kafāla placement.

As highlighted in the ISS' Kafalah study,[26] the consultation mechanism is frequently not known to involved professionals or simply not adequately applied in practice. For instance, the lack of implementation of the mechanism can lead to different *de facto* situations ('faits accomplis'), in which the child is already living with their kāfil parents, sometimes even in the receiving State. The mentioned situations are not only contrary to international standards but also and foremost to the best interests of the child.

Recommended practice:

---

[25] See above Principle 2.

[26] The same challenges have been stressed by ISS during its interventions in the 8th Special Commission on the practical operation of the 1980 Child Abduction Convention and the 1996 Child Protection Convention. See ISS interventions as an observer in the HCCH Special Commission (SC) 10 to 17 October 2023, available at https://iss-ssi.org/storage/2023/10/ISS-interventions-as-an-observer-at-8th-Meeting-of-the-HccH-Special-Comission-for-THC-1980-1996-2023.pdf.

- States should systematically comply with the mandatory co-operation mechanism laid down in Article 33 of the 1996 Child Protection Convention prior to any placement decision. By informing the receiving State, the State of origin makes sure that the latter is aware and well-prepared to receive the child in its territory. Indeed, a lack of consultation with the receiving State might result, among others, in the authorities of both States losing track of the whereabouts of the child with the latter possibly ending up in a vulnerable situation.[27]
- States should make use of the co-operation mechanisms under Article 33 of the 1996 Child Protection Convention also to follow-up and exchange information on the implementation *status* of the protection measure. The same mechanism can also be of help in dealing both with a kafāla breakdown, and the child's search for their origins.
- Immigration officers involved with the granting of the right of access and residence permit of children placed in kafāla should receive proper training to understand the complexities of this protection measure.

Principle 6: Applying the mechanisms of the 1996 Child Protection Convention to cross-border kafāla placements taking effect in non-Contracting States.

The respect for the best interests of the child in a cross-border kafāla placement shall be granted also in the case where the effects of the protection measure will take place in a non-Contracting State. Indeed, the non-applicability of the legal provisions of the 1996 Child Protection Convention should never be perceived as a way to enable unsupervised cross-border placements, which still seem to be frequent, possibly putting concerned children at risk of rights violations. To this end, Contracting States are encouraged to apply the same principles and standards laid down in the HCCH Conventions when dealing with non-Contracting States to ensure that also those placements that produce legal effects in the latter are supported with certain safeguards. In this scenario, diplomatic missions possibly of both States concerned can play a key role in helping exchange information and documents.

Recommended practice:

- When considering placing a child under a kafāla arrangement in a non-Contracting State, the consultation mechanism might occur with the diplomatic missions, which can help obtain the consent and relevant documentation to place a child in another territory.
- Diplomatic missions should receive proper training on the international applicable standards to cross-border kafāla placements given their significant role when dealing with non-Contracting States.[28]
- Non-Contracting States are encouraged to ratify the 1996 Child Protection Convention to grant minimum procedural guarantees for cross-border kafāla placements.

---

[27] See ISS' Kafalah study, at pp. 135 ff.

[28] See ISS' Kafalah study, at p. 180.

Principle 7: Finding a balance between respecting the original legal effects of a kafāla placement and ensuring equitable rights for children in care.

To proceed with the recognition and enforcement of a cross-border placement in a receiving State, a balance must be sought between the rights conferred by the protection measure and the child's access to the same rights as any other child in the receiving State.

Regarding the transfer of the child and related immigration questions, the legal certainty of the child is of paramount importance in choosing the lawful method for entering and residing in the receiving State.[29] Apart from the initial access approval, questions often remain as to the renewal of visas or permits, and the impact on the life of the child and the family as well as to access to social and family benefits.

Upon the arrival of the child (short-term effects), the effects of the protection measure in accordance with the law of the State of origin should apply[30] while implementing them into the receiving State's legal system. Currently, in the absence of a coordinated approach among receiving States, several possible private international law approaches exist in this regard (e.g. substitution or conversion; functional case-by-case equivalents). No matter which approach is taken, the receiving State is responsible for the legal status of the child and their protection and wellbeing on arrival. Therefore, to ensure legal certainty, provisions specific to kafāla should be foreseen to address not only the legal, but ideally also psycho-social aspects. For instance, the child's access to basic services (social, health and education, etc.) and the effective access to their origins (e.g. data collection and storage) must be guaranteed. After a few years, once the child is integrated into the receiving State (middle- and long-term effects), they should be fully subject to the national law of the receiving State. New circumstances such as the change in the child's habitual residence[31] or the acquisition of the nationality of the receiving State by the child[32] may then affect the original effects and functions of the kafāla placement in the receiving State.

As shown in ISS' Kafalah study, the uniqueness of kafāla makes it challenging to transpose its original effects and functions in the legal system of a receiving State with a civil or common law system. Significant differences can be observed between kafāla and other child protection measures that are generally available in receiving States (i.e. full, simple, or open adoption, foster care, kinship care, guardianship, placement in an institutional setting). Another difficulty lies also in the fact that, while in most States of origin, legal provisions clarify on the effects conferred by kafāla as to general care and maintenance obligations for the kāfil parent, matters related to name as well as inheritance rights of the makfūl child, the legal effects in

---

[29] See ISS' Kafalah study, Technical Note Cross-border kafāla, phase 3, at pp. 180 ff.

[30] See Article 15 para. 2 of the 1996 Child Protection Convention.

[31] See also Conclusions and Recommendations, 7th Special Commission on the practical operation of the 1980 Child Abduction Convention and the 1996 Child Protection Convention, para. 31, available at: https://assets.hcch.net/docs/edce6628-3a76-4be8-a092-437837a49bef.pdf.

[32] See ISS' Kafalah study, 'Technical note: Cross-border kafalah', phase 4, at pp. 18 ff.

relation to parental responsibility (legal representation, custody, etc.) are not clearly regulated nor understood and require further clarification.

Recommended practice:

- When dealing with access and residence rights, long-term solutions are encouraged as they provide essential protections and legal security for the child concerned. Given their crucial role, immigration authorities should be made aware of the impact of certain decisions on a child's life.
- In many legislations of States of origin, the exact legal effects as to parental responsibility conferred by kafāla are not comprehensively addressed, which adds a lawyer of complexity for the transposition of its legal effects in the receiving State. In this context a key role could be played by the International Hague Network of Judges in obtaining further information on the legal effects and the practical implementation of the protection measure in the State of origin.[33]
- The transposition of the protection measure in the receiving State should consider its short-term, middle, and long-term effects, until the child is fully integrated.
- The automatic assimilation or substitution of a kafāla placement by a protection measure in the receiving State should be dealt with extra caution. The principle of best interests of the child in any decision affecting their life requires to proceed on a case-by-case basis.
- The original kafāla placement might become "a hybrid measure" or *tertium genus* that would consider the specificities and uniqueness of kafāla as per the specific country-context and individual situation concerned.

Principle 8: Introducing additional safeguards to the co-operation mechanism under Article 33 of the 1996 Child Protection Convention.

While being a valuable tool to protect children placed under kafāla in other Contracting States, the sole application of Article 33 might still not be sufficient to fully safeguard the best interests of the concerned child and comply with the CRC. Indeed, as per Article 33, States of origin only have the obligation to consult with the Central Authority or other competent authority of the receiving State prior to making any decisions on the placement of the child and when doing so, provide them with a report on the child together with the reasons for the sought protection measure. No further requirements shall be fulfilled, with the consequence that if the receiving State does not request further action and provides its consent, the State of origin will issue said measure. While this allows for a "smooth" circulation of the measure among Contracting States, one can only but wonder if the cross-border kafāla placement is truly in the best interests of the child. Indeed, for instance, no obligations stand from the mentioned convention as to gathering the consents of the child

[33] See ISS' Kafalah study, Justice Victoria Bennett, 'The Judges' Network to foster direct judicial communication in cross-border kafalah placements', Annex IV.3, at pp. 211 ff.

or their birth family, ensuring the child's preparation, nor is there a reference to the evaluation of the suitability of the kāfils prior to the transfer of the child into their care.[34]

Recommended practice:

- Contracting States are encouraged to provide additional safeguards to cross-border kafāla placements by way, for example, of bilateral agreements to enable a cross-border placement in the best interests of the child.
- It is critical that the competent child protection authority take charge and lead the coordination efforts from a child's rights perspective, hence the importance of developing internal protocols and/or policies that clarify on the roles and responsibilities of each stakeholder concerned.[35]
- The establishment of additional safeguards should enable to carrying out of a structured case-management of each individual case, that ensures the respect for children's rights in each stage of the cross-border placement such as in the pre-placement (consultation), the placement decision, the transfer of the child, the implementation of the measure and its follow-up.[36]
- Bilateral agreements may mirror the legal safeguards foreseen by the UN Alternative Care Guidelines and for certain aspects the 1993 Child Adoption Convention to cover different aspects such as immigration and asylum matters, which do not fall under the scope of application of the 1996 Child Protection Convention. To this end, receiving States could subject their consent to the placement in their territory to the respect of their immigration and asylum laws to enable the child to enter and reside in the territory of the receiving State on a long-term basis and hence ensuring legal certainty for the child. Likewise, the State of origin could also determine certain requirements as to the exact treatment of a cross-border placement in the receiving State. A bilateral agreement could also ensure that the child and their birth family have been given the possibility to provide their informed consent to the issuing of the protection measure, as well as that mandatory preparatory courses for kāfils have been followed, and that periodical reports on the effective implementation of the protection measure in the receiving States will be provided.[37]
- If not done through a bilateral agreement, important additional procedural safeguards[38] could equally be foreseen and implemented unilaterally by a State through national laws, policies, or guidelines.
- The availability of additional safeguards should guide the States of origin in choosing the receiving States with whom to collaborate. Important elements to

[34] Minimum safeguards are extensively illustrated above in Principle 2.

[35] See above Principle 2.

[36] See ISS' Kafalah study, at pp. 179 ff.

[37] See ISS interventions as an observer in the HCCH Special Commission (SC) 10 to 17 October 2023, available at https://issssi.org/storage/2023/10/ISS-interventions-as-an-observer-at-8th-Meeting-of-the-HccH-Special-Comission-for-THC-1980-1996-2023.pdf.

[38] Ibid.

guide this choice are the availability and, *inter alia,* the duration of a residence permit, as well as the follow-up and support services available in the receiving State also regarding the child's access to origins.[39]

- As time is of the essence for a child, and to avoid unnecessary bureaucratic processes, States are encouraged to make their additional criteria publicly accessible, for instance, on their website or through the distribution of leaflets.

CASE STUDY

While doctrine and practice focus essentially on recognising and enforcing the legal effects of kafāla in a receiving State, the challenges go beyond these questions, influencing countless other child protection aspects as shown in the above-mentioned principles.

The case study developed by ISS in its Kafalah study illustrates these aspects and focuses on the key questions professionals concerned should ask themselves when dealing with a cross-border kafāla placement.

See ISS' Kafalah study, at pp. 129–132.

III. Final Remarks

ISS commends the enactment of the international project FAMIMOVE, which has touched upon topics that are at the core of ISS' mission, one of them being to safeguard the rights of children placed in kafāla. This project has served as a unique forum in raising awareness on the implementation of national and international legal frameworks regarding the protection of children across borders as well as the experienced challenges. It has provided an important contribution in the discussions around the importance of adopting common approaches among professionals across sectors entrusted with dealing with these complex cases. In its 100th year of existence dedicated to the protection of children and families across borders, ISS celebrates the global achievements in this field and hopes to see the number of States whose legislations are based on or influenced by Sharia Law and have ratified the 1996 Child Protection Convention increase in the coming years, and thus make an essential contribution to ensure decisions in the best interests of children.

[39] See ISS' Kafalah study, at pp. 178.

Recognition of Kafāla in European Member States: Need for a Uniform Approach?

Fabienne Jault-Seseke

I. Introduction

This chapter aims to answer the question if and under which conditions a kafāla issued in an Islamic state may be recognised in European member states. The way to deal with kafāla in the member states is heterogeneous.[1] The EU legislator has not adopted a uniform approach to the application and recognition of kafāla in the EU. This is not surprising, given that kafāla is not a protection measure known to the legislation of the member states. The European Court of Justice (CJEU) has dealt with the issue of kafāla only one time. Its ruling is promising.

The European legal framework is mainly given by the EU Charter of Fundamental Rights[2] which has the same legal value as the EU treaties. The Charter reflects the principles of the CRC.[3] The EU itself is not bound by the CRC but all EU member states have ratified it and the EU has incorporated the CRC into its policies and actions through various mechanisms When Article 7 of the Charter protects the right to a family and private life, Article 24 of the Charter obliges member states to "take into consideration the best interests of the child".[4] Moreover, the EU develops

[1] See above.

[2] EU Charter of Fundamental Rights (EU Charter).

[3] UN 1989 Convention on the Rights of the Child (CRC).

[4] Article 24: "1. Children shall have the right to such protection and care as is necessary for their well-being. They may express their views freely. Such views shall be taken into consideration on matters which concern them in accordance with their age and maturity; 2. In all actions relating to children, whether taken by public authorities or private institutions, the child's best interests must be a primary consideration. 3. Every child shall have the right to maintain on a regular basis a personal

F. Jault-Seseke (✉)
Faculty of Law and Political Science, Laboratory DANTE, University of Paris Saclay, Versailles Saint-Quentin-en-Yvelines, Paris, France
e-mail: fabienne.jault-seseke@uvsq.fr

S. Arnold, B. Heiderhoff (eds.), *Children in Migration and International Family Law*, https://doi.org/10.1007/978-3-031-71598-3_18

specific guidelines and strategies to support the implementation of children's rights, such as the EU Strategy on the Rights of the Child.

Regarding kafāla, Article 20 of the CRC is particularly relevant. It provides that kafāla is an alternative form of care for children deprived—temporarily or permanently—of their family environment. Article 20 emphasises the need to pay due regard to the desirability of continuity in a child's upbringing and to the child's ethnic, religious, cultural and linguistic background.[5]

In the light of this framework and in order to respect the cultural environment of the child, it should first be considered that kafāla is not an adoption (section "II. The Starting Point: Promoting Respect for Cultural Differences. Kafāla Is Not an Adoption"). Then, the best interests of the child should be protected outside the framework of the adoption. The child's interests must be taken into account at both the pronouncement of kafāla (section "III. The First Step: Promoting Respect for Fundamental Rights When Granting Kafāla") and recognition stages (section "IV. Second Step: Implement Best Practices for Recognising Kafāla").

II. The Starting Point: Promoting Respect for Cultural Differences. Kafāla Is Not an Adoption

The 1993 Child Adoption Convention[6] highlights the need to respect the distinct legal and cultural practices and states that kafāla is not an adoption. This is in line with the CRC which recognises the importance of different cultural practices in ensuring the welfare of children.

The question, nevertheless, arose as to whether respecting the principles of Muslim law, and specifically the prohibition of adoption, was detrimental to the interests of the child. The European Court of Human Rights (ECtHR) gave an answer in the famous case Harroudj.[7]

In this case, the French authorities refused the kāfil's request for the full adoption of an Algerian girl who had been abandoned at birth and placed in the applicant's care under kafāla. They considered that kafāla already gave the kāfil parental authority, allowing him or her to take decisions in the child's best interests. The ECtHR recalled the principle that, once a family tie is established, the State has to enable that tie to be developed and has to establish legal safeguards that render the

relationship and direct contact with both his or her parents, unless that is contrary to his or her interests."

[5] J. Tobin, In: Tobin (ed), The UN-Convention on the Rights of the child. A Commentary, 2019, Article 20, at p. 727.

[6] Convention of 29 May 1993 on Protection of Children and Co-operation in Respect of Intercountry Adoption (1993 Child Adoption Convention).

[7] ECtHR 4 October 2012, 43631/09, ECLI:CE:ECHR:2012:1004JUD004363109 (Harroudj versus France).

child's integration into the family possible. The Court also recalled the need to interpret the Human Rights Convention[8] in a manner consistent with the general principles of international law. The Court concluded that France sought to encourage the integration of children of foreign origin without cutting them off immediately from the rules of their country of origin, showed respect for cultural pluralism and struck a fair balance between the public interest and that of the kāfil.

III. The First Step: Promoting Respect for Fundamental Rights When Granting Kafāla

As stated in the ISS' Kafalah study,[9] most States of origin concerned with kafāla do not have a clear approach to processing cross-border kafāla. The practices are heterogeneous and can lead to "forum shopping". Illicit practices are not rare.

At the stage of the pronouncement of the kafāla, the EU is relatively powerless. However some actions can be taken. The EU does have some leverage through the conventions it has ratified, which establish a mechanism for cooperation between States of origin and receiving States.

The EU can encourage States of origin to provide a better framework for kafālas, so as to achieve ethic kafālas that respect the principle of subsidiarity. It can rely on the cooperation mechanism set up by the 1996 Child Protection Convention, which is satisfactory. We will not go into the role played by the 1996 Child Protection Convention, and in particular Article 33, again.[10] But we have to remember that the FAMIMOVE project highlighted that Article 33 of the 1996 Convention is not systematically applied. Even if France and the Netherlands consistently apply it, many Member States are unaware of it.[11] The roundtable organised in Paris shows, for example, that Belgium is not familiar with this cooperation mechanism. This can be explained through the late appointment of the central authority required by the 1996 Child Protection Convention. Nevertheless, there is place for improvement. This was recognised at the 2023 meeting of the Special Commission on the practical operation on this Convention. As a result, it was decided to establish a Working Group to develop a model form for cooperation and a guide on the operation of

[8] Convention for the Protection of Human Rights and Fundamental Freedoms (Human Rights Convention).

[9] See also above, G. Ricciardi and J. Wöllenstein-Tripathi, Principles to ensure a cross-border kafāla placement is in the best interests of the child, in this volume, at p. 271.

[10] See above M. Celis, Kafāla in the Netherlands, in this volume, 239, at pp. 240 ff., F. Jault-Seseke, Kafāla in France, in this volume, 225, at pp. 226 ff.

[11] See the responses to the 2023 Questionnaire on the 1996 Child Protection Convention, at pp. 109 ff. (see in particular, responses from Switzerland (at p. 111), France (at p. 119) and Norway (at p. 120)), https://assets.hcch.net/docs/79105a67-45d6-47ed-8ca5-2def687cf130.pdf.

Article 33.[12] The EU should strive to make this mechanism better known. The EU could also encourage States of origin to ratify the 1996 Child Protection Convention, as Morocco has done. It could also conclude agreements with countries of origin. In this regard the European decision empowering France to negotiate a bilateral agreement with Algeria concerning judicial cooperation in civil matters related to family law is interesting. Its Article 1 lit. b states that "France encourages Algeria to consider acceding to the core conventions concerning family law matters developed by the Hague Conference on Private International Law and to start an analysis of the most appropriate means to remove the obstacles which have prevented Algeria from acceding to the Hague Convention".[13]

Once a kafāla has been granted, it is essential that it is recognised in the EU, if the kāfil is a habitual resident there.

IV. Second Step: Implement Best Practices for Recognising Kafāla

Recognition of kafālas pronounced in the child's best interests must be ensured. This is the case when the cooperation mechanism set out in Article 33 of the 1996 Child Protection Convention has been respected. But this recognition only concerns civil matters. It could be useful to provide information for the national authorities responsible for migration issues who are outside of this cooperation process. This is currently not the case.

Recognition of kafālas pronounced outside the framework of Article 33 should also be favored to ensure child protection. This may even apply to non-ethical kafālas, particularly where the person to whom the child has been entrusted has succeeded in taking the child to the host country. A framework for the recognition of the kafāla in the EU does not exist. We can, however, draw on the case law of the CJEU and suggest going further.

The CJEU has dealt with the kafāla in the SM case.[14] It concerns the application of the Citizenship Directive.[15] SM, an Algerian girl, was abandoned at birth by her biological parents. She was placed, under the Algerian kafāla system, in the care of a French couple who lived in the UK and who were not able to have children of their own. When the husband returned to the UK to work, his wife stayed in Algeria to

[12] This conclusion was approved by the Council on General Affairs and Policy of the Hague Conference on Private International law in 2024, Conclusion & Decision, No. 26.

[13] Council Decision (EU) 2024/592 of 23 January 2024 empowering France to negotiate a bilateral agreement with Algeria concerning judicial cooperation in civil matters related to family law.

[14] CJEU 26 March 2019, case C-129/18, ECLI:EU:C:2019:248 (SM versus Entry Clearance Officer, UK Visa Section).

[15] Directive 2004/38/EC of the European Parliament and of the Council of 29 April 2004 on the right of citizens of the Union and their family members to move and reside freely within the territory of the Member States (Citizenship Directive).

look after the child while seeking entry clearance for her. The UK authorities refused the application. For the next six years the French couple fought for the UK authorities to accept the validity of their family relationship and also the child's right to enter and live in the UK. In February 2018 the UK Supreme Court referred some questions to the CJEU. The questions focus on two notions used in the Citizenship Directive, "direct descendant" and "any other family member".[16] In other words, could SM be treated as a direct descendant of an EU national for the purpose of free movement? Given that the Citizenship Directive pursues the objective of strengthening the primary and individual right of movement, the CJEU considers that its provisions had to be read broadly. A broad reading of the notion of "direct descendant" requires it to embrace both biological and legal parent-child relations. But the Algerian *kafāla* is a mere legal guardianship and not a parent-child relation. The child under legal guardianship is "only" embraced within the extended family. Under the Citizenship Directive, member states do not owe a duty of admission to extended family members. They only have an obligation to facilitate entry. They have to confer "a certain advantage" to their application for entry. Member states retain discretion in deciding on admission. Therefore, according to the letter of the directive, there is a gap between the treatment of core and extended family members for free movement purposes. Core family members have the same rights as the Union citizens where extended family members remain in the sphere of immigration law, where member states have a broader margin of appreciation. But in the SM ruling, the CJEU bridges the gap invoking fundamental rights: the discretion of the member states in deciding on the admission of an extended family member finds a clear limit in fundamental rights. The national authorities should make a balanced assessment of all relevant circumstances and have to take into account all interests in play, namely the age at which the child was placed under the protection of the kāfil, whether the child has lived with the kāfil, the personal relationship between the child and the kāfil and the dependence of the makfūl on the kāfil. If this assessment establishes that the child and his or her kāfil, who are citizens of the Union, lead a genuine family life and that the child is dependent on his or her kāfils, the fundamental right to respect for family life demands, in principle, that the child be granted a right of entry and residence as one of the other family members of the citizens of the Union for the purposes of Article 3 para. 2 lit. a of the Citizenship Directive.

Many lessons can be learned from this ruling.

The SM case underlines the primacy of children's best interests in decision making which leads *in casu* to grant entry and residence for a child who was still in her country of origin. If she has already stayed in the host State the consideration of her best interests would *a fortiori* have led to the issuance of a residence permit.

The SM ruling does not use Private International Law rule. It retains a case by case approach. At no point did the CJEU consider the law applicable to the protection measure or the method of recognising a decision taken by a foreign authority. It simply highlights the need for the national authority to respect

[16] Article 2 para. 2 lit. c and Article 3 para. 2 lit. a of the Citizenship Directive.

fundamental rights. Due to the growing importance of the fundamental rights in the PIL reasoning, namely through the public policy clause, the result would have probably been the same.[17]

Likewise, the Court does not directly address the issue of fraud. The question about refusing to admit a child if there was a risk of abuse, exploitation or trafficking was raised by the Supreme Court's question. The silence kept by the Court is not a missed opportunity: the risk of abuse is part of the whole assessment of the case.

The reasoning followed by the Court in the SM case concerns only the Citizenship Directive. However, a similar line could be applied to the interpretation of the Family Reunification Directive,[18] or to all texts relating to international protection.

Having that in mind, the CJEU has shown that migration rules need to be interpreted flexibly to allow for measures guided by consideration of the child's best interests. The protection afforded to de facto family life by the CJEU in migration matters should be extended to civil matters. In concrete terms, it should enable the Brussels IIter Regulation[19] to come into play once the child has acquired habitual residence in the territory of the Union, and lead to the recognition of the kāfil as the holder of parental responsibility, whenever this proves to be in the child's best interests.

In conclusion, it is to be hoped that, in the wake of the SM ruling, the case-by-case method inspired by the compass of the child's best interests will be followed by the various Member States.

[17] See R. Legendre, Droits fondamentaux et droit international privé, Réflexion en matière personnelle et familiale, 2020.

[18] Council Directive 2003/86/EC of 22 September 2003 on the right to family reunification (Family Reunification Directive).

[19] Council Regulation (EU) 2019/1111 of 25 June 2019 on jurisdiction, the recognition and enforcement of decisions in matrimonial matters and the matters of parental responsibility, and on international child abduction (recast) (Brussels IIter Regulation).

Part VI
Additional Topics

The Role of the Court of Justice in Shaping the Right to Maintain Family Unity for Beneficiaries of International Protection

Alessia Voinich

I. Introduction

The right to maintain family unity is one of the inherent guarantees of the content of international protection provided for in Chapter VII of the Qualification Directive.[1] This right extends to both refugees and beneficiaries of subsidiary protection, safeguarding the integrity of family units already present within the member state offering protection.[2]

This inclusion of family unity within the framework of international protection reflects a more specific application of broader principles enshrined in instruments like the EU Charter[3] (Articles 7 and 24) and the Human Rights Convention[4] (Article 8). Notably, the Geneva Refugee Convention[5] itself lacks an analogous provision, though the Final Act of the UN Conference of Plenipotentiaries on the Status of Refugees and Stateless Persons emphasises family unity as an "essential right" for refugees and urges the States to protect it.[6]

[1] Directive 2011/95/EU of the European Parliament and of the Council of 13 December 2011 on standards for the qualification of third-country nationals or stateless persons as beneficiaries of international protection, for a uniform status for refugees or for persons eligible for subsidiary protection, and for the content of the protection granted (recast) (Qualification Directive).

[2] CJEU 18 April 2023, case C-1/23, ECLI:EU:C:2023:296 (PPU Afrin) para. 37.

[3] EU Charter of Fundamental Rights (EU Charter).

[4] Convention for the Protection of Human Rights and Fundamental Freedoms (Human Rights Convention).

[5] 1951 Geneva Convention relating to the Status of Refugees.

[6] The Final Act highlights the right of refugee families to stay together, especially when the head of the household qualifies for admission to a specific country. It also calls for safeguarding refugee

A. Voinich (✉)
Faculty of Law, Milan Bicocca University, Milan, Italy
e-mail: alessia.voinich@unimib.it

S. Arnold, B. Heiderhoff (eds.), *Children in Migration and International Family Law*, https://doi.org/10.1007/978-3-031-71598-3_19

However, ensuring the practical application of this right presents significant challenges. The Qualification Directive mandates member states to uphold family unity while setting specific conditions and delegating aspects to national laws (see section "II. The Right to Family Unity of International Protection Beneficiaries Under the Qualification Directive"). This has resulted in a complex body of case law from the Court of Justice (CJEU), which has navigated this tension and developed innovative legal solutions within asylum law.

This chapter delves into this landscape and examines how the Court has addressed issues such as the flexibility of member states in establishing more favourable national regimes (see section "III. Family Unity and Access to International Protection (Under National Law)"), the complex link between the rights of family members and the asylum right of their relative who is a beneficiary of international protection (see section "IV. Family Unity as a Source of "Autonomous" Rights for Family Members"), and situations where responsibility for international protection and for ensuring family unity falls on different member states (see section "V. Family Unity as a Criterion for Responsibility Sharing in EU Asylum Law").

Finally, the article will examine the impact of recent reforms within the Common European Asylum System (CEAS) on this evolving legal landscape (see section "VI. Maintaining Family Unity Under the New "Qualification Regulation"") and some concluding remarks will be drawn (see section "VII. Conclusive Remarks").

II. The Right to Family Unity of International Protection Beneficiaries Under the Qualification Directive

The Qualification Directive's framework is driven by the overarching principle of upholding "human dignity and the right to asylum of applicants for asylum and their accompanying family members"; it also promotes "the application of Articles 1, 7, 11, 14, 15, 16, 18, 21, 24, 34 and 35 of that Charter".[7] The Qualification Directive aims to broaden the definition of family to include "different particular

minors, particularly unaccompanied children and girls. For an in-depth analysis of the right to family unity provided for by the Qualification Directive, also in relation to international sources, see H. Battjes, In: Thym/ Hailbronner (eds), EU Immigration and Asylum Law Commentary, 3rd ed. 2022, Chapter 20. Asylum Qualification Directive 2011/95/EU, Article 23, at pp. 1399–1404. For a broader perspective on the right to family life in migration contexts see H. Lambert, Family unity in migration law: the evolution of a more unified approach in Europe, In: Chetail/Bauloz (eds), Research handbook on international law and migration, 2014, at pp. 194–215; S. Marinai, La protezione giuridica della famiglia migrante, In: Calamia/Marinai/Gestri/Casolari/Di Filippo (eds.), Lineamenti di diritto internazionale ed europeo delle migrazioni, 2021, at pp. 359–390; S. Morgades-Gil, The protection of family life in the EU common policy on asylum, In: González Pascual/Torres Pérez (eds), The Right to Family Life in the European Union, at pp. 181–195.

[7] Recital 16.

circumstances of dependency" and to protect children's fundamental rights.[8] Accordingly, it calls upon member states to strengthen the protection of family unity through national law,[9] giving paramount consideration to the "best interests of the child" as defined by the CRC.[10] The Preamble of the Qualification Directive recognises the singular standing of family members of individuals granted protection, acknowledging that their familial bonds may expose them to the need for international protection themselves.[11]

On these premises, Article 23 para. 1 of the Qualification Directive prioritises the preservation of family bonds for beneficiaries of international protection setting forth a clear obligation for member states to "ensure that family unity can be maintained". To this end, the Qualification Directive establishes a set of mandatory guarantees that member states must provide to the "family members" of the individual granted international protection. As defined in Article 2 lit. j of the Qualification Directive, this encompasses the closest members of the family (i.e., nuclear family),[12] provided they are "present in the same member state in relation to the application for international protection" and "insofar as the family already existed in the country of origin".

Specifically, Article 23 para. 2 of the Qualification Directive mandates that member states grant "family members" who do not "individually" meet the criteria for refugee or subsidiary protection status the right to claim "in accordance with

[8] Recital 19.

[9] Under recital 38 the States "should take due account of the best interests of the child, as well as of the particular circumstances of the dependency on the beneficiary of international protection of close relatives who are already present in the Member State and who are not family members of that beneficiary. In exceptional circumstances, where the close relative of the beneficiary of international protection is a married minor but not accompanied by his or her spouse, the best interests of the minor may be seen to lie with his or her original family".

[10] UN 1989 Convention on the Rights of the Child (CRC). This entails taking due account of the principle of family unity, the minor's well-being and social development, safety and security considerations, and the views of the minor in accordance with their age and maturity. See recital 18. For a thorough exploration of the best interests of the child in this context, see E. Frasca/ J. Y. Carlier, The best interests of the child in ECJ asylum and migration case law: Towards a safeguard principle for the genuine enjoyment of the substance of children's rights?, In: Common Market Law Review, 2023, at pp. 345–390; C. Smyth, European Asylum Law and the Rights of the Child, 2014, at pp. 33–36.

[11] Recital 36.

[12] The definition includes the spouse and, according to the practices or laws of individual member states, "his or her unmarried partner in a stable relationship". It also encompasses unmarried minor children, irrespective of the nature of the filiation relationship. Furthermore, in cases where the protection status holder is an unmarried minor, the parents or "another adult responsible" for the minor "by law or by the practice of the Member State concerned" are considered family members.

national procedures" and "as far as is compatible with [their] personal legal status" the benefits outlined in Articles 24 to 35 of the Qualification Directive.

This entails the right to obtain a residence permit (Article 24) and to access the same guarantees related to the stay and integration[13] in the host state as those enjoyed by their close relatives granted international protection.[14]

The right to maintain family unity is not absolute. Article 23 para. 3 of the Qualification Directive carves out exceptions for family members who would be excluded from protection under Chapters III and V of the Directive. Additionally, Article 23 para. 4 of the Qualification Directive allows member states to refuse, reduce, or withdraw benefits for reasons of national security or public order. Finally, the Qualification Directive grants member states discretion to extend family unity beyond this core definition to "other close relatives" who cohabited "as part of the family" with the beneficiary in the country of origin and were "wholly or primarily dependent on the international protection beneficiary at that time".[15]

The Qualification Directive's framework presents certain critical junctures, affecting both the scope of application and the content of rights reserved for family members.

An example is the very notion of family accepted by the Qualification Directive which, limited to the closest ties and subject to conditions, may be itself challenging for beneficiaries.[16] Notably, the requirement that the family unit must have been formed in the country of origin[17] raises potential discriminatory concerns,

[13] In addition to the right to reside in that member state (Article 24 of the Qualification Directive), are included: the right to be issued with travel documents (Article 25); access to the labour market (Article 26), to the education system (Article 27) and to professional qualification recognition procedures (Article 28); the right to receive social (Article 29) and health (Article 30) assistance; rights set specifically for minors, first and foremost the right to legal representation (Article 31); access to accommodation (Article 32), freedom of movement within the territory of the State (Article 33), access to integration programmes (Article 34) and assistance for voluntary repatriation (Article 35).

[14] Provided they do not individually have the right to international protection (Article 23 para. 2 of the Qualification Directive), family member does not access some of the core guarantees reserved for refugees and individuals with subsidiary protection and closely linked to the effectiveness of the right to asylum, namely the protection from refoulement (Article 21) and the right to information (Article 22); see H. Battjes, In: Thym/Hailbronner (fn. 6), Chapter 20. Asylum Qualification Directive 2011/95/EU, Article 23, at pp. 1403 f. While Article 21 of the Qualification Directive does not apply in this case, the family member's right to protection against removal remains firmly established under the EU Charter (Articles 4 and 19). On the relationship between the principle of non-refoulement and the guarantees enshrined in the EU Charter see A. Lang, Il divieto di refoulement tra CEDU e Carta dei diritti fondamentali dell'Unione Europea, In: Amadeo/Spitaleri (eds), Le garanzie fondamentali dell'immigrato in Europa, 2015, at pp. 209–244).

[15] Article 23 para. 5 of the Qualification Directive.

[16] See, among others, J. Bastaki, "Not Without My Daughter": EU Asylum Law, Gender, and the Separation of Refugee Families, In: Refugee Survey Quarterly, September 2019, at pp. 266–289.

[17] Notably, this requirement is not waivable under Article 23 para. 5 of the Qualification Directive.

distinguishing between family ties of equal strength solely based on the time at which they are established.[18] The implications of this approach appear particularly prejudicial in the case of children of international protection beneficiaries who were born after their departure or even within the territory of the member states. Moreover, the CJEU seems to have implicitly rejected these arguments holding that a minor daughter of a refugee born in the host member state does not fall within the core definition of family members and therefore does not benefit from the family unity safeguards provided for in Article 23 of the Qualification Directive.[19]

From a different perspective, the Qualification Directive leaves national law with considerable discretion both in defining the procedures for accessing the guarantees provided for family members,[20] and in expanding the personal scope of application of the right to family unity. Implementation discretions can concretely determine that individuals with an identical need for international protection are treated differently, depending on the member state in which they are located. This risks not only undermining the fundamental rights of the person, but also ends up encouraging, indeed, precisely the secondary movements that CEAS instruments strive to prevent or repress.[21]

III. Family Unity and Access to International Protection (Under National Law)

The described regime for family members under Article 23 of the Qualification Directive is supplemented by practices, even of great favour, provided for by national law. These may include, under certain conditions and on the basis of

---

[18] These were raised by Advocate General Pitruzzella in his Opinion delivered on 20 April 2023, in case C-374/22, ECLI:EU:C:2023:902 (Commissaire général aux réfugiés et aux apatrides [Unité familiale]). Agreeing with the observations of the Commissioner for Human Rights, Advocate General Pitruzzella highlights that the condition is inappropriate for taking into account the reality of refugees' lives and could lead to a violation of the principle of equality enshrined in Article 20 of the EU Charter. The same condition, in the different context of family reunification, has already been condemned by the ECtHR as contrary to Articles 14 and 8 of the Human Rights Convention (ECtHR 6 November 2012, 22341/09, ECLI:CE:ECHR:2012:1106JUD002234109 [Hode and Abdi versus United Kingdom]). See AG G. Pitruzzella, Opinion delivered on 20 April 2023, case C-374/22, ECLI:EU:C:2023:318 (Commissaire général aux réfugiés e aux apatrides (Unité familiale) paras. 71–76.

[19] CJEU 9 November 2021, C-91/20, ECLI:EU:C:2021:898 (Bundesrepublik Deutschland [Maintien de l'unité familiale]) para. 37.

[20] In this context, the issue of the direct effect of these guarantees requires careful consideration. See AG Pitruzzella (fn. 18), paras. 49–54.

[21] For an analysis of the Court's case law on secondary movements, see E. Frasca/S. Rizzuto Ferruzza, Limits to intra-EU free movements rights and the Common European Asylum System: remarks on the CJEU case law and the activation of the temporary protection directive, In: Freedom, Security & Justice: European Legal Studies, 2023, at pp. 200–214.

national law, access to international protection even in the absence of the conditions provided for by the Qualification Directive for this purpose but by virtue of the sole family tie with a beneficiary of refugee or subsidiary protection.[22]

As already mentioned, the Qualification Directive is based on the assumption, expressed in recital 36, that the family members of an individual who is a victim of persecution are typically in a situation requiring international protection. Under EU law, however, the granting of refugee status or subsidiary protection must imperatively follow a concrete assessment of the existence of a risk of persecution or serious harm, to be examined in the specific case.[23]

Therefore, the Court has consistently ruled that the right to family unity under Article 23 of the Qualification Directive does not establish a right for family members to obtain international protection, even when considered alongside the fundamental rights secured by the EU Charter.[24]

In the "Ahmedbekova" judgment, which examined the situation of multiple applicants for protection who are members of the same family, the Court actually undertook to preserve precisely the individuality of the examination of the application for protection, including through the setting of limits on the procedural autonomy of member states.[25]

In these situations, the case law has nevertheless upheld the assumption expressed in recital 36 of the Qualification Directive. The "Ahmedbekova" judgment itself, in fact, established the obligation of the competent national authorities to take into account the risk of persecution or serious harm suffered by the applicant's family member "for the purpose of determining whether the applicant is, because of his family tie to the person at risk, himself exposed to the threat of persecution or serious harm".[26]

In other words, EU secondary law does not allow for any confusion between the need for international protection (safeguarded by the granting of an appropriate

---

[22] An analogous mechanism, initially proposed by the European Commission, was ultimately excluded from the final version of the former Qualification Directive (Directive 2004/86/EC) See H. Battjes, In: Thym/Hailbronner (fn. 6), Chapter 20. Asylum Qualification Directive 2011/95/EU, Article 23, at p. 1401. See also CJEU 9 November 2021, C-91/20, ECLI:EU:C:2021:898 (Bundesrepublik Deutschland [Maintien de l'unité familiale]) para. 50.

[23] See Article 4 para. 3 of the Qualification Directive. As the Court has repeatedly stressed "Article 4(3) requires the competent national authority to carry out a complete examination of all the circumstances specific to the applicant's individual case, which precludes any kind of automaticity". CJEU 29 February 2024, C-222/22, ECLI:EU:C:2024:192 (Bundesamt für Fremdenwesen und Asyl [Conversion religieuse ultérieure]) para. 37.

[24] For the latest cases, refer to CJEU 23 November 2023, C-614/22, ECLI:EU:C:2023:903 (Commissaire général aux réfugiés e aux apatrides [Unité familiale]) para. 20, and C-374/22, ECLI:EU:C:2023:902 (Commissaire général aux réfugiés e aux apatrides [Unité familiale]) para. 20.

[25] CJEU 4 October 2018, C-652/16, ECLI:EU:C:2018:801 (Ahmedbekova) paras. 52–65.

[26] Ibid., para. 50.

protection status[27]) and the needs of family unity (addressed in Article 23 of the Qualification Directive).

This clear distinction can, however, be overcome by the internal law of member states. The Court has, in fact, recognised the compatibility with the Qualification Directive of national law provisions that, more favourably, recognise international protection automatically and derivatively to family members of the refugee or the individual with subsidiary protection.

The derogation *in melius* option is based on Article 3 of the Qualification Directive, which allows member states to establish or maintain more favourable conditions for access to international protection, within the limits of compatibility with the Directive.[28] The CJEU has adopted a cautious approach to interpreting Article 3 of the Qualification Directive, imposing strict conditions to safeguard the overall credibility and uniformity of the EU's international protection system. Notably, it has affirmed that Article 3 of the Qualification Directive cannot be employed to grant international protection based on individual circumstances that are entirely unconnected to the "*rationale*" underlying principles of international protection.[29]

In the "Ahmedbekova" judgment, when faced with this issue for the first time in the context of family unity, the Court found that the extension of international protection status to family members as provided for by German law "is not, a priori, without connection to the rationale of international protection".[30]

Subsequent case law has provided a clearer foundation for the compatibility of national laws that recognise international protection for the beneficiary's family members. The courts have taken a proactive approach, reconstructing a positive connection between the goals of protecting family rights and the need for international protection, with Article 23 of the Qualification Directive (and the fundamental rights it incorporates) serving as the cornerstone.

In the "LW"[31] judgment, the referring court raised concerns about the compatibility with the Qualification Directive of national provisions that permitted the extension of derivative refugee status from a Syrian refugee father to a child born in Germany and holding Tunisian citizenship through her mother. As the family tie did not originate in the country of origin, the child does not meet the definition of

[27] See Article 78 para. 1 of the Treaty on the Functioning of the European Union.

[28] See H. Dörig, In: Thym/Hailbronner (fn. 6), Chapter 20. Asylum Qualification Directive 2011/95/ EU, Article 3, at pp. 1244–1248.

[29] Such as granting protection to individuals who are expressly excluded under Article 12 para. 2 of the Qualification Directive, provided they have perpetrated or are suspected of committing serious crimes. CJEU 9 November 2010, C-57/09, ECLI:EU:C:2010:661 and C-101/09, ECLI:EU:C:2009: 285 (B and D) para. 115. For a detailed analysis of this ground for exclusion from international protection and its implications for international protection, see S. Amadeo/F. Spitaleri, Il diritto dell'immigrazione e dell'asilo dell'Unione europea, 2022, at pp. 100–107.

[30] CJEU 4 October 2018, C-652/16, ECLI:EU:C:2018:801 (Ahmedbekova) para. 72.

[31] CJEU 9 November 2021, C-91/20, ECLI:EU:C:2021:898 (Bundesrepublik Deutschland [Maintien de l'unité familiale]).

"family members" as defined in the Qualification Directive. Additionally, the minor was not facing persecution in Tunisia, her country of nationality, rendering the recognition of refugee status incompatible with the principle of subsidiarity of protection enshrined in the Geneva Refugee Convention[32] and implicitly adopted by EU law itself.[33]

The Court clarified that the regime established by German law "is consistent with the rationale of international protection".[34] This conclusion is based on the family protection objectives pursued by the national legislator, in accordance with the spirit of the Geneva Refugee Convention;[35] as well as on the fact that "Directive 2011/95 itself recognises the existence of such a connection by laying down, in general terms in Art. 23(1), an obligation for Member State*s* to ensure that the family unity of the beneficiary of international protection is maintained".[36]

This interpretive approach ensures that the more favourable rule established under domestic law is integrated within the EU legal framework, particularly the right to maintain family unity as enshrined in the Qualification Directive and the fundamental safeguards incorporated therein. The link between family unity and the underlying principles of the international protection system does not automatically lead to the permissibility of more favourable national regimes. To this end, the specific requirements of Article 23 of the Qualification Directive must be met, particularly those aimed at safeguarding individual prerogatives.

This is illustrated by the compatibility reserve with the personal legal status of the family member under Article 23 para. 2 of the Qualification Directive, as examined in the same "LW" judgment.[37] The rationale behind the reserve lies in its function as a safeguard within the context of asylum law. The Court derives this function from the genesis of the rule and emphasises it in determining the reserve's scope. In essence, the reserve means that "it would, in particular, be incompatible with the personal legal status of the child of a beneficiary of international protection who does not individually satisfy the conditions necessary to obtain that protection to extend to that child the advantages referred to in Article 23(2) of Directive 2011/95 or the status granted to that beneficiary, where that child has the nationality of the host Member State or another nationality which gives him or her, having regard to all the elements of his or her personal legal status, the right to better treatment in that Member State than that resulting from such an extension".[38]

The determination of "better treatment" is left to the member states. However, this assessment cannot be based solely on the situation of the family member concerned

[32] Article 1 A para. 2 of the Geneva Refugee Convention.

[33] CJEU 9 November 2021, C-91/20, ECLI:EU:C:2021:898 (Bundesrepublik Deutschland [Maintien de l'unité familiale]) paras. 32–33.

[34] Ibid., para. 44.

[35] Ibid., para. 42.

[36] Ibid., para. 43.

[37] Ibid., para. 52.

[38] Ibid., para. 54.

but must also ensure the effective enjoyment of the right to asylum by the family member who is a beneficiary of international protection. Thus, in the case before the Court, it is irrelevant for the purposes of applying the compatibility clause to determine whether the family can safely relocate to the country of citizenship of the minor daughter and the mother "since such an interpretation would involve her father waiving the right to asylum conferred on him in Germany".[39]

IV. Family Unity as a Source of "Autonomous" Rights for Family Members

The rights granted to family members under Article 23 of the Qualification Directive or more favourable national laws are derived from the asylum rights (Article 18 of the EU Charter) of their family member who is a beneficiary of international protection. However, the interplay between these derived rights and the asylum rights can be nuanced in practice.

The case of "Bundesrepublik Deutschland versus SE"[40] serves as a clear illustration. The case involves the father of a son granted subsidiary protection in Germany. The father applied for protection himself while his son was still a minor asylum seeker. However, by the time the son's status was recognised, he had become an adult. Therefore, the German authorities consider that the father is not eligible for subsidiary protection as a family member and that he can be deported from the country. According to the national authorities, the father's right to protection should be assessed based on the situation existing at the time of the decision. Moreover, with the son's coming of age, the rationale for protecting the child's interests underlying the national rule extending international protection status to the parent would no longer apply.

The Court concludes that the proposed approach contravenes the rights and best interests of the minor as secured by the EU Charter. Essentially, it would hinge the actual guarantee of family unity on the varying promptness of asylum application decisions by the competent authorities, potentially compromising the principle of equality as well. With the aim of ensuring uniform protection for these fundamental guarantees, the Court determines that the relevant moment for exercising the rights related to family unity[41] in this case is the time of the parent's application for

[39] Ibid., para. 60.

[40] CJEU 9 September 2021, C-768/19, ECLI:EU:C:2021:709 (Bundesrepublik Deutschland versus SE).

[41] The Court used a comparable approach when it looked at this same issue in the context of the Family Reunification Directive. See C. Fratea, La tutela del diritto all'unità familiare dei minori migranti tra Sistema europeo comune di asilo e direttiva sul ricongiungimento familiare: una lettura alla luce della giurisprudenza della corte di giustizia dell'unione europea, In: Ordine Internazionale e Diritti Umani, 2023, at pp. 12–49.

international protection, even if informal.[42] Specifically, the benefits provided for in Article 23 of the Qualification Directive on family unity "including, as appropriate, the right to asylum where this is provided for by national law, must [. . .] be relied on by the parent concerned when his or her child, a beneficiary of international protection, is still a minor. Moreover, it follows from the wording of the third indent of Article 2(j) of Directive 2011/95 that the family must have already existed in the country of origin and that the family members concerned must have been present in the territory of the same Member State in relation to the application for international protection before that beneficiary reached the age of majority, which also means that that beneficiary applied for that protection before reaching the age of majority".[43]

The Court further holds that the enjoyment of the "benefits" associated with family unity cannot be contingent upon the actual resumption of family life in the host member state.[44] Indeed "although the relevant provisions of Directive 2011/95 and the Charter protect the right to a family life and promote its maintenance, they leave, in principle, to the holders of that right the decision as to the manner in which the latter wish to conduct their family life and do not impose, in particular, any requirement as to the intensity of their family relationship".[45]

Furthermore, these rights, once acquired, do not expire upon the termination of parental responsibility for the minor with international protection. They remain valid for the duration of the residence permit issued pursuant to Article 24 of the Qualification Directive.[46] It is incumbent upon member states to align the duration of the residence permit issued to the family member with that of the child beneficiary of subsidiary protection, if necessary.[47]

This interpretation safeguards family ties for minor beneficiaries of protection, preventing automatic severing upon reaching adulthood. It also implies a degree of autonomy for the rights granted to family members under Article 23 of the Qualification Directive (or national law). This autonomy stems from the Court's formalistic approach to the family bond, which justifies access to benefits regardless of the family relationship's intensity. Notably, this autonomy is evident in the separation between the duration of the family member's residence permit and their ongoing entitlement to benefits, ultimately establishing an independent position for family members vis-à-vis the host member state.

[42] CJEU 9 September 2021, C-768/19, ECLI:EU:C:2021:709 (Bundesrepublik Deutschland versus SE) paras. 42 and 51.

[43] Ibid., para. 43.

[44] Ibid., paras. 54–57.

[45] Ibid., para. 58.

[46] Ibid., paras. 63–64.

[47] Ibid., para. 65.

V. Family Unity as a Criterion for Responsibility Sharing in EU Asylum Law

The right to maintain family unity, along with the associated guarantees for family members, is intended to be exercised within a single legal system, the one that has granted international protection to the sponsor.

Nevertheless, diverse migratory events can cause family members to seek and obtain protection in different member states. These are situations that EU secondary law aims to prevent through the criteria for reconstituting family units established by the Dublin III Regulation[48,49] but which have materialised in practice.

With regard to these situations, the unresolved issue under secondary law is to determine which of the member states responsible for international protection should also guarantee family unity needs. The issue is particularly noteworthy because it also impacts the effective enjoyment of the right to asylum, which cannot be claimed by the beneficiary in legal systems other than the one that recognised the status.[50]

The Court addressed these issues in the judgment "XXXX versus Commissaire général aux réfugiés et aux apatrides".[51] The applicant in the case that has given rise to the preliminary ruling sought asylum in Belgium, where his daughters, including a minor, were beneficiaries of subsidiary protection. However, the Belgian authorities rejected his asylum application as inadmissible on the grounds that he had already been granted refugee status in Austria (Article 33 para. 2 lit. a of the Asylum Procedures Directive[52]). The applicant ultimately has no right to reside in Belgium. The referring court therefore asked the CJEU whether the principle of family unity and the best interests of the child can prevent Belgium from declaring the applicant's asylum request as inadmissible, as he is the only parent of a minor beneficiary of subsidiary protection in that State.

The Court finds that the situation at stake does not fall within the exceptional circumstances, based on the prohibition of inhuman and degrading treatment (Article

[48] Regulation (EU) No 604/2013 of the European Parliament and of the Council of 26 June 2013 establishing the criteria and mechanisms for determining the member state responsible for examining an application for international protection lodged in one of the member states by a third-country national or a stateless person (recast) (Dublin III Regulation).

[49] In setting the criteria for determining the competent state for examining an application for international protection, the Dublin III Regulation gives priority to those criteria that emphasise the applicant's family ties (Article 7 para. 1 and Articles 8–10). See U. Brandl, Family Unity and Family Reunification in the Dublin System: Still Utopia or Already Reality? In: Chetail/De Bruycker/Maiani (eds), Reforming the Common European Asylum System: The New European Refugee Law, 2016, at pp. 143–158.

[50] See CJEU 18 June 2024, C-753/22, ECLI:EU:C:2024:524 (Bundesrepublik Deutschland (Effet d'une décision d'octroi du statut de réfugié)) paras. 56–68.

[51] CJEU 22 February 2022, C-483/20, ECLI:EU:C:2022:103 (XXXX versus Commissaire général aux réfugiés et aux apatrides).

[52] Directive 2013/32/EU of the European Parliament and of the council of 26 June 2013 on common procedures for granting and withdrawing international protection (Asylum Procedures Directive).

4 of the EU Charter), which justify a derogation from the principle of mutual trust,[53] of which Article 33 para. 2 lit. a of the Asylum Procedures Directive is an expression. Indeed "the reason for the application for international protection made in Belgium by the appellant in the main proceedings is not a need for international protection as such, which is already satisfied in Austria, but his wish to ensure family unity in Belgium".[54] The Court further observes that the rights invoked by the applicant under Articles 7 and 24 of the EU Charter, while fundamental, are not absolute and can be subject to limitations under the conditions set forth in Article 52 para. 1 of the EU Charter.[55] Consequently, the right to family unity raised by the applicant do not provide sufficient grounds to compel Belgium to conduct a substantive examination of his asylum request.

Nonetheless, the applicant must be granted the right to reside in Belgium as the father of a minor child with subsidiary protection under Article 23 of the Qualification Directive. According to the Court, he falls within the definition of "family member" as set forth in the Qualification Directive, does not hold an individual right to international protection, and would not be subjected to treatment incompatible with his personal legal status.

On the first ground, the Court holds that "the fact that a parent and his or her minor child have had different migration paths before reuniting in the Member State in which the child has international protection does not prevent the parent from being regarded as a member of the family of that beneficiary within the meaning of Article 2(j) of Directive 2011/95, provided that that parent was present in the territory of that Member State before a decision was taken on the application for international protection of his or her child".[56]

On the second ground, concerning the individual right to international protection, the Court scrutinises the existence of concrete possibilities for the applicant to secure asylum in Belgium. The Court states that "with regard to the objective of Article 23(2) of Directive 2011/95 which consists of ensuring that the family unity of a

---

[53] For a comprehensive discussion of the characteristics and implications of the principle of mutual trust in the asylum sector, see G. Anagnostaras, The Common European Asylum System: Balancing Mutual Trust Against Fundamental Rights Protection, In: German Law Journal, 2020, at pp. 1180–1197; V. Moreno-Lax, Mutual (Dis-)Trust in EU Migration and Asylum Law: The Exceptionalisation of Fundamental Rights, In: Pascual/Sánchez (eds), Fundamental Rights in the EU Area of Freedom, Security and Justice, 2020; H. Labayle, Faut-il faire confiance à la confiance mutuelle?, In: Liber Amicorum per Antonio Tizzano - De la Cour CECA à la Cour de l'Union: le long parcours de la justice européenne, 2018, at pp. 472–485; P. Mori, Quelques réflexions sur la confiance réciproque entre les États membres: un principe essentiel de l'Union européenne, In: Liber Amicorum per Antonio Tizzano - De la Cour CECA à la Cour de l'Union: le long parcours de la justice européenne, 2018, at pp. 651–660; H. Battjes/E. Brouwer, The Dublin Regulation and Mutual Trust: Judicial Coherence in EU Asylum Law?, In: Review of European Administrative Law, 2015, at pp. 183–214.

[54] CJEU 22 February 2022, C-483/20, ECLI:EU:C:2022:103 (XXXX versus Commissaire général aux réfugiés et aux apatrides) para. 33.

[55] Ibid., para. 36.

[56] Ibid., para. 40.

beneficiary of international protection is maintained, and, moreover, taking into account the fact that the provisions of Directive 2011/95 must be interpreted in the light of Article 7 and Article 24(2) and (3) of the Charter [...], it must be found that a third-country national whose application for international protection is inadmissible and has therefore been refused in the Member State in which his or her minor child benefits from international protection owing to that national's refugee status in another Member State does not individually qualify for international protection in the first Member State, which gives rise to that national's right to be granted the benefits under Articles 24 to 35 of Directive 2011/95 in that Member State".[57]

Finally, regarding the third ground, the Court observes that "the grant of refugee status in a Member State does not, in principle, result in the person benefiting from that international protection receiving better treatment, in another Member State, than the treatment resulting from the benefits under Articles 24 to 35 of Directive 2011/95 in that other Member State".[58]

In the scenario presented, Article 23 of the Qualification Directive serves a distinct purpose, as it essentially empowers the individual to select the member state in which to establish family life. The Court, in this regard, reaffirms a particularly expansive interpretation of the fundamental right to family unity.

This, however, comes at the cost of the right to asylum claimed, in this instance by the father, in a different legal system. The Court refrains from asserting the father's right to enjoy international protection status under Belgian law, instead confining itself to mandating that the state provide the minimum guarantees of residence and integration for the family unit.

VI. Maintaining Family Unity Under the New "Qualification Regulation"

The current legal framework for family unity is set to undergo significant changes with the full implementation of the package of measures included in the New Pact on Migration and Asylum.

A notable aspect of the reform is the increased reliance on Regulations as the primary legislative instrument. This approach extends to the Qualification Directive which is repealed and replaced by the Qualification Regulation.[59] The shift towards

[57] Ibid., para. 41.

[58] Ibid., para. 43.

[59] Regulation (EU) 2024/1347 of the European Parliament and of the Council of 14 May 2024 on standards for the qualification of third-country nationals or stateless persons as beneficiaries of international protection, for a uniform status for refugees or for persons eligible for subsidiary protection and for the content of the protection granted, amending Council Directive 2003/109/EC and repealing Directive 2011/95/EU of the European Parliament and of the Council (Qualification Regulation).

Regulations aims to enhance uniformity and convergence of asylum systems across member states.[60] This objective aligns with the aim to ensure fair treatment for asylum seekers and beneficiaries of international protection, while also discouraging secondary movements within the EU.[61]

As regards the subjective scope of application and the content of the guarantees, the Qualification Regulation seems to achieve a higher level of protection of the right to family unity compared to the common minimum level currently set by the Qualification Directive. More protective outcomes then derive from the very nature of the secondary legal act in which these guarantees are contained. The right to stay and the access to other rights related to family unity will, in fact, find direct application in national legal systems, overcoming transposition defects.

The Qualification Regulation broadens the scope of application of the right to maintain family unity by expanding the definition of "family members", to encompass individuals who established family ties after leaving their country of origin but before arriving in an EU member state.[62] The provision seeks to prevent the discrimination "based on where a family was formed",[63] as previously raised in discussions regarding the condition set out by Article 2 lit. j of the Qualification Directive.

The Qualification Regulation's broader understanding of family also concerns the types of family ties, with the inclusion of the unmarried "adult dependent children" of the beneficiary of international protection[64] and of the adult siblings responsible for unmarried children with international protection.[65] Married children may access the more favourable family unity rights granted to unmarried minors, if appropriate in the light of their best interests.[66] The new rules require a case-by-case assessment to determine a minor's marital status under the Qualification Regulation, considering the marriage "would not be in accordance with the relevant national law had it been contracted in the Member State concerned, having regard, in particular, to the legal age of marriage".[67]

The spectrum of family members can be further extended at the discretion of member states to safeguard the right to maintain family unity with "other close relatives" who were already part of the family in the country of origin and are

[60] Recital 1.

[61] Recitals 5–7.

[62] Article 3 para. 9 of the Qualification Regulation.

[63] Recital 19.

[64] Recital 17 clarifies that the existence of a dependency relationship should be determined "on the basis of an individual assessment, only in circumstances where that child is unable to support him or herself due to a physical or mental condition linked to a serious non-temporary illness or severe disability".

[65] Article 3 para. 9 lit. c of the Qualification Regulation.

[66] This provision, when considered in conjunction with recital 20, may result in the denial of a residence permit for the minor's spouse in cases where the member state concerned determines that the minor's best interests lie with their parents.

[67] Article 3 para. 9 lit. b and c of the Qualification Regulation.

dependent on the person with international protection. The rule, already present in the Qualification Directive, now expressly mentions "siblings" and the "married minor", if this is in his or her best interests.[68]

The new Qualification Regulation further addresses the right to family unity by abrogating the general obligation enshrined in Article 23 para. 1 of the Qualification Directive. In its place, the Qualification Regulation outlines a more detailed set of rights for family members and substantially restricts the scope of discretion afforded to national law.[69]

The new Article 23 para. 1 of the Qualification Regulation establishes the right of family members to obtain a residence permit with a duration and validity matching that of their relatives who hold refugee or subsidiary protection status.[70]

The Qualification Regulation also addresses exceptions to the right to family unity by mandating the refusal of a residence permit on grounds of public order or public security,[71] mirroring those already outlined in the Qualification Directive, which nevertheless entrusted their implementation to the discretion of the States. The new rules provide for an additional ground for exclusion from the regime for family members (spouses or partners) to prevent abusive situations "where there are strong indications that the marriage or partnership was contracted for the sole purpose of enabling the person concerned to enter or reside in the Member State concerned".[72]

The high degree of harmonization resulting from the Qualification Regulation is counterbalanced by the elimination of the possibility for member states to establish more favourable standards as regards access to or the content of international protection (Article 3 of the Qualification Directive). Member states may still provide for permits for humanitarian reasons, provided that this does not "entail a risk of confusion" with the statuses governed by Union law.[73]

With the elimination of the faculty currently provided for in Article 3 of the Qualification Directive, the new Qualification Regulation puts an end to more favourable regimes for the recognition of international protection on grounds of family unity.[74] It should not, however, prevent considerations inherent to family

[68] Article 23 para. 7 of the Qualification Regulation.

[69] To counterbalance the reduced scope for discretion, the Qualification Regulation places particular emphasis on the need for member states to uphold their "values and principles". This entails that "in the event of a polygamous marriage, it is for each member state to decide whether they wish to apply the provisions on family unity to polygamous households, including to the minor children of a further spouse and a beneficiary of international protection". See recital 18.

[70] Article 23 paras. 2 and Article 24. The Qualification Regulation expressly states that the residence permit issued to the family member is renewable as long as that of the beneficiary of international protection is and prohibits its duration from being longer.

[71] Article 23 of the Qualification Regulation.

[72] Article 23 para. 4 and recital 19 of the Qualification Regulation.

[73] Article 2 para. 2 of the Qualification Regulation.

[74] See S. Peers, The New EU Asylum Laws, part 1: the Qualification Regulation, In: EU Law Analysis, https://eulawanalysis.blogspot.com/2023/12/the-new-eu-asylum-laws-part-1.html.

unity from being taken into account within humanitarian grounds and, therefore, from the issue of a residence permit on this basis under national law.

The limit of the clear separation between the "humanitarian" status and the forms of international protection provided for by Union law, however, makes it difficult to imagine a perfect alignment between the national regime reserved for family members and that to which they have access under the Qualification Regulation.

VII. Conclusive Remarks

The foregoing analysis allows us to draw some concluding considerations.

EU secondary law aims for high standards of protection for the right to family unity of individuals in need of international protection. It expresses a preference for granting international protection to family members, recognising their specific vulnerability. It establishes a "status" for family members who do not have an individual need for international protection, to ensure their residence, integration and decent living conditions in the host member state on a par with their refugee or subsidiary protection status family member. It sets this as a minimum level of guarantee, which can be raised at the discretion of member states.

The Court construed the Qualification Directive's provisions in line with their objective of effectively safeguarding respect for family life (Article 7 of the EU Charter), children's rights (Article 24 of the EU Charter), and the right to asylum (Article 18 of the EU Charter). In keeping with this, it consistently steered the exercise of state prerogatives towards an expansive interpretation of family protection.

Overall, the case law has thus achieved a consolidation of the right to family unity, particularly in cases involving minors (both in the position of family members and as beneficiaries of international protection). In situations concerning children, the Court has embraced the protection of their best interests as a standard for guiding the interpretive solution in the specific case, in line with developments in related fields.[75]

To achieve this result, the Court did not overturn the framework established by EU legislators but rather utilised its inherent potential in an innovative way. It acknowledged the potential role of family unity in determining eligibility for international protection. It emphasised the right to maintain the family unity of the beneficiary of international protection as a means of providing guarantees for family members, recognising, within certain constraints, the autonomous standing of the

[75] On the need of "case-by-case assessment" when dealing with family unity and children's fundamental rights see L.S. Rossi, The interaction between the directive 2003/86 and the Charter of fundamental rights of the European Union in the family reunification of a third country national, In: Freedom, Security & Justice: European Legal Studies, 2024, at pp. 25–40, specifically at p. 37; on the best interests of the child as a 'safeguard principle' see E. Frasca/J. Y. Carlier, Common Market Law Review, 2023, at pp. 345–390.

latter. In specific instances, it employed this fundamental right of the individual to reinforce the individual choice of the member state in which to establish family life.

The recognition of rights granted to family members, as well as their "autonomous" standing, appears to be reinforced by EU legislators. However, in the new Qualification Regulation, the increased uniformity potentially limits the further expanding of such protections. The Court of Justice's future decisions will be crucial in determining how this balance is struck, ensuring uniformity while allowing for necessary flexibility in individual cases.

Polygamous Marriages and Reunification of Families on the Move Under EU Law: An Overview

Giovanni Zaccaroni

I. Introduction

Families on the move, to be understood as groups of more than one person travelling from the outside to the inside the EU, pose a number of challenges to our legal framework. One of these challenges is represented by the fact that, in particular contexts, the family partnership might involve more than one spouse or partner. This second (or third) partner might follow the family nucleus in the first place or might, once the first family members have already settled, attempt to exercise family reunification at a later stage. This situation is common in the case of polygamous marriages. As known, so far, there has been very little room for the recognition of polygamous marriages in Europe.[1] The reason is that polygamous marriages are considered to be at odds with the principle of equal treatment between men and women, a fundamental cornerstone of the EU as well as of the national legal orders in Europe. Polygamous marriages in Europe are also, according to a Pew Research Centre analysis, quite rare and are usually involving one male partner and a plurality of female ones (polygyny), while the contrary, a plurality of male partners and one female partner (polyandry) is even more rare.[2] Several countries where polygamy used to be the practice and the majority of the population is Muslim have also adopted a restrictive interpretation of the concept of polygamy (Morocco and

[1] M. Jänterä-Jareborg, Populism and Comparative Law as Tools not to Recognise Foreign Marriages, Journal of International and Comparative Law, 2019, 347, at pp. 355, 359.

[2] S. Kramer, Polygamy is rare around the world and mostly confined to a few regions (7 December 2020), available at https://www.pewresearch.org/short-reads/2020/12/07/polygamy-is-rare-around-the-world-and-mostly-confined-to-a-few-regions/.

G. Zaccaroni (✉)
Faculty of Law, Milan Bicocca University, Milan, Italy
e-mail: giovanni.zaccaroni@unimib.it

S. Arnold, B. Heiderhoff (eds.), *Children in Migration and International Family Law*, https://doi.org/10.1007/978-3-031-71598-3_20

Indonesia) and others exclude completely the possibility to make use of it.[3] Thus, it can be said that the situation of polygamous marriages represents a niche into the broader picture of private international law as well as in the rights of EU migrant families.[4]

II. Polygamous Marriages and Family Reunification in Certain EU Member States: The Examples of France, Italy and Spain

It is difficult to find a consistent approach to the plurality of issues raised by polygamous marriages in Europe, perhaps in light of the changing value that the institute of marriage itself interprets in the member states.[5] France, Italy and Spain are examples of these competing trends at national level and currently there seems to be a considerable degree of uncertainty for marriages that involve more than two partners. It is true that polygamous marriages are — per se — unlawful in all the EU members states.[6] However, as it will be seen, the situation becomes more complex when the marriage has been contracted abroad and the partner(s) attempt(s) to exercise the civil and social rights attached to status of spouse (as pension rights and family reunification).

In France, for instance, an important judgment of the French *Cour de Cassation* of 17 November 2021 questioned the well-known automatic non-recognition of a foreign polygamous marriage.[7] The *Cour de Cassation*, in a judgment assessing the validity of a previous decision of the Court of Appeal of Orleans, maintained that a bigamous marriage is not automatically void under French law and that the lower court judging the case is required to designate the applicable law to the marriage in order to correctly assess its validity.[8] This case is interesting because it does not

[3] A. Trigiyatno/D. Rahmawati/P. Utomo/Mujadid, Comparative Analysis of the Polygamy Regulations in Indonesia and Morocco, Diktum: Jurnal Syariah dan Hukum, 2023(1), 34, at p. 35.

[4] On the contextualisation of polygamy and other Islamic legal institutions in European and private international law see D. Zannoni, Cultural Diversity as a Test Bench for the Future of Private International Law: What Legal Treatment for Islamic Institutions in Europe?, Anuario Espanol Derecho Int'l Priv. 2023 (23), at p. 255.

[5] R. Probert/A. Barlow, Displacing Marriage - Diversification and Harmonisation within Europe, Child & Fam L Q 2000(2), 153, at pp. 155 f.

[6] At the following link a summary of the legislation regulating polygamy in the EU member states is available (although updated only up to 2016): https://www.refworld.org/reference/themreport/euemn/2016/en/115576.

[7] Cour de Cassation 17 November 2021, case n. 20-19.420, ECLI:FR:CCASS:2021:C100708, available at https://www.legifrance.gouv.fr/juri/id/JURITEXT000044352185?isSuggest=true.

[8] M. Ho Dac, French Supreme Court Opens Door for Recognition of Foreign Bigamous Marriage, EAPIL Blog, (6 January 2022), available at https://eapil.org/2022/01/06/french-supreme-court-opens-door-for-recognition-of-foreign-bigamous-marriage/.

discuss only the validity of the polygamous union but it focuses on its effects. The facts of the appealed decision originated from the request of a woman to file a divorce against her husband whom she had married in Libya. However, since the French legal order does not recognise polygamous marriages, the Court of Appeal ruled that it was impossible to dissolve a non-existing marriage. On the contrary, with this decision, the *Cour de Cassation* confirmed that, under French law, polygamous marriages can produce effects in order to protect the rights acquired abroad.[9] This should allow the national court to select the legislation applicable to the case, despite the lack of an explicit conflict-of-laws rule in the French civil law.[10]

French scholars hoped that this position could have been partially reflected into the French draft reform codifying private international law in the national legal order.[11] However, Article 44 of the draft law excludes the possibility to enter into a polygamous marriage in France and Article 45 of the draft law extends the possibility to recognise the foreign double marriage contracted abroad only to couples where no one of the spouses is of French nationality, thus creating a potential discrimination between French and non-French couples. In France it is also not possible for family members of a polygamous family to obtain a residence permit relying on the Code on entry, residence and asylum, according to the amendments made by Article 25 of the law of 24 august 2021.[12]

The legal status of polygamous marriages in Italy is also complex, but more fragmented. The criminal legislation prohibits the marriage of a person with more than one other person,[13] and the civil law also considers the polygamous union to be void, thus excluding the possibility to recognise the polygamous union legitimately contracted abroad.[14] To this should be added that a strict interpretation of

[9]See C. Campiglio, Il diritto di famiglia islamico nella prassi italiana, Rivista di diritto internazionale privato e processuale, 2008, 43, at p. 50; V. Petralia, Ricongiungimento familiare e matrimonio poligamico. Il riconoscimento di valori giuridici stranieri e la tutela delle posizioni deboli, University of Catania - Online Working Paper, n. 49, 2013, available at http://www.cde.unict.it/quadernieuropei/giuridiche/49_2013.pdf.

[10]M. Ho Dac, EAPIL Blog (fn. 8): "the lower court should have verified, in accordance with the personal law of the spouses pursuant to article 202-1 of the Civil Code, whether the foreign bigamous marriage was valid (so that, in the affirmative, it could be dissolved). At that stage of the reasoning, the French prohibition of bigamy pursuant to article 147 of the Civil Code did not matter".

[11]F. Jault-Seseke, Recognition of Marriages Celebrated Abroad under the French Draft PIL Code, EAPIL Blog, (4 July 2022), available at https://eapil.org/2022/07/04/recognition-of-marriages-celebrated-abroad-under-the-french-draft-pil-code/.

[12]F. Jault-Seseke, La loi du 24 août 2021 confortant le respect des principes de la République: Aperçu des dispositions relatives au droit des étrangers et au droit international privé, Actualité Juridique Famille, 2021(9), 472, at p. 476.

[13]Article 556 of the codice penale (Italian Criminal Code). An OSCE/ODHIR sponsored database with the translation of the Italian Criminal Code can be found online at: https://legislationline.org/.

[14]Article 86 of the codice civile (Italian Civil Code). See N. Tonti, L'eterno ritorno dell'uguale? La poligamia nello spazio giuridico contemporaneo Tra identità religiosa e (nuove) istanze di legittimazione, CALUMET – intercultural law and humanities review, 2024(19), 1, at p. 13, available at https://calumet-review.com/index.php/2024/01/15/leterno-ritorno-delluguale-la-

Article 3,[15] read in combination with Article 29[16] of the Italian Constitution, prohibits a spousal relationship that is asymmetrical in nature, as the polygamous one.[17]

The exercise of the right to family reunification in Italy, on the other side, is characterised by a more complex approach. As it will be detailed in paragraph IV., since the entrance into force and the transposition of the Family Reunification Directive,[18] member states are free to establish obstacles to the right to family reunification of polygamous spouses. Notwithstanding that, as noted by Tonti, the position of scholarship on polygamy and family reunification before the entrance into force of Family Reunification Directive was more nuanced, with several advocating in favour of the non-discrimination between the spouses and of the unity of the family household.[19] The reader could then be allowed to think that, after the transposition within the Italian legislation of the rather express prohibition of family reunification in the directive, the problem was then resolved.[20] However, the Supreme Court of Cassation was forced to intervene in 2013 when the Court of Appeal of Venice was confirming the decision of the Court of First Instance to allow the family reunification of a spouse in a polygamous marriage filed not by the husband but by the son.[21] As noted by Petralia, a situation where the application

---

poligamia-nello-spazio-giuridico-contemporaneo-tra-identita-religiosa-e-nuove-istanze-di-legittimazione/.

[15] Article 3 of the Italian Constitution: "All citizens have equal social dignity and are equal before the law, without distinction of sex, race, language, religion, political opinion, personal and social conditions. It is the duty of the Republic to remove those obstacles of an economic or social nature which constrain the freedom and equality of citizens, thereby impeding the full development of the human person and the effective participation of all workers in the political, economic and social organisation of the country". English translation courtesy of the Senato della Repubblica, available at https://www.senato.it/documenti/repository/istituzione/costituzione_inglese.pdf.

[16] Article 29 of the Italian Constitution: "The Republic recognises the rights of the family as a natural society founded on marriage. Marriage is based on the moral and legal equality of the spouses within the limits laid down by law to guarantee the unity of the family". English translation courtesy of the Senato della Repubblica.

[17] Ibid.

[18] Council Directive 2003/86/EC of 22 September 2003 on the right to family reunification (Family Reunification Directive).

[19] N. Tonti, CALUMET – intercultural law and humanities review, 2024(19) (fn. 14) mentions at p. 16, the scholarship in J. Witte, A. Pin, Il rifiuto della poligamia in Occidente: gli argomenti, Diritto pubblico comparato ed europeo, 2020, 57, at. p. 58.

[20] Decreto legislativo n. 5, 8 January 2007 *Attuazione della direttiva 2003/86/CE relativa al diritto di ricongiungimento familiare*, subsequently modified by Decreto legislativo n. 160, 3 October 2008, *Modifiche ed integrazioni al decreto legislativo 8 gennaio 2007, n. 5, recante attuazione della direttiva 2003/86/CE relativa al diritto di ricongiungimento familiare*. This change was also reflected into the Italian immigration legislation, with the introduction of the prohibition of family reunification for more than one spouse in Article 29 para. 1-ter of the decreto legislativo n. 286 of 25 July 1998, *Testo unico delle disposizioni concernenti la disciplina dell'immigrazione e norme sulla condizione dello straniero*, as amended by Article 1 para. 22 lit. s of the legge 94 of 15 July 2009, *Disposizioni in materia di sicurezza pubblica*.

[21] Court of Appeal of Venice 27 July 2011, case n. 804/2010.

for family reunification is filed by a different person from the spouse does not give rise to a challenge to the public order per se.[22] There was also a precedent by the Court of Bologna where a minor, a Moroccan national, filed an application for a visa for family reunification that was rejected by the Italian embassy in Rabat.[23] The local Court of Bologna decided that the rejection of the visa was unlawful since the Italian legislation on migration that was prohibiting family reunification in the case of polygamy was only applicable if it was the spouse filing the application for family reunification.[24] A judgment of a different tone was however rendered by the Juvenile Court of Torino a couple of years earlier, where, under similar circumstances, the Court argued that, if the main interest of the minor was to live with his mother, then the family should have moved back to the country of residence of the mother.[25] This decision was however appealed and the Court of Appeal of Torino reversed the decree of the Juvenile Court, arguing in favour of the interest of the child to live with his mother.[26]

The Italian Supreme Court, with its order, rejected the precedents of the Court of Appeals by arguing in favour of the integrity of the legal order, recognising that, after the entrance into force of the provision of Article 29 of the Italian immigration code amended after the transposition of the Family Reunification Directive, it was not possible to distinguish between the application for family reunification filed by the child and the one filed by the spouse.[27]

Spain is another EU member state where polygamous marriages are prohibited by the national legislation, but where the social rights attached to the status of spouse might be, in certain conditions, recognised.[28] A polygamous marriage is not allowed by the Spanish legislation, but the husband (or, although more difficult, the wife) is allowed to choose freely the wife with whom he wants to reunite, thus not considering the chronological order of marriages.[29] The chronological order of marriages is however more important in the case of the social rights following the condition of wife, and in particular the situation of the survivor's pension. In this case, the Spanish case law produced a series of judgments that were first denying the right

[22] V. Petralia, University of Catania - Online Working Paper, n. 49, 2013 (fn. 9), at p. 10.

[23] Court of Bologna 12 March 2003, case n. 469/2003. This precedent is also mentioned by V. Petralia, University of Catania - Online Working Paper, n. 49, 2013 (fn. 9), at p. 13.

[24] V. Petralia, University of Catania - Online Working Paper, n. 49, 2013 (fn. 9), at p. 13.

[25] Juvenile Court of Torino 21 December 2000, see Diritto, Immigrazione e Cittadinanza, volume 2, 2001, at p. 172; also mentioned by V. Petralia University of Catania - Online Working Paper, n. 49, 2013 (fn. 9), at p. 13 and by N. Tonti, CALUMET – intercultural law and humanities review, 2024(19) (fn. 14), at p. 19.

[26] Court of Appeal of Torino (Juvenile section) 11 April 2001, see Diritto, Immigrazione e Cittadinanza, volume 2, 2001, at pp. 173 ff.

[27] Italian Court of Cassation 28 February 2013, case n. 4984/2013.

[28] N. Tonti, CALUMET – intercultural law and humanities review, 2024(19) (fn. 14), at p. 21.

[29] Ley Orgánica n. 4/2000, sobre derechos y libertades de los extranjeros en España y su integración social. Mentioned by N. Tonti, CALUMET – intercultural law and humanities review, 2024(19) (fn. 14), at p. 22.

of the spouses following the first one to enjoy the survivor's pension, while, in 2018, a judgement of the Spanish Supreme Court allowed the second wife to see her application for the survivor's pension to be welcomed.[30] The case law on family reunification in Spain, on the contrary, gives rise to less ambiguity compared to the Italian one, as there is the possibility to obtain only one residence permit for family reunification with the spouse per family.[31]

In all these cases, as it will be further discussed in paragraph IV., it is possible that the codification of the prohibition of family reunification for polygamous marriages in the Family Reunification Directive, while protecting non-discrimination between men and women in the marital relationship, introduces a conflict with the right to family life of the minor.

III. Polygamous Marriages and Family Reunification: Instruments of Private International, EU and Human Rights Convention[32] Law

The 1978 Marriage Convention[33] states that "a marriage validly entered into under the law of the State of celebration or which subsequently becomes valid under that law shall be considered as such in all Contracting States".[34] The Convention, however, has been ratified only by a limited number of States.[35] Interestingly, however, out of three parties that have fully ratified the Convention, two of them are EU member states (Luxembourg and the Netherlands). The status of children born to the married couple might be protected under other private international law instruments, as the CRC[36] and the 1996 Child Protection Convention.[37] The Brussels IIbis Regulation[38] and its successor the Brussels IIter

---

[30] This case law is discussed into details by N. Tonti, CALUMET – intercultural law and humanities review, 2024(19) (fn. 14), at pp. 23 f.

[31] See also F. Di Pietro, La poligamia e i ricongiungimenti di famiglie poligamiche in Spagna e Italia, Cuadernos de Derecho Transnacional, 2015, 56, at pp. 63–65.

[32] Convention for the Protection of Human Rights and Fundamental Freedoms (Human Rights Convention).

[33] Convention of 14 March 1978 on Celebration and Recognition of the Validity of Marriages (1978 Marriage Convention).

[34] Article 9 of the 1978 Marriage Convention.

[35] See the Status Table of the Convention, available at https://www.hcch.net/en/instruments/conventions/status-table/?cid=88.

[36] UN 1989 Convention on the Rights of the Child (CRC).

[37] Convention of 19 October 1996 on Jurisdiction, Applicable Law, Recognition, Enforcement and Co-operation in respect of Parental Responsibility and Measures for the Protection of Children (1996 Child Protection Convention).

[38] Council Regulation (EC) No 2201/2003 of 27 November 2003 concerning jurisdiction and the recognition and enforcement of judgments in matrimonial matters and the matters of parental responsibility.

Regulation[39] are also relevant to the situation of polygamous marriages, as they provide for the possibility to refuse the recognition of matrimonial decisions on the ground of public policy, eventually leading to the very likely refusal of any marriage decision coming from an EU member state that tolerates polygamy.[40]

The lack of recognition of polygamous marriages eventually impacts the recognition of the right to family reunification, under EU law and private international law. The right to respect for private and family life is also a fundamental right protected by both the EU Charter[41] as well as by the Human Rights Convention. The European Court of Human Rights (ECtHR) dealt with the issue of the recognition of polygamous marriages in at least three cases. The cases consider the refusal of national authorities to allow family reunification of family members from polygamous marriages. Interestingly, in the first case, E.A. and A.A. v. the Netherlands, the European Commission of Human Rights considered the question on the compliance of the refusal of recognition of polygamous marriages with the Human Rights Convention as inadmissible, considering the act of the local authority as a legitimate measure of immigration control.[42]

Two more applications, M. and O.M. v. the Netherlands[43] and R.B. v. the United Kingdom[44] were also found inadmissible by the European Commission of Human Rights, as the national authority was also pursuing the legitimate aim of controlling internal migration and the Court again declined to examine the cases.[45] In all these cases, the European Commission of Human Rights followed a similar approach: to reject the application as inadmissible, since the refusal of recognition was to be considered as an internal measure adopted to control migration. Such a justification is only partially satisfactory from a legal standpoint but allowed the European Commission of Human Rights to avoid a subject which might have been divisive for the parties of the convention at least for a while. One thus would wonder what could happen if a similar case would reach the ECtHR in the near future.

---

[39] Council Regulation (EU) 2019/1111 of 25 June 2019 on jurisdiction, the recognition and enforcement of decisions in matrimonial matters and the matters of parental responsibility, and on international child abduction.

[40] Article 38 of the Brussels IIter Regulation. Polygamous marriages are unlawful in all the EU member states, so a decision in matrimonial matters about polygamy coming from EU member states is not realistic. However, since Luxembourg and the Netherlands have ratified the 1978 Marriage Convetion, although only hypothetical, this situation can happen if another State that recognises polygamy joins the 1978 Marriage Convention.

[41] Charter of Fundamental Rights of the European Union (EU Charter).

[42] ECtHR 6 January 1992, 14501/89, ECLI:CE:ECHR:1992:0106DEC001450189 (E.A. and A.A. against the Netherlands).

[43] ECtHR 5 October 1987, 12139/86, ECLI:CE:ECHR:1987:1005DEC001213986 (M. and O.M. against the Netherlands).

[44] ECtHR 29 June 1992, 19628/92, ECLI:CE:ECHR:1992:0629DEC001962892 (R.B. against the United Kingdom).

[45] Recitals 10 and 11 of the Family Reunification Directive.

The Family Reunification Directive, consistently with the Strasbourg case law mentioned above, recognises the possibility for EU member states not to authorise family reunification in case of polygamous marriage, referring to the need to respect the rights of women and children.[46] Article 4 para. 4 of the Family Reunification Directive states that "[i]n the event of a polygamous marriage, where the sponsor already has a spouse living with him in the territory of a Member State, the Member State concerned shall not authorise the family reunification of a further spouse".[47]

The lack of recognition observed by several EU member states and also found at the level of the EU legislation reflects the determination that polygamous marriages can undermine equal treatment between women and men and also foster violence against women.[48] Other scholars challenged this view by saying that it reflects a culturally biased and Western-centred interpretation of fundamental rights of women and that it conceals a sense of superiority from the Western legal culture towards other interpretations of fundamental rights.[49] Another counter-argument is that the lack of recognition of the second marriage might eventually leave too much power to the decision of the man as of the wife to reunite with and leave the other family members in a legal and societal limbo in the country of origin, thus eventually producing more inequality than the one that it is aspired to challenge. This, known also as the accommodation argument, attempts to preserve the rights of women involved in a polygamous marriage, instead of challenging its situation from a position of cultural superiority.

IV. The Prohibition of Family Reunification in Article 4 para. 4 of the Family Reunification Directive: In Search of a Balance Between Rights Protected by the EU Charter?

The analysis of the condition of polygamous marriages and the distinction between on the one side, the refusal to recognise a polygamous union and, on the other side, its effects on the social and free movement rights operated in the EU leads to the conviction that the introduction of an express prohibition of family reunification in Article 4 para. 4 of the Family Reunification Directive might have eventually contributed to foster the situation of discrimination already present in several polygamous unions.

---

[46] Article 4 para. 4 of the Family Reunification Directive.

[47] See J. Bornemann/C. Arevalo, In: Thym/Hailbronner (eds), EU Immigration and Asylum Law, 3rd ed. 2022, Article 4 of the Family Reunification Directive paras. 41–44.

[48] J. Witte, Diritto pubblico comparato ed europeo, 2020(1) (fn. 19), at pp. 75 f.

[49] N. Stybnarova, Teleology behind the prohibition of recognition of polygamous marriages under the EU family reunification directive: A critique of rule effectiveness. Journal of Muslim Minority Affairs, 2020(1), at pp. 104–116.

This is because, in a situation of existing difference of treatment (as the one between first and second or third wives) another difference of treatment will be added: the one between the child of the first spouse and the ones of the other spouse.

On the other side, the EU legal orders pursue the legitimate aim to protect and promote equal treatment between women and men, which is also protected in the EU Charter as well as by the national constitutions.

There is, accordingly, a potential balance to be struck between the best interests of the child read together with the right to family unity, connected to the right of family life, and the right of non-discrimination of women involved in a polygamous marriage.[50]

In the EU Charter, the best interests of the child principle is to be found under Article 24 para. 2, that cites: "In all actions relating to children, whether taken by public authorities or private institutions, the child's best interests must be a primary consideration."[51]

The case law of the Court of Justice of the European Union (CJEU) on the best interests of the child as derived by the EU Charter is not extremely abundant and even more so when the situation of application of the EU Charter itself is referred to a third country national.[52] However, in the last five years, there has been an increase in the use of Article 24 para. 2 in front of the CJEU, although not directly related, again, to the case of third-country nationals. The EU Charter applies to the EU institutions and to the EU member states "only when they are implementing EU law".[53] Thus, it cannot be limited or restricted only to EU citizens, and it is also applicable to all the third country nationals that find themselves on the territory of the EU.

In a recent case, the CJEU, ruling on a European Arrest Warrant addressed against a Belgian woman with two young children, had an occasion to update its interpretation of Article 24 para. 2 of the EU Charter.[54] The Court, in particular, confirms that "Article 7 of the Charter enshrines the right of every person to respect for his or her private and family life, and second, Article 24(2) of the Charter provides that, in all actions relating to children, whether taken by public authorities or private institutions, the child's best interests must be a primary consideration".[55]

---

[50] As noted by F. Di Pietro, Cuadernos de Derecho Transnacional (fn. 31), at p. 68.

[51] Here is the full text of Article 24 para. 2: "1. Children shall have the right to such protection and care as is necessary for their well-being. They may express their views freely. Such views shall be taken into consideration on matters which concern them in accordance with their age and maturity. 2. In all actions relating to children, whether taken by public authorities or private institutions, the child's best interests must be a primary consideration. 3. Every child shall have the right to maintain on a regular basis a personal relationship and direct contact with both his or her parents, unless that is contrary to his or her interests."

[52] A search on the database available on curia.europa.eu based on Article 24 para. 2 gives 39 results.

[53] Article 51 of the EU Charter.

[54] CJEU 21 December 2023, case C-261/22, ECLI:EU:C:2023:1017 (Criminal proceedings against GN).

[55] CJEU 21 December 2023, case C-261/22, ECLI:EU:C:2023:1017 (Criminal proceedings against GN) para 40.

The fact that the Court reinforces the reference to Article 24 para. 2 of the EU Charter with a reference to Article 7 of the EU Charter (right to respect of private and family life) seems to suggest that an EU Charter-oriented interpretation of the legal acts of EU law should take into account the child's best interests not by itself but in the context of the family unity of the child.

Applying the reasoning of the CJEU in this recent case to the situation of a minor third-country national that files a request for family reunification with regard to his or her parent should then lead to the conclusion that this request is considered in light of Article 24 para. 2 of the EU Charter read together with Article 7. It should be then possible to strike a balance between the legitimate aim pursued by the EU member states while applying the prohibition in Article 4 para. 4 of the Family Reunification Directive — the promotion of equal treatment between women and men — and the best interests of the minor child who files an application for family reunification. Accordingly, it should be difficult, in a potential case in front of the CJEU about polygamy, to deny the possibility of applying the EU Charter.[56] The only real obstacle seems to be to know if such a situation falls within the concept of implementation of EU law according to the EU Charter. But the only way to know this for sure is to address a question for a preliminary ruling to the Court itself, and there is the scope also perhaps to target a similar issue with strategic litigation.

This call to action to the Court has been upheld also by scholars, making also reference to the seminal case law of the CJEU in Zambrano.[57] As I maintained above, one should avoid to not consider Zambrano and other case law of the CJEU that might be relevant to the solution of the case of family reunification of the child of a polygamous marriage simply because they are referred to EU citizens. Although we know that certain rights (as free movement) are exclusive to EU citizens, the EU Charter applies to everyone. Thus, it will be for the CJEU to decide, when it will be invested of the question, if the EU Charter (the combination of Article 24 para. 2 and Article 7) applies to the situation of the child of a polygamous marriage.

V. Conclusion

The prohibition of polygamous marriages in the law of the EU member states still stands, perhaps also in light of the complexity of its impact on society.[58] On the other side, however, the recognition of the civil and social rights of the partners

---

[56] At present, however, there is no case law of the CJEU on polygamy, as recognised by the Commission in its report on the application of the directive on family reunification.

[57] P. Rodrigues/M. Klaassen, The Best Interests of the Child in EU Family Reunification Law: A Plea for More Guidance on the Role of Article 24(2) Charter, European Journal of Migration and Law, 2017, at pp. 191–218.

[58] M. Husni/A. Pakarti et al, The Role of Family Law in Confronting Polygamy Practices in Contemporary Society, Syakhshiyyah Jurnal Hukum Keluarga Islam, 2023, 132, at p. 136, available at https://e-journal.metrouniv.ac.id/index.php/syakhsiyah/article/download/7614/3685.

legitimately involved, in the State of provenience, in a polygamous marriage should be considered more carefully. This is in order, surely, to protect the rights of the weaker parts of the relationship (the plurality of wives) and to avoid the creation of partners of first and second class, thus discriminating among persons in a similar situation and violating their fundamental rights as expressed in the EU Charter and in the national constitutions. Even more so when children are involved, and they (their guardians) are the subjects filing an application for family reunification. The best interests of the child, resulting, in the EU legal order, from the combined reading of the Articles 7 and 24 para. 2 of the EU Charter, should be carefully weighted with the competing legitimate aim of promoting equality between men and women and avoiding discrimination. At the same time, it is worth to be reflected upon the variety of solutions present at the level of the EU member states before the entrance into force of the prohibition in Article 4 para. 4 of the Family Reunification Directive, and favoured by the framework of private international law, that was much richer and more protective for the rights of the weaker categories. Going back to the previous framework seems indeed to be difficult, but perhaps an EU Charter-oriented reading of the instruments of private international law that have been embodied into the EU legal order can help in finding a middle ground between competing interests.

The manufacturer's authorised representative in the EU is Springer Nature Customer Service Centre GmbH, Europaplatz 3, 69115 Heidelberg, Germany. If you have any concerns regarding our products, please contact ProductSafety@springernature.com

Printed and bound by CPI Group (UK) Ltd, Croydon, CR0 4YY
01/10/2026
02225925-0016